Computer Science Applications

REVISED FIRST EDITION

Edited by Joslyn A. Smith

cognella™
San Diego, CA

First published in the United States of America in 2013 by Cognella, Inc.

Printed in the United States of America

ISBN: 978-1-62131-256-7 (pbk)

cognella™

www.cognella.com 800.200.3908

CONTENTS

Part I: Classes and Objects

Part I: Classes and Objects

INTRODUCTION

The articles in this section lay the foundation for understanding **O**bject **O**riented **P**rogramming (**OOP**). They discuss fundamental concepts such as **Objects** and **Classes**, and how they relate to **Object Oriented** Programming. These two concepts form the cornerstone to **OOP**.

As you will learn, object oriented programming (OOP), is that type of programming that defines both the data and any operations that can be perform on the data, as a complete program unit. In this way, the entire unit, both data and operations, is referred to as the object. In this paradigm the data declarations are called fields, and the operations are called methods. Both the fields and the methods are stored as one unit, typically called a class.

SOME BENEFITS OF OOP

- Modularity—each object forms a separate entity with its own set of data and its own set of operations. This concept called encapsulation protects the data, which makes it difficult, if not impossible for objects outside of the system to access the data.
- Modifiability—it is easy to make minor changes to the entity in terms of the data representation or operations. In addition, changes inside a class often do not affect any other part of the program.

To help us understand the concept of objects, we must first understand that the general description of an object is an entity. Any particular reference to this entity is the object. For instance, one mode of transportation is motor car. The general description of motor car is the entity. **Figure 1** shows a partial description of the entity motor car. It consists of four attributes and four operations. I am sure you can list some more attributes and some more operations for motor car.

Figure 1 The entity motor car

Name of Entity	Possible Attributes	Possible Operations
Motor car	make	accelerate
	model	reverse
	engine size	set cruise control
	maximum speed	brake

The object, however, is as a specific example of the entity, as we mentioned earlier. We sometimes refer to an object as an instance of the entity. For example, motor car is the entity, but a Ford Mustang with **V**ehicle **I**dentification **N**umber (VIN) is a specific instance of motor car. Hence, this particular vehicle is an object of the entity motor car.

There are four articles in this section. The first, Object Oriented Program Fundamentals discusses the fundamental pillars of OOP–Encapsulation, Inheritance, and polymorphism. The second, Object Oriented Language Basics I, explains how to declare classes, and create objects. The third, Object Oriented Language Basics II, elaborates on Java modifiers, the role of constructors, access specifiers, and overloading; and the fourth, A Pedagogical Approach to Discussing Fundamental of Object Oriented Programming Principles—using ADT Set, serves as a application to the foregoing ones.

Object-Oriented Programming Fundamentals

BY JIM BOOTH

INTRODUCTION

Object orientation: these words can wreak havoc in the minds of developers everywhere. It doesn't need to be this way though. Object orientation is actually a much more direct method of mapping business problems to program code than any methods we have had in the past.

As an approach to system design and construction, object orientation is not a drastic change in how we build things. The same principles that we have always used still apply. Spaghetti code is bad, structured code is good. Encapsulating functionality into discrete blocks of code results in better maintainability.

However, object orientation requires that we adjust the way we think about what we do. Changing methodology is fairly easy. Most of us have learned more than one programming language in our careers and it wasn't the end of the world. But changing the way we think, well that is another beast altogether.

WHAT IS OBJECT ORIENTATION?

Object orientation is an approach to software development in which we focus on objects and their attributes and responsibilities. All business problems involve things. These things can be mapped to a set of objects, such as customers, invoices, etc.. In any given business problem the various things have attributes like name, color, weight, etc., and they have responsibilities such as initiate an order, fulfill an order, pay an invoice, etc..

The object-oriented approach of system building starts with the earliest phase of analysis of the business problem. In this early phase we center on identifying the objects involved and what their attributes and responsibilities are. One interesting part of object orientation is that it closely parallels the real world, much more so than the traditional structured approach of system design. This allows for a more thorough and accurate modeling of the business problem in the system design.

Object orientation can be defined as a system of components which encapsulate data and function, inherit these things from other components, and communicate via messages with one another.

In the object-oriented approach we not only identify the objects required, but we also organize them into classes of objects.

WHAT IS THE DIFFERENCE BETWEEN A CLASS AND AN OBJECT?

Edward Yourdan defines a class as, "A collection of one or more objects with a uniform set of attributes and services, including a description of how to create new objects in the class."

Grady Booch defines an object as, "An object has state, behavior, and identity; The structure and behavior of similar objects are defined in their common class; The terms instance and object are interchangeable."

From these two definitions we can see that there is a difference between a class and an object. A class is the definition, or blueprint, for an object. Classes don't really ever exist, they are plans. We use the class to create an object which has identity. That is, an object exists, has values in its properties, and can execute behaviors.

This difference between a class and an object is a subtle but very important one. It is analogous to visiting an architect to have a new house built. The architect will draw up plans for the house that show all the rooms and elevations etc.. However, you cannot move into the plans and live there. The plans must be used to build a house. The house is an object while the plans are a class.

CONCEPTS OF OBJECT ORIENTATION

Object orientation is more than classes and objects, it is a whole thought process about building applications. An object-oriented development language has many qualities that support the object-oriented approach to system design and construction.

The concepts we will investigate are abstraction, specialization, encapsulation, inheritance, polymorphism, communication, and reuse. The following sections discuss each of these concepts in detail. You may find situations where the various concepts are in conflict with each other; that is fine because in the real world we often find our goals in conflict and we must make a decision and go with it.

ABSTRACTION

This is the ability to represent a complex problem in simple terms. In the object-oriented approach, it is seen in the ability to create a high-level class definition that has little or no detail included in it. We are able to "abstract" the problem to a simple class definition and only add detail later in the process.

The ability to support abstraction is instrumental in being able to model very complex business problems in our designs.

SPECIALIZATION

Seen in class structures, specialization is the ability to make lower-level subclasses more detailed than their parent classes. Technically, specialization is defined as the ability of an object to inherit operations and attributes from a superclass (parent class) with possible restrictions and additions.

These first two concepts work in conjunction with one another. Abstraction allows us to define high-level classes that lack minute details of implementation while specialization supports the introduction of those details later in the class design.

ENCAPSULATION

Defined as hiding the implementation of the object, encapsulation is really the process of making an object as self sufficient as is possible. An object contains not only code but also data. Encapsulation, in the structured design, is the process of enclosing all of the code necessary to a particular operation into a single module and limiting the external dependencies of that module.

In object orientation, not only is the code encapsulated, but also the data required by that code (in the form of object properties).

INHERITANCE

Just as you and I have inherited certain traits from our ancestors, so do classes in an object-oriented system. There are superclasses (classes that have subclasses) and there are subclasses (classes that inherit from another class). These terms, superclass and subclass, are relative in that a given class may be a subclass of one class and a superclass for another.

Microsoft has opted to use the term parentclass instead of superclass in Visual FoxPro. Don't let this confuse you; a parentclass and a superclass are exactly the same thing.

Inheritance is the ability of one class to incorporate all or part of another class's definition in its own definition. An example may help to understand this.

Assume a class named cmdBase is derived from the Visual FoxPro baseclass of CommandButton. In this class, cmdBase, we change the FontName to Times New Roman. We then create a new class named cmdSpecial as a subclass of cmdBase. The cmdSpecial class will have Times New Roman as its default font because it inherits this trait from the parentclass cmdBase. If we later change the font for cmdBase then the font for cmdSpecial will also change (as long as we have not overridden the inherited font name).

POLYMORPHISM

Ah, the 35 cent word. An aside, it has been noticed that we get compensated for our work proportionally to the length of the words we used to describe that work. If this is true then polymorphism should get us all a raise.

The word is composed of poly, meaning many, and morph meaning shape. So polymorphism means many shapes and that is correct.

The general definition of polymorphism is the ability of different things to use the same name. There are two types of polymorphism seen in object-oriented systems, inherent and ad hoc.

Inherent Polymorphism

The ability of an operation to apply to different classes. Basically the ability to define a method in a class and have that method exist for all subclasses of that class even when the subclasses are very different in their behavior. For example, if we create a form class and give it a PrintMe method, then all subclasses of that form class will have a PrintMe method. Now we may create subclasses of this form class for Invoices and Customers, each of which will have specific code in the PrintMe method for printing the respective information. The fact that they both have a PrintMe method is inherent polymorphism.

Ad Hoc Polymorphism

With ad hoc polymorphism we are concerned with the specific behavior of the PrintMe methods. Ad hoc polymorphism is defined as the ability of different operations of different types to have the same name.

In our example, ad hoc polymorphism is seen in the fact that the invoice class prints an invoice and the customer class prints a customer ledger but both methods have the same name, PrintMe. The printing of an invoice and a customer ledger are very different processes, however, they both have the same name.

This ad hoc polymorphism allows us to create reusable components easily. Since the forms both have the same method name, we can create a print button that simply says Thisform.PrintMe() and not be concerned with what form that button may appear in.

Object Communications

Probably the simplest and yet most misunderstood aspect of object orientation is the fact that all behavior in an object-oriented system is the result of objects communicating with other objects.

How do objects communicate? By calling methods or assigning values to properties. In our example above, the Print button communicates with the form by calling the form's PrintMe method. The form is responsible for the actual action of printing, the button's responsibility is to provide a way for the user to communicate their desires to the form.

Where does the user fit in this scenario? The user is another object in the design. We provide objects that the user can communicate with (buttons, TextBoxes etc..) and then code those objects to respond to the user's interaction. The user uses the keyboard and mouse to send messages and our objects use the screen and printer to send messages to the user.

Reuse

The concept of code reusability has been around for much longer than object orientation. In structured programming we were always looking for ways to create reusable routines or functions that could reduce the effort required on later projects. We were working toward encapsulation and loose external coupling in the effort to get things to be reusable.

In object-oriented programming we have new tools that allow for an even better level of reusability. By taking advantage of things like polymorphism and inheritance we can create class definitions that are truly universal in their applicability. In the example above about the PrintMe method, by combining the form class with the PrintMe method and the button class with the Thisform.Printme() call in its click event, we have just removed the need to ever make a print button again.

DESIGN FIRST

Many folks find the transition to object-oriented programming a difficult one. The major reason for this is a tendency to "code from the hip." That is, to invent the solution as you write the code. While this approach can cause problems in any programming style, it is especially harmful in object-oriented programming.

Object-oriented development requires the design and creation of objects that have specific responsibilities and behaviors. These objects must interact with one another. Without careful planning up front, the likelihood that these objects will communicate well together is slim to none. The vary goals of OO will be lost in the monolithic code segments that are trying to handle complete problems without benefit of individual objects with specific responsibilities.

I have heard some folks say that doing things in VFP is difficult, I say that is not true. Doing things in VFP is easy, figuring out what to do is the hard part. Figuring out what to do is the design. VFP gives you a multitude of approaches to each problem you face. There is invariably more than one way to attack each situation. The difficulty, or complexity, that VFP presents is in making the decision as to which approach you will take.

Any trip will be easier if you know where you want to go before you start. Just as you would make plans for a vacation, you should also make plans for a project. If you were to get in your car one day to leave on vacation with no plans or goals for the trip, it is unlikely that you will have a truly enjoyable vacation. The same is true for your development efforts. If you start a project with no plan of what it will do and how it will do it, you are headed down a long and tortuous path of difficulty and complexity.

OBJECT ORIENTATION AND VISUAL FOXPRO THE CONCEPT OF CONTAINERSHIP

Visual FoxPro has a containership model built into it. This model is the implementation of the concept of one object containing other objects. Containership is defined as the ability of one object or class to contain other objects, including other containers.

This containership model dictates the way we address various objects with our code. Just like addressing a letter to someone, where we must supply the postal code, state, city, street and name, in VFP we must tell Fox where the object exists that we want to address. Below is a diagram showing a containership. In this diagram there is a TextBox in a Page of a PageFrame that is in a Form. To address the TextBox it is necessary to tell VFP where the TextBox is, as in, Thisform.PageFrame.Page.TextBox. Notice that the syntax lists the containership for the TextBox as being in the form, in the PageFrame, and in the page.

EXAMPLE:

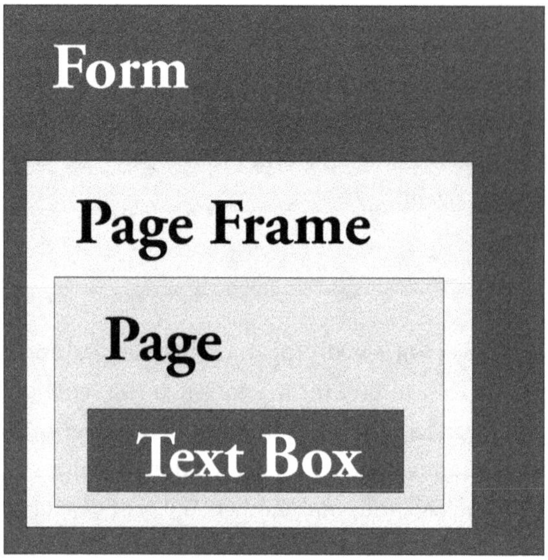

The syntax of containership can be made simpler through the use of certain FoxPro keywords that provide for relative addressing, that is addressing starting from the location of the object that contains the code. ThisForm, ThisFormSet, and This are three examples of this relative addressing.

ThisForm refers to the form that the code is contained in regardless of which control or object in that form has the code. ThisFormSet does the same thing as ThisForm except that it refers to the formset containing the code. This refers to the immediate object that contains the code. By using these keywords we can write code that is independent of the names of the objects.

There is one more keyword that can be helpful here: Parent. Every object in Visual FoxPro has a parent property. This property holds an object reference to the immediate container of the object. In the example above, the TextBox's parent is the Page, the page's parent is the PageFrame, the PageFrame's parent is the form, and the form has no parent.

This concept of containership is instrumental in understanding how to best use the features of Visual FoxPro. You can construct complex classes with multiple controls and provide all the behavior for those controls in the class definition. Then using them is as simple as dropping them on a form, setting some properties and that's it.

THE BASECLASSES

Every class we define in Visual FoxPro must derive from a Visual FoxPro base class. These base classes are the default class definitions that come with Visual FoxPro. If you open the form designer and look at the Form Controls toolbar, you will see many of the Visual FoxPro base classes. Not all of them are on that toolbar, but many of them are.

The following table is a list of all of the base classes provided with Visual FoxPro 6.0.

Baseclass	Container	Visual Design
CheckBox	No	Yes
ListBox	No	Yes
ComboBox	No	Yes
CommandButton	No	Yes
OptionButton	No	Yes
Spinner	No	Yes
TextBox	No	Yes
EditBox	No	Yes
ActiveDoc	Yes	Yes
Column	Limited	No
CommandGroup	Limited	Yes
Container	Yes	Yes
Control	Yes	Yes
Cursor	No	No
Custom	Yes	Yes
DataEnvironment	Limited	No
Form	Yes	Yes
FormSet	Limited	Yes
Grid	Limited	Yes
Header	No	No
HyperLink	No	Yes
Image	No	Yes
Label	No	Yes
Line	No	Yes
OLEContainer	Limited	Yes
OLEBoundContainer	Limited	Yes
OptionGroup	Limited	Yes
PageFrame	Limited	Yes
Page	Yes	No
ProjectHook	No	Yes

Relation	No	No
Separator	No	Yes
Shape	No	Yes
Timer	No	Yes
ToolBar	Limited	Yes

The above table shows you all of the Visual FoxPro base classes and tells you if they are a container and if they can be used in the Visual Class Designer to build your own subclasses. Any of the base classes can be in program code to define subclasses, but some of them are not available to design in the Visual Class Designer.

Certain of the base classes are limited containers, this means they are restricted as to what other base classes they may contain. For example, a Grid may only contain Columns, or a PageFrame may only contain Pages.

THE VISUAL CLASS DESIGNER

Visual FoxPro provides two ways to create your own classes; one is the Visual Class Designer the other is in program code. First let's look at the Visual Class Designer. This tool is similar to the Form Designer except instead of designing a form you are designing a class.

Most of the FoxPro base classes can be subclassed using the Visual Class Designer. The exceptions are Column, Header, Page, DataEnvironment, Cursor, Relation, and Session. These base classes can only be subclassed in program code.

The Visual Class Designer can be used to write code in the events and methods of your class. You can also add new properties or methods to the class definition using the Class-New Property or Class-New Method options on the Class menu.

The classes created with the class designer are stored in a VCX file (visual class library). This file has a sister file with a VCT extension. The VCX is actually a FoxPro DBF file with fields for all of the information regarding the class definitions.

DEFINING CLASSES IN CODE

Classes can also be defined in program code using the DEFINE CLASS command. An example is seen below;

```
DEFINE CLASS Employee AS Custom
  cName = "John Smith"

  PROCEDURE Launch
    PARAMETERS pcForm
    DO FORM (pcForm)
    RETURN
  ENDPROC
ENDDEFINE
```

In this example a class named Employee is being defined as a subclass of the VFP Custom base class. The line cName = "John Smith" creates a property named cName for this class and assigns it the value of "John Smith". The PROCEDURE declaration is defining a custom method named Launch. The code inside of the PROCEDURE is the code that will run when the Launch method is called.

The employee class defined in the example will have all of the properties and methods of the Custom base class because it inherits from that base class. The cName property and the Launch method will be additional things for this particular class.

You can also subclass your own classes like the following example;

```
DEFINE CLASS FullTimeEmployee AS Employee

   PROCEDURE Bonus
     PARAMETERS  pnPay
     RETURN pnPay * 1.1
   ENDPROC

ENDDEFINE
```

In this example we have created a class named FullTimeEmployee and added a bonus method. This new class will have the cName property and the Launch method, but it will also have a Bonus method. The behavior of the Launch method will be the same as it is for the Employee class.

WHY SUBCLASS?

You may ask, why do I want to create a hierarchy of subclasses? The reason is somewhat elusive at first. Your first impression may be that having a hierarchy of subclasses creates a complex reservoir of code that will be difficult to maintain and debug. Well that is partly correct. In a class hierarchy the code that provides the behaviors we see is often scattered around in different places.

However, there is one object-oriented programming concept that requires that class hierarchies be used, that is *programming to interface.*

Programming to Interface

This idea is that we should be writing our systems based on the properties, methods and the arguments and return values from those methods rather than on the actual code that implements the behaviors. This may seem like a mouth full of garbage right now, but rest assured it is not.

Let's look at an example of this in practice.

```
DEFINE CLASS frmperson AS form
    Name = "frmperson"
    PROCEDURE ask
        LPARAMETERS pcQuestion
        * Delegate to the person inside
        THIS.Person.Ask(pcQuestion)
    ENDPROC
    PROCEDURE Init
        LPARAMETERS pcName
        * Receive a name for this person
        IF EMPTY(pcName)
            * If no name is passed
            pcName = "Who Am I?"
        ENDIF
        THIS.Name = pcName
        THIS.Caption = pcName
        THIS.Visible = .T.
    ENDPROC
ENDDEFINE
DEFINE CLASS frmfemale AS frmperson
    Height = 325
    Width = 274
    Name = "frmfemale"
    ADD OBJECT person AS female WITH ;
```

```
        Top = 14, ;
        Left = 20, ;
        Name = "Person", ;
        HEAD.Name = "HEAD", ;
        LeftEye.Name = "LeftEye", ;
        RightEye.Name = "RightEye", ;
        HAIR.Name = "HAIR", ;
        NOSE.Name = "NOSE", ;
        MOUTH.MOUTH.Name = "MOUTH", ;
        MOUTH.Timer1.Name = "Timer1", ;
        MOUTH.Name = "MOUTH", ;
        Label1.Name = "Label1", ;
        tmrBlinker.Name = "tmrBlinker", ;
        tmrYawn.Name = "tmrYawn", ;
        LeftPigTail.Name = "LeftPigTail", ;
        RightPigTail.Name = "RightPigTail"
ENDDEFINE
DEFINE CLASS frmmale AS frmperson
    Height = 325
        Width = 274
    Caption = "Form1"
    Name = "frmmale"
    ADD OBJECT person AS male WITH ;
        Top = 14, ;
```

```
Left = 19, ;
Name = "Person", ;
HEAD.Name = "HEAD", ;
LeftEye.Name = "LeftEye", ;
RightEye.Name = "RightEye", ;
HAIR.Name = "HAIR", ;
NOSE.Name = "NOSE", ;
MOUTH.MOUTH.Name = "MOUTH", ;
MOUTH.Timer1.Name = "Timer1", ;
MOUTH.Name = "MOUTH", ;
Label1.Name = "Label1", ;
tmrBlinker.Name = "tmrBlinker", ;
tmrYawn.Name = "tmrYawn"
```

In these class definitions you can see that frmFemale and frmMale are both subclasses of frmPerson. As such both the frmFemale and frmMale classes have an Ask method and the behavior of that method is the same for both of them.

This means that both the frmFemale and frmMale can be used interchangeably without requiring the alteration of code that interacts with their Ask methods. You see all code that interacts with a frmFemale using the Ask method is programmed to the interface, that is the name of the method and the arguments it takes. There is no code that is dependent on the implementation of the Ask method. Because of this, we could substitute the frmMale for the frmFemale without changing any code.

We could even specialize the Ask method for one or both of the subclasses and, as long as we preserve the interface of the method, the two subclasses could have different behaviors without requiring the recoding of any calling code. The two subclasses now would do different things when their Ask method was called, but they are still interchangeable.

PROGRAMMING BY EXCEPTION

The inheritance model used in Visual FoxPro is called programming by exception. In this model a subclass will inherit the code from its parent class unless there is any code in the subclass's method. When code is written in the subclass's method it overrides the otherwise inherited code. For example;

```
DEFINE CLASS Widget AS TextBox
PROCEDURE Click
        WAIT WINDOW "OooH!, That tickles."
ENDPROC
ENDDEFINE

DEFINE CLASS BlueWidget AS Widget
PROCEDURE Click
        WAIT WINDOW "I am blue"
ENDPROC
ENDDEFINE
```

In the example we define a class named widget and give it some click behavior. We then define a subclass of widget and modify the click procedure. The BlueWidget class will NOT exhibit the behavior seen in the Widget class as that behavior is overridden in the subclass definition.

If we want both the parent class behavior and the subclass behavior, we must explicitly call the parent class code. This can be done in one of two ways. Using the DoDefault() function or using the scope resolution operator (::). Below are two examples of the BlueWidget class using each of these methods to call the parent class's code.

```
DEFINE CLASS BlueWidget AS Widget
PROCEDURE Click
        DoDeafult()
        WAIT WINDOW "I am blue"
ENDPROC
ENDDEFINE
DEFINE CLASS BlueWidget AS Widget
PROCEDURE Click
        Widget::Click() && scope resolution
        WAIT WINDOW "I am blue"
ENDPROC
ENDDEFINE
```

The preferred method of doing this is to use the DoDefault() call, as it has no binding to the name of the parent class. With the scope resolution operator it is necessary to hard code the parent class's name into the subclass's code. This could cause problems later if the class structure is modified and BlueWidget becomes a subclass of some child of the Widget class.

Any code, including a comment, in a subclass's method will override the behavior of its parent. At first this may seem unusual as inheritance is one of the goals of object-oriented programming. However, you would soon realize that when you are specializing the behavior for a class you need to have control over when the parent class's code is run. This programming by exception approach gives you complete control over how and when the parent class code will be done from your subclass.

THE NODEFAULT COMMAND

Certain events and methods of the Visual FoxPro base classes have a default behavior associated with them. For example, a form's release method will release the form from memory and destroy it or the KeyPress event of a control will process the key pressed.

These default behaviors are not overridden by your coder, they will always execute after your code runs. If you want to suppress the default behavior you can use the NODEFAULT command. This command tells VFP to not execute the default behavior. In a form's release method it will stop the release of the form, in a keypress it will stop the processing of the keystroke.

You can combine the DoDefault() function with the NODEFAULT command to control when the default behavior will occur. For example;

```
* Some textbox's KeyPress
DoDefault() && Process the keystroke
* put your code here
NODEFAULT && stop the automatic processing of the keystroke
```

The DoDefault() function will call the default VFP behavior as well as any behavior in the parent classes.

SUMMARY

Visual FoxPro is an object-oriented development environment. As such it has the capability of exploiting the full feature set of object oriented languages. At first, OO may seem overwhelming however given time and experience you will reach the point where you will find it difficult to imagine how you ever built systems in any other fashion.

The concepts of OO can seem academic, but they are important. The major difference between procedural programming and object-oriented programming is how we think about what we do. Just as there is good and bad procedural code, there is also good and bad object oriented code. The things that make code good or bad don't change, just the approach to writing it changes.

The obtuseness of OO development will fall away for you as soon as you begin to think about your systems as collections of objects with each one having specific responsibilities. Where no object steps on the domain of any other object, rather it calls the other object for services. An environment where each and every object is capable of standing on its own and doing what it does. Where no object is dependent on exactly how any other object functions, but only on what it does and how to call it.

Object-Oriented Language Basics, Part I

INTRODUCTION

OBJECTIVES

On completing this article you will:

1. Know how to declare classes and create objects
2. Know the distinction between classes and java programs
3. Learn how to create objects
4. Learn how Java destroys objects that are no longer in existence

TERMINOLOGIES

Object Oriented Programming • Declaring classes • Creating objects • Destroying objects • Encapsulation • Information hiding

Object-Oriented Language Basics, Part I

BY JEFF FRIESEN

LEARN HOW TO DECLARE CLASSES AND CREATE OBJECTS

Back in the mid-1980s, I used the prevailing software development methodology of the time—structured programming—to help me write computer programs. Structured programming emphasizes separating a program's data from its functionality. As I discovered, separating data from functionality typically leads to software that is difficult to maintain and understand—especially in large programs.

In the early 1990s, I learned a new software development methodology—object-oriented programming (OOP). OOP-created software more realistically models real-world entities—such as cars, bank accounts, and dogs—in source and executable code. Structured programming emphasizes making an entity's representation fit the constraints of the programming language; OOP emphasizes making the programming language fit the constraints of the representation. For example, in a structured programming language, a car is represented by a set of functions (named bodies of code) for starting, braking, parking, accelerating, and so on. A separate set of variables defines the car's color, number of doors, make, model, and so on. You initialize the car's variables and call some functions that operate on those variables—and voilà, you have a car!

An OOP language sees a car as an integration of its *behaviors*—the functions—and the variables that hold the car's *state*—the data values. The integration of state variables and behaviors results in an *object.* You create that object simply, at the same time initializing the variables. At any time, the object-oriented program identifies the object it wants to work with and calls the object's functions. Essentially, the object-oriented program thinks in terms of objects (e.g., cars)—not in terms of separate functions (e.g., parking) and variables (e.g., number of doors).

The integration of state variables and behaviors into objects is called *encapsulation.* Encapsulation promotes *information hiding*—a concept that facilitates program maintenance by hiding state variables and behaviors that don't need to be externally accessed—and is one of the three fundamental principles of OOP. (I'll explore the other two, inheritance and polymorphism, in later series articles.)

OOP has been widely available to developers for about 15 years, mainly because of the popularity of the C++ programming language. However, because of its C heritage, C++ is not completely object-oriented; you can write C++ programs that do not use object-oriented features. In contrast, Java is completely object-oriented: every Java program requires the presence of at least one class (an object-oriented feature). Furthermore, Java's official language definition includes the term object-oriented. (See Resources.)

This article begins an in-depth examination of OOP from Java's perspective. I'll start by examining classes and objects; I'll also discuss the javadoc tool for documenting packages, classes, fields, and methods. For more about javadoc, see the sidebar "Documenting Java."

Read the whole series on object-oriented language basics:

- Part 1: Learn how to declare classes and create objects
- Part 2: Declare and access fields and methods
- Part 3: Composition: Build objects from other objects
- Part 4: Inheritance: Build objects in layers
- Part 5: The root of all classes
- Part 6: Use interfaces for safe multiple inheritance and a great deal more
- Part 7: Learn about Java's many shapes and find out how to accommodate generalities in your class hierarchies

Objects don't just appear out of thin air. Just as a contractor needs access to an architect's blueprint before creating a building based on that blueprint, a running program needs access to a class before creating objects based on that class.

Declaring Classes

A *class* is a source code blueprint for objects. That blueprint specifies each object's behaviors and state variables. Use the following Java syntax to declare a class in source code:

```
[ 'public' ] [ ( 'abstract' | 'final' ) ] 'class' class_name
'{'
// behaviors and state variables are declared between the { and } characters
'}'
```

To introduce a class declaration, specify keyword class and follow it with an identifier—represented by class_name —that names the class. The identifier cannot be a reserved word. For example, class Account introduces a class declaration where Account names the class. (By convention, class names are capitalized.) Keywords public and/or abstract or final, but not abstract and final, because the resulting class would be meaningless—and can optionally precede keyword class.

Use keyword public in conjunction with packages. Specify public to make class_name accessible to all classes in all packages. Do not specify public if class_name is to be accessed only by classes in the same package as class_name. (I'll explore packages in an upcoming article.)

Remember the following rule when declaring a public class: only one public class can be declared in a source file. Furthermore, the source filename must match class_name. Consider the following example:

```
// MyClass.java
public class MyClass
{
```

Java requires that MyClass be declared in a source file called MyClass.java. Declaring that class in another file—such as Fred.java, or even MyClass.java—is unacceptable. Specify the exact identifier, used as class_name; case is significant. (For MyClass, you specify a capital letter m and a capital letter c. All other letters must be lowercase.)

You can choose any name for the source file if it does not contain a public class. However, the file still must end with a.java extension. The following example demonstrates that:

```
// Fred.java
class MyClass
{}
```

The above example declares a nonpublic class called MyClass and specifies (via the comment) that the class declaration is stored in a file called Fred.java.

Use keyword abstract to identify class_name as the name of an abstract class. Objects cannot be created from abstract classes. (I will present the concept of abstract classes later in this series.)

Use keyword final to identify class_name as the name of a final class. You cannot create a class that inherits behaviors and state variables from a final class. (I'll explore the concepts of inheriting and final classes later in this series.) Keywords public, abstract, and final can be specified in any order. For example, specify public abstract class fred, final public fred, abstract fred, and so on.

Each class has a body where you declare behaviors (known as methods) and state variables (known as fields). The body begins with a `{` character and ends with a `}` character. Although you don't need to declare methods or fields between `{` and `}` (see the aforementioned `MyClass` examples), there is almost no point in declaring a class without methods or fields. Therefore, you'll almost always declare fields, methods, or some combination of both in your class bodies. (I will provide a detailed exploration of fields and methods later in this series.)

Classes and Java Programs

Each Java program consists of one or more classes. One of those classes is known as the *starting class,* because it is the first program class that the JVM loads. Actually, the classfile that implements the starting class—by providing code to implement behaviors and variables to hold state—is loaded by the JVM.

As you saw in previous Java 101 articles, a Java application contains a starting class with a main () method. For a quick refresher on what a simple application looks like, check out Listing 1 for the CODemo1 application:

Listing 1. CODemo1.java

```
// CODemo1.java
class CODemo1
{
        public static void main (String [] args)
        {
                System.out.println ("Hello");
        }
}
```

CODemo1—class/object demo number 1—is a simple Java application. The CODemo1 class's body is a single method named main(). After you compile that code and issue the java CODemo1 command to run the program, the JVM loads the starting classfile—CODemo1. class—and executes the byte codes that constitute the main () method. That execution results in the Hello message appearing on the standard output device.

Creating Objects

An *object* is an instance of a class. Use the following syntax to create an object:

'new' *constructor*

The new keyword, often called the *creation operator,* allocates an object's memory and initializes that memory to default values. An object's field values are stored in memory. Because new is an operator, it takes an operand: constructor, which is the name of a special method that constructs the object. Once new finishes allocating and initializing memory, it calls the constructor to perform object initialization.

Listing l's CODemo1 source code demonstrates the simplest possible useful application. Although Listing 1 clearly shows that an application requires a class declaration, no objects have been created from that class. How do you go from executing code in a class's main() method to creating an object from that class and manipulating the object by accessing its fields and calling its methods? For an answer, check out Listing 2 for the CODemo2 application:

Listing 2. CoDemo2.java

```
// CODemo2.java
class CODemo2
{
```

```
    int i = 3;
    public static void main (String [] args)
    {
          CODemo2 obj1 = new CODemo2 ();
          System.out.println ("obj1.i = " + obj1.i);
          obj1.printHello ();
          CODemo2 obj2 = new CODemo2 ();
          obj1.i = 5;
          System.out.println ("obj1.i = " + obj1.i);
          obj1.printHello ();
          System.out.println ("obj2.i = " + obj2.i);
          obj2.printHello ();
    }
    void printHello ()
    {
          System.out.println ("Hello! i = " + i + "\n");
    }
}
```

Field declaration statement int i = 3; specifies a field named i, which is of type integer (as specified by the int keyword) and initializes i to 3 (as specified by the integer literal 3).

CODemo2 obj1 = new CODemo2 (); creates an object from the CODemo2 class. CODemo2 obj2 = new C0Demo2 (); creates a second object from CODemo2. Because an object is an instance of a class, class instance is often used as a synonym for object.

CODemo2 obj1 and CODemo2 obj 2 declare variables in a manner similar to int count or double balanceOwing. Data type keywords int and double declare storage locations named count and balanceOwing for holding values of primitive data types: integer and double-precision floating-point, respectively. CODemo2, on the other hand, declares a storage location for holding a value of a reference or address data type. In other words, because obj1 and obj2 have the CODemo2 data type and CODemo2 is a reference data type, any value assigned to either obj1 or obj2 is a reference to (that is, the address of) an object created from the CODemo2 class.

CODemo2's new operator calls CODemo2() to build the object. But wait! No CODemo2() constructor method is declared in the CODemo2 class. What's going on? For an answer, check out the next article in this series.

Once the constructor has finished building the object, creation operator new returns the address of that object. In Listing 2, the first-returned CODemo2 object-address assigns to variable obj1; the second address assigns to variable obj2. Figure 1 conceptualizes both objects, referenced by their respective variables.

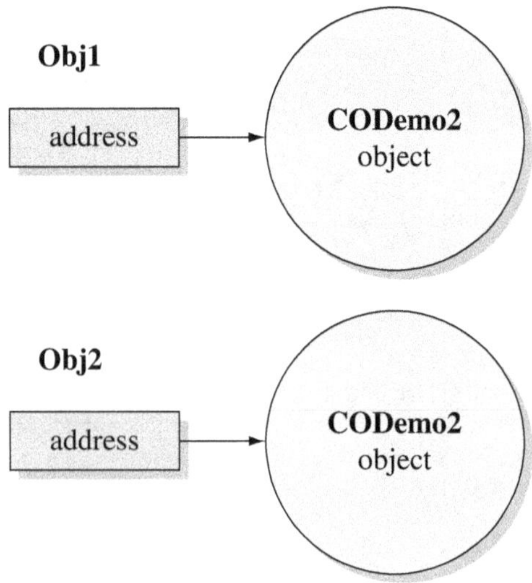

Figure 1. *A conceptualization of two CODemo2 objects and their respective reference variables*

Personally, I imagine an object as one or more arrows pointing to a circle. Each arrow represents a reference to the object, and originates from a rectangle containing the object's address.

Check out Listing 2's System.out.printin ("obj1.i = " + obj1.i); method call. What does obj1.i mean? Well, i is an integer field variable that initializes to 3. An object created from CODemo2 is capable of having its own copy of that variable (with a different value), so we must distinguish between multiple variable copies. Therefore, we must tell the program which copy to use. The period character following variable name obj1 identifies the i variable that belongs to the object referenced by obj1 (as opposed to the i variable that belongs to the object referenced by obj2). The period character is often referred to as the dot operator. (I will say more about fields in next month's article.)

obj1.printHello (); calls the printHello() method. As in obj1.i, obj1. prefixes printHello () Because Listing 2 also contains obj2.printHello ();, you might think there are two copies of printHello()—one for each object. Actually, only one copy exists. Its byte codes are loaded when the CODemo2 classfile loads. How does the single copy of printHello () distinguish between the i field in the object referenced by obj1 and the i field in the object referenced by obj2? The answer involves the obj1. and obj2. prefixes. The dot operator that appears between obj1 and printHello () tells printHello () that it can access the i field belonging to obj1 (as opposed to accessing the i field belonging to obj2). The same idea holds for the dot operator that appears between obj2 and printHello(). (I will say more about methods in next month's article.)

Why doesn't obj1 or obj2 prefix the i variable in printHello ()? If you're curious, check out next month's article.

Now that you have some insight into what an object is and how it is referenced, you might be curious about its internal structure. Figure 2 sheds some light on that structure.

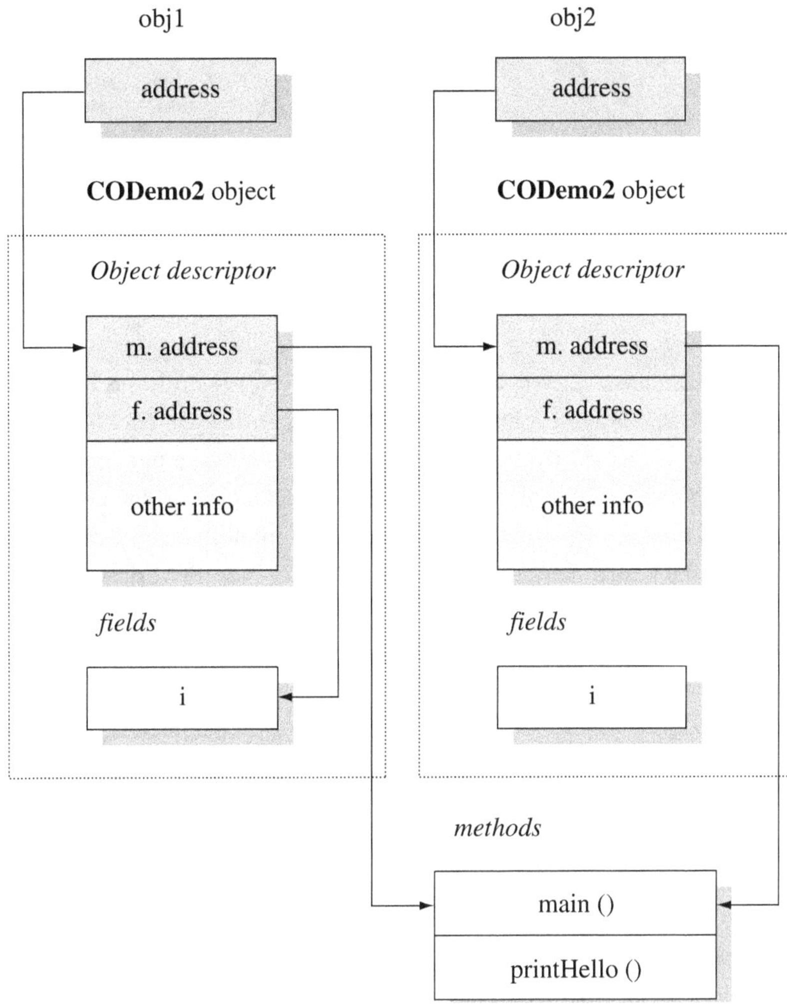

Figure 2. *Inside a CODemo2 object*

Figure 2 shows two reference variables—obj1 and obj2—that reference two CODemo2 objects. Actually, each variable contains the address of an object descriptor that contains information about the object. Among other things, the descriptor holds the addresses to one block of memory that contains the object's fields, and one that contains the byte code of each CODemo2 method.

A close look at Figure 2 gives the impression that Java supports *pointers*—variables that contain the addresses of other variables. At the language level, Java does not support pointers. Instead, Java supports *references*—abstract object identifiers. The underlying JVM determines how to implement a reference. For example, one kind of JVM might assign a number to a reference variable that indexes into a table of pointers to objects, whereas another kind of JVM might assign the object's memory address to the reference variable. (In this case, the reference variable is basically a pointer to the object.) Because you don't know (and don't need to know) what assigns to a reference variable, just think of a reference variable as being able to reference an object in some fashion—and forget about pointers!

Destroying Objects

C++ requires all heap-created objects to be explicitly destroyed—by using C++'s delete keyword. Java, however, assumes responsibility for destroying created objects. The JVM's garbage collector, which runs at periodic intervals, examines each object to see if it is referenced by at least one variable. If not, the garbage collector destroys the object, freeing memory in the process.

Internally, the JVM maintains a reference count for each object. When the creation operator first creates an object (as in new coDemo2 ();), and the assignment operator assigns that reference to an object reference variable (as in coDemo2 obji = new coDemo2 ();), the reference count initializes to one (behind the scenes). Whenever that reference assigns to another variable of the same reference data type, the reference count increments by one. However, if the null literal assigns to the variable, the reference count decrements by one. As soon as the reference count reaches zero—and the next time the garbage collector runs—the JVM destroys the object. Consider the following example:

```
// Create an object and assign its reference to myObjectReference.
CODemo2 myObjectReference = new CODemo2 ();          // Internal reference count set to 1.
// Assign myObjectReference's reference value to anotherObjectReference.
CODemo2 anotherObjectReference = myObjectReference;  // Internal reference count set to 2.
// Destroy one of the references.
myObjectReference = null;                            // Internal reference count set to 1.
// Destroy the other reference.
anotherObjectReference = null;                       // Internal reference count set to 0.
// At this point, the object will be destroyed when the garbage collector runs.
```

About the author

Jeff Friesen has been involved with computers for the past 20 years. He holds a degree in computer science and has worked with many computer languages. Jeff has also taught introductory Java programming at the college level. In addition to writing for JavaWorld, he wrote his own Java book for beginners—Java 2 By Example (QUE, 2000)—and helped write a second Java book, Special Edition Using Java 2 Platform (QUE, 2001). Jeff goes by the nickname Java Jeff (or JavaJeff). To see what he's working on, check out his Website at http://www.javajeff.com.

Object-Oriented Language Basics, Part II

INTRODUCTION

OBJECTIVES

On completing this article you will:

1. Learn how to declare and access fields and methods
2. Be able to differentiate between instance fields, class fields, and constants
3. Learn about Java's access specifiers – private, public, and protected.
4. Learn how to difference between instance methods and class methods.
5. Learn about modifiers such as abstract, static, final, native and synchronized.
6. Learn about method overloading
7. Learn about constructors and the role they play in constructing objects.

TERMINOLOGIES

Instance fields • Class fields • Constants • Enumerated types • Access specifiers • Instance method • Class method • Overloading • Constructor

Object-Oriented Language Basics, Part II

BY JEFF FRIESEN

DECLARE AND ACCESS FIELDS AND METHODS

Ever hear the expression, "I can't see the forest for the trees"? That expression refers to specific details that cloud your understanding of the big picture. And what could be cloudier than a detailed examination of fields and methods during an introduction to Java's classes and objects? That is the reason I chose to minimize fields and methods while maximizing the big picture—classes and objects—in Part 1 of this object-oriented language series. However, because you eventually have to step back from the forest and focus on the trees, this month's article examines fields and methods in great detail.

Read the whole series on object-oriented language basics:

- Part 1 : Learn how to declare classes and create objects
- Part 2: Declare and access fields and methods
- Part 3 : Composition: Build objects from other objects
- Part 4: Inheritance: Build objects in layers
- Part 5: The root of all classes
- Part 6: Use interfaces for safe multiple inheritance and a great deal more
- Part 7: Learn about Java's many shapes and find out how to accommodate generalities in your class hierarchies

Java's variables can be divided into three categories: fields, parameters, and local variables. I'll present fields here and leave an exploration of parameters and local variables for a later section that discusses methods.

DECLARING FIELDS

A *field* is a variable declared in a class body that holds either part of an object's state (an instance field) or part of a class's state (a class field). Use the following Java syntax to declare a field in source code:

```
[ ( 'public' | 'private' | 'protected' ) ]
  [ ( 'final' | 'volatile' ) ]
    [ 'static' ] [ 'transient' ]
      data_type field_name [ '=' expression ] ';'
```

A field declaration specifies the field's name, data type, optional expression (which initializes the field), access specifiers, and modifiers. Choose identifiers for the data type and name that are not reserved words. Consider this example:

```
class Employee
{
  String name;     // The employee's name.
  double salary;  // The employee's salary.
  int jobID;       // The employee's job identification code (e.g., accountant, payroll clerk, manager, and so on).
}
```

The Employee class declares three fields: name, salary, and jobiD. When you create an Employee object, name eventually holds a reference to a string object that contains the employee's name. The salary field will hold the employee's salary, and jobiD will hold an integer that identifies the employee's job category.

Access Specifiers

You can optionally declare a field with an access specifier keyword: public, private, or protected. The access specifier determines how accessible the field is to code in other classes. Access ranges from totally accessible to totally inaccessible.

If you do not declare a field with an access specifier keyword, Java assigns the field a default access level, which makes the field accessible within its class and to all classes within the same package. (Think of packages as libraries of classes a concept I'll explore in a future article.) Any class not declared in the same package as the class that contains the field cannot access the field. Take a look at the following example:

```
class MyClass
{
  int fred;
}
```

Only code contained in MyClass and other classes declared in the same package as MyClass can access fred.

If you declare a field private, only code contained in its class can access the field. That field becomes inaccessible to every other class in every other package. Examine the code below:

```
class Employee
{
  private double salary;
}
```

Only code contained in Employee can access salary.

If you declare a field public, code contained in its class and all other packages' classes can access the field. Refer to the code below:

```
public class Employee
{
  public String name;
}
```

Code contained in Employee and all other packages' classes can access name. (Employee must also be declared public before code in other packages can access name.)

Declaring every field in a given class public defeats the concept of information hiding. Suppose you create a Body class to model the human body and Eye, Heart, and Lung classes to model an eye, the heart, and a lung. The Body class declares Eye, Heart, and Lung reference fields, as demonstrated by the following example:

```
public class Body
{
  public Eye leftEye, rightEye;
  private Heart heart;
  private Lung leftLung, rightLung;
}
```

The leftEye and rightEye field declarations are public because a body's eyes are visible to an observer. However, the heart, leftLung, and rightLung declarations are private because the organs they represent are hidden inside the body. Suppose heart, leftLung, and rightLung were declared public. Wouldn't that be the equivalent to having a body with its heart and lungs exposed?

```
public class Employee
{
  protected String name;
}
```

Finally, a field declared protected resembles a field with the default access level. The only difference between the two access specifiers is that subclasses in any package can access the protected field. The following example demonstrates that:

Only code contained in Employee, other classes declared in the same package as Employee, and all Employee's subclasses (declared in any package) can access name.

Modifiers

You can optionally declare a field with a modifier keyword: final or volatile and/or static and/or transient.

If you declare a field final, the compiler ensures that the field is initialized and subsequently treats the field as a *constant,* a read-only variable. The compiler can now perform internal optimizations on a program's byte codes because it knows the constant will not. change. Consider the example below:

```
class Employee
{
  final int ACCOUNTANT = 1;
  final int PAYROLL_CLERK = 2;
  final int MANAGER = 3;
  int jobID = ACCOUNTANT;
}
```

The example above declares three final int fields: accountant, payroll_clerk, and manager.

Note: It is customary to use all capital letters and separate multiple words with underscores when declaring constants. That helps distinguish constants from read/write variables when analyzing source code.

If you declare a field `volatile,` multiple threads can access thASZASe field, and certain compiler optimizations are prevented so that the field is accessed appropriately. (You'll learn about volatile fields when I discuss threads in a future article.)

If you declare a field static, all objects share one copy of the field. When you assign a new value to that field, all objects can see the new value. If static is not specified, the field is known as an instance field, and each object receives its own copy.

Finally, the value of a field declared transient will not be saved during object serialization. (I explore the topics of transient fields and object serialization in a future article.)

Instance fields

An *instance field* is a field declared without the static keyword modifier. Instance fields are associated with objects—not classes. When modified by an object's code, only the associated class instance—the object—sees the change. An instance field is created when an object is created and destroyed when its object is destroyed.
The following example demonstrates an instance field:

```
class SomeClass1
{
  int i = 5;
  void print ()
  {
    System.out.println (i);
  }
  public static void main (String [] args)
  {
    SomeClass1 sc1 = new SomeClass1 ();
    System.out.println (sc1.i);
  }
}
```

SomeClass1 declares an instance field named i and demonstrates two common ways to access that instance field from an instance method or from a class method. Both methods are in the same class as the instance field.

To access an instance field from an instance method in the same class, you only specify the field's name. To access an instance field from another class's instance method, you must have an object reference variable that contains the address of an object created from the class that declares the instance field you want to access. Prefix the object reference variable along with the dot operator to the instance field's name. (You'll explore instance methods later in this article.)

To access an instance field from a class method in the same class, create an object from the class, assign its reference to an object reference variable, and prefix that variable to the instance field's name. To access an instance field from another class's class method, complete the same steps as when you accessed that field from a class method in the same class. (I'll present class methods later in this article.)

When the JVM creates an object, it allocates memory for each instance field and subsequently zeroes the field's memory, which establishes an instance field's default value. The way you interpret a default value depends on the field's data type. Interpret a reference field's default value as null, a numeric field's default value as 0 or 0.0, a Boolean field's default value as false, and a character field's default value as \u0000.

Class Fields

A *class field* is a field declared with the `static` keyword modifier. Class fields are associated with classes not objects. When modified by a class's code, the class (as well as any created objects) sees the change. A class field is created when a class is loaded and destroyed if and when a class is unloaded. (I believe some JVMs unload classes whereas other JVMs do not.)

The example below illustrates a class field:

```
class SomeClass2
{
  static int i = 5;
  void print ()
  {
    System.out.println (i);
  }
  public static void main (String [] args)
  {
    System.out.println (i);
  }
}
```

SomeClass2 declares a class field i and demonstrates two common ways to access i—from an instance or class method (both methods are in the same class as the class field).

To access a class field from an instance method in the same class, you only specify the field's name. To access a class field from another class's instance method, prefix the class field with the name of the class in which the class field is declared. For example, specify SomeClass2.i to access i from an instance method in another class which is in the same package as SomeClass2, because SomeClass2 isn't declared public.

To access a class field from a class method in the same class, you only specify the field's name. To access a class field from another class's class method, follow the same procedure as you did when accessing the class field from an instance method in another class.

Once a class loads, the JVM allocates memory for each class field and establishes a class field's default value. Interpret a class field's default value just as you would interpret an instance field's default value.

Class fields are the closest things to global variables in Java. Check out the example below:

```
class Global
{
  static String name;
}
class UseGlobal
{
  public static void main (String [] args)
  {
    Global.name = "UseGlobal";
    System.out.println (Global.name);
  }
}
```

The above example declares a pair of classes in a single source file: Global and UseGlobal. If you compile and then run the application, the JVM loads UseGlobal and then begins executing the main() method's byte codes. After seeing Global.name, the JVM searches for, loads, and then verifies the Global class. Once Global is verified, the JVM allocates memory for name and initializes that memory to null. Behind the scenes, the JVM creates a String object and initializes that object to all characters between the pair of double quote characters—UseGlobal. That reference assigns to name. Then, the program accesses Global.name and retrieves the String object's reference, which subsequently passes to System.out.println(). Finally, the contents of the String object appear on the standard output device.

Because neither Global nor UseGlobal are explicitly marked public, you can choose any name for the source file. Compiling that source file results in a pair of class files: Global.class and UseGlobal.class. Because UseGlobal contains the main() method, use that class to run the program. Type java UseGlobal to run the program at the command line.

If you type java Global instead, you would receive the following error message:

```
Exception in thread "main" java.lang.NoSuchMethodError: main
```

The word main at the end of the error message indicates that java couldn't find a main() method in class Global.

Constants

A *constant* is a read-only variable; once the JVM initializes that variable, the variable's value cannot change.

Declare constants with the final keyword. Just as there are two kinds of fields, instance and class, constants come in two flavors—instance and class. For efficiency, create class constants, or final static fields. Consider this example:

```
class Constants
{
  final int FIRST = 1;
  final static int SECOND = 2;
  public static void main (String [] args)
  {
    int iteration = SECOND;
    if (iteration == FIRST) // Compiler error.
      System.out.println ("first iteration");
    else
    if (iteration == SECOND)
      System.out.println ("second iteration");
  }
}
```

The above example's Constants class declares a pair of constants—FIRST and SECOND. FIRST is an instance constant because the JVM creates a separate copy of FIRST for each Constants object. In contrast, because the JVM creates a single copy of SECOND after loading Constants, SECOND is a class constant.

Note: A compiler error occurs when you attempt to directly access FIRST in main (). Constant FIRST does not exist until an object is created, but then FIRST is only accessible to that object—not the class.

Use constants for the following reasons:

1. In source code, it is easier and less error-prone to change a constant's initial value than to replace all occurrences of a hard-coded magic number.
2. Constants facilitate reading and understanding source code. For example, the constant num_array_elements is more meaningful than the number 12.

Enumerated Types

Suppose you write a Java program, Zoo1, that models a zoo of circus animals:

Listing 1. Zool.java

```
// Zoo1.java
class CircusAnimal
{
  final static int TIGER = 1;
  final static int LION = 2;
  final static int ELEPHANT = 3;
  final static int MONKEY = 4;
}
class Zoo1
{
  private int animal;
  public static void main (String [] args)
  {
    Zoo1 z1 = new Zoo1 ();
    z1.animal = CircusAnimal.TIGER;
    // Some time later ...
    if (z1.animal == CircusAnimal.TIGER)
      System.out.println ("This circus animal is a tiger!");
    else
    if (z1.animal == CircusAnimal.MONKEY)
      System.out.println ("This circus animal is a monkey!");
    else
```

```
      System.out.println ("Don't know what this circus animal is!");
  }
}
```

Zoo1.java declares a pair of classes: circusAnimal and Zoo1. Class circusAnimal declares some convenient integer constants that represent various circus animals, whereas Zoo1 is the starting class—its main() method runs the Zoo1 application.

The main () method creates a Zoo1 object, assigns that object's reference to z1, and initializes the object's animal instance field to CircusAnimal.TIGER. Even though animal is private, method main() has access to that variable—through the z1 object reference variable—because main() is part of the same class in which animal is declared. Later, main() checks animal's current value and outputs an appropriate message based on its findings.

Zoo1 features a problem: animal's int data type keyword. Suppose we assign z1.animal to 978324 which is legal because both animal and 978324 have the integer data type. The resulting assignment would be meaningless. What animal does 978324 represent? Using an integer as animal's data type makes it possible to create irrational code, which often leads to bugs. A solution to that problem is to give animal a more appropriate data type and restrict the set of values that can assign to animal. That is the rationale behind using enumerated data types.

An *enumerated data type* is a reference data type with a restricted set of values. Each value is an object created from the enumerated data type, as shown below:

Listing 2. Zoo2.java

```
// Zoo2.java
class CircusAnimal
{
  static final CircusAnimal TIGER = new CircusAnimal ("Tiger");
  static final CircusAnimal LION = new CircusAnimal ("Lion");
  static final CircusAnimal ELEPHANT = new CircusAnimal ("Elephant");
  static final CircusAnimal MONKEY = new CircusAnimal ("Monkey");
  private String animalName;
  private CircusAnimal (String name)
  {
    animalName = name;
  }
  public String toString ()
  {
    return animalName;
  }
}
class Zoo2
{
```

```
    private CircusAnimal animal;
    public static void main (String [] args)
    {
        Zoo2 z2 = new Zoo2 ();
        z2.animal = CircusAnimal.TIGER;
        // Some time later ...
        if (z2.animal == CircusAnimal.TIGER)
            System.out.println ("This circus animal is a tiger!");
        else
        if (z2.animal == CircusAnimal.MONKEY)
            System.out.println ("This circus animal is a monkey!");
        else
            System.out.println ("Don't know what this circus animal is!");
    }
}
```

The Zoo2 class closely resembles Listing 1's Zoo1 class, with the major difference being animal's data type. Instead of int, animal now has the CircusAnimal data type—only references to objects created from CircusAnimal can be assigned to animal.

The CircusAnimal class declares four CircusAnimal constants: TIGER, LION, ELEPHANT, and MONKEY. Each constant initializes to a CircusAnimal object.

A special CircusAnimal constructor, which takes a single string argument, is declared. The string passed to the constructor is saved in a private animalName field. (I discuss constructors later in this article.)

The constructor is declared private to prevent the creation of CircusAnimal objects beyond those four objects declared as constants. You don't want someone to create a CircusAnimal object equivalent to the meaningless 978324. Only the four CircusAnimal constants are valid for the Zoo2 program.

Why is a toString() method declared in CircusAnimal? That method returns the value of the String object, whose reference is assigned to animalName. Suppose you call System.out.println (z2.animal) after initializing z2.animal to CircusAnimal.TIGER. The result: Tiger will print, which is the value passed to CircusAnimal's constructor when the TIGER constant was created. System.out.println () acquires Tiger behind the scenes by calling the toString() method. (I'll have more to say about toString() in a later article.)

Now that you know how to declare and access fields, you need to learn how to declare and access methods.

Declaring Methods

Java uses the term *method* to refer to named bodies of code that are associated with classes. Whereas fields hold either an object's state or class values, methods describe the behaviors of either an object or a class. Furthermore, Java's methods are completely declared inside classes. To declare a method in source code, use the following Java syntax:

```
[ ( 'public' | 'private' | 'protected' ) ]
  ( [ 'abstract' ] | [ 'final' ] [ 'static' ] [ 'native' ] [ 'synchronized' ] )
    return_data_type method_name '(' [ parameter_list ] ')'
    compound_statement
```

A method declaration consists of a method signature followed by a compound statement. The method signature specifies the method's name, return data type, parameter list, access specifiers, modifiers, and the types of exceptions the method can throw. (I discuss throwing exceptions in a future article.) The compound statement is a *block* (group) of statements that executes when the method is called by code executing in another method. Code that calls a method is known as the method's *caller.* See "Non-Object-Oriented Language Basics, Part 3" for the syntax of a compound statement.

The method's name identifies the method. Choose an identifier for the method name that is not a reserved word.

Preceding each method is a return data type, which either identifies the kind of data values that the method returns or indicates that the method returns nothing. Apart from void, *return_data_type* is either:

- One of the primitive data type keywords boolean, byte, char, double, float, int, long, or short
- A reference data type identifier

If a reference data type identifier is specified, the method returns a reference to an object created from that data type instead of a primitive value.

A pair of round brackets follows each method. You can optionally declare a comma-delimited list of variables between the brackets. Each variable in the declaration is known as a *parameter.* When the method is called, an optional comma-delimited list of expressions, known as *arguments,* passes to the method. The number of arguments and data type of each argument (in a left-to-right order) must match the number of parameters and data type of each parameter (in a left-to-right order). A method's parameter list is often referred to as a *params operator.*

To call a method, pass zero or more arguments to the method. The method accesses those arguments, processes the values in those parameters, and then (optionally) returns a value to the method's caller. For example, suppose you create a method designed to calculate a number's square root. Your code passes a value to the square root method and then calls that method. The method grabs that argument via the corresponding parameter; after some processing, the square root method returns the value's square root back to the caller.

The following example demonstrates a simple method with four compiler errors:

```
class MathUtilities
{
  int sum (int limit)
  {
    System.out.println ("limit = " + limit);
    System.out.println ("total = " + total); // Compiler error.
    int total;
```

```
        for (int i = 1; i <= limit; i++)
            total += i; // Compiler error.
        System.out.println ("i = " + i); // Compiler error.
        return total; // Compiler error.
    }
}
```

In the code above, MathUtilities declares a method named sum() with a single int parameter named limit. Method sum() calculates the sum of integers ranging from 1 to limit and returns that total. Let's examine sum() in detail.

Notice that limit is a parameter to sum(). The JVM creates the limit variable and assigns the argument value—passed to sum() during the call—to limit. Any statement in the block following sum()'s method signature can access the argument value contained in limit. In other words, the *scope*—or visibility—of limit is the entire block. However, the parameter cannot be accessed outside the block; another method declared in MathUtilities cannot access limit. Once a program's execution leaves a method in which a parameter is declared, the JVM destroys that parameter.

Also note the variable declaration statement int total; it declares a local variable named total. Like a parameter, a *local variable* is a variable that is local to a method block. A local variable cannot be accessed from outside the block. Unlike a parameter, a local variable's scope is not the entire block. Instead, its scope ranges from the point in the block where the local variable is declared to the block's end. Suppose you attempt to access a local variable before it is declared. What happens? For an answer, notice the // Compiler error. comment to the right of System. out.println ("total = " + total);. Never attempt to access a local variable prior to that variable's declaration.

Furthermore, the above code shows that blocks can be nested—as the code's for loop statement illustrates. The total += i; simple statement following for (int i = 1; i <= limit; is a block. That block nests within the method block. Local variable i is local to the total += i; block. If you try to access i from the enclosing method block, another compiler error results. Never attempt to access a local variable declared in an inner block from an outer block.

Local variables introduce another potential problem: They must be explicitly initialized before they are accessed. Otherwise, the compiler reports an error. If total is not initialized, total += i; and return total; result in compiler errors. To correct those errors, change int total; to int total = 0;. Always initialize your local variables to avoid errors that arise from uninitialized local variables.

Examine the return total; statement at the end of sum() in the code above. That return statement returns a value to the method's caller. Use the following syntax to express a return statement in source code:

'return' [*expression*];

A return statement consists of keyword return optionally followed by *expression*. Unless a method's return data type is void, you must always follow return with an expression whose data type matches the method's return data type. Furthermore, if a method's return data type is not void, execution must always exit from a method via a return statement. Otherwise, the compiler reports an error. (Stay tuned to this article for more examples of return statements.)

After fixing the four compiler errors in the code above, how would you call sum()? Check out the following code fragment: MathUtilities mu = new MathUtilities (); int sumTotal = mu.sum (10);. That fragment creates an object from the MathUtilities class and then calls sum() via the mu object reference variable, with 10 as sum()'s sole argument. sum() calculates the sum of integers ranging from 1 to 10 and returns the result. The sum is then assigned to sumTotal.

Once a return statement executes, where does program execution continue? If a method call is not part of an expression, execution continues with the statement that immediately follows the method call. However, if the method call is an operand to some operator in an expression, execution continues with the operator that evaluates its other operand(s).

How does the JVM know the return location at which to continue program execution? Internally, the JVM maintains a data structure known as a *method call stack*. Before the JVM calls a method, it pushes the address of the next instruction following the method-call byte code instruction onto the method call stack. When execution leaves the method block either from a return statement or from falling off the method's bottom, the JVM pops this address from the method call stack and execution picks up with the first byte code instruction following the original method-call byte-code instruction. (I explore data structures and stacks in a future article.)

Access Specifiers

You can declare a method with an access specifier keyword: public, private, or protected. The access specifier determines how accessible the method is to code in other classes (for calling purposes). Access ranges from totally callable to totally uncallable.

If you do not declare a method with an access specifier keyword, Java assigns a default access level to the method, making the method callable within its class and to all classes within the same package. Any methods of any class not declared in the same package as the class that contains the method to be called cannot call that method. Examine the code below:

```
class Temperature
{
   private int degrees;
   void setDegrees (int d)
   {
      degrees = d;
   }
   int getDegrees ()
   {
      return degrees;
   }
}
```

Only methods declared in Temperature and other classes declared in the same package as Temperature can call setDegrees() and getDegrees().

If you declare a method private, only code contained in its class can call that method. The method becomes inaccessible to every other class in every other package. Consider the example below:

```
class MathUtilities
{
  private int factorial (int n)
  {
    if (n == 0)
      return 1;  // 0! (0 factorial) returns 1
    int product = 1;
    for (int i = 2; i <= n; i++)
      product *= i;
    return product;
  }
  int permutation (int n, int r)
  {
    return factorial (n) / factorial (n - r);
  }
}
```

Only code contained in the above example's MathUtilities class can call factorial(). The factorial() method is a *helper method* to permutation() because it helps permutation () calculate a permutation. As such, factorial() isn't designed to be called from outside its class. (A case could be made for not declaring factorial() private because that method is quite useful. However, for the purpose of the above example, let's just say that factorial() should be declared private.) When a method only exists to serve other methods in a class, that helper method should be declared private. Declaring helper methods private helps promote information hiding and keeps class design clean and easy to maintain.

If you declare a method public, code contained in its class and other packages' classes can call that method, as shown in the example below:

```
public class Color
{
  private int color;
  public int getColor () { return color; }
}
```

Declaring Color public makes Color accessible to other packages. However, getc.olor() is not callable from code in those packages unless it is also marked public.

Finally, if you declare a method protected, that method resembles a method with default access level. The only difference: subclasses in any package can access protected methods. Examine the following code:

```
class Employee
{
  // Several fields are declared but not shown in this example.
  protected double computeSalary ()
  {
    return hoursWorked * hourlyRate;
  }
}
```

Only code contained in Employee, other classes declared in the same package as Employee, and all Employee's subclasses (declared in any package) can call computeSalary().

Modifiers

You can declare a method with a modifier keyword: abstract or final and/or static and/or native and/or synchronized.

If you declare a method abstract, it only consists of a method signature; there is no block. Furthermore, the class in which the abstract method is declared must also be declared abstract. Finally, an abstract method cannot be declared final, static, native, synchronized, or private at the same time.

If you declare a method final, the compiler ensures that the method cannot be overridden by subclasses.

If you declare a method static, that method is known as a class method because it can only access class fields. However, if static is not specified, the method is known as an instance method because it can access instance fields as well as class fields.

If you declare a method native, only a method signature is present. The method body is written in C++ and stored in a platform-specific library.

Finally, if you declare a method synchronized, only one thread at a time can execute method code.

Note: I will discuss abstract, native, and synchronized methods as well as method overriding in future articles.

Instance methods

An *instance method* accesses the instance fields and class fields declared in its class. To declare an instance method, do not specify the static keyword in the instance method signature. Check out the following code:

```
class Employee
{
  private double salary;
  void setSalary (double s)
  {
    salary = s;
  }
}
```

set Salary() is an instance method; it accesses the salary instance field.

Suppose you have an instance method with a parameter that has the same name as an instance field. Is it possible to assign the parameter's value to the same-named field? For an answer, examine the following example:

```
class Employee
{
  private double salary;
  void setSalary (double salary)
  {
    this.salary = salary;
  }
}
```

The setSalary () instance method declares a parameter named salary. That method's body assigns the parameter salary to the instance field salary. To accomplish that task, setSalary() uses keyword this.

One of the stranger keywords in Java and other object-oriented languages, this identifies the current object at the source code level. When you prefix a field name with this, you say, "Access the field belonging to this object."

Suppose you want to call an instance method. The manner in which you make that call depends on whether the instance method is being called from another instance method in the same class, from another instance method in another class, from a class method in the same class, or from a class method in another class.

Call an instance method from another instance method in the same class by specifying the method's name and argument list. The following example demonstrates that:

```
class MyClass
{
  void first () { second (true); }
  void second (boolean firstFlag)
  {
    if (firstFlag)
       System.out.println ("First flag.");
    else
```

```
        System.out.println ("Second flag.");
    }
}
```

The above example's first() instance method calls the second() instance method with a default argument value set to true. You don't have to prefix the method call with an object reference variable.

Call an instance method from another class's instance method by completing the following: Create an object from the former instance method's class, assign that object's reference to an object reference variable, and prefix the object reference variable to the instance method. This code demonstrates that:

```
class AnotherClass
{
    void callSecond ()
    {
        MyClass mc = new MyClass ();
        mc.second (false);
        new MyClass ().second (false);
    }
}
```

AnotherClass's callSecond() method creates a MyClass object and assigns its reference to mc. callSecond(), then uses the mc. prefix to call MyClass's second() instance method with a false argument value.

AnotherClass also demonstrates that you don't need an object reference variable to call an instance method. Instead, the new MyClass ().second (false); expression creates an object from MyClass and then implicitly uses that object's reference to call second().

Finally, to call an instance method from either a class method in the same class as the instance method or a different class's class method, follow the same approach as you did when you called the instance method from another class's instance method.

Instance method calls can be chained together using a technique called *method chaining*, which the following example demonstrates:

```
class HelloGoodBye
{
    public static void main (String [] args)
    {
        new HelloGoodBye ().hello ().goodbye ();
    }
    HelloGoodBye hello ()
    {
        System.out.println ("Hello");
```

```
    return this;
  }
  void goodbye ()
  {
    System.out.println ("Goodbye");
  }
}
```

HelloGoodBye's main() method creates a new HelloGoodBye object and calls its hello() method. Because hello() returns a reference to that same object (via hello()'s return this statement), a goodbye() method call is chained to the end of the hello() method call. (You will sometimes see method chaining used in Java source code, so it's good to know what's happening.)

Class Methods

A *class method* is a method that accesses the class fields declared in its class. To declare a class method, specify the static keyword in the class method signature. Check out this code:

```
class Employee
{
  private static int numEmployees;
  static void setEmployeeCount (int numEmp)
  {
    numEmployees = numEmp;
  }
}
```

The above example's setEmployeeCount() class method assigns the value of its numEmp parameter to Employee's numEmployees class field. If the parameter had been named numEmployees, could you use this to assign the parameter to the same-named class field? For an answer, check out the example below:

```
class Employee
{
  private static int numEmployees;
  static void setEmployeeCount (int numEmployees)
  {
    this.numEmployees = numEmployees; // Compiler error.
  }
}
```

You cannot use this within a class method because this refers to the current class instance, and a class method is not associated with any class instance.

The manner in which you call a class method depends on whether the class method is being called from another class method in the same class, from another class's class method, from an instance method in the same class, or from another class's instance method.

You can call a class method from another class method in the same class by specifying the method's name and argument list as in the following code:

```
class FirstAndSecond
{
  static void first ()
  {
    System.out.println ("first");
    second ();
  }

  static void second ()
  {
    System.out.println ("second");
  }
}
```

The above example's first() class method calls the second() class method. You don't have to prefix the method call with a class name.

To call a class method from another class's class method, prefix the class method call with the name of its class and the dot operator:

```
class UseFirstAndSecond
{
  public static void main (String [] args)
  {
    FirstAndSecond.first ();
    FirstAndSecond.second ();
  }
}
```

The above example's main() method calls the first() and second() methods in FirstAndSecond. The main() method accomplishes that task by prefixing FirstAndSecond. to each class method.

To call a class method from an instance method in the same class, specify the method's name and argument list. That is the same as calling the class method from another class method in the same class.

Finally, you call a class method from another class's instance method just as you do when calling the class method from another class's class method.

So far, I have said nothing about how to pass arguments to either instance or class methods during a method call. In the C++ world, there are two approaches to this task: call-by-value and call-by-reference. *Call-by-value* makes a copy of each method argument and passes that copy to the method. Because the method receives only a copy of the argument value, that method cannot modify the original value. In contrast, *call-by-reference* passes the address of an argument's variable to the method. That implies the method does not receive a copy of the argument value, but receives the address of that value's storage location—and can modify the original value.

Java supports call-by-value and does not support call-by-reference. Therefore, only a copy of each primitive or reference argument passes to a Java method during a method call That method can modify the copy's value, but cannot modify the original value. To put this idea into perspective, take a close look at Listing 3:

Listing 3. CBDemo.java

```
// CBDemo.java
class Employee
{
    private double salary;
    double getSalary () { return salary; }
    void setSalary (double salary) { this.salary = salary; }
}
class CBDemo
{
        public static void main (String [] args)
    {
        int v = 12;
        Employee e = new Employee ();
        e.setSalary (50000.0);
        System.out.println ("v = " + v);
        System.out.println ("e salary = " + e.getSalary ());
        changeArgs (v, e);
        System.out.println ("v = " + v);
        System.out.println ("e salary = " + e.getSalary ());
    }
    static void changeArgs (int x, Employee y)
    {
      x = 30;
      y.setSalary (30000.0);
    }
}
```

CBDemo declares and initializes two variables in its main() method: v and e. Variable v is based on the integer primitive data type, whereas e is a reference variable that holds a reference to an object created from Employee. At the start of the changeArgs(), method call, the JVM allocates memory (on the method call stack) for temporary storage. From a source code perspective, one of the temporary storage locations is named x, whereas the other temporary storage location is named y. The JVM then copies the value in v to x, and copies the value in e to y. Within changeArgs(), an assignment is made to x, and an attempt is made to change the salary field of the Employee object that y references. (The JVM destroys both x and y when execution leaves changeArgs().) Take a look at the following output:

```
v = 12
e salary = 50000.0
v = 12
e salary = 30000.0
```

Clearly, x = 3 0; did not change the value in v. Therefore, v must have been passed call-by-value to changeArgs(). But was e also passed call-by-value? The answer is yes. The JVM placed a copy of e's reference value in y. At that point, both e and y referenced the same Employee object, and could call that object's setsalary() method to manipulate its salary field. If the JVM had used call-by-reference, y would contain a reference to variable e, and not a reference to the object—and y.setSalary (30000.0); would probably crash the JVM.

Are you still skeptical about e being passed call-by-value? If so, perform the following experiment: Add y = null; to the end of changeArgs()—just after y.setSalary (30000.0);—and recompile. Run the program. If you see the previous output, e was passed call-by-value. But if you see an error message stating something about NullPointerException, e was passed call-by-reference. That error message arises from the e.getsalary() method call that follows the changeArgs() method call. If e's value was passed call-by-reference, y = null; would assign null to e, and the attempt to call the getsalary() method, via e's null reference, would cause the JVM to terminate that program with a NullPointerException message. However, you will not see that message because e was passed call-by-value.

NOTE

As with other object-reference arguments, the JVM uses call-by-value to pass array reference arguments to a method. As a result, a method can modify an array's element values. However, the method cannot assign an array's reference to the original array variable (located outside the method).

Overloading Methods

Declaring multiple methods with the same name but with different parameter lists is known as *overloading* a method. The compiler selects the appropriate method by choosing a method whose name, number of parameters, and parameter data types match a method call's name, number of arguments, and argument data types. Examine the code below:

```
void print ()
{
    System.out.println ("Default");
}
void print (String arg)
{
    System.out.println (arg);
}
```

The above example demonstrates two overloaded print() methods. Specifying print() results in a call to the top method, whereas specifying print ("Hello"); results in a call to the bottom method.

A method **cannot** be overloaded by only changing return data types. The compiler reports an error if it encounters two method declarations in the same class with the same names and parameter lists:

```
int sum (int x, int y)
{
    return x + y;
}
long sum (int x, int y)
{
    return x + y;
}
```

The above example demonstrates two nonoverloaded sum() methods. The compiler will report an error because declaring a method that is identical to an existing method except for a different return data type does not give the compiler enough information to tell those methods apart. How can the compiler distinguish between the above example's sum() methods when confronted with sum (3, 2)?

Constructors

A *constructor* is a special method called by the creation operator to initialize an object. Place your own custom initialization code in the constructor. Because constructors are methods, they can be declared with parameter lists and access specifiers. However, a constructor must be given the same name as the class in which it is declared. Furthermore, a constructor must not be declared with a return data type.

Refer to Listing 2 in Part 1, which presents a CODemo2 class along with the following line of code: CODemo2 obj1 = new CODemo2 ();. I noted that CODemo2() is a constructor. However, there was no CODemo2() constructor declared in CODemo2. What's going on? Basically, when you declare a class and do not specify a constructor, the compiler creates a default constructor with an empty parameter list. Take a look at this example:

```
class X
{
}
```

X looks empty, but it's not. In reality, the compiler sees X with a default no-argument constructor, as demonstrated by the following example:

```
class X
{
   X ()
   {
   }
}
```

The compiler only creates a default no-argument constructor when no other constructors are explicitly declared in the class. If you declare any constructor in the class, the compiler will **not** generate a default no-argument constructor. See the code below:

```
class X
{
  private int i;
  X (int i)
  {
    this.i = i;
  }
}
class UseX
{
  public static void main (String [] args)
  {
    X x1 = new X (2);
    X x2 = new X (); // Compiler error.
  }
}
```

In the preceding example, an attempt to call the default no-argument constructor results in a compiler error because there is no default no-argument constructor.

Constructors initialize instance fields to explicit values. The compiler inserts initialization code that explicitly initializes instance fields into the constructor prior to any developer-provided code. For proof, check out the following example:

```
class X
{
   int i = 5;
   X ()
   {
      System.out.println (i);
   }
}
class UseX
{
   public static void main (String [] args)
   {
      X x = new X ();
   }
}
```

If you run UseX, you'll discover 5 as that program's output. Obviously, the compiler must have initialized i prior to the System.out.println (i); method call in X().

You can declare multiple constructors in a class. Multiple constructors make it possible to perform different kinds of initialization. To see an example, check out Listing 4:

Listing 4. Geometry.java

```
// Geometry.java
class Circle
{
  private int x, y, r;
  Circle ()
  {
    // System.out.println ("Before");
    this (0, 0, 1);
    System.out.println ("After");
  }
  Circle (int x, int y, int r)
  {
    this.x = x;
    this.y = y;
    this.r = r;
  }
```

```
  int getX () { return x; }
  int getY () { return y; }
  int getRadius () { return r; }
}
class Geometry
{
  public static void main (String [] args)
  {
    Circle c1 = new Circle ();
    System.out.println ("Center X = " + c1.getX ());
    System.out.println ("Center Y = " + c1.getY ());
    System.out.println ("Center Radius = " + c1.getRadius ());
    Circle c2 = new Circle (5, 6, 7);
    System.out.println ("Center X = " + c2.getX ());
    System.out.println ("Center Y = " + c2.getY ());
    System.out.println ("Center Radius = " + c2.getRadius ());
  }
}
```

Geometry.java declares a pair of classes: Circle and Geometry. Class Circle declares a pair of constructors. The first constructor takes no arguments and contains the following line of code: this (0, 0, 1);, which calls the second three-argument constructor. (Java requires use of keyword—this in place of a constructor name.)

A constructor call, via this(), must be the first developer-provided code in a constructor method. Otherwise, the compiler reports an error. (That is the reason for turning System.out.println ("Before"); into a comment.) Because a constructor call must be the first line of code, you cannot specify two constructor calls in a constructor. For example, you cannot state this (0, 0, 1); this (60, 30, 30);. If you try, the compiler reports an error.

If you study the source code to Java's class library, you'll come across class declarations consisting of only a single constructor declared private. In addition, you might encounter a method called getInstance() that allows only a single object from that class to be created. These types of classes are singletons.

A *Singleton* is a *design pattern*—frequently occurring code specification—in which only a single object can ever be created from a class. The reason for the restriction is the cost and the probability of error associated with the creation of multiple objects from that class. For example, suppose you declare a class that mimics a network connection. You only need a single object to communicate with the network connection because establishing the connection is time-intensive and subject to error (the connection might be down). The following example declares a singleton class that provides network access:

```
public class NetworkConnection
{
  private static NetworkConnection singleton;
  private NetworkConnection ()
  {
```

```
    // The code in this constructor establishes the network connection.
    // This code deals with situations in which the connection is down.
  }
  public static NetworkConnection getInstance ()
  {
    if (singleton == null)
      singleton = new NetworkConnection ();
    return singleton;
  }
}
```

Because NetworkConnection declares a single private constructor, it is not possible to specify NetworkConnection nc = new NetworkConnection ();. Only one instance of NetworkConnection can be created, by calling getInstance. The following code demonstrates that:

```
NetworkConnection nc = NetworkConnection.getInstance ();
```

Review

In this article, you learned how to declare fields and methods by using various access specifiers and modifiers. Furthermore, you learned how to distinguish between class and instance fields, and how to distinguish between class and instance methods. Finally, you learned about enumerated types and singletons.

A Pedagogical Approach to Discussing Fundamentals of Object Oriented Programming Principles: Using ADT Set

INTRODUCTION

OBJECTIVES

After reading this article you will:

- Understand the concepts: decomposition, modularity, and encapsulation
- Clearly understand Java's implementation of sets.

TERMINOLOGIES

Set • Union • Intersection • Containment

A Pedogogical Approach to Discussing Fundamental Object-Oriented Programming Principles: Using the ADT Set

BY NOA RAGONIS

Computer science (CS) instructors look for "good" examples that allow in-depth discussion of the fundamental concepts of object-oriented programming (OOP), yet keep the implementation framework simple. This paper presents a case study that uses the abstract data type (ADT) Set as such a "good" example. Familiarity with the Set type and the need for relatively basic programming tools for its implementation enable to delve quickly into the desirable discussions. The paper suggests a teaching sequence that includes introducing the problem and different design considerations that relate to the structures of classes and operations; a discussion of the projection of the different designs chosen, focusing on the relations between the classes; and an additional presentation of different representations of the Set values involving efficiency aspects. The teaching sequence takes into account authentic inputs from students obtained while studying this example, and offers pedagogical guidelines for its use. The example can be used within diverse educational contexts and has already been applied in high school classes, pre-service teacher preparatory courses, and study programs for in-service teachers.

*****

1.0 INTRODUCTION

Educators are constantly looking for examples that provide opportunities to discuss fundamental principles of object-oriented programming (OOP) and, at the same time, are simple to implement. Researchers, on their part, have expressed various concerns about choosing such examples [1,3,4]. Börstler et al. emphasized the importance of using appropriate examples since learners use examples as templates, guidelines, and inspiration for writing their own programs [1]. They also proposed an evaluation instrument to evaluate examples of object-oriented programs that identifies three main properties: technical quality, object-oriented quality, and didactic quality. The first stage in solving a problem within the OOP framework is the design path—choosing the appropriate, required classes. In this stage, learners must apply the fundamental OOP principles that influence the comprehensive problem-solving process until reaching a complete solution. This stage involves abstraction, the application of which is recognized as being difficult for students [e.g., 2,5]. Our recommendation, therefore, is to guide learners through these processes to facilitate their own skill acquisition process.

This paper discusses the use of the mathematical type Set as such an appropriate example. Sets are frequently used as exercises in CS studies but the focus is usually on manipulating the array data rather than on the conceptual aspect of regarding the set as an *object*. The students' previous knowledge of the *Set* concept and its relevant functions (such as union and intersection), enable one to focus on the application of the fundamental OOP principles—decomposition, modularity and encapsulation—based on recognizing the problem entities, and to consider the structure, meaning and context of different designs.

The paper suggests a teaching sequence that includes introducing the problem and different design considerations that relate to the structures of classes and operations; a discussion of the projection of the different designs chosen, focusing on the relations between the classes; and an additional presentation of different representations of the *Set* values involving efficiency aspects.

The case study is limited to a set of same-type elements and relates specifically to sets of integers. Implementation is in Java.

The exercise and the discussion that accompany the development of the different solutions follow the spirit of the constructivist teaching approach. The teaching guidelines are based on extensive use of the exercise in various educational contexts and takes into account authentic inputs from students obtained while studying this example.

2.0 THE SET PROBLEM

2.1 Mathematical Requirements

2.1.1 *Definition of a set*

The basic characteristics of a mathematical set are (a) A set is a collection of elements; (b) the size of a set is unlimited; (c) the order of the elements in the set is irrelevant; (d) duplicate values in a set have no meaning.

The basic function defined for a set is does the set contain an element.

2.1.2 *Functions on two sets*

Four basic two-sets functions are defined: union, intersection, inclusion, and complementation. Due to space limitations, we chose the union function to serve as an example of a function on two sets. The other functions can be addressed similarly.

2.2 The Student Exercise

The main aim of the exercise is to implement the mathematical set functions in the programming language using the object-oriented approach. The pre-programming structures students need are conditions, loops, and arrays. The student worksheet starts with the basic set definitions followed by simple examples to illustrate the different functions. Students are asked to develop a project according to the following steps:

1. Choose the appropriate class/classes needed in order to perform the specified required operations.
2. For each class, plan the required attributes and methods.
3. Define the type of each attribute.
4. Define the header of each method.
5. For each method, write an example of the method invocation.
6. Implement the class/classes in Java.
7. Implement a test class.

3.0 DIDACTIC ASPECTS

3.1 Preliminary Discussion

First, the instructor must decide, according to the population, whether to let the students cope with the requirements on their own or in small groups, or whether to guide them through the process. When the instructor chooses to guide students, thus easing their entrance into the problem-solving process, we recommend starting with a discussion about what needs to be implemented. The implementation in a given programming language requires the addition of "administration" methods, such as a set construction method, to enable the use of sets.

The solution to the proposed exercise includes the minimal, additional methods that enable the use of sets: *set init* and *is set empty*. The following two tables can be presented to the students: Table 1 presents the basic set operations and Table 2 presents some of the operations that can be performed on two sets. Neither of them dictates the choice of a specific class structure, but only clarifies what needs to be implemented.

TABLE 1. SET OPERATIONS

Operation	Documentation
Set init	Returns a set
Is set empty?	Returns true if set is empty, or false if not
Is element in set?	Returns true if a given element is in the set and false if not

The insertion or removal of an element to or from a set is not defined as a mathematical concept. These operations, therefore, are not presented as requirements in the exercise, but can be added according to need. These considerations are also a suitable subject for discussion with students.

TABLE 2. OPERATIONS ON TWO SETS

Operation	Documentation
Union	Returns the union set of the two sets
Intersection	Returns the intersection set of the two sets
Containing	Returns *true* if one set is a subset of the other set and *false* if not

3.2 Didactic Guidelines

We recommend that instructors consider the following didactical guidelines for discussions on fundamental OOP concepts:

- Tables 1 and 2 can be given to the students instead of being developed as part of the exercise.
- Different options exist for decomposing classes to solve the problem and for implementing the set attributes. It is important to let students consider their own versions and test them throughout the entire design process.
- Stages 4 and 5 are important since it is here that students validate their design and better understand the choices they made in previous stages. This is the time to go back and make changes according to the insights gained.
- Implementing the classes is not too demanding due to the limited number of methods and the fact that no difficult algorithmic thinking is required. The implementation enables the students to examine the semantic and syntactic relations between the classes they design.
- Implementing a test class is essential. Students tackle object creation and methods invocation, and test their ideas. The main issue here is to test the students' design rather than to check their programming skills.

3.3 Recommended Teaching Sequence

The recommended teaching sequence is as follows:

1. Present the exercise and give students time to think about it;
2. Decide whether to discuss the basic requirements and present Tables 1 and 2;
3. Give students time to work through Stages 1–5 of the exercise. Students can work on their own or in groups of two or three. It is important not to interrupt the work until Stage 5 is completed; at this stage, the students address the relations between the chosen classes. In some cases this stage can lead to changes in the students' previous decisions, and as a result, some stages are repeated accordingly;
4. When the majority of students have completed Stage 5, conduct a class discussion about their solutions. We recommend including the design considerations presented in Section 4.
5. Let the students choose whether to continue with their own original design or adopt a different design following the class discussion, before continuing on to Stages 6 and 7.
6. Further discussion can be offered on the representation of the set values, as presented in Section 5.
7. Section 6 presents additional directions in which the exercise may be expanded

The time dedicated to the teaching-learning process depends on the target population. For high school students, four 45-minute lessons usually suffice, whereas for academic classes we recommend two sessions of 1.5 hours each.

4.0 DESIGN CONSIDERATIONS

This section discusses the basic implementation of the Set class and examines four different approaches to implementing operations on two sets, of which three are "appropriate" and one is "inappropriate". In this section, we focus on the decomposition of the classes, and in Section 5 we discuss the implementation of the Set class attributes.

4.1 Implementing the Basic Set Class

Table 3 presents the interface of the basic methods in the Set class. The constructor method returns an object of the *Set* class and the other methods are invoked on an object of the *Set* class.

TABLE 3. BASIC METHODS IN THE SET CLASS

Method Header	Documentation
public Set (int[] elements)	Returns a set object containing the elements that appear in *elements*
public boolean isEmpty ()	Returns *true* if the set is empty, else returns *false*
public boolean isInSet (int element)	Returns *true* if the element is in the set, else returns *false*

A constructor method must be used to initialize a set and several such methods should be considered: (1) A method that initializes a set whose values are received by the parameter array; (2) a method that returns an empty set; or (3) a method in which the set values are received from input. The second method leads to the need to implement an additional method to enable insertion of an element into the set. The third method involves an unacknowledged constructor that involves input. The first method, on the other hand, requires no additional methods. An empty set can be returned when the parameter array is an empty array or, alternatively, an exchangeable *Set* constructor can be added that returns an empty set. Although we recommend using the first method (as shown in Table 3), instructors can, nevertheless, leave this issue to the discretion of the students. If the second method is chosen, the set constructor and the insert method should be developed. The class interface will include the methods presented in Table 4 in addition to the methods *isEmpty()* and *isInSet(int element)* presented in Table 3.

TABLE 4. EXPANSION OF THE BASIC METHODS IN THE SET CLASS

Method Header	**Documentation**
public Set ()	Returns an empty set
public insert (int element)	Inserts an *element* into the current set

4.2 DESIGN AND IMPLEMENTATION OF OPERATIONS ON TWO SETS

In this section, we discuss three appropriate design alternatives for implementing operations on two sets: (a) Including the two-set operations in the Set class (4.2.1); (b) defining operations on two sets as static methods (4.2.2); and (c) enclosing the static operations on two sets into a special service class (4.2.3). We will then discuss an inappropriate solution that defines an additional class whose attributes are two (or three) sets (4.2.4). The discussion will relate to semantic and syntactic issues and several misconceptions held by students will be addressed as well. Since each of the design alternatives is based on the previous one, we recommend that instructors guide their students in a discussion about the various alternatives. It is important for students to be aware of the different considerations, whether their own solution is satisfactory or not and whether it is correct, (i.e. works) or not.

TABLE 6. THE STATIC UNION METHOD

Method Header	*public static Set union (Set a, Set b)*
Documentation	The method accepts two sets a, b and returns a new set that is their union
Method Invocation within the class in which the method is defined	*Set c = union (a, b)*;

Method Invocation from an external class of the class in which the method is defined	*Set c = Set.union (a, b);*

4.2.1 *Including two-set methods in the Set class*

The first alternative is to include the two-set operations in the Set class. The outcome is that a method is invoked on one set while the second set serves as a parameter. Table 5 presents the interface of the union method according to this design and the way it is invoked.

TABLE 5. THE UNION METHOD IN THE SET CLASS

Method Header	*public Set union (Set b)*
Documentation	The method accepts a set b and returns a new set that is the union of the current set and set *b*
Method Invocation	*Set c = a.union (b);*

Although this alternative can be considered to be consistent with OOP principles, we can argue that there are still some semantic problems. From a mathematical point of view, the syntax of the method invocation is not natural since the two sets, which are supposedly equivalent, are used differently. The fact that the operation is invoked on one of the sets, while the second set serves as a parameter, can lead to an incorrect perception of the operation by project users. Specifically, one could conclude that the elements of the set that serves as a parameter are added to the set on which the method is invoked. Emphasizing these considerations to the students can lead to an examination of the second alternative approach.

Student misconception

One characteristic misconception that frequently appears in students' solutions is their intuitive use of a method with two set parameters like they use the mathematical union notation Thus, many students' first attempt consists of writing the union method using two parameters—the two sets needed for the union function. The implementation of the method header is thus:

public Set union (Set a, Set b)

Some students examine their design only when writing the method invocation. Since the method is defined in the *Set* class, it should be invoked on a *Set object.* So, which object should it be invoked on? What is the relationship between the "current" set and the sets that appear as parameters? Some students do not reveal this misconception even at this stage, ignore the problem and proceed to write the next, incorrect invocation:

Set c = union (a, b);

4.2.2 *Implementing static two-set methods*

The second alternative is to implement static methods for operations on two sets. This alternative seems to fit better the mathematical concept and its invocation does not seem "strange". Table 6 presents the interface of the union method when designed as a static method and the way it is invoked.

The static methods can be defined in a main class in which the main method is defined. Alternatively, they can be defined in the *Set* class (see the following paragraph) or in a service class (see Section 4.2.3).

Clarifying the concepts and the student misconception

The alternative of including the static two-set methods in the Set class is less consistent with OOP principles. We believe that with novice learners it is better to adhere to an elementary distinction: a class that represents an entity should include only methods that are invoked on an object of the class—in our case, a *Set object.* Moreover, using the word Set when identifying and creating a Set object, as it appears in a variable declaration: Set c or when using a constructor: *Set c = new Set(elements),* could be confused with the use of the word Set to indicate the class in which the method is defined: *Set.union(a,b).* Novice students might interpret this as the creation of an object using the constructor method.

4.2.3 *A service class for the static two-set methods*

A service class, according to our interpretation, is a class that contains static methods, and thus serves other classes. A service class does not represent an entity. The static methods for two sets can be included in a special service class called, for example, *SetOperations.* The class is dedicated to methods that relate to operations on two sets. Table 7 presents the interface of the union method as a static method in a service class and the way it is invoked.

This alternative, which is based on the previous one, adheres to the principle of separating operations on two sets from the basic Set class, and enables modular inclusion of all required operations. Using such a service class, however, requires that each application that uses sets has access to both classes: (1) The *Set* class, which represents the set entity; and (2) the service class *SetOperations,* which contains the operations on two sets.

TABLE 7. THE UNION STATIC METHOD IN THE SETOPERATIONS CLASS

Method Header	*public static Set union (Set a, Set b)*
Documentation	The method accepts two sets *a, b* and returns a new set that is their union
Method Invocation	*Set c = SetOperations.union (a, b);*

4.2.4 *An inappropriate solution: Define a TwoSets class*

To overcome the need to define operations that relate to two sets, some students suggested the following misleading solution. They defined an additional class, whose attributes are two sets. Figure 3 presents a partial implementation of this class.

The consequences of choosing this solution is the creation of an object whose attributes are two sets. Table 8 presents an example of such an interface.

TABLE 8. THE UNION METHOD IN THE TWOSETS CLASS

Method Header	*public static Set union ()*
Documentation	The method returns a new set that is the union of the sets that serve as attributes of the current object
Method Invocation	*Set setsObj = new TwoSets (a, b); Set c = setsObj.union ();*

This solution is inappropriate for three main reasons. First, an entity of two sets does not really exist nor is one needed. Second, it seems rather strange, semantically, to use the union operation with no parameters. Third, according to this interpretation, before performing any operation on two sets, a *TwoSets* object must be created. Such an object, however, has no semantic meaning and its creation is needed only due to the misleading design of the *TwoSets* class.

We also encountered students who designed a similar version, but with three set attributes. The purpose of the third set attribute was to contain the computed set that is the result of the union operation.

5.0 REPRESENTING THE SET VALUES

In Section 4 we explored different designs of classes. In this section, we will discuss different possible representations of set values. This discussion is beyond OOP considerations and involves other related programming considerations needed to obtain a solution. After choosing the OOP design version, the way of implementing the set values, and accordingly the way of implementing the body of set operations, must be decided on. When teaching according to the object-first approach, the initial focus is on the fundamental OO concepts. Still, students simultaneously acquire other programming skills as well. This case study enables us to discuss additional programming concepts, such as different representations of required data, and their impact on the operations' efficiency. The different possible representations of the set values can be integrated into each of the previous designs. Instructors who teach OOP after imperative programming may find the next discussion superfluous.

The assumption is that *array* is the only programming tool students can use to implement a set. Two main data structures can be considered: (a) an array that contains the set elements; or (b) a *boolean* array that specifies the existence of the sets' elements. While discussing these two approaches, instructors can bring to their students' awareness the various considerations and decisions that programmers make during the implementation path, such as algorithmic considerations, efficiency considerations, and generalization issues. We will present the two versions and illustrate the different considerations accordingly. Appendix A presents some programming code according to the two versions.

5.1 Arrays of Set Elements

A set can be implemented using an array that contains the set elements. Choosing this option leads to the following alternatives:

a. Using a fixed-size array in which the elements are assigned consecutively, beginning at the first array cell, and the current number of elements must be smaller than the fixed array size. When choosing this implementation, students must address the following considerations:
   i. Since each new element must be inserted into the set in the next "empty" cell in the array, the way in which an empty cell is represented must be determined and all class methods must treat the chosen representation consistently.
   ii. The fixed array size must be predetermined. One option is to use a static constant to represent the maximum size of all sets created. A second option is to use an attribute that represents the maximum optional size of each set created. Choosing the second approach requires updating the constructor methods in the class *Set* to allow initialization of the *maxSize* attribute. For example, the header of the constructor method that returns an empty set will be *public Set (int maxSize)*
   This option is not recommended since it digresses too much from the mathematical concept of the set.
b. Using a fixed-size array in which, instead of relating to an empty cell, an attribute is added that represents the number of actual elements in the set, i.e. a *counter* attribute. The management of the counter attribute is the responsibility of the class methods: initializing to zero in the constructor, increasing by one when inserting an element, and decreasing by one when removing an element. The counter attribute can be used as a limit index when searching for an element in the array. Reviewing this option with the students enables the instructor to discuss data hiding aspects. The counter should not be presented to users of the *Set* class since it is needed only to manage the data and is not part of the Set concept. Therefore, all other uses of the counter, other than the class, must be forbidden. This means, for example, that no *geter* or *seter* methods are defined for the counter attribute.
c. Some languages allow the declaration of variables at runtime. This may lead to a dynamic implementation of the array size. Each operation that causes a change in the set size will allocate a new array. The size of the new array will be either greater or smaller by one than the current array size, depending on the operation. The values are copied from the current array to the new array, and the new array is assigned to the attribute. In this version, at any given time, the data contains exactly the set values. Even though this option seems to be inefficient in terms of programming, it is better suited to the idea of an unlimited set size.

5.2 A Boolean Array

A set can also be implemented using a *boolean* array. Each of the array's cells represents an optional element value of the set—the cell index. If an element is in the set, the value will be *true,* otherwise the value will be *false.* The advantage of this representation is that the index of a cell can be used to directly access that cell. This representation can be used only if the range of values that can be included in the set is final and of an ordinal type (integer or char), otherwise direct access is not applicable.

5.3 Efficiency Comparison

A comparison can be made between the efficiencies of the set operations according to the different representations. Table 9 presents the efficiency of a sample of set methods and their efficiency according to the different representations. Even if formal measures of efficiency (such as the Big-O) have not yet been introduced to students at their current stage of learning, this issue can be discussed intuitively.

TABLE 9. A COMPARISON OF THE EFFICIENCY OF SET METHODS WHERE N IS THE SET SIZE

Operation Representation	**Is the set empty**	**Is the element in the set**	**Union of two sets**
Array of set elements (5.1 - a)	0(1)	0(n)	0(n2)
Array of set elements and the current size (5.1 - b)	0(1)	0(n)	0(n2)
Boolean array (5.2)	0(n) (searches for any element)	0(1)	0(n)

6.0 FUTURE DIRECTIONS

The version of the exercise we have presented deals with a set of integers. The exercise can however be expanded in four main directions:

a. Expand the basic tools for performing operations on sets by adding methods such as "input a set" or "print a set". This will lead to a discussion about the appropriate place in which to define such tools.
b. Use different kinds of set element types such as a set of dates or a set of cards.
c. Expand the context of the exercise (see Section 6.1).
d. Define a generic class *SET<T>* (see Section 6.2).

e. Use built-in classes and compare them to the self-implemented class. For example: *interface Set<E>extends Collection<E>; Class HashSet<E>; Class AbstractSet<E>.*

The discussion of those options exceeds the scope of the current paper.

6.1 Expanding the Context

After the design and implementation of the mathematical set are understood, the context in which the set is used can be expanded. This is important for several reasons: Students should experience the actual use of the ADT set, and the discussion should not be limited only to the implementation of the ADT. Furthermore, when the *Set* class is used in a realistic context, students can apply knowledge gained while developing the ADT.

Following are two examples of possible scenarios:

Example 1: In a project that deals with teachers' time schedules, one of the attributes of a teacher can be a set of working days. Possible tasks can be to find common free days for teachers who teach a particular subject, or to find a day in which the most teachers are scheduled to teach.

Example 2: In a project that deals with a person's activities, one of the attributes can be a set of hobbies. Possible tasks can be to find hobbies common to two people, to find a person with a unique hobby, or to find the most frequent hobby of group of people. This context enables to discuss a group or a set of people in which each person has his or her own set of hobbies. Students must understand that using different kinds of set element types requires the definition of separate classes for each type. This could lead to future discussions on generic classes (as discussed below).

6.2 Generic Set Classes

The Set elements type, specifically integers in the presented implementation, can be easily changed into any built-in type (for example: double, char) or any user-defined type (for example: Card, Ball). Furthermore, in order to gain generalization, the Set class can be defined as a generic class *Set<T>*. In this case, the use of any set elements type is possible (built-in or user-defined). Use of a generic type for the set elements requires the following definition for the array of set elements:

private T[] values = (T[]) new Object[MAX_ELEMENTS];

In addition, the elements should be compared using the "equals" method; for example, *if (values[i].equals(element))*.

More changes that are significant are needed for the two-sets methods since generic types can not be used in a static context. This leads to a rejection of the version of the class *SetOperations,* and therefore to the selection of the implementation version of the two-sets methods within the Set class (see Section 2.4.1).

Generic types are taught at a later stage of learning. We recommend returning to this exercise after learning the implementation and uses of generic types and revisiting the various implementation considerations presented in Section 4.

7.0 SUMMARY

In this paper we described a case study that can be used as a summary exercise when teaching the basic OOP principles of decomposition, modularity, and encapsulation. The programming skills needed are mostly elementary and are not at the center of the discussion. The case study enables a discussion of class decomposition, the outcomes of the design decisions regarding semantic and syntactic issues, static and non-static issues, classes that represent entities versus service classes, and the implementation of attributes and their influence on method efficiency. The case study also enables instructors to emphasize the meaning of developing a code for implementing an ADT, and present its use in different contexts. The exercise can be extended to use in higher stages of learning and can involve generic and advanced built-in classes.

We recommend discussing with students the various considerations presented in the paper according to their academic level. The suggested investigation of the various class decomposition, the various implementation options, determining tradeoffs between different solutions, and the efficiency considerations involved are the essence of learning to program. This teaching-learning process gives students the opportunity to broaden their perspectives, to construct their own knowledge, and to refine it.

After slight adaptation, the case study can be used in diverse learning environments, such as high school classes, academic courses, and pre-service or in-service teacher preparatory courses. It is our experience that the kind of discussion presented here is beneficial for all respective populations.

REFERENCES

[1] Börstler, J., Christensen, H. B., Bennedsen, J., Nordström, M., Kallin Westin, L., Moström, J. E., and Caspersen, M. E. 2008. Evaluating OO example programs for CS1. In *Proceedings of the 13th Annual Conference on innovation and Technology in Computer Science Education* (Madrid, Spain, June 30–July 02, 2008), 47-52.

[2] Fleury, A. E. 2000. Programming in Java students-constructed rules. *SIGCSE Bulletin,* 32(1), 197-201.

[3] Malan, K. and Halland, K. 2004. Examples that can do harm in learning programming. In *Companion to the 19th Annual Conference on Object-Oriented Programming Systems, Languages, and Applications,* 83-87.

[4] Lin, J., Lin. K. and Wu, C. 1999. A content analysis of programming examples in high school computer textbooks in taiwan. *Journal of Computers in Mathematics and Science Teaching,* 18(3), 225-244.

[5] Ragonis, N. and Ben-Ari, M. 2005. A Long-Term Investigation of the Comprehension of OOP Concepts by Novices. *Computer Science Education,* 15(3), 203–221.

APPENDIX A

We now present a part of the project implementation to demonstrate different representations of the set values and their projection in the desired methods. The OOP design version that serves as the basis for the class implementation was presented in Section 4.2.3: The Set class is used to create and manipulate set objects, and the *SetOperations* service class is used for methods of two-sets functions.

The implementation code tends to prefer code readability and suppleness over programming sophistication.

Since all versions are supposed to serve the same application, the *TestSet* main method is identical in all of them and will be presented in Section A1 below.

Readers who will delve deeper into the codes will find additional relevant issues that must be considered and determined. One such question is whether or not to adhere to the rule that forbids direct access to the set value array using the next method: *public int[] getValues()*. In the next solutions, it is not permitted.

A1: Implementing an Array of Set Elements Using a Fixed-Size Array (presented in Section 5.1-a)

```
public class Set   {
    public static final int MAX_ELEMENTS = 100;
    private int[] values = new int[MAX_ELEMENTS];
    // The set values range is (0..1000)
    // -1 represents an empty cell
    public Set(int[] elements)   {
        for (int i= 0; i < elements.length; i++)
                values[i] = elements[i];
        for (int i= elements.length; i < values.length; i++)
                values[i] = -1;
    }
    public boolean isEmpty ( )   {
        return values[0] == -999;
    }
    public boolean isInSet (int element)   {
        for (int i= 0; i < values.length; i++)
                if (values[i] == element)
                    return true;
        return false;
    }
}
```

```
public class SetOperations   {
    public static Set union(Set a, Set b)
    {
          int[] elements = new int[Set.MAX_ELEMENTS];
          int counter =0;
          for (int i = 0;i < 1001; i++)   {
                if ( a.isInSet(i) || b.isInSet(i) )  {
                      elements[counter] = i;
                      counter++;
                }
          }
          return new Set(elements);
    }
}


public class TestSet   {
    public static void main(String [] args)   {
          int[] elements1 = {1,4,9,3};
          Set a = new Set (elements1);
          if ( a.isEmpty ( ) )
                {  System.out.println("The set is empty");       }
          if ( a.isInSet (3)  )  {
                {  System.out.println("The number 3 is in set"); }
          int[] elements2 = {1,2,8,3,7};
          Set b = new Set (elements2);
          Set c = SetOperations.union (a,b);
          if ( c.isInSet (1)  )
                {  System.out.println("The number 1 is in the union
                                                        set");   }
    }
}
```

A2: Implementing an Array of Set Elements Using an Attribute that Represents the Number of Actual Elements in the Set (presented in Section 5.1-b)

The difference in the *Set* class is that the restriction of representing an empty cell by -1 is no longer needed since a counter attribute is added.

```
public class Set    {
    public static final int MAX_ELEMENTS = 100;
    private int[] values = new int[MAX_ELEMENTS];
    private int counter = 0;
    // The set values range is (0..1000)
    public Set(int[] elements)    {
         for (int i= 0; i < elements.length; i++)
                   values[i] = elements[i];
         counter = elements.length;
    }
    public boolean isEmpty ( )    {
         return counter == 0;
    }
    public boolean isInSet (int element)    {
         for (int i= 0; i < counter; i++)
                   if (values[i] == element)
                          return true;
         return false;
    }
}
```

The difference in the *SetOperations* class is that since the counter is an attribute that is concealed even from class *SetOperations,* the constructor of the union set must be implemented with an array parameter whose size is identical to that of the new set.

```
public class SetOperations    {
    public static Set union(Set a, Set b)
    {
         int[] elements = new int[Set.MAX_ELEMENTS];
         int counter =0;
         for (int i = 0;i < 1001; i++)    {
                   if ( a.isInSet(i) || b.isInSet(i) )    {
                        elements[counter] = i;
                        counter++;
                   }
         }
         int[] clearElements = new int[counter];
         for (int i= 0; i < counter; i++)
                   clearElements[i] = elements[i];
         return new Set(clearElements);
    }
}
```

Thus, an additional manipulation is performed using the array *clearElements.*

A3: Implementing a Boolean Array (presented in Section 5.2)

```
public class Set  {
    public static final int MAX_ELEMENTS = 1001;
    private boolean[] values = new
                                boolean[MAX_ELEMENTS];
    // The set values range is (0..1000)
    public Set(int[] elements)    {
         for (int i= 0; i < elements.length; i++)
                   values[ elements[i] ] = true;
    }
    public Set(boolean[] elements)    {
         this.values = elements;
    }
    public boolean isEmpty ( )    {
         int i;
         for ( i = 0; (i<MAX_ELEMENTS) && (!values[i]);
                                              i++) {}
         return ( i == MAX_ELEMENTS);
    }
    public boolean isInSet (int element)    {
         return ( values[element] );
    }
```

The *SetOperations* class of this version can be identical to that of the version presented in Section A1. This can be discussed to emphasize that changing the representation of the set does not require changes in other classes.

```
public class SetOperations    {
    public static Set union(Set a, Set b)    {
         int[] elements = new int[Set.MAX_ELEMENTS];
         int counter =0;
         for (int i = 0;i < 1001; i++)     {
              if ( a.isInSet(i) || b.isInSet(i) )   {
                   elements[counter] = i;
                   counter++;
              }
         }
         return new Set(elements);
    }
}
```

Further discussion can lead to consider adding an alternative union method, the *unioni* method presented above, which requires an alternative *Set* constructor as well.

Part II: Inheritance and Polymorphism

Part II: Inheritance and Polymorphism

INTRODUCTION

In Object Oriented Programming the concept of inheritance simply means defining new classes from an existing one. That is, the new class is an extension of the existing class. Another way to say this is that the new class is derived or inherited from an existing class. This concept is a key feature of Object Oriented Programming. The existing class is called the direct super class and the new or derived class is called the direct subclass. A direct super class does not have any intervening class between itself and its direct subclass; conversely, a direct subclass does not have any class between itself and its direct super class. With this understanding, whenever the word subclass is used, it means direct subclass; and vice versa. Figure 2 is a conceptual drawing of the concept of inheritance. In the diagram **A** represents the super class and **B** represents the subclass.

Figure 2 A the direct super class and B the direct subclass

Java allows one and only one direct super class for any direct subclass. **A** super class on the other hand can have any number of subclasses. In addition, a subclass can serve as a super class for other subclasses. Figure 3 shows that class **A** has two subclasses—**B** and **C**; and subclass **C** is the super class for class **D**, making **D** an indirect subclass of **A**.

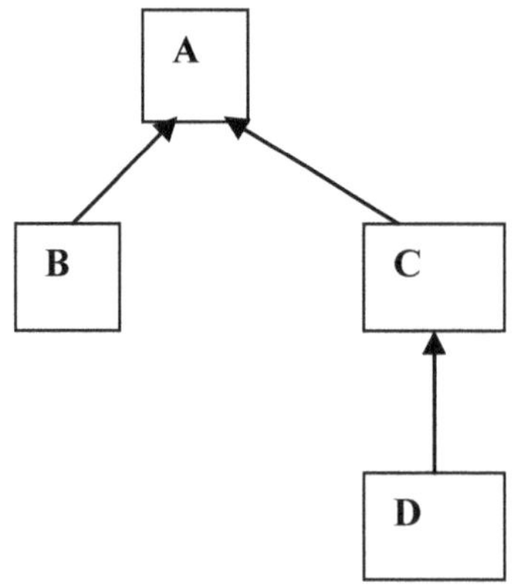

Figure 3 Classes B and C are direct subclasses of class A, and class D is a subclass of C

Conceptually two or more classes can be combined to form a new one. Although this is true with some programming paradigm, Java does not support this idea. **Figure 4** shows that class **R** is derived from class **P** and class **Q**. As we said before, Java does not support this form of inheritance.

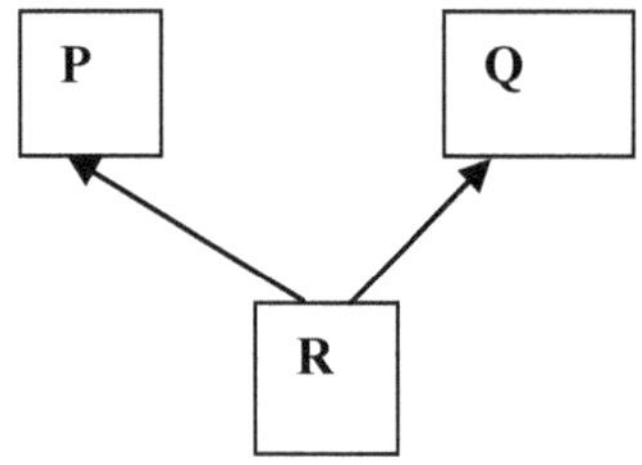

Figure 4 Class R inherits classes P and Q. (NOT SUPPORTED BY JAVA)

Some benefits of Inheritance are:

- Extensibility: the concept of inheritance allows you to create new entities from existing ones, and add new features to the new entity. This extended entity becomes a unique feature of the original entity.
- Maintainability: because each object is distinct, it makes it easier to maintain an entire system by modifying only those entities that require changes. Any changes made to an entity usually has little or no change to existing modules; thereby reducing programming time, reduces maintenance costs, and reduces program development time.

Some notes about Constructors

- Constructors are not considered inherited, but rather they are considered to be included as part of the definition of the subclass, as such they can be used to initialize variables in the super class.

- You may use constructors in the super class to assist with the initialization of variables in the derived class. To do so, you must use the Java method **super()**. Its format is as follows: ***super***(*<argument>*); When used, the statement must be the first executable statement in the constructor of the subclass.

Some notes about Data Members and Methods

- Non-private variables in the super class can be referenced directly by their names in the subclass.
- Private members of the super class cannot be accessed directly by its subclasses. Instead, you must provide public accessor methods to return their values.
- You can use the Java modifier **super** to reference the method in the super class. The format of using it is as follows: ***super*.nameOfMethod();**
- A subclass class can override the definition of its inherited method. That is, a subclass can redefine a method it inherits from a super class. The new method will undoubtedly have the same signature as the super class, but usually they have different code in the body. At runtime the object type determines which method is invoked.

The term polymorphism simply means that a substance or an object can exist in multiple forms. When applied to Object Oriented Programming, it means a reference variable can be used to create objects from different classes, and you can use this reference variable to call on methods from the different objects. Of course we could use different variable declarations for each object, but our intention is to understand the concept of polymorphism as it relates to Object Oriented programming. The programmer does not have to know the exact type of object in advance, so its behavior is implemented at runtime. This concept is called late binding or dynamic binding. In terms of Java, polymorphism exhibits itself in four basic forms, as you will see in the following three articles—overloading, inclusion, parametric, and coercion or casting.

Polymorphism: Prose of Java Programmers

INTRODUCTION

OBJECTIVES

After reading this article you will:

1. Understand the term polymorphism.
2. Be able to differentiate between universal polymorphism and ad-hoc polymorphism
3. Be able to differentiate between the two major forms of universal polymorphism – parametric polymorphism and inclusion polymorphism
4. Be able to differentiate between the two major forms of ad-hoc polymorphism – coercion polymorphism and overloading polymorphism
5. Know what overriding means
6. Be able to differentiate between method overloading and method overriding

TERMINOLOGIES

Universal polymorphism • Inclusion polymorphism • Parametric polymorphism • Ad-hoc polymorphism • Coercion • Operator overloading • Method overloading • Method overriding

Polymorphism: Prose of Java Programmers

BY ZDZISLAW SPLAWSKI

Abstract. In Java programming language as implemented in JDK 5.0 there appear rather advanced kinds of polymorphism, even if they are hidden under different names. The notion of polymorphism unifies many concepts present in typed programming languages, not necessary object-oriented. We briefly define some varieties of polymorphism and trace them in Java. Java shows that "industrial" programming languages are able to express more abstract patterns using rather involved theoretical means, hence the "working programmer" has to be better educated in order to understand them, recognize them in different programming languages under different names and superficial syntax, and make good use of them.

Monsieur Jourdain.

Par ma foi! il y a plus de quarante ans que je dis de la prose sans que j'en susse rien, et je vous suis le plus oblige du monde de m'avoir appris cela.
Molière

Zdzislaw Splawski, "Polymorphism: Prose of Java Programmers," from XXI Fall Meeting of Polish Information Processing Society Conference Proceedings, pp. 223–s231.

1. INTRODUCTION

Polymorphism <gr. πολυς = many + μορφη = form> in general means "multiform" and allows the same code to be assigned multiple types. This may be achieved in many ways, hence there are varieties of polymorphism in computer science and still new kinds of it are being proposed, but most of them are known only to theoreticians. The unqualified term "polymorphism" may cause some confusion, since among programmers it is often used to mean concrete kinds of polymorphism. For object-oriented programmers it almost always means inclusion polymorphism, for functional programmers—shallow parametric polymorphism, for theoreticians it usually means impredicative parametric polymorphism, as used in System F (called also polymorphic or second-order lambda-calculus). The "working programmer" usually identifies this term with inclusion polymorphism, but it does not mean that he did not unconsciously use other kinds of polymorphism (*vide* monsieur Jourdain, who all of his life has spoken prose not being aware of this fact). Our goal is to disclose other kinds of polymorphism which may be found in Java in order to make these mechanisms more accessible to the working programmer.

Since a long time people discussed how to include in Java programming language parametric polymorphism which allows abstracting over types. Some proposals were considered, among them GJ [2]. However it turned out that importing this mechanism from functional programming languages, e.g., Standard ML, raises some problems in connection with inclusion polymorphism. Thorup and Torgersen [13] proposed a variant of bounded polymorphism which integrates the merits of virtual types with F-bounded polymorphism. Their type system has been further developed, formalized, and proven sound by Igarashi and Viroli [10] within the Featherweight GJ calculus [9]. This mechanism is now available in JDK 5.0. Its short description can be found e.g., in [3, 14].

2. VARIETIES OF POLYMORPHISM

Many kinds of polymorphism can be found in modern programming languages. Below we provide necessary definitions (somewhat simplified, but suitable for this paper) and shortly characterize polymorphisms discussed in this paper.

Objects are programming units that associate data (called instance variables) with the operations (called methods) that can use or affect these data.

Classes are extensible templates for creating objects, providing initial values for instance variables and the bodies for methods. New objects can be created from a class with the new operator.

In terms of implementation we can recognize *universal polymorphism* when the same code is executed for any admissible type, whereas in case of *ad-hoc polymorphism* different code is executed for each type. There are two major kinds of universal polymorphism: *parametric* and *inclusion polymorphism,* and two major kinds of ad-hoc polymorphism: *coercion* and *overloading.*

Parametric polymorphism allows a simple piece of code to be typed "generically", using variables in place of actual types. These type variables are instantiated with concrete types. Parametric polymorphism guarantees uniform behavior on the range of types.

In *inclusion polymorphism* an object can be viewed as belonging to many different classes that need not to be disjoint; that is, there may be inclusion of classes. Inclusion polymorphism models *subtyping* and *subclassing (inheritance)*.

Subtyping. The type of an object is just the set of names and types of its methods. We say type S is a *subtype* of T (written S <: T), if a value of type S can be used in any context in which a value of type T is expected. We say T is a *supertype* of S if S is a subtype of T. Subtyping relation should be reflexive and transitive. Because values may have multiple types in languages supporting subtyping, we say these languages support *subtype polymorphism.* Object types fit naturally into the subtype relation.

Subclassing (inheritance). Classes are used not only to create objects, but also to create richer *subclasses* by inheritance that allows new classes to be derived from old ones by adding implementations of new methods or *overriding* (i.e. replacing) implementations of old methods. Subclass relation is defined analogically to the subtype relation. We will write S <: T to mean also that class S is a *subclass* of T, which is a *superclass* of S. The meaning of "<: " should be clear from the context. The reference to an object of a subclass can be used anywhere that a reference to an object of its superclass is expected.

In general we have two hierarchies, one induced by inheritance, the other one corresponding to the subtyping relation. These two hierarchies are, in principle, completely distinct, e.g., in Objective Caml [11], but in many typed object-oriented languages the two hierarchies coincide.

Bounded polymorphism integrates parametric and subtype polymorphism, and allows restriction on type variables by specifying upper and/or lower bounds.

Ad-hoc polymorphism allows to us use the same name for different piece of code that may behave in unrelated ways for each type.

Coercion is a semantic operation that converts an argument to the expected type in a situation that would otherwise result in a type error. The special well-known case of coercion is *promotion.*

In *overloading* the same name is used to denote different functions or methods and the context is used to decide which function or method is denoted by a particular instance of the name.

In languages with subtyping we differentiate at least two disciplines of method (or function) selection:

early binding is based on static (compile-time) type information;

late binding is based on dynamic (run-time) type information.

Classification of type systems can be found in [5], see also [6]. Theoretical foundations of type systems in programming languages are contained in monographs [1,4,7,12].

3. POLYMORPHISM "AD HOC"

There are two major kinds of ad-hoc polymorphism: *overloading* and *coercion,* but the boundary between them in many cases is not sharp and depends on the implementation.

3.1 Operator Overloading

Operators for arithmetical operations in Java are overloaded for all numeric types and strings, but both arguments must be of the same type. In the expression '5+3.4' operator '+' denotes addition of two numbers of type double and left argument is coerced to the type double. In the expression '5+3.4F' two numbers of type float are added with appropriate coercion of the left argument. Of course different object code is generated by the compiler in both cases. However, one may imagine that operator '+' is overloaded for four combinations of argument types (int and double). The same situation may be observed for other arithmetic operators.

In this example we may consider the same expression to exhibit overloading or coercion (or both), depending on implementation decision.

3.2 Method Overloading

Most object-oriented programming languages, including Java, allow programmers to overload method names on classes. A method name is overloaded in a context if it is used to represent two or more distinct methods, and the method represented by the overloaded name is determined by its signature, like the method name `m` from the class `C` defined below. As long as their signatures are different, Java treats methods with overloaded names as though they had completely different names. The compiler statically (using early binding) determines what method code is to be executed.

```
public class C {
   void m( ) { System.out.print("C.m()  "); }
   void m( C other ) { System.out.print("C.m(C)  "); }
}
```

In Java, the overloading can happen when a method in a superclass is inherited in a subclass that has a method with the same name, but different signature.

```
public class SubCOverload extends C {
   void m( SubCOverload other )     // overloading m
   { System.out.print("SubCOverload.m(SubCOverload)  "); }
}
```

Class **SubCOverload** has three overloaded methods with name m.

```
public class TestOverload {
  public static void main(String[] args) {
    C c = new C();
    C c1 = new SubCOverload();
    SubCOverload sc = new SubCOverload();
                                          System.out.print(" c: ");
    c.m(); c.m(c); c.m(c1); c.m(sc);      System.out.print("\nc1: ");
    c1.m(); c1.m(c); c1.m(c1); c1.m(sc);  System.out.print("\nsc: ");
    sc.m(); sc.m(c); sc.m(c1); sc.m(sc);  System.out.println();
  }
}
```

Executing code of the class **TestOverload** we obtain the following result.

```
 c: C.m()  C.m(C)  C.m(C)  C.m(C)
c1: C.m()  C.m(C)  C.m(C)  C.m(C)
sc: C.m()  C.m(C)  C.m(C)  SubCOverload.m(SubCOverload)
```

It illustrates the fact, that the class `SubCOverload` has three overloaded methods `m`, and that Java uses early binding for overloaded methods.

3.3 Coercion between Primitive Types and Wrapper Classes

The type of an object is just the set of names and of its methods. In Java these types are called *reference types* (since objects in Java are accessed exclusively by references). But Java has also *primitive types* like int, double, or boolean. Values of these types are not objects, but for each primitive type there exists wrapper class, e.g., Integer, Double, Boolean, which can be used in contexts where primitive types are not allowed.

Converting between primitive types, like int or boolean, and their wrapper classes like Integer and Boolean was very annoying in old Java. Unfortunately, these back and forth conversions could not be avoided since only objects can be stored in collections. Below the essential part of the wrapper class Integer is shown.

```
public final class Integer {
  private int i;
  public Integer(int i) { this.i = i; }
  public int intValue() { return i; }
}
```

The following code illustrates the operations of "wrapping" and "unwrapping" integer value.

```
Integer wi1 = new Integer(5);  // wrapping
int i1 = wi1.intValue();       // unwrapping
```

Using autoboxing/unboxing mechanism the code is much more concise and easier to follow. This is an example of coercion, hence ad-hoc polymorphism.

```
Integer wi2 = 5;  // autoboxing
int i2 = wi2;     // unboxing
```

In old Java (without generic types) the terms *subtype* and *subclass* were basically interchangeable, but in Java 5.0 this relationship is more complicated, as we shall see later.

4 POLYMORPHIC CLASSES

4.1 Inclusion Polymorphism

Suppose we want to define a class which provides the basic functionality of a pair without regard for specific types. In old Java this could have been done using inclusion polymorphism. We had to define a pair whose both elements are instances of the `Object` class, since every class in Java inherits from it, hence every object can be stored in such a pair.

```
public class ObjectPair {
  private Object e1;
  private Object e2;

  public ObjectPair(Object e1, Object e2)
  { this.e1 = e1; this.e2 = e2; }
  public Object getFst() { return e1; }
  public Object getSnd() { return e2; }
  public String toString() { return "(" + e1 + ", " + e2 + ")"; }
}
```

Unfortunately, when we use this class, downcasts (with time and memory overhead) are required.

```
ObjectPair p;
p = new ObjectPair("Five", new Integer(5));

String numeral = (String) p.getFst();
Integer number = (Integer) p.getSnd();

p = new ObjectPair(new Integer(5), "Five");
numeral = (String) p.getFst();  // throws ClassCastException
```

Java compiler generates code, which checks dynamically correctness of downcasting operation and possibly throws ClassCastException. This affects program efficiency.

Method overriding with late binding exhibits quite different behavior than method overloading with early binding. When "object-oriented working programmer" speaks about polymorphism, he usually refers to this mechanism. In Java, when a method is redefined in a subclass with exactly the same signature as the original method in the superclass, then we have overriding and the binding of method calls occurs at run time (late binding). If the new method has the same name, but different signature, then we have overloading as described in Subsection 3.2 and the binding occurs at compile time (early binding).

In the example below both classes SubC1Override and SubC2Override inherit from the class C, defined in Subsection 3.2, and they override (redefine) inherited method m.

```
public class SubC1Override extends C {
   void m( ) { System.out.print("SubC1Override.m()  "); }
}

public class SubC2Override extends C {
   void m( ) { System.out.print("SubC2Override.m()  "); }
}
```

In the code below the list of instances of these classes is traversed, and for each object its method m is invoked. This method prints the name of a class in which its body has been defined. LinkedList is a standard collection, which contains instances of class Object. We need downcasting (C)i.next() to make use of method m. This is a typical program with collections and inclusion polymorphism.

```
import java.util.*;
public class TestOverrideIncl {
   public static void main(String[] args) {
      LinkedList l = new LinkedList();
      l.add(new C());
      l.add(new SubC1Override());
      l.add(new SubC2Override());
      for (Iterator i = l.iterator(); i.hasNext(); ) {
          ( (C)i.next()).m();
      }
      System.out.println();
   }
}
```

Program output is given below. Observe, that the code of the method m comes from classes objects are instantiated, and not necessary from class C, to which they were downcast. This proves that late binding was used (in C++ terminology these methods are virtual).

```
C.m()  SubC1Override.m()  SubC2Override.m()
```

Unfortunately, downcasting is always dangerous, since there is no guarantee that all objects in the collection are instances of class C (or its subclasses).

4.2 Parametric Polymorphism

A class for a pair can be defined using parametric polymorphism (or generic class in Java terminology).

```
public class Pair<A, B> {
   private A e1;
   private B e2;

   public Pair(A e1, B e2)
   { this.e1 = e1; this.e2 = e2; }

   public A getFst() { return e1; }
   public B getSnd() { return e2; }
   public String toString() { return "(" + e1 + ", " + e2 + ")"; }
}
```

Below this class is used to create a pair for strings and integers. In Java generic class can be instantiated with reference types only. We do not need downcasting. All type checking is done statically during compilation and ClassCastException will never be thrown.

```
Pair<String, Integer> p;
p = new Pair<String, Integer> ("Five", 5);

String numeral = p.getFst();
Integer number = p.getSnd();
```

The code below illustrates the advantages of Java generics over code which uses inclusion polymorphism (class **TestOverrideIncl** from the previous section). Again, there are no casts. Notice also shorter form of the for loop.

```
import java.util.*;
public class TestOverrideParam {
   public static void main(String[] args) {
      LinkedList<C> l = new LinkedList<C>();
      l.add(new C());
      l.add(new SubC1Override());
      l.add(new SubC2Override());
      for (C e:l) { // read: for each e of type C in l
          e.m();
      }
      System.out.println();
   }
}
```

This is a typical program with collections and parametric polymorphism.

4.3 Integrating Parametric and Inclusion Polymorphism

Java 5.0 integrates parametric and inclusion polymorphism as illustrates class **PairMut.** It extends functionality of class **Pair** with two new methods, which allow to change objects stored in a pair.

```
public class PairMut<A, B> extends Pair<A,B>{
   public PairMut(A e1, B e2) { super(e1, e2); }
   public void setFst(A e) { e1 = e; }
   public void setSnd(B e) { e2 = e; }
}
```

5 IMPLEMENTATION OF GENERICS

When generating bytecode for a generic class, Java compiler replaces type parameters by their *erasure.* Basically, erasure gets rid of (or *erasures*) all generic type information, and generates *one* bytecode for a generic class, which contains nothing but ordinary types, and which is executed for each instantiation of this class. This guarantees backward compatibility with legacy code. For an unbounded type parameter its erasure is `Object.` For an upper-bounded type parameter its erasure is the erasure of its upper bound.

With the addition of generics, the relationship between subtyping and subclassing has become more complex. In the code below (references to) objects pS and pI have distinct types (Pair<String, String> and Pair<Integer, Integer>, respectively), but are instances of the same class Pair, which is called *raw type.* All reference types in old Java were raw types in this terminology and they are legitimate in Java 5.0.

```
Pair<String, String> pS = new Pair<String, String>("fst","snd");
Pair<Integer, Integer> pI = new Pair<Integer, Integer>(1,2);
System.out.println(pS.getClass());        // prints: class Pair
System.out.println(pI.getClass());        // prints: class Pair
System.out.println(pS instanceof Pair);   // prints: true
System.out.println(pI instanceof Pair);   // prints: true
```

Consequently, the expression pS instanceof Pair<String, String> is illegal and gives rise to the compilation error *"illegal generic type for instanceof"*.

This erasure implementation enforces some limitations on generics in Java, e.g., type variables in parametric polymorphism cannot be instantiated with primitive types. This limitation is not serious in presence of autoboxing/unboxing mechanism.

For comparison, templates in C++ are generally not type checked until they are instantiated. They are typically compiled into disjoint code for each instantiation rather then a single code, hence problems arise with code bloat, but type variables *can* be instantiated with primitive types.

6 GENERIC TYPES ARE NOT COVARIANT

We say that type operator G is *covariant* (or that subtyping is covariant for G) if S <: T implies G<S> <: G<T>. We call it is *contravariant* if S <: T implies G<T> <: G<S>. We say that G is *invariant* if the conjunction of S <: T and T <: S implies G<S> <: G<T>.

Subtyping is invariant for generic types. We show only why it cannot be covariant. Suppose we want to have a method that prints elements of any pair. Here is a naive attempt using generics:

```
public static void printPairOfObjects(Pair<Object,Object> p) {
   System.out.println( "(" + p.getFst() + ", " + p.getSnd() + ")");
}
```

The problem is that it only works for Pair<Object,Object> which is *not* a supertype of all pairs! Compiling the following code we obtain compilation errors in lines 2 and 3.

```
PairMut <String, Integer> pSI;
pSI = new PairMut <String, Integer> ("Five", 5); // 1
printPairOfObjects(pSI);                          // 2
PairMut<Object, Object> pOO = pSI;        // 3: incompatible types
```

Suppose that assignment in line 3 was accepted. Then the following instructions must also be accepted.

```
pOO.setFst(new Object());    // 4
String s = pSI.getFst();     // 5
```

Accessing pair **pSI** through the alias pOO arbitrary object can be inserted to the pair, as was done in line 4. Now in line 5 we attempt to assign an **Object** to a **String!** For the same reason line 2 is illegal.

The argument against covariant subtyping for generic classes also applies to arrays, but Java actually permits covariant subtyping of arrays. This feature is now generally considered a flaw in the language design, since it seriously affects the performance of programs involving arrays. The reason is that the unsound subtyping rule must be compensated with a run-time check on *every* assignment to *any* array, to make sure the value being written belongs to the actual type of the elements of the array. If this type checking fails, the **Array Store Exception** is thrown. In the example below we refer to classes C and SubCOverload defined in Subsection 3.2. Assignment arrC = arrSC is legal, because of covariant subtyping: SubCOverload < : C hence SubCOverload [] <: C[].

```
SubCOverload[] arrSC = {new SubCOverload(), new SubCOverload()};
C[] arrC = arrSC;
arrC[0] = new C();
arrSC[0].m(new SubCOverload()); // throws ArrayStoreException
```

Since arrays in Java are covariant, but generic types are invariant, one cannot create an array of a generic type using named variables (but unbounded wildcards are allowed). The declaration:

```
Pair <Integer, Integer>[] iPArr = new Pair <Integer, Integer>[5];
```

is illegal and causes compilation error *"generic array creation"*.

7 WILDCARDS AND BOUNDED POLYMORPHISM

The supertype of all kinds of pairs is **Pair**<?,?>, where wildcard '?' stands for some unknown type. Here is the code for our printing method.

```
public static void printPair(Pair<?,?> p) {
   System.out.println("(" + p.getFst() + ",  " + p.getSnd() + ")");
}
```

Syntactically, a wildcard is an expression of the form '?', possibly annotated with an upper bound, as in '? extends T', or with a lower bound, as in '? super T'. As demonstrated in Section 6 subtyping is *invariant* for parameterized types. Using wildcards one may also express *covariant* and *contravariant* subtyping. Parameterized types with extends-bounded wildcards give rise to covariant subtyping: if A<:B then G<? extends A> <: G<? extends B>. Dually, super-bounds give rise to contravariant subtyping: if A<:B then G<? super B> <: G<? super A>.

Similarly one can specify upper bounds for named type parameters 'S extends Foo'. In the absence of a type bound, a type parameter is assumed to be bounded by Object. Only wildcards can have lower bounds. A named type parameter can have more than one upper bound, but a wildcard can have only a single (upper or lower) bound.

8 POLYMORPHIC METHOD

Methods can also be made generic, independently of the class in which they are defined by adding a list of formal type arguments to its definition. Suppose we want to write static utility method `max`, which returns greater of its two arguments. Static methods are outside the scope of class-level type parameters (this is another limitation caused by erasure semantics), so we have to use generic method, parameterized by a type of its argument. But arguments must be comparable, hence the type must specify appropriate method for comparison, which can be assured by a bound.

Java standard library contains generic interface Comparable<T>.

```
public interface Comparable<T> {
  public int compareTo(T o);
}
```

It specifies a method that compares 'this' object with the specified object for order. Here is our polymorphic method we were looking for:

```
public class Test{
   public static <T extends Comparable<T>> T max(T e1, T e2) {
        return e1.compareTo(e2) > 0 ? e1 : e2;
   }

  public static void main(String[] args) {
        System.out.println(max("Adam", "Dick"));
        System.out.println(max(6, 2));  // autoboxing to Integer
  }
}
```

Notice, that when extends is used to denote a type parameter bound, it does not denote a subclass-superclass relationship, but rather a subtype-supertype relationship.

9 CONCLUSIONS

The notion of polymorphism unifies many concepts present in typed programming languages. We briefly defined some varieties of polymorphism and traced them in Java 5.0. Java shows that "industrial" programming languages are able to express more abstract patterns using rather involved theoretical means, hence the "working programmer" has to be better educated in order to understand them, recognize them in different programming languages under different names and make good use of them. Programmers are often unpleasantly surprised when a mechanism exhibits different behavior in another language, or if different names turn out to denote the same mechanism.

It would be also interesting to compare polymorphic features of some other "industrial" programming languages (e. g. C++, C#) from more abstract perspective than used in manuals or tutorials. "Working programmer" should have a command of many programming languages which quickly evolve, and deeper understanding of underlying concepts would greatly alleviate his task.

REFERENCES

1. Abadi M., Cardelli L.: *A Theory of Objects,* Springer-Verlag (1996).
2. Bracha G., Odersky M., Stoutamire D., Wadler P.: *Making the future safe for the past: Adding genericity to the Java programming language,* In: Proceedings of ACM Symposium on Object-Oriented Programming: Systems, Languages and Applications (OOPSLA), ACM Press (1998) pp. 183-200.

3. Bracha, G.: *Generics in the Java programming language,* (2004) **http ://java. sun.com/j2se/1.5/pdf/generics-tutorial.pdf**
4. Bruce K. B.: *Foundations of Object-Oriented Languages,* MIT Press (2002).
5. Cardelli L., Wegner P.: *On understanding types, data abstraction and polymorphism,* Computing Surveys 17 (1985) pp. 471-522.
6. Cardelli L.: *Type systems,* In: Tucker A. B., ed.: Handbook of Computer Science and Engineering. CRC Press (1997) pp. 2208-2236.
7. Castagna G.: *Object-Oriented Programming. A Unified Foundation,* Birkhäuser (1997).
8. Cook W. R., Hill W. L., Canning P. S.: *Inheritance is not subtyping,* In: Proceedings of ACM Symposium on Principles of Programming Languages (POPL), ACM Press (1990) pp. 125-135.
9. Igarashi A., Pierce B., Wadler P.: *Featherweight Java: A minimal core calculus for Java and GJ,* In: Proceedings of ACM Symposium on Object-Oriented Programming: Systems, Languages and Applications (OOPSLA), ACM Press (1999) pp. 132-146.
10. Igarashi A., Viroli M.: *On variance-based subtyping for parametric types,* In: Proceedings of European Symposium on Object-Oriented Programming (ECOOP). LNCS 2374, Springer-Verlag (2002) 441-469.
11. Leroy X.: *The Objective Caml System, release 3.08. Documentation and users manual,* INRIA. (2004) http://caml.inria.fr.
12. Pierce B. C.: *Types and Programming Languages,* MIT Press (2002).
13. Thorup K. K., Torgersen M.: *Unifying genericity. Combining the benefits of virtual types and parameterized classes,* In: Proceedings of European Symposium on Object-Oriented Programming (ECOOP). LNCS 1628, Springer-Verlag (1999) 186-204.
14. Torgersen M., Ernst E., von der Ahe P., Bracha G., Gafter N.: *Adding wildcards to the Java programming language,* In: Proceedings of ACM Symposium on Applied Computing (SAC), ACM Press (2004).

Polymorphism and Interfaces

INTRODUCTION

OBJECTIVES

After reading this article you will:

1. Be able to define the term polymorphism.
2. Understand the concept of upcasting
3. Understand how to invoke (call) methods
4. Know what is meant by static binding and dynamic binding
5. Know what is an abstract class
6. Know what is an interface
7. Know how to extend abstract classes and how to implement interfaces

TERMINOLOGIES

Polymorphism • Upcasting • Interfaces • Implementing Interfaces • Static binding • Dynamic binding • Abstract class

The following article concentrates on the concept of polymorphism from the stand point of abstract class and interface. Though the explanations to the concepts are concise, they are to the point. In addition, each concept is followed by diagrams that are self explanatory, and program codes that are short and simple enough so as to engage the reader.

Polymorphism and Interfaces

AGENDA

- Define polymorphism
- Talk about upcasting and method invocation
- Compare static and dynamic binding
- Talk about abstract classes and interfaces
- Look at interfaces

POLYMORPHISM GIVES YOU SUBSTITUTABILITY

In addition to code reuse, inheritance gives you polymorphism.

- Polymorphism means "many shapes."
- Gives you substitutability: Code that works with a Cup will work with a CoffeeCup, because a CoffeeCup *is-a* Cup.

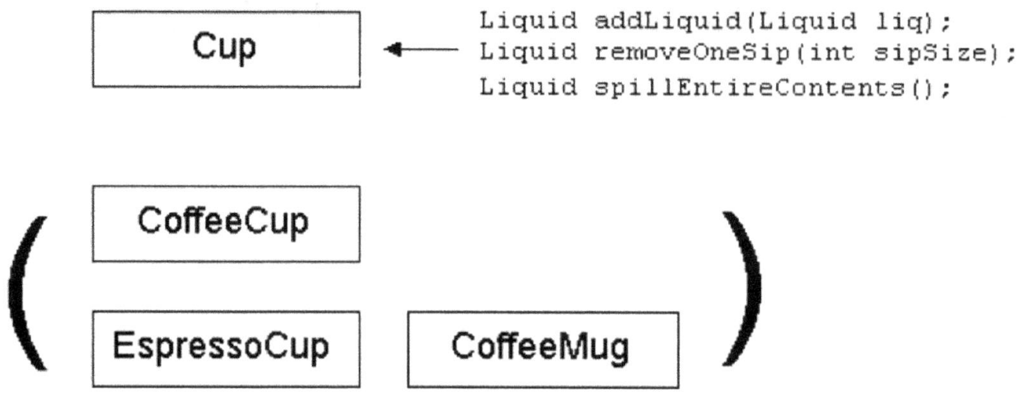

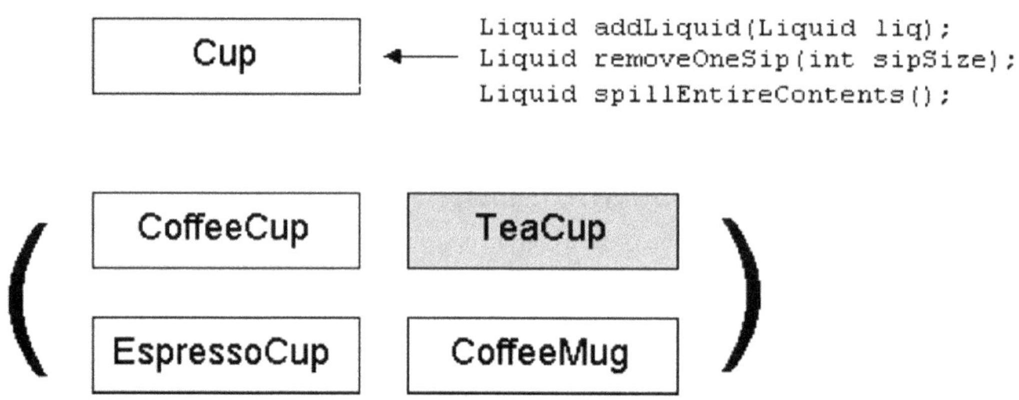

POLYMORPHISM GIVES YOU EXTENSIBILITY

- Can add new subclasses, and old code that worked with the base class will still work, even on new subclasses.

INTERFACE AND IMPLEMENTATION

- Polymorphism works because a base class establishes a common interface:

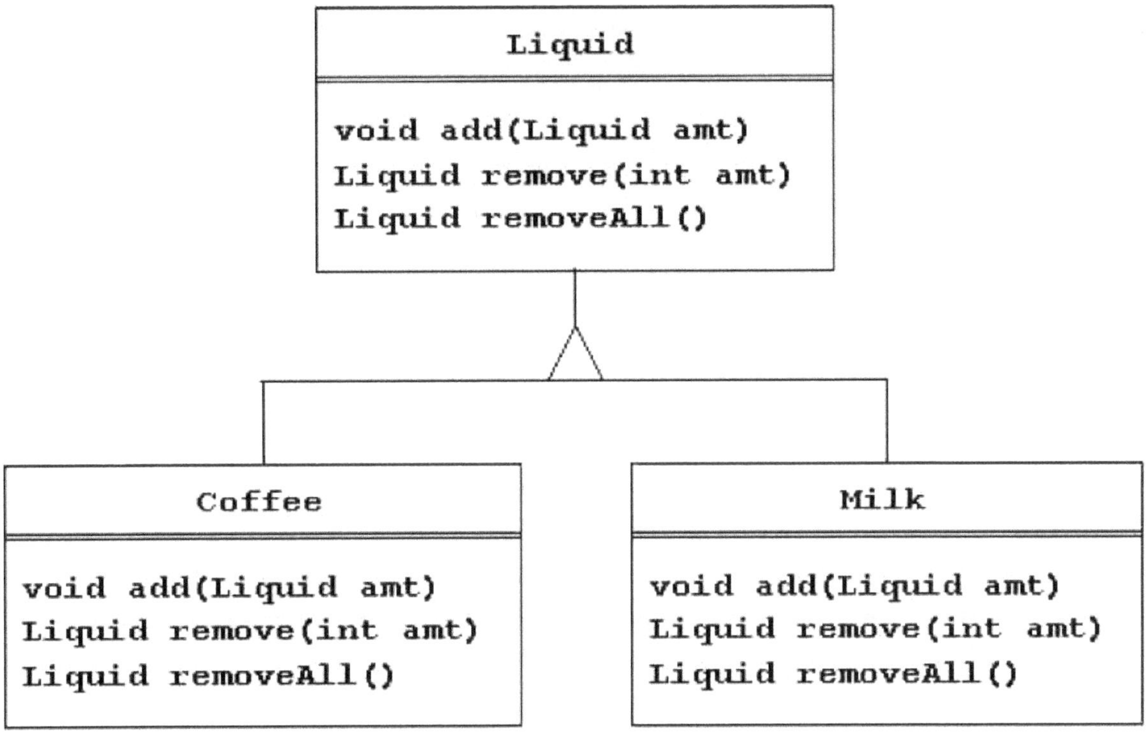

- Subclasses *implement* the common interface, each in a way unique to its particular class.

UPCASTING

- Polymorphism enables you to use a variable of a base type to hold a reference to an object of a derived type:

```
Liquid myFavoriteBeverage = new Coffee();
```

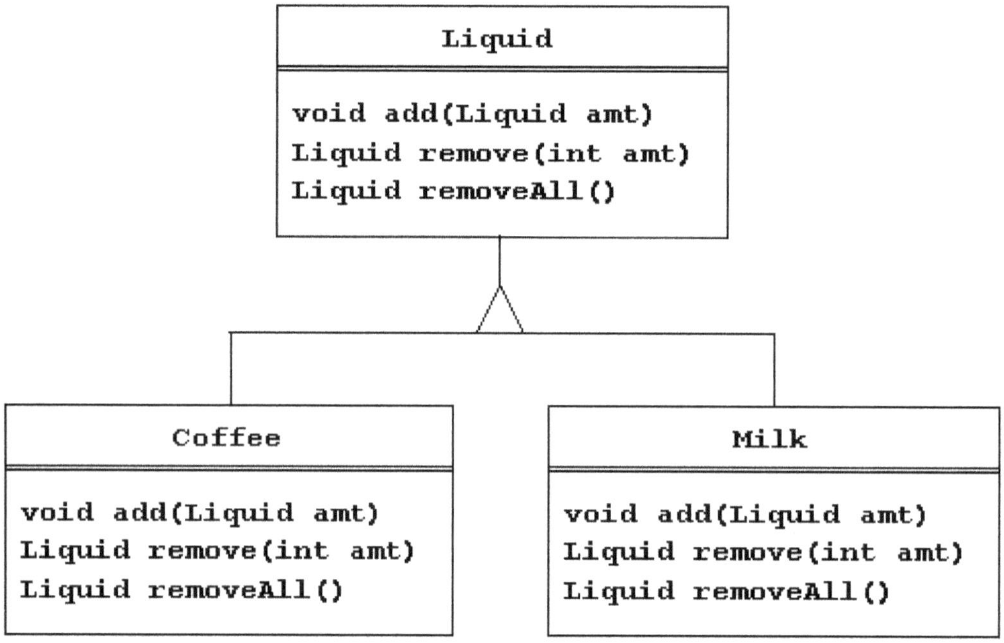

- This is called "upcasting" because a Coffee reference is being cast up the inheritance hierarchy to a **Liquid** reference.

INVOKING METHODS

- Which implementation of **add**() gets invoked?

```
Liquid myFavoriteBeverage = new Coffee();
myFavoriteBeverage.add(new Milk(25));
```

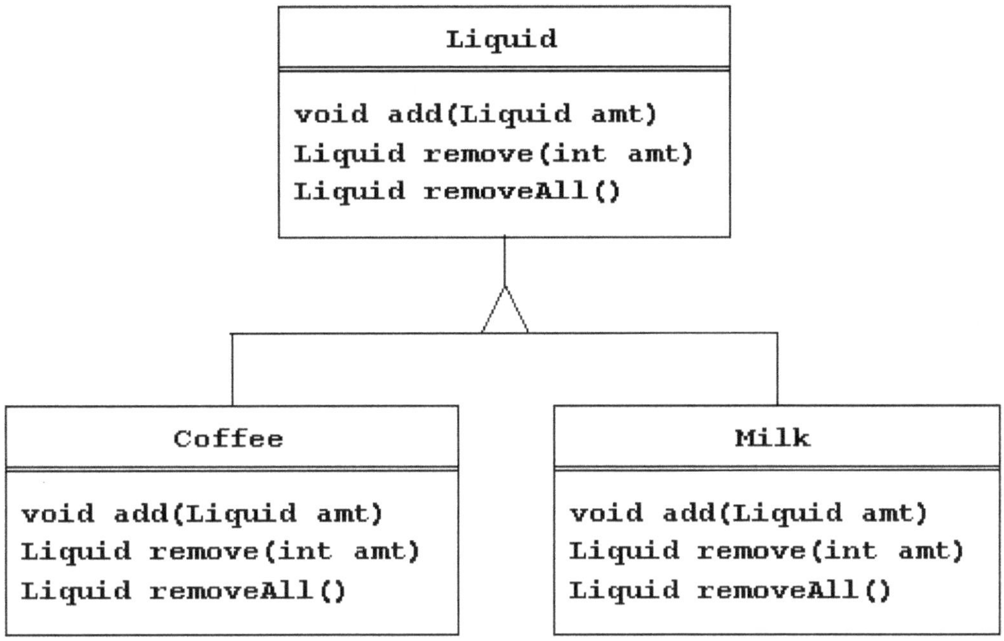

- The type of the reference, myFavoriteBeverage, is Liquid.
- The class of the object is Coffee.

STATIC BINDING

- *Static binding* is deciding at compile time which method to invoke.
- With static binding, the method that gets invoked is determined by the type of the reference.
- In Java, class methods (static methods) are statically bound.

DYNAMIC BINDING

- *Dynamic binding* is deciding at run time which method to invoke.
- With dynamic binding, the method that gets invoked is determined by the class of the object.
- In Java, instance methods (with 3 exceptions) are dynamically bound.
- Which implementation of add() gets invoked?

```
Liquid myFavoriteBeverage = new Coffee();
myFavoriteBeverage.add(new Milk(25));
```

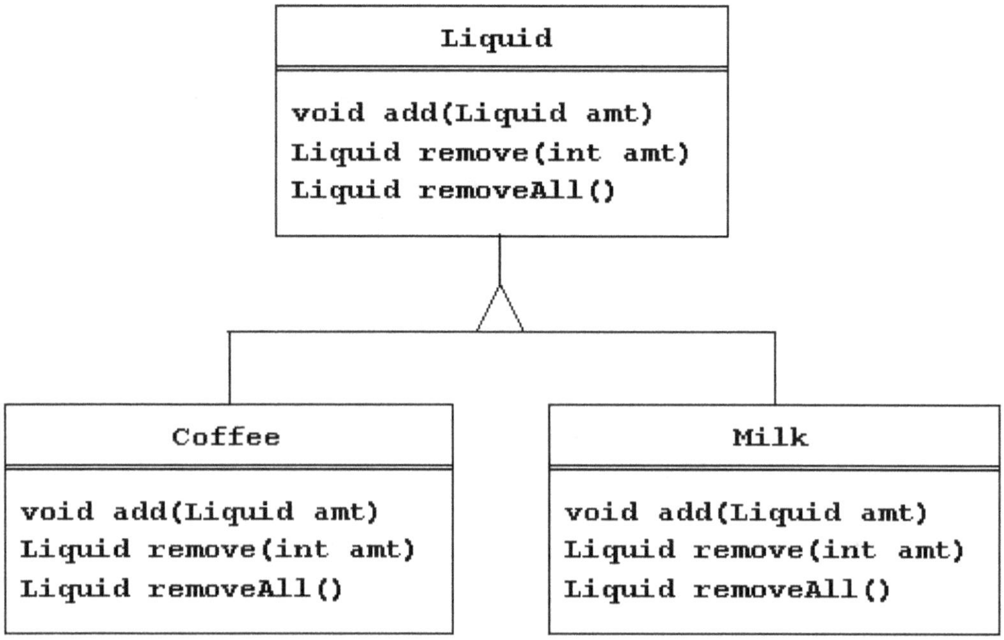

- Three kinds of instance methods get special treatment by the JVM: private methods, <init> methods, and super invocations.

POLYMORPHISM EXAMPLE

- To fully realize the wonders of polymorphism, you must send a message to an object without knowing the actual class of the object:

```
// In file PolymorphInt/examples/ex1/Liquid.java
public class Liquid {

    void swirl(boolean clockwise) {

        // Implement the default swirling
        // behavior for liquids
        System.out.println(
            "Swirling Liquid");
    }
}
```

```
// In file PolymorphInt/examples/ex1/Coffee.java
class Coffee extends Liquid {

    void swirl(boolean clockwise) {

        // Simulate the peculiar swirling
        // behavior exhibited by Coffee
        System.out.println(
            "Swirling Coffee");
    }
}
```

```
// In file PolymorphInt/examples/ex1/Milk.java
class Milk extends Liquid {

    void swirl(boolean clockwise) {

        // Model milk's manner of swirling
        System.out.println("Swirling Milk");
    }
}
```

```
// In file PolymorphInt/examples/ex1/Cup.java
class Cup {

    private Liquid innerLiquid;

    Cup(Liquid liq) {
        innerLiquid = liq;
        // Swirl counterclockwise
        innerLiquid.swirl(false);
    }
}
```

```
// In file PolymorphInt/examples/ex1/Example1.java
class Example1 {

    public static void main(String[] args) {

        // First you need various kinds
        // of liquid
        Liquid liquid = new Liquid();
        Liquid coffee = new Coffee();
        Liquid milk = new Milk();

        // Now create cups that contain
        // various kinds of liquid
        Cup cup1 = new Cup(liquid);
        Cup cup2 = new Cup(coffee);
        Cup cup3 = new Cup(milk);
    }
}
```

- Output of Example2 application will be

```
Swirling Liquid
Swirling Coffee
Swirling Milk
```

INHERITANCE AND POLYMORPHISM

- Subclasses will inherit what they don't implement:

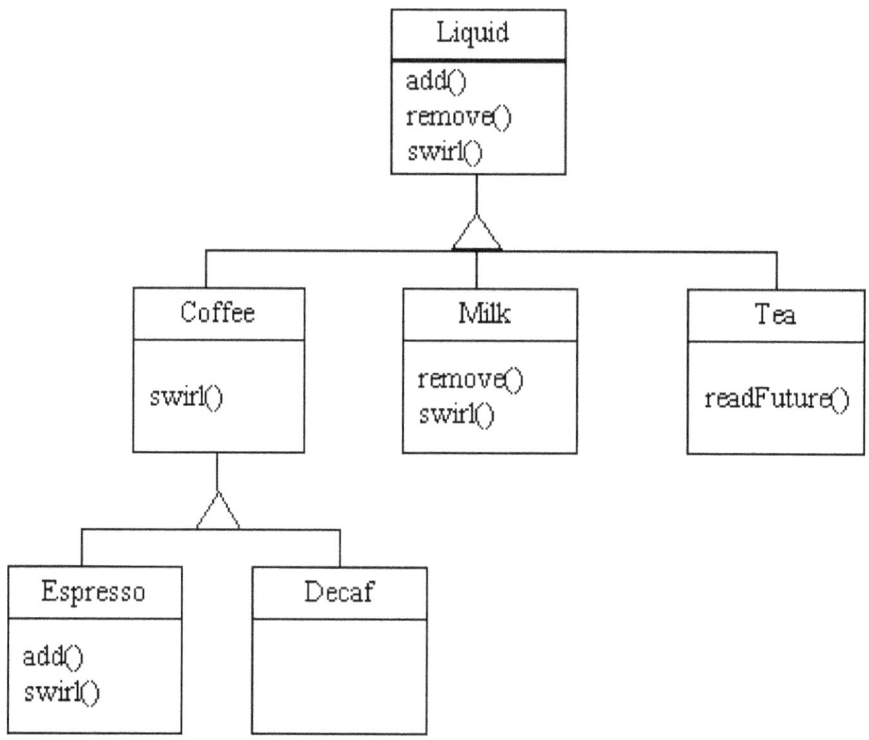

- Subclasses will always have the base class interface, so can always use subclasses polymorphically as if they were a base class.

ABSTRACT CLASSES AND METHODS

- Can declare classes abstract with the abstract keyword:

```java
// In file PolymorphInt/examples/ex2/Animal.java
public abstract class Animal {

    public void talk() {
        System.out.println("Hi there.");
    }
}

```

```java
// In file PolymorphInt/examples/ex2/Dog.java
public class Dog extends Animal {

    public void talk() {
        System.out.println("Woof!");
    }
}

```

```java
// In file PolymorphInt/examples/ex2/Cat.java
public class Cat extends Animal {

    public void talk() {
        System.out.println("Meow.");
    }
}

```

```java
// In file PolymorphInt/examples/ex2/Example2.java
public abstract class Example2 {

    public static void main(String[] args) {

        Animal dog = new Dog();
        Animal cat = new Cat();

        // THIS WOULDN'T COMPILE
        // Animal animal = new Animal();

        dog.talk();
        cat.talk();
    }
}

```

- Can also declare methods abstract:

```
// In file PolymorphInt/examples/ex3/Animal.java
public abstract class Animal {

    public abstract void talk();
}

```

```
// In file PolymorphInt/examples/ex3/Dog.java
public class Dog extends Animal {

    public void talk() {
        System.out.println("Woof!");
    }
}

```

```
// In file PolymorphInt/examples/ex3/Cat.java
public class Cat extends Animal {

    public void talk() {
        System.out.println("Meow.");
    }
}

```

```
// In file PolymorphInt/examples/ex3/Example3.java
public abstract class Example3 {

    public static void main(String[] args) {

        Animal dog = new Dog();
        Animal cat = new Cat();

        // THIS WOULDN'T COMPILE
        // Animal animal = new Animal();

        dog.talk();
        cat.talk();
    }
}

```

INTERFACES

- An interface in Java is like an abstract class in which all methods are also abstract:

```
// In file PolymorphInt/examples/ex4/Washable.java
interface Washable {

    int MAX_SUDS = 10;

    // Returns true if the object needs to be
    // washed
    //
    boolean needsWashing();

    // Washes the object
    //
    void wash();
}

```

- Methods declared in an interface are implicitly public and abstract.
- Fields declared in an interface are implicitly public, static, and final.
- The interface represents a special syntax for a special kind of abstract class.
- Classes and interfaces are *types.*

IMPLEMENTING INTERFACES

- Interfaces enable a special kind of multiple inheritance in Java: multiple inheritance of interface, but not of implementation:

```
// In file PolymorphInt/examples/ex4/Washable.java
interface Washable {

    int MAX_SUDS = 10;

    // Returns true if the object needs to be
    // washed
    //
    boolean needsWashing();

    // Washes the object
    //
    void wash();
}

```

```
// In file PolymorphInt/examples/ex4/Cup.java
public abstract class Cup {

    private int innerLiquid;

    public void add(int amount) {
        //...
    }

    public int releaseOneSip(int sipSize) {
        //...
        return 0;
    }

    public int spillEntireContents() {
        //...
        return 0;
    }
}
```

```
// In file PolymorphInt/examples/ex4/CoffeeCup.java
public class CoffeeCup extends Cup
    implements Washable {

    public boolean needsWashing() {
        return true;
    }

    public void wash() {
        //...
    }
}
```

INTERFACES CAN "EXTEND" OTHER INTERFACES

- Interfaces can multiply inherit from other interfaces via the **`extends`** keyword:

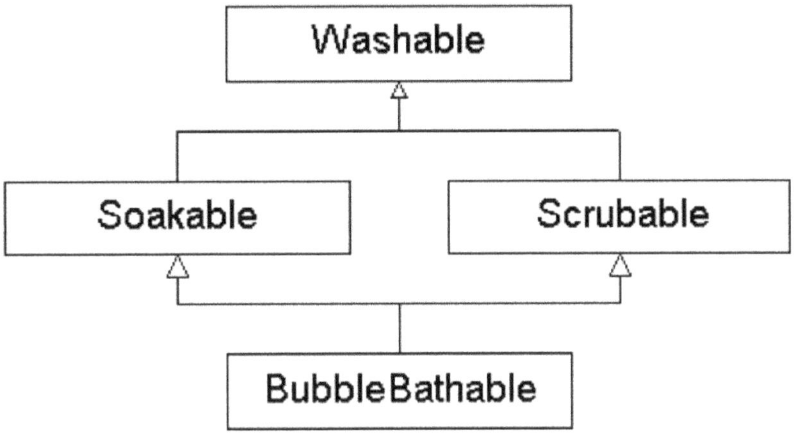


```java
// On CD-ROM in file interface/ex8/Washable.java
interface Washable {
      void wash();
}
```

```java
// On CD-ROM in file interface/ex8/Soakable.java
interface Soakable extends Washable {
      void soak();
}
```

```java
// On CD-ROM in file interface/ex8/Scrubable.java
interface Scrubable extends Washable {
      void scrub();
}
```

```java
// On CD-ROM in file interface/ex8/BubbleBathable.java
interface BubbleBathable extends Soakable, Scrubable {
      void takeABubbleBath();
}
```

CLASSES CAN IMPLEMENT MULTIPLE INTERFACES

Classes can multiply and inherit from multiple interfaces via the **implements** keyword:

```
// On CD-ROM in file interface/ex8/Washable.java
interface Washable {
      void wash();
}

```

```
// On CD-ROM in file interface/ex8/Soakable.java
interface Soakable extends Washable {
      void soak();
}

```

```
// On CD-ROM in file interface/ex8/Scrubable.java
interface Scrubable extends Washable {
      void scrub();
}

```

```
// On CD-ROM in file interface/ex8/BubbleBathable.java
interface BubbleBathable extends Soakable, Scrubable {
      void takeABubbleBath();
}

```

```
// In file PolymorphInt/examples/ex5/Breakable.java
interface Breakable {
    void breakIt();
}

```

```
// In file PolymorphInt/examples/ex5/CoffeeCup.java
class CoffeeCup
     implements BubbleBathable, Breakable {

    public void wash() {
    }

    public void soak() {
    }

    public void scrub() {
    }

    public void takeABubbleBath() {
    }

    public void breakIt() {
    }
}

```

- If CoffeeCup had neglected to implement all methods declared or inherited by BubbleBathable and Breakable, CoffeeCup would have to be declared abstract.

EXERCISES

Problem 1.

Take the code from Problem 4 from the *Composition and Inheritance* exercises and replace class **`Rodent`** with an interface. To refresh your memory, here's Problem 4 from *Composition and Inheritance:*

> Create an inheritance hierarchy of Rodent: Mouse, Gerbil, Hamster, etc.. In the base class, provide methods that are common to all Rodents, and override these in the derived classes to perform different behaviors depending on the specific type of Rodents. Create an array of Rodent, fill it with different specific types of Rodents, and call your base-class methods to see what happens.

Problem 2.

In a class named Dictionary (in a file named Dictionary.java), create a class (static) variable named WORD_COUNT of type long. Make WORD_COUNT public and final. Initialize WORD_COUNT in a static initializer to the value 1234567. (A static initializer is just an "= <value>" after the declaration of the static variable and before the semicolon.) Create a static initialization block inside Dictionary that prints the value of WORD_COUNT out to the standard output with this string message: "Dictionary: WORD_COUNT == <value>".

Create a class named SpellChecker (in a file named SpellChecker.java) that has a main() method of the usual signature (public, static, void, a String array as its only parameter). In the main() method, print the value of Dictionary.WORD_COUNT to the standard output with this message: "SpellChecker: WORD_COUNT == <value>".

Compile these classes and run them to see the output. Take a moment to ponder the deep significance of this output.

Problem 3.

In class SpellChecker from Problem 2, create a new Dictionary object with the new keyword. Place this new statement first in the main method. Store the reference returned from new in a local variable.

Compile these classes again and run them to see the output. Why is this output different from that of Problem 2?

Problem 4.

Since you've been having so much fun with Dictionary and Spell Checker, please return to this code one last time. Take the classes from Problem 3 and edit Dictionary. java. Change the value of WORD_COUNT in Dictionary to 7654321. Recompile just Dictionary.java. It is important that you compile Dictionary.java without recompiling SpellChecker.java. Make sure you type: javac Dictionary.java

Run the SpellChecker program one last time and observe its startling output. What went wrong?

Problem 5.

In the PolymorphInt/examples/ex1 directory of the sample code, create a class Tea that extends Liquid. Define a swirl() method in Tea that overrides Liquid's implementation. In the body of Tea's swirl() method, just print "Swirling Tea" to the standard output.

Edit Examplel.java in the PolymorphInt/examples/ex1 directory. At the end of the main() method, add two more statements. In the first statement, create a new Tea instance and store the reference in a local variable. In the second statement, create a new Cup instance, passing a reference to the Tea object to Cup's constructor. Execute the Example1 application and observe the results.

Problem 6.

In the PolymorphInt/examples/ex5 directory, create a new class Puppy. Make Puppy implement Bubblebathable, but don't actually implement any methods in the body of Puppy (just declare that "Puppy implements Bubblebathable".) Attempt to compile your program and observe the error messages generated by the compiler.

Problem 7.

In the Puppy.java class from Problem 6, implement whatever methods you need to implement to get class Puppy to compile. In each method, just print out a message to the standard output saying which method is being called, such as "Puppy: wash() invoked.".

Type in this Problem7 application and run it:

```
class Problem7 {

    public static void main(String[] args) {

        Puppy puppy = new Puppy();
        soakIt(puppy);
    }

    public static void soakIt(Soakable s) {
        s.wash();
        s.soak();
    }
}
```

Problem 8.

Copy Problem7.java to Problem8.java, and rename the class it contains Problem8. Changing only the body of thesoakIt() method in class Problem8, find a way to invoke, in addition to wash() and soak(), the takeABubble-Bath() method on any passed object that happens to implement BubbleBathable. (Do not change the type of the passed s parameter. Your revised soakIt() method should also accept a Soakable reference.) Run the Problem8 program and observe the output.

An Introduction to Polymorphism in Java

INTRODUCTION

OBJECTIVES

After reading this article you will know the five categories or types of run-time polymorphism:

- Polymorphic assignment statements
- Polymorphic parameter passing
- Polymorphic return types
- Polymorphic (Generic) array types • Polymorphic exception handling

TERMINOLOGIES

Polymorphic assignment statements • Polymorphic parameter passing• Polymorphic return types• Polymorphic (Generic) array types • Polymorphic exception handling

This article treats each topic as a tutorial. While the topic is being discussed program codes are immediately shown to support the ideas. Also the entire program is listed. Follow up exercises and their answers are also provided.

An Introduction to Polymorphism in Java

BY DAN UMBARGER

The term **homonym** means "a word the same as another in sound and spelling but with different meaning." The term **bear** could be a verb (to carry a burden) or it could be a noun (a large, hairy mammal). One can distinguish between the two usages through the use of context clues. In computer science the term **polymorphism** means "a method the same as another in spelling but with different behavior." The computer differentiates between (or among) methods depending on either the method signature (after compile) or the object reference (at run time).

```
// A Java program written to demonstrate compile-time
//   polymorphism using overloaded methods

public class OverLoaded
{
  public static void main(String [] args)
  {
     DemoClass obj = new DemoClass();
     System.out.println(obj.add(2,5));            // int, int
     System.out.println(obj.add(2, 5, 9));        // int, int, int
     System.out.println(obj.add(3.14159, 10));    // double, int
  } // end main
}// end OverLoaded
```

```
public class DemoClass
{
   public int add(int x, int y)
   {
      return x + y;
   }// end add(int, int)

   public int add(int x, int y, int z)
   {
      return x + y + z;
   }// end add(int, int, int)

   public int add(double pi, int x)
   {
      return (int)pi + x;
   }// end add(double, int)
}// end DemoClass
```

In the example above polymorphism is demonstrated by the use of multiple `add` methods. The computer differentiates among them by the method signatures (the list of parameters: their number, their types, and the order of the types).

This form of polymorphism is called **early-binding** (or **compile-time) polymorphism** because the computer knows after the compile to the byte code which of the `add` methods it will execute. That is, after the compile process when the code is now in byte-code form, the computer will "know" which of the add methods it will execute. If there are two actual int parameters the computer will know to execute the add method with two formal int parameters, and so on. Methods whose headings differ in the number and type of formal parameters are said to be **overloaded methods.** The parameter list that differentiates one method from another is said to be the **method signature list.**

There is another form of polymorphism called **late-binding** (or **run-time) polymorphism** because the computer does not know at compile time which of the methods are to be executed. It will not know that until "run time." Runtime polymorphism is achieved through what are called **overridden methods** (while compile-time polymorphism is achieved with overloaded methods). Run-time polymorphism comes in two different forms: run-time polymorphism with abstract base classes and run-time polymorphism with interfaces. Sometimes run-time polymorphism is referred to as **dynamic binding.**

TYPES OF RUN-TIME POLYMORPHISM

There are five categories or types of run-time polymorphism:

1. Polymorphic assignment statements
2. Polymorphic Parameter Passing
3. Polymorphic return types
4. Polymorphic (Generic) Array Types
5. Polymorphic exception handling (not in AP subset)

1. POLYMORPHIC ASSIGNMENT STATEMENTS

When learning a new concept, it is often helpful to review other concepts that are similar and to use the earlier, similar skill as a bridge or link to the new one. Look at the following declaration:

```
int x = 5;
double y = x;      // results in y being assigned 5.0
```

This is an example of "type broadening." The int x value of 5, being an int which is a subset of the set of doubles, can be assigned as the value of the double y variable.

On the other hand,

```
double x = 3.14;
    int y = x;
```

results in the compile error message "Possible loss of precision." The JVM knows that it will have to truncate the decimal part of 3.14 to do the assignment and is fearful to do so, thinking that you have made a mistake. You can assure the JVM that you really do know what you are doing and really do wish to effect that truncation by coding a "type cast."

```
double x = 3.14;
   int y = (int) x;
```

Below is some curious code to analyze. The variable value y received from x was originally an int value (5), but we are not allowed to assign that value (5) to the int variable z without a type cast on y. It seems as though the "type broadening " from 5 to 5.0 has somehow changed the nature of the value. This situation will be helpful to remember in another few pages when we discuss a concept called "down-casting."

```
public class DownCast
{
        public static void main(String [] args)
        {
                int x = 5;
                double y = x;
                //int z = y;   y = x = 5 right???
                int z = (int)y;  // now it's O.K.
        }// end main
}// end class

Possible loss of precision (compile error)
```

Consider the following example. In the figures shown here boys and girls enter a gymnasium where they become generic sports fans, but are not allowed to enter gender-specific restrooms without first being converted back (type cast) to their specific gender types.

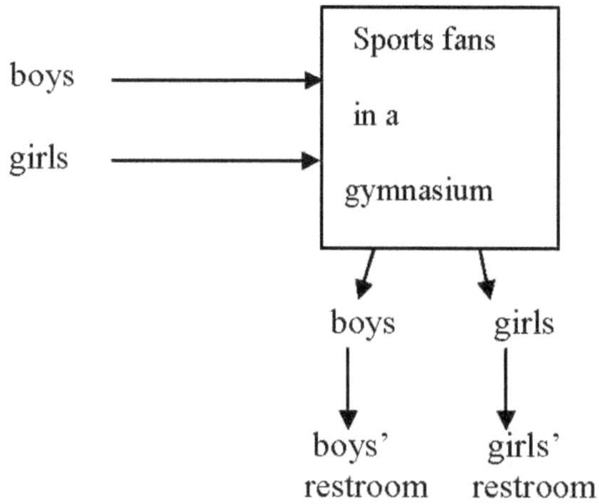

We now move from discussing primitive variables to object reference variables. The figure at the right pictorially represents an "is-a" relation between two classes. ClassB is an extension of ClassA. ObjY is a type of ClassA, but objX is not a type of ClassB. This relation is not symmetrical.

```
public class PolymorphicAssignment
{
        public static void main(String [] args)
        {
            ClassA obj1 = new ClassA();
            ClassA obj2 = new ClassA();
            ClassB obj3 = new ClassB();

1)          obj1 = obj2;  // no problem here...same data types
2)          obj1 = obj3;  // obj3 is a type of ClassA...ok
3)          //obj3 = obj2;  // "incompatible types" compile message
4)          //obj3 = obj1;    // still incompatible as the obj3 value
                              // stored in obj1 (see line 2 above)
                              // has lost its ClassB identity
5)          obj3 = (ClassB)obj1; // the ClassB identity of the object
                           // referenced by obj1 has been retrieved!
                           // This is called "downcasting"
6)          obj3 = (ClassB)obj2; // This compiles but will not run.
                           // ClassCastException run time error
                           // Unlike obj1 the obj2 object ref. variable
                           // never was a ClassB object to begin with

        } // end main
}// end class
```

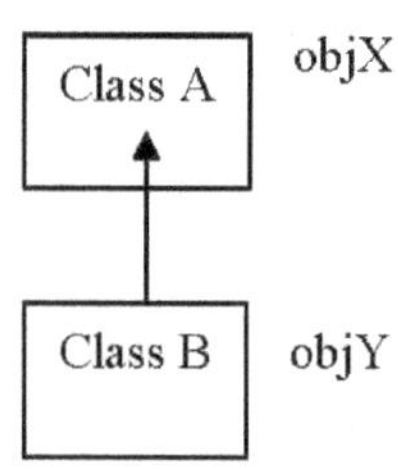


```
public class ClassA
{

}// end ClassA
```

```
public class ClassB extends ClassA
{

}// end ClassB
```

In the previous code, **line 1** is a snap. Both object reference variables obj1 and obj2 are of ClassA() type. Life is good. **Line 2** works because obj3 is an object reference variable of type ClassB, and ClassB type variables are a type of ClassA. Obj3 is a type of ClassA. Life is still good. **Line 3** will not compile, as the code is attempting to assign a ClassA variable value to a variable of ClassB type. That is analogous to trying to assign a double value to an int variable. **Line 4** is more complicated. We know from **line 2** that obj1 actually does reference a ClassB value. However, that ClassB information is now no longer accessible as it is stored in a ClassA object reference variable. **Line 5** restores the ClassB class identity before the assignment to ClassB object reference variable obj3 with a type cast. Life is good again. **Line 6** is syntactically equivalent to **line 5** and will actually compile because of it, but will result in a "ClassCastException" at run time because obj2 never was ClassB data to begin with.

Exercise 1

1. How is **line 2** above conceptually similar to the discussion of "type broadening?" Use the term "is-a" in your response.
2. What is wrong with the code in **lines 3 and 4** above? Relate to the discussion on the previous page.
3. Why isn't **line 4** okay? From **line 2** aren't you assigning a ClassB value to a ClassB variable?
4. **Lines 5 and 6** are syntactically equivalent. They both compile but **line 6** will not execute. Why? Explain the difference between those two lines.

Code to Demonstrate Polymorphic Assignment

```
import java.util.Random;

public class PolyAssign
{
    public static void main(String [] args)
    {
        Shape shp = null;

        Random r = new Random();
        int flip = r.nextInt(2);

        if (flip == 0)
            shp = new Triangle();
        else
            shp = new Rectangle();

        System.out.println("Area = " + shp.area(5,10));
    } // end main
}// end class
```

```
abstract class Shape
{
  public abstract double area(int,int);

} // end Shape

public class Triangle extends Shape
{
    public double area(int b, int h)
    {
      return 0.5 * b * h;
    }

}// end Triangle.

public class Rectangle extends Shape
{
    public double area(int b, int h)
    {
      return  b * h;
    }
}// end Rectangle
```

Output is chosen at random: either
Area = 25 (area triangle) or Area = 50 (area rect)

Here we see run-time polymorphism at work! The JVM will not know the value of variable "shp" until run time, at which time it selects the area() method associated with the current object assigned to "shp." The "abstract" specification on class Shape means that that class cannot be instantiated and only exists to indicate common functionality for all extending subclasses. The "abstract" specification on the area method means that all extending subclasses will have to provide implementation code (**unless they also are** abstract).

2. POLYMORPHIC PARAMETER PASSING

Early in the Java curriculum we encounter the syntax requirement that actual (sending) and formal (receiving) parameters must match in number, type, and sequence of type. With polymorphism we can write code that appears to (but does not actually) break this rule. As before, we use the idea of "type broadening" of primitives as a bridge to understanding how polymorphism works with parameter passing of objects. If we write the code:

int actual = 5;	and the method	public void method(double formal)
method(actual);		{ *implementation code* }

the int actual parameter is "broadened" to a 5.0 and received by parameter formal.

Note that

double actual = 5.0;	and the method	public void method(int formal)
method(actual);		{ *implementation code*}

would result in a "type incompatibility" compile error message unless a type cast were made on the actual (sending) parameter first: method((int) actual).

We now move from the discussion of type broadening of primitives to the idea of polymorphic parameter passing. We create objects for each of the two classes shown at right here and proceed to show their objects being passed as parameters to a method.

```
public class PolymorphicParameterPassing
{
        public static void main(String [] args)
        {
            ClassA obj1 = new ClassA();
            ClassA obj2 = new ClassA();
            ClassB obj3 = new ClassB();

        1)    method1(obj1);
        2)    method1(obj3);
        3)    //method2(obj1);
        4)    obj1 = obj3;
        5)   //method2(obj1);
        6)    method2((ClassB) obj1);
        7)   // method2((ClassB) obj2);
        } // end main

public static void method1(ClassA formal) {}

public static void method2(ClassB formal) {}

}// end class
```

```
public class ClassA
{

}// end ClassA
```

```
public class ClassB extends ClassA
{

}// end ClassB
```

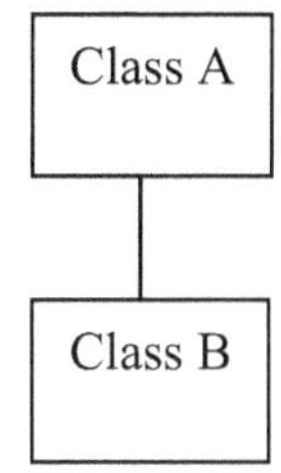

In **line 1,** at left, an object reference variable of classA type is passed to method1 and received as a ClassA object reference variable. Actual and formal parameter types are the same. Life is good! **Line 2** shows a ClassB object reference variable passed to and received as a ClassA type variable. This is okay, as a ClassB type variable "is-a" type of ClassA variable. **Line 3** fails, as you are passing a superclass type variable to be received as a subclass type. It seems as though **line 5** should work, as obj1 received the value of a ClassB variable, but it doesn't work unless the ClassB identity is restored through a type cast as shown in **line 6. Line** 7 will compile, as it is syntactically the same as **line 6,** but **line** 7 will result in a "type cast exception" upon program execution.

CODE TO DEMONSTRATE POLYMORPHIC PARAMETER PASSING

```
import java.util.Random;
public class PolyParam
{
        public static void main(String [] args)
        {
            Shape shp;
            Shape tri  = new Triangle();
            Shape rect = new Rectangle();
            Random r = new Random();
            int flip = r.nextInt(2);
            if (flip == 0)
               shp = tri;
            else
               shp = rect;

            printArea(shp);  // output will vary
        } // end main

        public static void printArea(Shape s)
        {
                System.out.println("area = " + s.area(5, 10));
        }// end printArea()
} //   end class
```

```
abstract class Shape
{
  abstract double area(int a, int b);
}// end Shape

public class Triangle extends Shape
{
        public double area(int x, int y)
        {
           return 0.5 * x * y;
        }

}// end Triangle

public class Rectangle extends Shape
{
        public double area(int x, int y)
        {
           return x * y;
        }
}// end Rectangle
```

Exercise 2 What is the output of this program? Why?

3. POLYMORPHIC RETURN TYPES

When returning values from return methods we know that there must be a type compatibility between the type of the variable receiving the value and the value being returned. For example:

```
int x = retMethod();      and   public int retMethod(){ return 5;}
```

We can code:

```
double x = retMethod();   and   public int retMethod(){ return 5;}
```

because the value being returned (5) is a type of double and, after the int 5 is "broadened" to a 5.0, that value can be assigned to the double variable x.

The code `int x = retMeth2();` with `public double retMeth2() { return 5;}`

results in a "type compatibility" error message (even though 5.0 was originally an integer value) unless we type cast the double return value as:

```
int x = (int) retMeth2();
```

Again we move from discussion of type broadening of primitives to the idea of polymorphic return types. We create objects for each of the two classes shown at right here and proceed to show their objects being used in return methods.

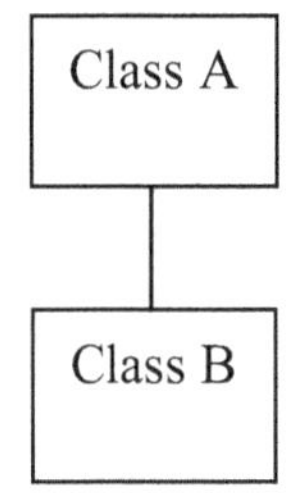


```
public class PolymorphicReturnTypes
{
   public static void main(String [] args)
   {
      ClassA obj1 = new ClassA();
      ClassA obj2 = new ClassA();
      ClassB obj3 = new ClassB();

      1.) obj1 = method1();
      2.) obj1 = method2();
      3.) //obj3 = method1();  // incompatible types
      4.) //obj3 = method3();  // incompatible...why?
      5.) obj3 = (ClassB) method3();
      6.) //obj3 = (ClassB) method1();

   } // end main

   public static ClassA method1()  { return new ClassA(); }

   public static ClassB method2()  { return new ClassB(); }

   public static ClassA method3()  { return new ClassB(); }

}// end class
```

```
public class ClassA
{

}// end ClassA
```

```
public class ClassB extends ClassA
{

}// end ClassB
```

Exercise 3

1. Why does **line 1** compile and execute?
2. Why does **line 2** compile and execute?
3. Why does **line 3** fail to compile and execute?

4. Why does **line 4** fail to compile and execute? How is **line 4** different from **line 3?**
5. **Line 5** is similar to **line 4.** How does it succeed when **line 4** fails to compile?
6. **Line 6** is similar to **line 5. Line 6** will compile but not execute. Why?

CODE TO DEMONSTRATE POLYMORPHIC RETURN TYPES

Exercise 4 What is the output of the preceding code? Why?

```
import java.util.Random;

public class PolyReturn
{
        public static void main(String [] args)
        {
            Shape shp = retMethod();
            System.out.println(shp.area(5, 10));
        } // end main

        public static Shape retMethod()
        {
                Random r = new Random();
                int flip = r.nextInt(2);
                if (flip == 0)
                    return new Triangle();
                else
                    return new Rectangle();
        }// end retMethod()
}// end class
```

```
abstract class Shape
{
   public abstract double area(int a, int b);
}// end Shape

class Triangle extends Shape
{
        public double area(int x, int y)
        {
          return 0.5 * x * y;
        }
}// end Triangle

class Rectangle extends Shape
{
        public double area(int x, int y)
        {
            return x * y;
        }
}// end Rectangle
```

4. POLYMORPHIC (GENERIC) ARRAY TYPES

Arrays in Java, as with other languages, are homogeneous data types. This means that every array position must have the same type, hence the same length.

`int arr = new int[1000];` // every array position reserves space for 4 bytes (in Java)

The declaration above reserves 4000 (1000 * 4) bytes of contiguous memory—each 4 bytes of memory storing an int value. Combining homogeneous position length together with contiguous memory is what gives arrays their O(1) access. In the figure below, storage or retrieval of data in position x can be determined by the formula "address of arr[x] = base + (x * 4)." Hence if the first item in the array is located in memory position 3b4f then the xth position in the array would be 3b4f + (x * 4).

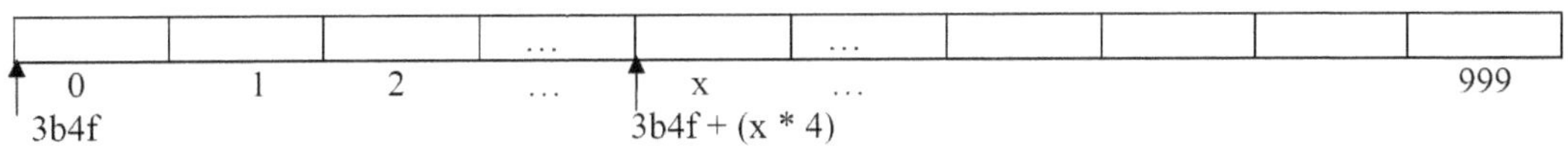

With "one-based counting" the same addressing formula would be "address of data in array = base + **(x - 1)** * 4." This is why computer scientists like "zero-based counting." Thus contiguous memory arrays allow us to use a single identifier for many, many different items of data while still having O(1) access. We need only to observe the restriction that every position in the array reserves the same amount of memory. If, instead of working with an array of primitives, we declare an array of objects, we can still achieve O(1) access but also achieve the effect of a "virtual" heterogeneous array. This effect will require some background to understand but is important as it is the "trick" behind polymorphic arrays.

The code example below is used to prepare the reader for the idea of polymorphic arrays.
<APPLET CODE="Poly1.class" WIDTH=900 HEIGHT = 600> </APPLET>

```
public class Poly1 extends java.applet.Applet
{
   public void paint(Graphics g)
   {
         Head objRef0 = new Head();
         objRef0.draw(g);
         RightEye objRef1 = new RightEye();
         objRef1.draw(g);
         LeftEye objRef2 = new LeftEye();
         objRef2.draw(g);
         Nose objRef3 = new Nose();
         objRef3.draw(g);
         Mouth objRef4 = new Mouth();
         objRef4.draw(g);
   }// end paint
}// end class poly1
```

```
public class Head
{
         public void draw(Graphics g)

         {  g.drawOval(75, 75, 400, 400);  }

}// end class Head

public class RightEye
{
         public void draw(Graphics g)

         {  g.drawOval(150, 200, 60, 40);  }

}// end class RightEye


public class LeftEye
{
         public void draw(Graphics g)

         {  g.drawOval(300, 200, 60, 40);  }

}// end class LeftEye

public class Nose
{
         public void draw(Graphics g)

         {  g.drawOval(250, 300, 30, 30);  }

}// end class Nose

public class Mouth
{
         public void draw(Graphics g)

         {  g.drawArc(175, 300, 200, 100, 180, 180);  }

}// end class Mouth
```

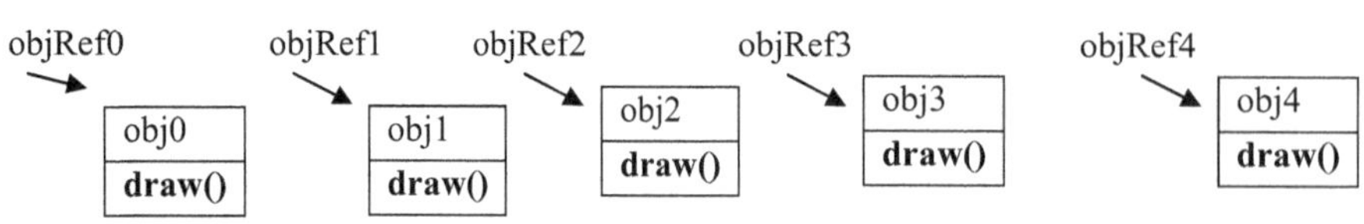

What we wish to do is to rewrite the code above so that the effect will be as follows:

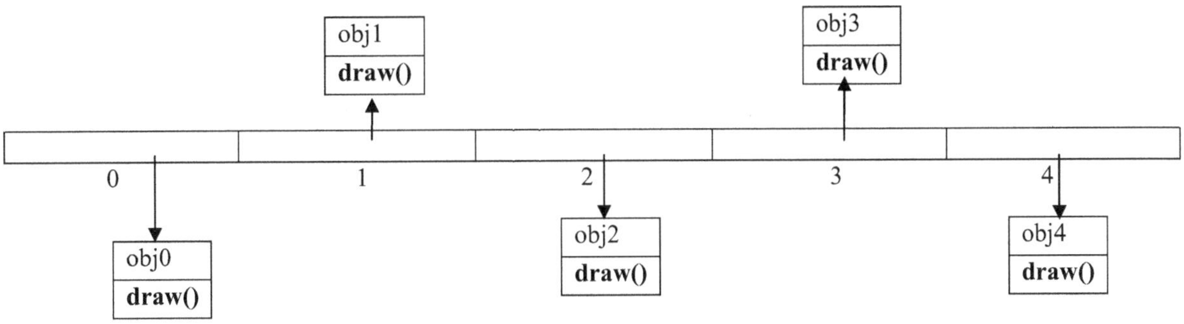

If we could place all the object references inside an array, then the code

```
objRef0.draw(g);
objRef1.draw(g);
objRef2.draw(g);
objRef3.draw(g);
objRef4.draw(g);
```

could be replaced by

```
for (int k = 0; k < 5; k++)
        refArray(k].draw(g);
```

Run-Time Polymorphism

Compile-Time Polymorphism

The benefit of this new code would increase as the number of desired draw methods increased. The problem of achieving such code is the requirement that all contiguous memory arrays be typed—the same type—so that each array position will be the same length. What type could we choose? We might try Object refArray = new Object[5]. But then there would be the problem of "type casting" each object back to its reference variable subclass type. Java 1.5 automatically unboxes for the ArrayList but only if a common type can be specified when the ArrayList is declared: ArrayList <type> refArray = new ArrayList<type>(); What could we use for <type>? What we need is an abstract "place-keeper" type—sort of like a variable in Algebra I, but representing an unknown type as opposed to an unknown value.

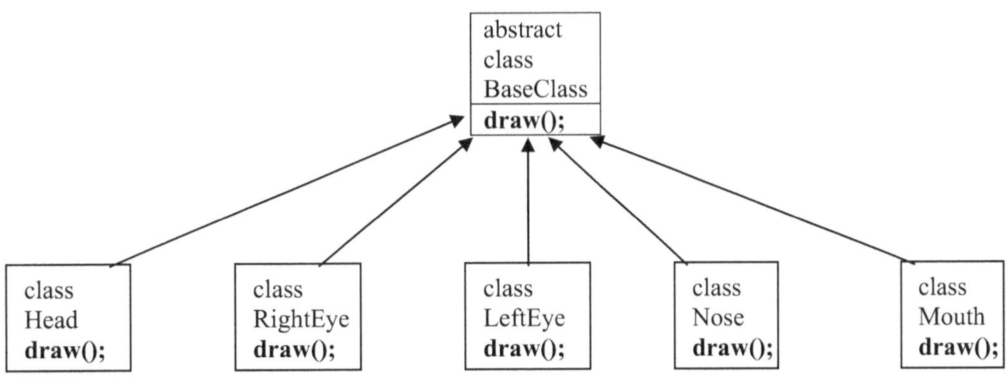

Classes `Head`, `RightEye`, `LeftEye`, `Nose`, and `Mouth` all extend from abstract class `BaseClass`. Therefore each of those classes "is-a" type of `BaseClass`. Hence the code we are looking for to instantiate an array of generic type would be:

```
BaseClass [] refArray = new BaseClass[5];
```

Below is the code to draw the happy-face figure using a "polymorphic array" with an abstract base class type.

```
import java.awt.*;

public class PolyArray extends java.applet.Applet
{
        public void paint(Graphics g)
        {
            BaseClass [] refArray = new BaseClass[5];

            refArray[0] = new Head();
            refArray[1] = new LeftEye();
            refArray[2] = new RightEye();
            refArray[3] = new Nose();
            refArray[4] = new Mouth();

            for (BaseClass e: refArray)
                e.draw(g);

        }// end paint
}// end class PolyArray

abstract class BaseClass
{
        abstract void draw(Graphics g);
}
```

```
class Head extends BaseClass
{
        public void draw(Graphics g)

        {   g.drawOval(75, 75, 400, 400);  }

}// end class Head

class RightEye extends BaseClass
{
        public void draw(Graphics g)

        {   g.fillOval(150, 200, 60, 40);  }

}// end class RightEye


class LeftEye extends BaseClass
{
        public void draw(Graphics g)

        {   g.drawOval(300, 200, 60, 40);  }

}// end class LeftEye
```

```
class Nose extends BaseClass
{
        public void draw(Graphics g)

        {   g.drawOval(250, 300, 30, 30);  }

}// end class Nose
```

```
class Mouth extends  BaseClass
    {
        public void draw(Graphics g)

        {  g.drawArc(175, 300, 200, 100, 180, 180);  }

    }  // end class Mouth
```

Exercise 5 Using a polymorphic array and abstract base class, draw the house below.

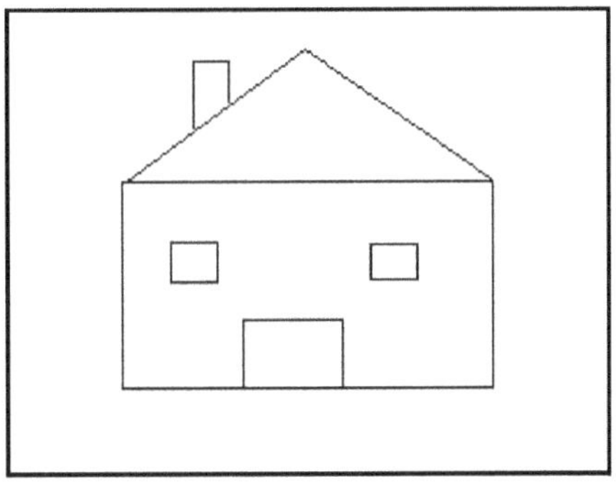

There is another way to effect a polymorphic array, through a technique known as using a generic interface (base class). An interface (base class) is similar to an abstract base class but with differences. The table below compares an abstract base class with an interface base class. They both can serve as "generic" types.

Abstract Base Class	**Interface (abstract by default)**
1) Must be specified as abstract. Classes are concrete by default.	1) Abstract may be specified but is default abstract regardless. Does not implement code!
2) Can have both variables and constants	2) Can only have constants, no variables.
3) Usually has a mix of concrete and abstract methods.	3) Can only have abstract methods. Interface methods may be specified as abstract but are default abstract regardless.
4) Subclasses **extend** abstract base classes.	4) Subclasses **implement** an interface (base class).
5) Subclasses can only extend 1 abstract base class.	5) Subclasses can implement more than 1 interface.
6) Methods can be private, public, or protected.	6) All methods (actually method headings) are public.

Below is the code to draw the happy-face figure using a "polymorphic array" with an abstract interface class type.

```
import java.awt.*;

public class PolyArray extends java.applet.Applet
{
   public void paint(Graphics g)
   {
        BaseInterface [] refArray = new BaseInterface[5];

        refArray[0] = new DrawHead();
        refArray[1] = new DrawLeftEye();
        refArray[2] = new DrawRightEye();
        refArray[3] = new DrawNose();
        refArray[4] = new DrawMouth();

        for (BaseInterface e: refArray)
            e.draw(g);

   }// end paint
}// end class poly1

interface BaseInterface
{
        /* abstract */ void draw(Graphics g);
}
```

```
public class Head implements BaseInterface
{
        public void draw(Graphics g)

        {  g.drawOval(75, 75, 400, 400); }

}// end class DrawHead

public class RightEye implements BaseInterface
{
        public void draw(Graphics g)

        {  g.fillOval(150, 200, 60, 40);  }

}// end class RightEye

public class LeftEye implements BaseInterface
{
        public void draw(Graphics g)

        {  g.drawOval(300, 200, 60, 40);  }

}// end class LeftEye
```

```
public class Nose implements BaseInterface
{
        public void draw(Graphics g)

        {  g.drawOval(250, 300, 30, 30);  }

}// end class Nose
```

```
public class Mouth implements BaseInterface
{
    public void draw(Graphics g)

        {  g.drawArc(175, 300, 200, 100, 180, 180); }

} // end class Mouth
```

5. POLYMORPHIC EXCEPTION HANDLING (OPTIONAL, NOT IN AP SUBSET)

To catch only the large fish in the figure below we would use the net with the large mesh, which would allow the two other smaller fish to swim right through the net. Then, to catch the middle-sized fish, we would use the net with middle-sized mesh, allowing the smaller fish to swim through the net. On the other hand, if we used the net with the smallest mesh on our first cast we would catch all three fish at once. Catching exceptions with try-catch blocks is similar to catching fish of different sizes, due to the polymorphic relation of the exception classes.

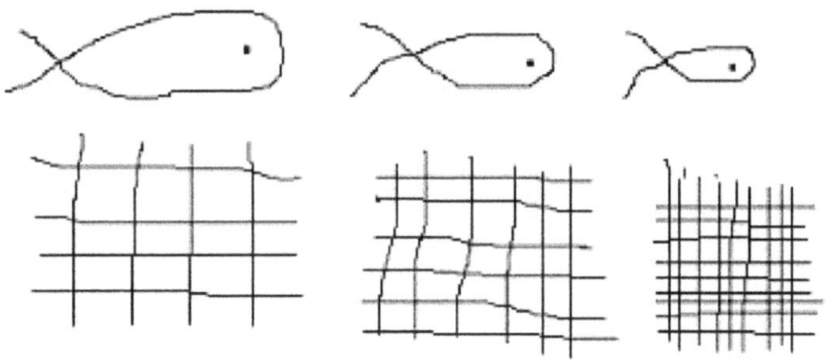

In the API segment below, you can see that the bottom class in the extended inheritance relation indicated is the "ArrayIndexOutOfBoundsException." Catching an exception with a "ArrayIndexOutOfBoundsException" object is analogous to catching the fish with the large mesh. It can only catch the largest fish. Due to polymorphism, the higher up one goes in the chain of inheritance the more errors can be caught (analogous to using a finer-mesh fishnet). The ability to catch errors selectively allows for different sections of recovery code targeted at specific error situations.

```
java.lang.Object
  └ java.lang.Throwable
      └ java.lang.Exception
          └ java.lang.RuntimeException
              └ java.lang.IndexOutOfBoundsException
                  └ java.lang.ArrayIndexOutOfBoundsException
```

```
import java.util.ArrayList;
import static java.lang.System.*;

public class PolyException
{
 public static void main(String [] args)
 {
  int [] x = new int[10];
  String str = "Dallas";
  try{  x[-1] = 3;                // error #1
        int y = str.charAt(-1); // error #2
        int z = 5/0;             // error #3
   }
   // catches all three errors shown in try block
   catch(RuntimeException e) {
        out.println("RuntimeException");
   } // end catch RuntimeException
```

```
// catches "big fish", then "middle fish", then "little fish"
/*
catch (ArrayIndexOutOfBoundsException e) {
    System.out.println("ArrayIndex OutOfBoundsException");
 }// end catch ArrayIndexOutOfBoundsException

catch(IndexOutOfBoundsException e){
    System.out.println("IndexOutOfBoundsException");
 } // end IndexOutOfBoundsException

 catch(RuntimeException e) {
    System.out.println("RuntimeException");
 }// end RuntimeException
*/
```

```
  }// end main
}// end class
```

Exercise 6

1. Type in and execute the code above.
2. One at a time, comment out errors 1 and 2, recompile, and rerun. Explain the resulting outputs from the three executions.
3. Reactivate all three errors, comment out the single catch block shown in this code example, then activate the commented three catch blocks shown to the right. Recompile and rerun. Again, one at a time, comment out error 1 and 2 as before, and rerun. Explain the resulting outputs.

ANSWERS

Exercise 1

1. Line 2 of PolymorphicAssignment.java assigns a Class B type object reference variable as the value of a Class A object reference variable. This is okay as ClassB extends ClassA and therefore obj3's type "is-a" type of Class A.
2. Line 3 is attempting to assign a superclass type object variable as the value of a subclass object reference variable. This is like trying to assign a double value to an int. This is also true for line 4, but lines 3 and 4 differ from each other as the value being assigned in line 3 (obj2) never was a ClassB object while the value being assigned in line 4 (obj1) was originally a ClassB object prior to the conversion to superclass type (like type broadening from int to double). This distinction between lines 3 and 4 is crucial to understanding the difference between lines 5 and 6.
3. Line 4 is not allowed because even though obj1 was, in line 2, assigned the value of a ClassB variable, obj1's internal format was somehow changed after line 2 to the superclass type in a manner analogous to the type broadening from int to double.
4. Line 5 works because obj1's value was originally a ClassB type (see line 2) but line 6 does not work as obj2 never was a ClassB type to begin with.

Exercise 2

The output of PolyParam.java is chosen at random to be either "area = 50" or "area = 25." Assignment of the variable shp is made at random to be either tri, a variable of class type Triangle, or rect, a variable of class type Rectangle. Both those respective classes have overridden the method area in the abstract superclass to reflect the different areas for the triangle and the rectangle. Both the assignment statements shp = tri; and shp = rect; are syntactically possible due to polymorphism—tri and rect are both subclasses (hence types of) abstract class Shape.

Exercise 3

1. In line 1 method1() returns a ClassA object reference variable and assigns it to obj1, which is also a Class A object reference variable.
2. In line 2 method2() returns a ClassB object reference variable (which is a subclass type of Class A) and assigns it to a ClassA object reference variable. The type assignment is still compatible.
3. In line 3 method1() returns a ClassA object reference and attempts to assign it to a ClassB type variable. This is analogous to assigning a double value to an int variable.
4. In line 4 method3() returns a ClassA object reference value and attempts to assign it to a ClassB object reference variable. Although lines 3 and 4 look very much alike, the "incompatible types" mismatches are actually different because the value returned by method3() was originally a ClassB object type that was "broadened" to ClassA format. This latter point is important to understanding the difference between lines 5 and 6.
5. Line 5 converts the underlying object reference type (a ClassB object value that was broadened to a ClassA value) back to its original type though the use of a type cast.
6. Line 6 cannot type cast the ClassA object reference value returned by method1 () as, unlike the object returned in line 5, the object returned in line 6 never was a ClassB object reference to begin with.

Exercise 4:

The answer to Exercise 4 is the same as the answer for Exercise 2 except that this time the result is obtained by polymorphic return types instead of polymorphic assignment statements.

Exercise 5

<APPLET CODE="HouseBuild.class" WIDTH=800 HEIGHT = 600> </APPLET>

```
import java.awt.*;

public class HouseBuild extends java.applet.Applet
{
   public void paint(Graphics g)
   {
         BuilderClass [] refArray = new BuilderClass[5];

         refArray[0] = new Framer();
         refArray[1] = new Windows();
         refArray[2] = new Door();
         refArray[3] = new Roof();
         refArray[4] = new Chimney();

         for (BuilderClass e: refArray)
            e.build(g);

   }// end paint
}// end class

abstract class BuilderClass
{
         abstract void build(Graphics g);
}// end BuilderClass
```

```
public class Framer extends BuilderClass
{
         public void build(Graphics g)
         {
            g.drawRect(250, 300, 200, 100)         ;
         }// end build
}// end class Framer
```

```
public class Windows extends BuilderClass
{
   public void build(Graphics g)
   {
         g.drawRect(280,340, 20, 20);
         g.drawRect(400,340, 20, 20);
   }// end build
}// end class Windows
```

```
public class Door extends BuilderClass
{
         public void build(Graphics g)
         {
            g.drawRect(330, 360, 40, 40) ;
         }// end build
}// end class Door
```

```
public class Roof extends BuilderClass
{
      public void build(Graphics g)
      {
            g.drawLine(250, 300, 350, 200);
            g.drawLine(350, 200, 450, 300);
      }// end build
}// end class Roof
```

```
public class Chimney extends BuilderClass
{
         public void build(Graphics g)
         {
            g.drawLine(300, 250, 300, 200);
            g.drawLine(300,200, 330, 200);
            g.drawLine(330, 200, 330, 218);
         }// end build
}// end class Framer
```

Exercise 6

1. *Type in and execute given code.*
2. Errors 1 (ArrayIndexOutOfBoundsException), 2 (IndexOutOfBoundsException) and 3 (RuntimeException) will all be caught by the RuntimeException object. This is analogous to catching all three fish at once with the fine-mesh net. This catch is nonselective and does not allow for recovery code specified to correct specific error situation.
3. Here the errors are caught one at a time by the polymorphic exception catches. This allows for recovery code written to correct specific error situations as they occur.

Part III:
Problem Solving Before Programming

The Problem-Solving Process

OBJECTIVES

In this article you will learn:

1. The steps necessary in problem solving before writing codes.
2. What it means by defining the problems

TERMINOLOGIES

Defining the problem • Input Process Output (IPO)

INTRODUCTION

When you use your computer, in most cases you are pleased with its performance. You type letters using a word processor, you access the Internet, you enter chat rooms, and the list goes on. But have you ever stopped to think about what causes the computer to respond so well to your concerns? The answer is of course the programs. Some programs take years to develop to what they are today; and some are being updated as we speak. No matter what the situation is however, it is programmers who write the necessary codes so that the computer can function the way that we expect it to.

When programmers decide to write programs they all have certain activities in common to perform. They just do not sit at the computer and start typing the program codes. There is a series of eight significant steps that they generally follow. These steps are

1. Define the problem
2. Outline a solution to the problem
3. Develop the outline into an algorithm
4. Test the algorithm for correctness
5. Code the algorithm into a specific programming language
6. Execute the program (run the program)
7. Document the program
8. Maintain the program until it proves flawless over time.

Most times beginning programmers think that they can go directly from the problem definition to programming (writing codes) without first having a detailed plan as stated in steps 1 through 4. Oftentimes when these steps are not followed, this is where frustration begins. The program that they so anxiously wanted to write ends up with errors—from syntax errors (incorrect statements) to logic errors (wrong answers). Experienced programmers on the other hand will first try to comprehend the problem; design an algorithm solution; check the solution for correctness, and then code the solution using a programming language of choice. They will code the program only if they are satisfied with the solution algorithm.

DEFINE THE PROBLEM

This first step in problem solving requires careful reading, and re-reading of the problem until you understand completely what data (if any) will be required, what processing is to be done, and what output is required. To help you understand this initial step, you should first divide the problem into three major components—what input is required, what the processing steps are, and what output is to be generated. When reading the problem you should actually analyze each word, noting those words that are sort of descriptive, and those that are action words. This will give you a clue as to what to consider for each of the components. In some cases the components will be clearly defined, but in other cases you will have to decipher them for yourself.

DECOMPOSE PROBLEM: INPUT – PROCESS – OUTPUT (IPO)

When defining the problem, you should use the **I**nput–**P**rocess–**O**utput chart (**IPO** for short) as a technique for helping to understand the problem. This is nothing more than a table that outlines the input, the process, and the output. The input requirements are placed in the left column of the table, the output on the right, and the process statements in the middle; hence the name Input–Process–Output (IPO) chart. See **Figure 1**.

Input	Process	Output
Input1 Input2 : :	First action Second action : :	Information 1 Information 2 : :

Figure 1 The format of the IPO chart

EXAMPLE

A shopper picks up three items at the supermarket. The cashier scans the price of each of the items, adds the price of each of the items, and then prints the total. Design a solution to this problem.

DEFINING THE PROBLEM.

First, read problem, and re-read it if necessary; then underline the key terms, especially in the first two sentences.

> A shopper picks up <u>three items</u> at the supermarket. The cashier <u>scans</u> the price of each of the item, <u>adds</u> the <u>price</u> of each of the item and then <u>prints</u> the <u>total</u>.

In analyzing each underlined word we see that the input for this problem requires three numbers; the output one number; and the process consists of three actions—scan, add, and print. See Figure 2.

Input	Process	Output
price1 price2 price3	Scan three prices Add the prices Print the total	Total

Figure 2 IPO chart defining the problem.

EXAMPLE

A program is required to prompt the user for two numbers, one representing the length of a rectangle, and the other its width. Use these numbers to find the area and the perimeter of the rectangle. You are to print the area and the perimeter.

DEFINING THE PROBLEM

Underline the key terms in the passage. Look for nouns, descriptive phrases, and action words or phrases.

A program is required to prompt the user for two numbers, one representing the length of a rectangle and the other its width. Use those numbers to find the area and the perimeter of the rectangle. You are to print the area and the perimeter.

From the analysis we see that the input requires two numbers, and the output requires two numbers also. The processing requires a few things to be done—prompt user, calculate the area, calculate the perimeter, and print both the area and the perimeter. See **Figure 3.**.

Input	**Process**	**Output**
length width	Prompt user for length Prompt user for width Calculate area Calculate perimeter Print area, perimeter	Area Perimeter.

Figure 3 IPO chart defining the problem to find area and perimeter of rectangle.

Although the actual word calculate does not appear in the passage, it is introduced here, since finding area and the perimeter are computational activities.

EXERCISE

1. Name the first three steps that should be carried out before writing computer code.
2. What does the term IPO mean?
3. What are the three columns of an IPO chart?
4. What is the purpose of an IPO chart?
5. There are eight significant steps that are necessary when considering writing a computer program. List these steps in the order that they should be done.
6. Design an IPO chart for the following: Input a number. Add 20 to the number, subtract 10 from it. Multiply the result by 2, and print the result.
7. Design an IPO chart that does the following: Read two numbers, the larger followed by the smaller. The larger represents money, and the smaller represents the interest rate. Use these values to find the interest payable on this amount at simple interest for 12 months. Print the amount, the interest rate and the interest amount for the 12 months.

Algorithm and Data Representation

BY JOSLYN A. SMITH

OBJECTIVES

In this article you will learn about:

1. What an algorithm is
2. Data representation
3. Variables
4. Constants

TERMINOLOGIES

Data representation • Variables • Constants

CONCEPT OF ALGORITHMS

Once you have defined the problem, the next step is to develop an algorithm to represent the solution. In the most general sense, an algorithm is a set of detailed step by step instructions that tell how something gets done, from the beginning of the process, to the end of the process. In terms of programming, an algorithm is a finite sequence of step by step instructions, for solving a problem on the computer. People use algorithms every day, but probably don't know it. They give directions to others how to get from one place to another; or how to prepare a meal; or in the case of a motor mechanic, how to fix a vehicle related problem.

A worthy algorithm has four properties—it must be precise and unambiguous; it must provide some flow of control from one process to another, it must give correct results in all cases; and it must eventually terminate. All algorithms, and ultimately programs, are designed from the following four basic concepts: data representation, sequential statements, selection statements, and iteration statements. The following sections explain each of these concepts.

REPRESENTING DATA

In programming the concept of data type is like what the bolts and nuts are to a piece of machinery. It is almost impossible to construct any meaningful computer program, if you do not understand data types, data values, and the permissible operations that can be performed on data. Most programming languages define a minimum of four types of data—integer numbers, floating point (real) numbers, characters (single character), and string (a series of characters).

Integers are the set of numbers that do not have decimal values associated with them. For example, the numbers 10, 255, 0, -200, 100,009 are all integer numbers. Floating point numbers on the other hand is the set of numbers that contain decimal values. For example, the numbers 1.5, 0.0, 0.25 -200,000.59, are all floating point numbers. The character type is represented by any of the printable symbol found on the keyboard. Single quotation marks are used around a single character to indicate its value. Example, 'H', 'h', 'x', '8', and '(, are all characters. The type string as mentioned is a series of characters. Double quotation marks are used around zero or more characters to denote a string value. For example, "", "a", "hello", "hello there", are all string values. In this example there are four strings. The first is the empty string, the second is a string consisting of only one character; the third is a string consisting of five characters; and the fourth is a string consisting of two words separated by a single space.

When designing algorithms, it is important to indicate the type of data that the computer will encounter when the program is written. This is done through the concept of variables and constants. The following two sections describe these two concepts.

UNDERSTANDING VARIABLES

In Mathematics, we will recall that a variable is a name together with a value associated with it. In programming, we use similar concept. That is, a variable is a memory location where values are stored during the execution a program. Rather than the programmer having to specify the exact memory address, the programmer supplies a name, called variable name. This name represents the memory location. When the program is executing, the variable may take on different values at different stages of the execution process. **Figure 1** shows the concept of a variable called price with value 89.95. In this illustration the rectangle represents a memory location labeled price. The value 89.95 is stored in that location. Only one value can be stored in the location at any one time.

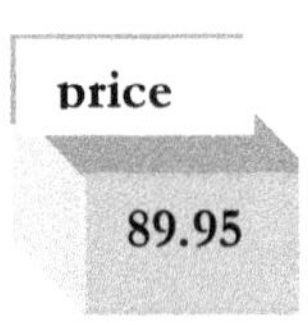

When we write programs we generally specify or declare the variables that will be used in the program. For the purpose of algorithm development we will use the following words to denote variable types: **Integer**, **Float**, **Char**, and **String**. Individual programming language will specify the names it chooses to use, and the syntax it uses. **Figure 2** explains the meaning and use of each of these types:

Data Type	Variables and Meaning	Example
Integer	Used to denote integer variables. Variables can take on integer values only. No decimal value.	**Integer** people
Float	Used to denote floating point variables. Variables can take on integer values or decimal values.	**Float** price
Char	Used to denote character variables. Variables can take on only one character at a time.	**Char** indicator
String	Used to denote string values—a series of any of the printable character on the keyboard.	**String** title

Figure 2 shows the four most common data types that are used in programming

Once a variable has been declared, it can be set an initial value. For example, in **Figure 3** each of the statements denotes a declaration and assignment of an appropriate value to the respective one.

- Integer people = 100
- Float price = 89.95
- Char indicator = ‘c’
- String title = “Information Technology”

Figure 3 Variable declaration and assignment of appropriate value

UNDERSTANDING CONSTANTS

In Mathematics, a fixed value is called a constant. The value for pi (π) is a typical example. Programming uses similar concept. For instance, you might write a program that uses sales tax rate in its calculations. Tax rates rarely change; hence, you can code sales tax as a constant. For the purpose of defining algorithm we will use the word **CONST** to denote constant. Each programming language will provide its exact syntax. For instance, if the sales tax on goods is 5%, we could define 5% as a constant this way:

CONST Float SALES_TAX = 0.05

EXERCISE

1. When an experienced programmer is about to write a program, what steps must he be fully aware of and apply?
2. When developing a computer program there are three basic control structures that can be used. What are these control structures?
3. Define the term variable and give one example.
4. Define the term constant and give one example.
5. A contractor is paid twenty five thousand dollars to construct a garage. He soon realizes that he needs five workers, so that the work can be finished in four days. The workers agree to work at a rate of fifty dollars and fifty cents per hour for eight-hour days. In making the agreement each worker supplies his/her name, along with their telephone number.

   From the above description do the following:

   a) Identify those underlined phrases which represent variables.
   b) Identify those underlined phrases which represent constants.
   c) For each underlined phrase that represents variable give it a variable name and tell the data type.
   d) For each underlined phrase that represents constant give it a name, tell the data type, and assign it a value based on its description.

Control Structures

BY JOSLYN A. SMITH

OBJECTIVES

To understand the three concepts on which programs are built—sequence, selection, and iteration.

TERMINOLOGIES

Sequence • Selection • Iteration • Relational operators • Logical operators • Boolean logic

Computers execute program statements in sequence, unless there are instructions that require it to alter the course of operation by either skipping the code, or repeating the code. To skip any code relies on the concept of selection, and to repeat any code relies on the concept of iteration.

SEQUENCE

Sequence means that the computer executes the program in a linear fashion, from the first statement to the last; none is skipped, and none is repeated. **Figure 1** shows the linear/sequential path of executing each statement.

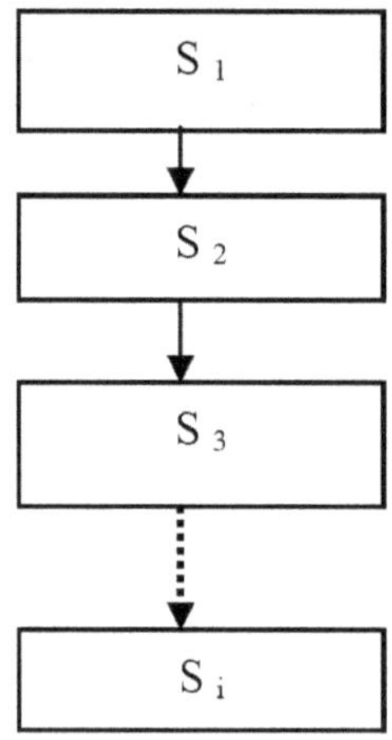

Figure 1 Statements are excuted in a linear fashion

Sequence takes the form of any of the following four concepts:

1. Input data. The typical verbiages used are – *read*, *input*, or *get*. For example,
- Read three numbers
- Input three numbers, or
- Get three numbers.

2. Output information. The typical verbiages used are – *print, write, display, or store.* For example,
- Print "The sum is", sum
- Write "The sum is", sum
- Display "The sum is", sum.
- Store sum

3. Perform computation. The typical wordings are – *add, total, sum.* For example,
- Add number to total
- Total = Total + number
- Sum the numbers

4. Assign data value to a variable. Some typical wordings are – initialize number, set number to, assign a number to. For example,
- Initialize number to 0.
- Set number to 0
- Assign 0 to number
- number = 0

In most cases we use arithmetic operators to write program statements for items 3 and 5. **Figure 2** shows the arithmetic operators that are used to perform calculations when writing computational statements.

Symbol	Meaning
+	Addition, sum, total
-	Subtract, minus, difference
*	Multiply, product, times
/	Division

Figure 2 Arithmetic operators used in programming

EXAMPLE 1

The following set of statements defines the sequence of activities to read two numbers representing the dimensions of a rectangle; find the area, find the perimeter; and print both the area and the perimeter.

```
Input length
Input width
Area = length * width
Perimeter = (length + width) * 2
Print area
Print perimeter.
```

EXERCISE 1

- As it pertains to computer programming, what does the term *sequence* means?
- Write a sequence of steps for the following narrative, to show how the computer would execute them. Read three numbers, one after the other, find the average of the numbers, and print the average.
- A telephone service provider charges a flat fee of $25.00 per month for all local telephone calls, and 45 cents per minutes for international calls. Use the concept of sequence to show we can solve this problem. That is, enter the number of minutes, and calculate and print the total bill.

SELECTION STATEMENTS

Selection statements are those statements that allow a choice of action to be taken. The decision for making a choice is based on the result of a conditional expression. **Figure 3** represents a decision-making process. In the figure, the parallelogram is used to denote decision, and the directional arrows show the flow of activities. Notice also that the result of the conditional expression representing a decision is either **true** or **false**. In programming these two values are called Boolean values. They are named after the English Mathematician George Boole who developed the Boolean logic, a system of how to determine the validity of statements.

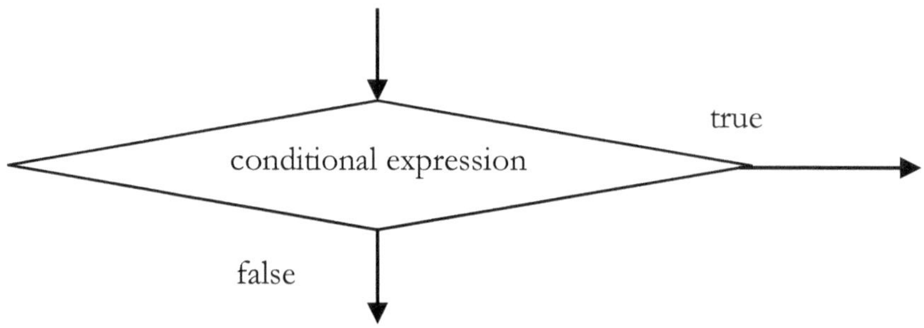

Figure 3 Diagram representing selection

Selection statements allow the programmer to select which statement gets executed. Selection statements use words such as **IF**, **THEN**, **ELSE**, **ENDIF**, **SWITCH**, **CASE** and **ESAC**. There are two basic forms of selection statements—**IF** (**IF** – **ELSE**) statement and the **SWITCH** statement.

RELATIONAL AND LOGICAL OPERATORS

Selection statements are based on two kinds of tests—relational test and logical test. Relational tests use relational operators in Mathematics to form what are called conditional expressions. Logical tests however, use the Boolean operators found in Boolean algebra to form conditional expressions. **Figure 4** summarizes the relational operators, their meaning and their associated operation.

Operator	Operation	Usage Pattern	Example
<	Strictly less than	x < y	100 < 200
<=	Less than or equal to	x <= y	100 <= 200
>	Strictly greater than	x > y	200 > 100
> =	Greater than or equal to	x >= y	200 >= 100
=	Is equal to	x = y	200 = 100
<>	Not equal to	x <> y	200 <> 100

Figure 4 Relational operators and their meanings

The Boolean operators are **AND**, **OR** and **NOT**, are used to form logical expressions. **Figure5** summarizes the boolean operators, their meaning and their associated operation.

Operators	Meaning	Example—logical expressions
AND	Two relations must be true for the result to be true	(2 < 5) **AND** (20 – 3 > 10)
OR	At least one of a pair of relations must be true for the result to be true	(2 > 10) **OR** (6 = 3 + 3)
NOT	The Boolean result of a conditional is reversed. True becomes false, and false becomes true	NOT((2 > 10) **OR** (6 = 3 + 3))

Figure 5 Boolean operators AND, OR and NOT

Relational operators and logical operators enable us to write conditional expressions which are required for selection statements and iterative statements. When evaluating logical expressions, you must first evaluate the relational expressions, and then apply the Boolean operator to the result of the relational operations.

EXAMPLE 2

Given that **a** and **b** are two integers, write a relational expression that will determine if the sum of these two numbers is larger than their product.

Solution

The sum of the numbers is (**a** + **b**), and their product is (**a*****b**). The desired result is **(a + b) > (a*b)**.

EXAMPLE 3

Evaluate the following conditional expression: (2 < 5) AND (20 – 3 > 10)

Solution

In this example the conditional expression is composed of two relational expressions. On the left is (2 < 5), and the right is (20 – 3 > 10). The result of the first expression is true, and the second also true. Because both expressions are true, the entire conditional expression is true. **Figure 6** shows how the process works. Notice that the relational expressions are evaluated first, and then the Boolean operator AND is applied after.

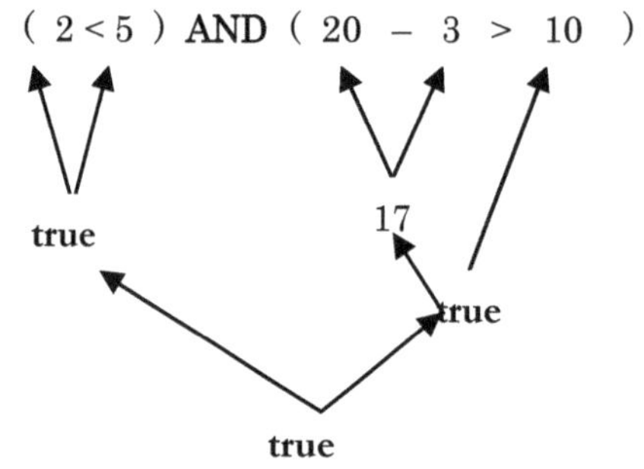

Figure 6 Using Boolean AND

EXAMPLE 4

Evaluate the following conditional expression: (2 > 10) OR (6 = 3 + 3)

Solution

In this example the Boolean operator OR is applied to the relational expression on its left, (2 > 10) and the one on its right, (6 = 3 + 3). Again, resolve both relational expressions first, then apply the logical operator after. This time the first evaluates to false. This does not stop the process, because the OR says, one or the other, or both, so we go on to evaluate the second expression. This expression evaluates to true. So, applying the logical operator, OR, we see that the result of the original expression evaluates to true. The process is shown in **Figure** 7.

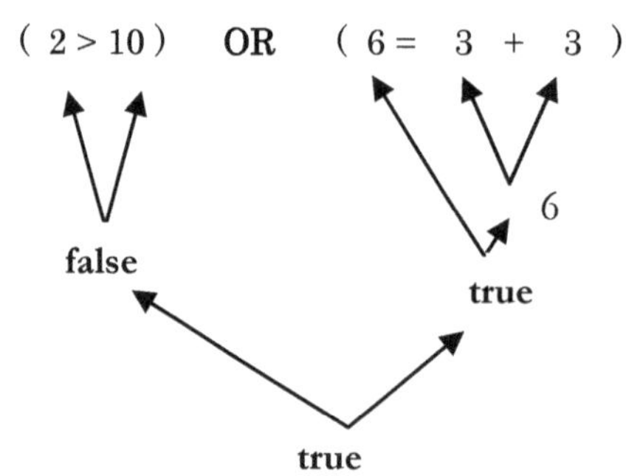

Figure 7 Using Boolean OR

EXAMPLE 5

Evaluate the following conditional expression: **NOT**((2 > 10) OR (6 = 3 + 3))

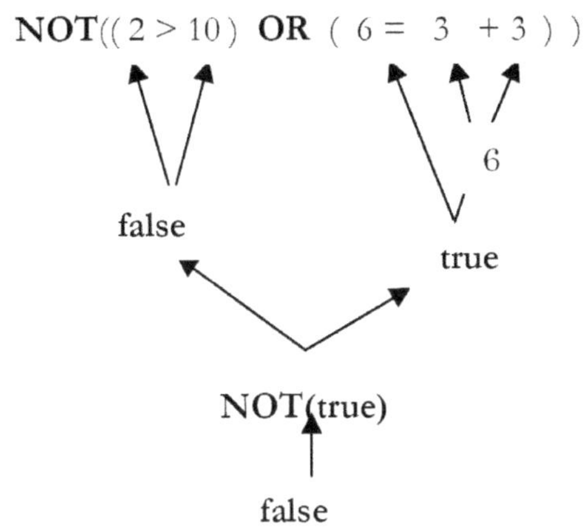

Figure 8 Using Boolean NOT

Solution

The solution to this problem is the same as this previous case, except that its result must be negated. When the value true is negated the result is false, as shown in **Figure 8**.

EXAMPLE 6

Formulate a conditional expression for the following:
Is the sum of two positive integers, **a** and **b**, larger than their products, or is twice their sum smaller than four times their difference?

Solution

The sum of **a** and **b** larger than their products is **(a + b) > a * b**, and
Twice their sum smaller than four times their difference: **2 * (a + b) < 4 * (a - b)**.
The solution therefore is **((a + b) > a * b) OR (2 * (a + b) < 4 * (a - b))**

THE IF STATEMENT

The **IF** statement allows the program to select which statements get executed. The statement has two forms, namely, **IF** without an alternate choice, and **IF** with alternate choice, symbolized by the word **ELSE**. The general format of the **IF** statement without an alternate choice is as follows:

```
IF (conditional_expression) THEN
      a_single_statement;
ENDIF
```

or

```
IF ( conditional_expression ) THEN
BEGIN
      Two or more statements;
ENDIF
```

For the sake of algorithm development we use the words **BEGIN** and **END** to denote group of statements. If it is a single statement then we do not use them.

EXAMPLE 7

Suppose you were given a number, determine if the number is positive. If it is positive, print it.

Solution

Figure 9 shows a flow diagram of how the process works. First we decide on the variable name. In this case it is called number. The parallelogram is used to denote decision. If the result of the test is true then the number is printed; otherwise, nothing happens.

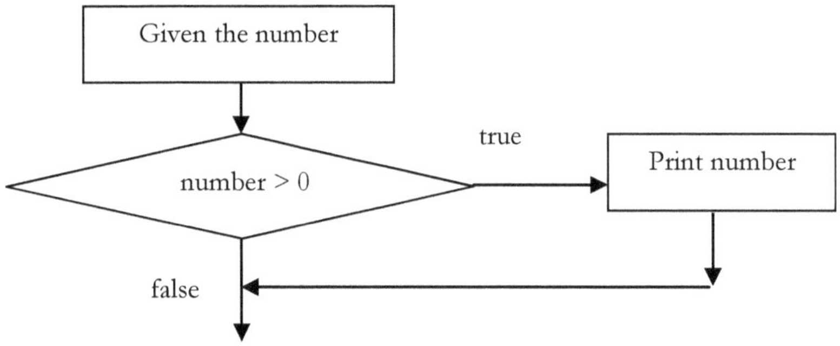

Figure 9 Flow diagram denoting the IF construct

The IF – THEN – ENDIF statement which follows is a direct translation of **Figure 9**

```
IF (length > 0) THEN
      PRINT "length is positive"
ENDIF
```

The interpretation of this form of the **IF** statement is that, if the conditional expression evaluates to **true**, then the statement or the block of statements that follow the condition will be executed. If the result is false, then the statements or block of statements that follow the condition is skipped.

THE IF.. ELSE STATEMENT

The **IF.. ELSE** statement specifies at least one alternate choice. The general format of this statement is

```
IF (condition1) THEN
        statement1;
ELSE IF (condition2) THEN
        statement2;
            :
            :
ELSE IF (conditioni) THEN
        statementi;
ELSE
        statement;
ENDIF
```

EXAMPLE 8

Suppose you were given a number, determine if the number is positive, negative, or zero. Print whichever it is.

Solution

Figure 10 shows a flow diagram of how the process works. Again we decide on the variable name. We use number as before. Since we are required to account for all three possibilities, we have to use the decision box twice. That is, whatever the result, is the number must be printed along with a message saying what it is.

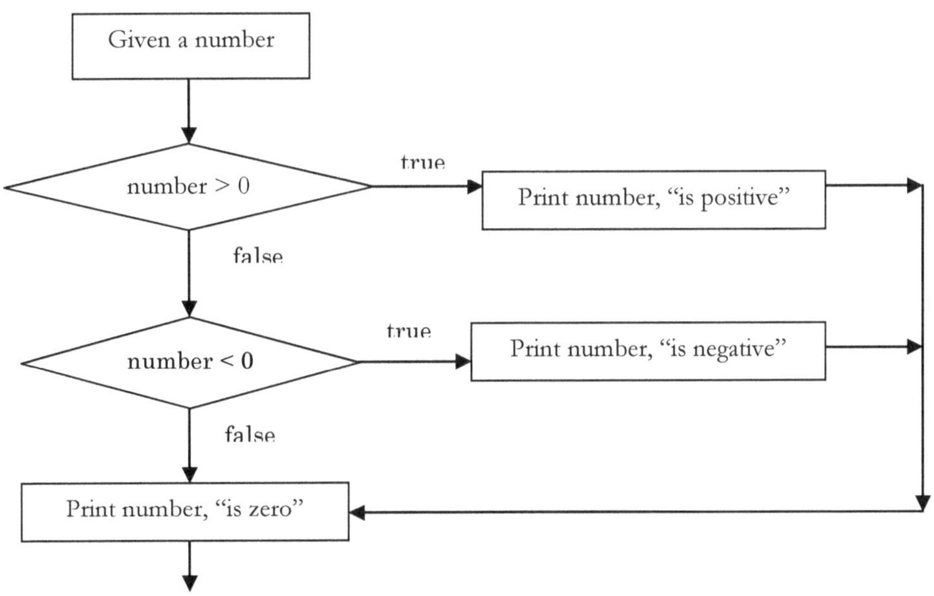

Figure 10 Flow diagram denoting the IF-THEN-ELSE construct

The IF-THEN-ELSE-ENDIF statement which follows is a direct translation of **Figure 10**

```
IF (length > 0) THEN
    PRINT "length is positive"
ELSE IF (length  < 0 ) THEN
    PRINT "length is negative"
ELSE
    PRINT "length is zero"
ENDIF
```

THE SWITCH STATEMENT

The **SWITCH** statement is an alternate method for multi-way selection. It is a special case of the **IF-THEN-ELSE** statement. This multi-way selection statement can only test discrete values such as integer values and character values. It cannot be used to test floating-point values, nor string values. The general format of the **switch** statement is:

```
SWITCH (selectionVariable)
BEGIN
        CASE value1:
                statement1;
        ESAC;
        CASE value2:
                statement2;
        ESAC;
          :
          :
        CASE valuei;
                statementi;
        ESAC;
        DEFAULT:
                statement;
        ESAC;
END
```

EXAMPLE 9

You are required to write a program segment that will display a student's status in a university, based on the **Figure 11**. As part of the solution write a **switch** statement to select a student

Code	Student status
1	Freshman
2	Sophomore
3	Junior
4	Senior

Figure 11 Student status code

Solution

Let us use a variable called **code** to denote the student status. First let us make a flow diagram showing how the process should work. **Figure 12** shows the flow chart depicting the situation. If there is a code that does not match any of those digits, print a message to that effect.

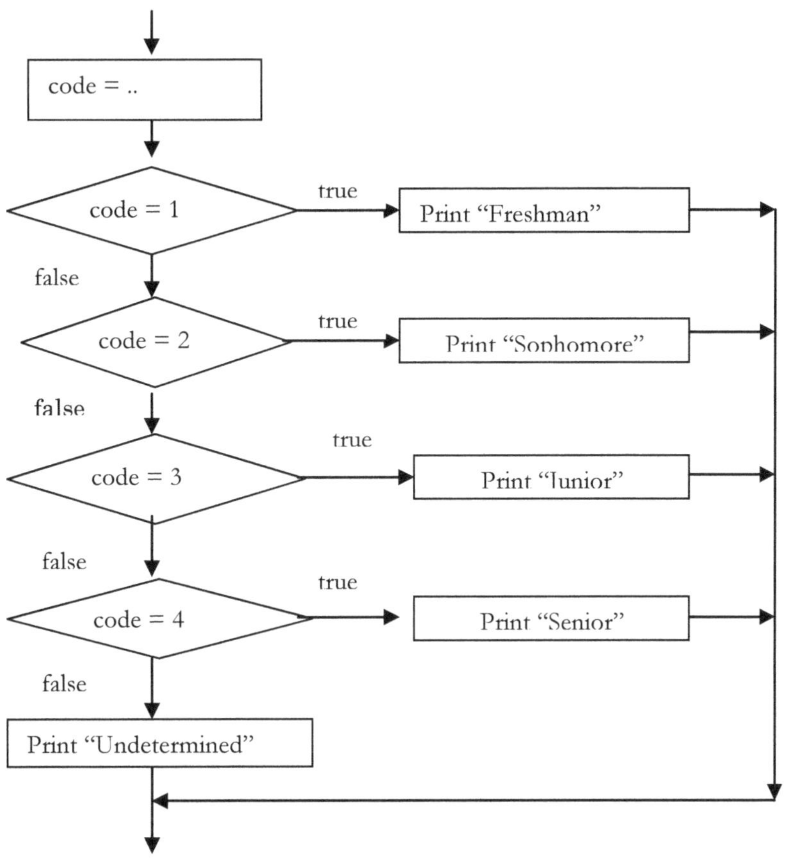

Figure 12 Diagram depicting the SWITCH statement

We now use the multi-way diagram of Figure 12 to construct the **SWITCH** statement.

EXERCISE 2

1. Complete the following sentences by supplying the missing word(s) in the space provided.
   (a) ______________ statements allow choices of action.
   (b) Selection statements use words such as __________, __________ and ______.
   (c) Two types of tests that can be used when constructing selection statements are __________test and ________ test.
   (d) The three Boolean operators are __________, __________, and __________.
   (e) The ______________ is a special form of the **if-else** statement.
2. Name one similarity and one difference between the IF statement and the SWITCH statement.
3. Use the concepts of sequence and selection to solve the following:
   a) Read two numbers
   b) Find the product of the numbers
   c) Find the sum of the numbers
   d) Determine which is bigger, the sum or the product. If the product is bigger, print a message to say so, if not print a message to the contrary.
4. Given a number N, write an if/else construct to determine if the number is odd or even. Note, a number is even if it is exactly divisible by 2, and odd otherwise.
5. Evaluate the following Boolean expressions. For each expression, assume that x is 10, y is 15, and z is 20.
   a) $z < (x + y)$
   b) $2 * (x - 5) > (2*z - y)$
   c) $(x > y)$ AND $(y > z)$
   d) $(x < y + z)$ OR $(x + 10 = z)$
   e) NOT$(x > y)$ AND $(y > z)$
6. The price of an airfare ticket between two cities varies, depending on the type of passenger. If the passenger is a senior citizen the fair is 75% the regular fare, if the passenger is a child, the fare is 60% the regular fare. Any other passenger pays full fare. A computer program must be designed to calculate the fare for an individual. The input consists of a character code that represents the type of passenger [s – senior citizen, c – child, a – adult], and a number that represents the full fare. Use the **SWITCH** statement to determine the fare that a passenger must pay.

ITERATIVE STATEMENTS

Iterative statements, commonly called loops, cause a program to repeat certain statements or block of statements. The statements or block of statements is referred to as the loop body. For example, if you were asked to add all the integers from 1 to 1000, and the only method that you know was addition, you would more than likely write something like this:

$1 + 1 = 2$
$2 + 1 = 3$
$3 + 1 = 4$

4 + 1 = 5
5 + 1 = 6
:
:

Surely it would not be long before you realize that this approach is repetitive and laborious. The concept, iteration, which is a fundamental tool to programming, relieves us from this drudgery. Computers on the other hand are capable of carrying out tasks repetitively without ever getting tired as humans can.

There are three forms of iterative statements. These are the ***while*** statement, the ***do…while*** (same as **repeat – until**) statement, and the ***for*** statement. The typical words that are used in algorithm design are **WHILE, DO.. WHILE**, (**REPEAT – UNTIL**), and **FOR**.

The While Statement

The format of the ***while*** statement is as follows:

```
WHILE (conditional expression) BEGIN
      Loop body
  ENDWHILE
```

where the word **WHILE** indicates a repetitive construct. Within the pair of parentheses is the conditional expression that is to be tested, to determine if the loop body must be executed. If the conditional expression is initially false, the loop body is skipped immediately.

EXAMPLE 10

Write a **while** loop that prints the partial sum of all the integers from 1 and 1000.

Solution

This problem focuses on two key issues—counting from 1 to 1000, and printing partial sum of the numbers. The solution is depicted in **Figure 13**. The variable counter is used as the loop control variable. It is used in the decision box to determine if the loop body is to be repeated or stop. Notice also that it is updated each time that the loop body gets executed. The loop terminates when the loop variable value is 1001.

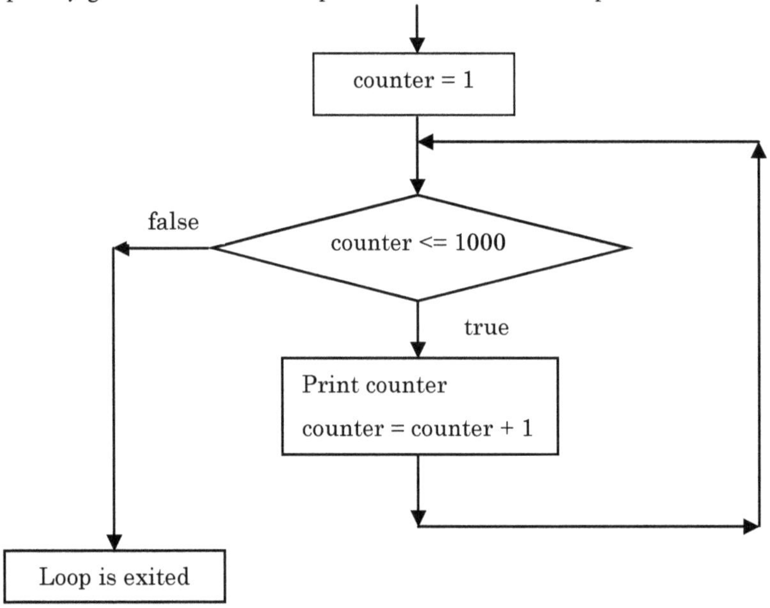

Figure 13 Looping construct for the while statement

Figure 14 shows how the WHILE statement which is based on Figure 13.

```
counter = 1;
WHILE (counter <=1000) BEGIN
      PRINT counter
      counter = counter + 1;
ENDWHILE
```

Figure 14 Using the WHILE loop

The first line declares and initializes the loop variable, counter. It is used as the basis for the conditional expression (counter <= 1000), in the WHILE clause. The loop body is enclosed within the BEGIN and ENDWHILE statements.

THE DO..WHILE AND THE REPEAT..UNTIL STATEMENTS

The **do..while** and the **repeat** statements have the same effect. Some programmers will prefer one over the other. Both statements are opposite to the ***while*** statement, in that the conditional expression comes after the loop body. The format of the **DO.. WHILE** *and the* **REPEAT.. UNTIL** statement are shown in **Figure 15** and **Figure 16**, respectively.

```
DO
        Loop body
WHILE(conditional_expression)
```

Figure 15 The DO..WHILE loop

```
REPEAT
        Loop body
UNTIL(conditional_expression )
```

Figure 16 The REPEAT..UNTIL loop

EXAMPLE 11

Write a DO..WHILE loop and a REPEAT..UNTIL loop that prints the partial sum of all the integers from 1 and 1000.

Solution

This example is the same as the Example 10, except that this time we use the DO..WHILE and the REPEAT.. UNTIL constructs. Before writing the statements, let us make a flow diagram to show how the process works. First we get a counter variable and initialize it. Next is to execute the loop body, then we test the condition. If the condition is true, the loop body is executed, otherwise the loop is terminated. See **Figure 17.**

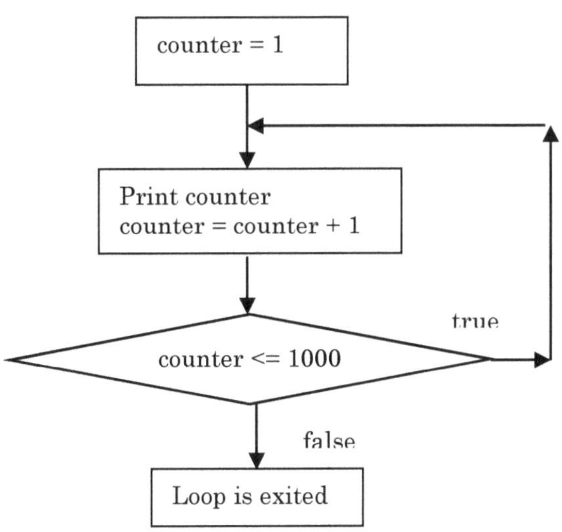

Figure 17 Flow chart showing the DO..WHILE and the REPEAT –UNTIL constructs

In **Figure 17,** notice that the loop body begins before the test is made. **Figure 18** and **Figure 19** show the DO..WHILE and the REPEAT..UNTIL constructs translated from **Figure 17.**

```
counter = 1
DO
    PRINT counter
    counter = counter + 1
WHILE(counter <= 1000)
```

Figure 18 The DO..WHILE

```
counter = 1
REPEAT
    PRINT counter
    counter = counter + 1
UNTIL(counter <= 1000)
```

Figure 19 The REPEAT ... UNTIL

THE FOR STATEMENT

The **FOR** statement, like the **WHILE** statement and the **REPEAT** statement, is a looping construct that continually executes the loop body if the condition is true. When the condition becomes false the loop body is skipped, and the statement following it is executed. The general format of the **FOR** statement is as follows:

```
FOR ( counter = initialValue TO limit)
    Loop body;
ENDFOR
```

FOR **loo**p statement consists of two major parts—the loop heading, following the word **FOR**, and the loop body. The loop heading includes the implied conditional expression within the pair of parentheses. In this case, the loop variable is implicitly updated. **Figure 20** shows the construct of the **FOR** loop.

The **FOR** statement behaves the following way:

- First, the control loop variable is declared and initialized.
- Second, the condition is tested. If the result of the condition is true, the loop body is executed, if not, the loop terminates.
- Third, the loop variable is implicitly updated. That is, the control variable is reassigned, and the second step is repeated.

EXAMPLE

Print the partial sum of all the integers from 1 to 1000.

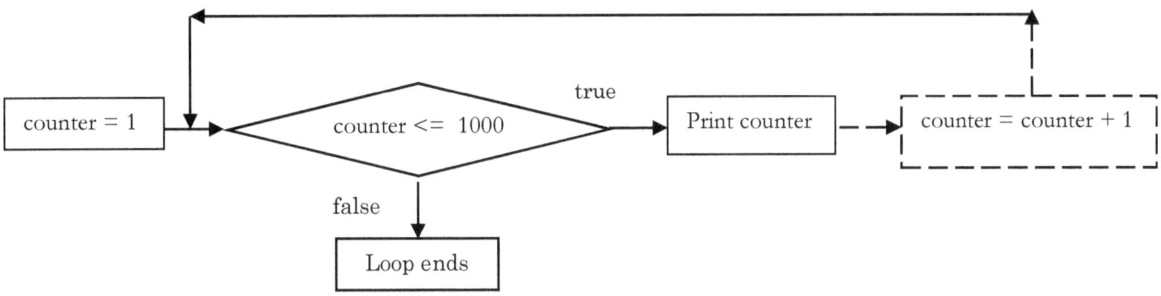

Figure 20. Flow chart showing the way the FOR loop works

Figure 21 shows the FOR loop construct. Notice that in this case the loop control variable **counter** is implicitly incremented by 1.

```
FOR (counter = 1 TO 1000)
    PRINT counter
ENDFOR
```

Figure 21 Using the FOR loop construct

Remember that these control structures are generic. Each programming language will specify its own implementation and syntax. What you need to understand at this point is that these three constructs are used to define algorithm solutions.

EXERCISE 3

1. Complete the following sentences by supplying the missing word(s) in the space provided.
   (a) Iterative statements are commonly called ______________________.
   (b) The ________________ loop and the _____________ loop are similar.
2. In this section you learned about three control structures. Name these structures and differentiate among them.
3. Make a diagram that shows how to read ten numbers.
4. Write a **FOR** loop, **WHILE** loop, a **DO/WHILE** loop and a **REPEAT/UNTIL** loop for each of the following:

(a) $1 + 2 + 3 + 4 + 5 + \ldots. + 120$

(b) $5 + 10 + 15 + \; + 45 + 50$

(c) $1 + \frac{1}{2} + \frac{1}{3} + \frac{1}{4} + \ldots\ldots.. + \frac{1}{120}$

SUMMARY

We also learned about the three control structures that are used to develop algorithms—sequence, selection, and iteration.

PROBLEMS

1. What output is produced from each of the following:

a)
```
x = -14, y = 0
IF (x < y) THEN
    Print x
ELSE
    Print y
ENDIF
```

b)
```
x = 50, y = 25, count = 0, sum = 10
IF (x = y) THEN
    Print "x and y have the same value", x, y
ELSE
BEGIN
    count = count + 1
    sum = sum + x + y
    Print "x is " x, " and y is ", y
ENDBEGIN
ENDIF
Print x, y, count, sum
```

c)
```
p = -8, q = 21
r = p + q
IF ( p > q) THEN
BEGIN
      p = q
      r = p * q
ENDBEGIN
ELSE IF (P < 0)
```

```
BEGIN
        p = -(p)
        q = q – p
        r = p * q
ENDBEGIN
ELSE
    r = 0
ENDIF
Print "p is " p, "q is ", q, " and r is ", r
```

d) x = 3, y = 5, b = 10

```
SWITCH(x)
    CASE 1:
        b = x
    ESAC
    CASE 2:
        x = x * y
    ESAC
    CASE 3:
        y = x * x * y
    ESAC
ENDSWITCH
Print "x is ", x, "y is ", y, " and b is ", b
```

2. A substance floats in water if the density of the substance is less than 1 gram/cm3, and sinks if it is 1 or more. The density of a liquid is mass/volume. Given the mass and the volume of an object, calculate its density and determine if it floats or sinks. Do the following:
   a) Write the arithmetic expression to calculate the density of the substance.
   b) Write an IF-THEN-ELSE statement that will print whether or not the substance will float or sink.

3. What output is produced from the following?

```
i = 1, m = 3
WHILE (m < 20)
BEGIN
      Print m
      i = i + 1
      m = m * i
END
```

4. How many times does the body of the while statement below get executed?

```
int x = 3;
WHILE (x < 9)
    x = x + 2;
```

5. Consider the following two loops (a) and (b), what will be printed by each of them?

```
(a)
i = 10
WHILE (i <= 9 )
BEGIN
    Print i
    i = i + 1
ENDWHILE
```

```
(b)
i = 10
DO
BEGIN
    Print i
    i = i + 1
WHILE(i <= 9 )
```

6. Write a FOR statement that prints all the odd number years from 1970 to 2009.

Develop Algorithm and Desk Check for Correctness

BY JOSLYN A. SMITH

OBJECTIVES

In this article you will learn:

- How to present solution in pseudocode.
- How to design and construct decision tables
- How to test the algorithm for correctness

TERMINOLOGIES

Pseudocode • Algorithm development • Decision table • Trace table • Desk checking

INTRODUCTION

As we have mentioned in the overview, before an experienced programmer starts coding, he/she defines the problem, and outlines a solution to the problem. The third step in the process is to develop an algorithm. This step is followed by a testing of the algorithm for correctness. If the algorithm cannot pass the test, then the programmer must go back and re-read the problem to make sure that no part of the problem was missed. The programmer must then correct, or re-design the solution and also the algorithm. This article uses the technique called pseudocode to define algorithms. It also discusses decision table as a technique used to test the correctness of the algorithm.

ALGORITHMS DEVELOPMENT

Once you have defined the problem, the next step is to develop an algorithm to represent the solution. In the most general sense, an algorithm is a set of detailed step-by-step instructions that tell how something gets done, from the beginning of the process, to the end of the process. In terms of programming, an algorithm is a finite sequence of step by step instructions, for solving a problem on the computer.

A worthy algorithm has four properties—it must be precise and unambiguous; it must provide some flow of control from one process to another, it must give correct results in all cases; and it must eventually terminate. All algorithms, and ultimately programs, are designed from the following four basic concepts: data representation, sequential statements, selection statements, and iteration statements.

PSEUDOCODE

Pseudocode is a kind of structured English for describing algorithms. That is, it uses short, English-like phrases to explain each specific task. The data values are represented by variables. The programmer decides the names for the variables. The name you choose can be one word such as *tax* or multiple words grouped to form one name, for example *taxRate*. Pseudocode algorithm uses any of the following six concepts to form a solution algorithm.

1. Input data.
2. Output information.
3. Perform computation.
4. Assign data value to a variable.
5. Compare values and make selection, using selection statements.
6. Repeat a statement or a group of statements, using repetitive statements.

When writing pseudocode, you should begin it with a tag. A tag is a short descriptive word or phrase that reflects the problem you are solving. The pseudocode solution should also have an ending tag that indicates that the algorithm solution is completed.

Example 1

Define a pseudocode algorithm for the following problem.

A shopper picks up three items at the supermarket. The cashier scans the price of each of the items, adds the price of each of the items, and then prints the total. Design a solution to this problem.

Solution

First we define the problem by designing a IPO diagram. See **Figure 1**

Input	Process	Output
price1	Scan three prices	Total
price2	Add the prices	
price3	Print the total	

Figure 1 IPO diagram

Since the pseudocode should be enclosed between a beginning tag and an ending tag, let us call the beginning tag *Find_Total_Cost*, and the ending tag, *End_Find_Total_Cost*, as shown in **Figure 2**.

```
Find_Total_Cost
    Input price1, price2, price3           <---- Input
    Total = price1 + price2 + price3       <---- Process
    Print "Your total is", Total           <---- Output
End_Find_total_Cost
```

Figure 2 Finding total cost for three items.

It is always a good practice to isolate the body of the pseudocode from the tags by indenting the statements. This allows for ease of reading, and understanding of where the pseudocode begins and where it ends. Notice that the actual pseudocode solution begins with the phrase *Input price1*, and follows through to the statement, *Print "Your total is", Total.* In addition, the first line of the pseudocode denotes the input. The words *price1*, *price2*, and *price3* represent the variables that will be used to store the price of each item. The second line denotes the process that is to be performed with these values. When the addition is performed, the value is stored in the variable called *Total.* The last line denotes the output. The value in the variable *Total* is printed.

There are situations where input statements are interspersed with process statements. Generally, this is where it is expected that the computer prompts the user for the input.

Example 2

Define a pseudocode algorithm for the following problem.

> A program is required to prompt the user for two numbers, one representing the length of a rectangle, and the other its width. Use these numbers to find the area and the perimeter of the rectangle. You are to print the area and the perimeter.

Solution

Let us assume that we had defined the problem using an IPO chart. **Figure 3** shows the pseudocode algorithm for the problem.

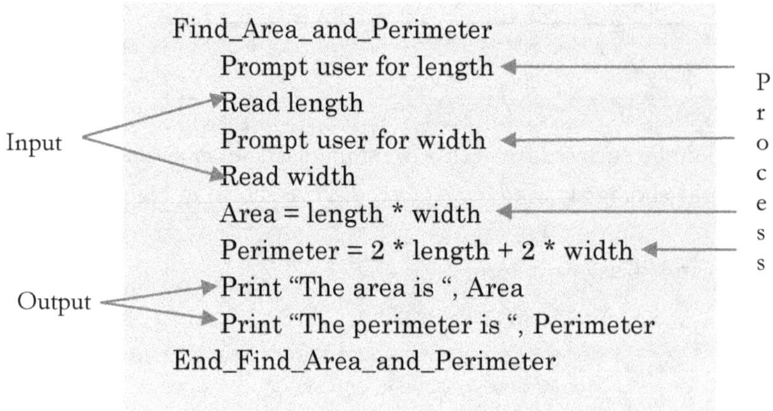

Figure 3 Find area and perimeter of rectangle

Notice the opening tag and the closing tags referred to as *Find_Area_and_Perimeter* and *End_Find_Area_and_Perimeter*, respectively. In this example we see that the user will be prompted each time that input is required. This interactive approach is best used when you desire an interaction between the user and the computer. It helps to reduce, if not eliminate input errors, such as keying in the wrong entry.

You will notice that these two examples use only the sequence construct, where each step is executed once and in a linear fashion. That is, there is no selection nor iteration statement in these solutions. The following examples illustrate the concepts of selection and iteration, respectively.

Example

The postal service wants to convert its manual system of determining the cost for sending packages. You are required to design a program that will automate the cost for shipping packages. **Figure 4** shows the rates for determining the shipping cost. Design a solution algorithm in pseudocode to show how the selection is made.

Parcel weight(kg)	Cost per kg ($)
Under 5 kg	$5.50 per kg
5 – 10 kg	$4.50 per kg
Over 10 kg	$4.00 per kg

Figure 4 Rate table

DEFINING THE PROBLEM

After carefully reading and analyzing the problem, we see that the solution requires one number representing the input for the weight. The process requires determining the range in which the weight falls, applying the correct charge from the rate table, and calculating the cost. The output is simply the shipping cost. See the IPO chart shown in **Figure 5**.

Input	Process	Output
Weight	Prompt user for the weight	Cost
	Determine the range of weight	
	Assign the charges per kilogram	
	Calculate the shipping cost	
	Display	

Figure 5 IPO diagram to determine shipping cost

DEFINING THE PSEUDOCODE

Once we get the weight of the parcel, we must determine the price range for posting the parcel. To do this requires the use of the **IF-THEN-ELSE** construct. But first we must validate the data by disallowing zero and negative values. The pseudocode is shown **in Figur**e 6.

```
    Begin_shipping_cost
        Prompt user for weight
        Read weight
        IF (weight <= 0) THEN
            PRINT "Sorry, you entered an invalid; cannot calculate cost"
        ELSE
        BEGIN
            IF (weight > 10) THEN
                charge = weight * 4.00
            ELSE IF (weight > 5) THEN
                charge = weight * 4.50
            ELSE
                charge = weight * 5.50
            ENDIF
            PRINT charges
        END_BEGIN
        ENDIF
End_shipping_cost
```

Figure 6 pseudocode solution for finding shipping cost

In this example the pseudocode algorithm simply gets the number representing the weight of the parcel and makes sure that the value entered was a positive value. Once the weight is determined to be valid, the appropriate charge is applied. In order to apply the right charge, the IF-THEN-ELSE construct is used to find the range in which the weight falls.

DECISION TABLE

Sometimes logic problems that deal with selection statements are better handled in a tabular form called decision table. Decision tables serve as a means of ensuring that the programmer understands the logic of the problem. Decision tables are typically divided into quadrants as shown in **Figure 7**. However, there are variants of this format.

Conditions	Condition alternatives
Action entries	Action taken

Figure 7 A simple decision table

We will study this concept by using an example.

Example 3

The ABC courier company offers services for shipping packages domestically. It calculates delivery charges for each package as follows:

- If the weight of the package is under 2 lbs and the distance to transport it is less than 100 miles, the delivery charge is $25.00. If the distance is 100 miles or more, the delivery charge is $30.00.
- If the weight of the package is 2 lbs or more, and the distance it has to go is less than 100 miles, the charge is $35.00. If the distance is 100 miles or more, the charge is $40.00. Design a decision depicting the solution to the problem.

Solution

As you may have noticed in the problem, there are two attributes—the weight and the distance. Each of these attributes has its respective set of conditions; and corresponding action. See **Figure 8**.

	Under 2 Lbs	2 Lbs or over	$25	$30	$35	$40
Under 100 miles	x	√				
		x			√	
100 miles or more	x			√		
		x				√

Figure 8 Decision table for calculating shipping charges

We can now design the pseudocode algorithm from this table. Let distance and weight be the names of the variables representing the situation. Also, let us validate each data entry. **Figure 9** shows the pseudocode solution to the problem. Notice that the action (charges) to be taken is based on distance versus weight. For instance, if weight > 100 and weight is less than 2 lbs, the corresponding action entry that is checked is $30. Another case, if the weight is less than 100 miles, the weight is more than 2 lbs, the corresponding charge is $35. Figure 8.12 shows the entire pseudocode solution.

```
Begin_service
        Read distance, weight
        IF (distance <= 0) THEN
             Print "Invalid – distance must be positive"
        ELSEIF (weight <= 0) THEN
             Print "Invalid – weight must be positive"
        ELSE
        BEGIN
             IF ((distance < 100) AND (weight < 2)) THEN
               charge = 25
             ELSEIF ((distance < 100) AND (weight >= 2)) THEN
               charge = 35
             ELSEIF ((distance >= 100) AND (weight < 2)) THEN
               charge = 30
             ELSEIF ((distance >= 100) AND (weight >= 2)) THEN
             charge = 40
             ENDIF
             Print "Your cost is $", charge
        ENDBEGIN
        ENDIF
End_service
```

Figure 9 Pseudocode solution for calculating shipping charges, using the decision table.

In this solution you will notice two major decisions to be made:

1. We have prevented negative values from entering the decision process by validating the data, and
2. The use of the logical expression to determine the relevant cost that is associated with the corresponding distance and weight relationship.

There is an alternate way that we can use the decision table to arrive at the answer. This solution would do away with the logical expression, and simply use relational expression. We begin with **Figure 10**. In this figure we focus first on the distance.

```
IF (distance >= 100)
BEGIN
        Calculate charges for distance 100 miles or more
ENDBEGIN
ELSE
BEGIN
        Calculate charges for distance under 100 miles
ENDIF
```

Figure 10 Partial solution determines the boundaries for the distance

Once we have established the boundaries for the distance we turn next to the weight. **Figure 11** shows the complete result. Notice the solution is achieved without mentioning logical expression.

```
Begin_service
        Read distance, weight
        IF (distance <= 0) THEN
                Print "Invalid – distance must be positive"
        ELSEIF (weight <= 0) THEN
                Print "Invalid – weight must be positive"
        ELSE BEGIN
            IF (distance >= 100)
            BEGIN
                IF (weight >= 2)
                    charges = 40
                ELSE
                    charges = 30
            ENDBEGIN
            ELSE BEGIN
                IF (weight >= 2)
                    charges = 35
                ELSE
                    charges = 25
                ENDBEGIN
        ENDIF
End_service
```

Figure 11 Pseudocode using relational expressions only.

Earlier we learned that iterative statements cause certain statements or block of statements to be executed, repeatedly. Iteration sometimes require that the statements are to be repeated a specified number of times, as well as an unspecified number of times. When the number of iterations is unknown in advance, it usually occurs when the process approaches an acceptable value, or the process must terminate when a sentinel value is set in the input. Also, when reading from files, the end-of-file (EOF) marker is usually used as the sentinel to determine when to stop reading.

Repeat a specified number of times.

Example 4

Design an algorithm that reads the name and price of 20 products, and displays the name of the product with the highest price. (Assume that the prices are different.)

DEFINING THE PROBLEM

After carefully reading the problem we see that the input requires 20 pairs of data items—product and price. The required output is one item, the highest priced product. The process has two parts—validate the price and determine which of the valid price is the highest. **Figure 12** shows the IPO chart.

Input	Process	Output
Product	Determine if price is positive	Product
Price	Find highest price	Highest price
	Print product	
	Print price	

Figure 12 IPO chart for finding highest price of a set of items

This problem requires a loop that iterates for 20 valid pairs of data. If the price is negative or is zero, that entry is skipped and the counter is not updated. **Figure 13** shows the variables that are required.

Variables	Meaning
product	The input variable to store the name of the product
price	The input variable to store the price of the product
counter	The loop variable that keeps track of the 20 valid pairs of data
highest Price	The variable which stores the highest priced product

Figure 13 Required variables and their meanings

Figure 14 shows the solution algorithm for the problem.

```
Begin_Find_highest_Price
        counter = 1
        price
        product
        highestPrice = 0
        theProduct= ""
        WHILE (counter <= 20)
              Read product, price
              IF (price <= 0) THEN
                  PRINT "invalid price"
              ELSE
                  IF (price > highestPrice) THEN
                  BEGIN
                      highestPrice = price
                      theProduct= product
                  ENDBEGIN
                  counter = counter + 1
              ENDIF
        ENDWHILE
        PRINT theProduct, "highest price", highestPrice
End_Find_highest_Price
```

Figure 14 solution algorithm for finding the highest priced item

In this solution there are some key things worth noting:

- Initially the counter is set to 1; the highestPrice is set to 0; and the product with the highest price is set to the empty or blank string.
- The **WHILE** loop may run more than 20 times, but the variable counter is updated only when valid price is encountered.
- The **IF**-THEN-**ELSE st**atement is used to validate the data.
- Once the data is known to be valid, the IF statement (without alternate choice) is used to determine which value is higher. If the current price is known to be higher than the previous price, then the previous price is set to the current price as the highest price so far. Also, the current product is set as the product for the corresponding highest price.
- Notice also that the counter variable is updated by 1 only if the price is positive.

Repeat an unspecified number of times.

There are two ways that you can encounter repetition an unspecified number of times. These may occur when reading data from the keyboard or reading data from a file. In either case, the program reads a sentinel value that determines when the loop must stop. Let us re-visit the problem and change it slightly.

Example 5

Design an algorithm that reads the name and price of a number of products, and displays the name of the product with the highest price. (Assume that the prices are different.)

Solution

This problem is the same as the previous example, with the exception that we do not know how many products to expect. In this case the programmer has to design an artificial way to stop reading when there is no more data. The technique that is commonly used is to follow the last data set with a sentinel value. In this example we use an asterisk (*) to signal the end of the data. In this case we do away with the counter variable, unless you were specifically asked to keep track of the number of products; or, if you were asked to find the average price of the products, then you would have to count the number of products. Let us re-write the pseudocode algorithm without the counter variable. See **Figure 15**.

```
Begin_Find_highest_Price
        price
        product
        highestPrice = 0
        theProduct= “”
        Read product
        WHILE (product != “*”)
              Read price
              IF (price <= 0) THEN
                  PRINT “invalid price”
              ELSEIF (price > highestPrice) THEN
                  BEGIN
                      highestPrice = price
                      theProduct= product
                  ENDBEGIN
               Read product
              ENDELSE
        ENDWHILE
        PRINT theProduct, “highest price”, highestPrice
End_Find_highest_Price
```

Figure15 Reading an unspecified number of times.

Notice that we read the name of the product code before entering the loop, because we cannot assume that there is any data at all to be read. Once we determine that the input read is not the sentinel value, then we go on to reading the price. In order to stay in the loop we read again at the bottom of the loop body. Control takes us back to determine if the sentinel was read.

Repeat an unspecified number of times from a file.

When the data is to be read from a file, in most cases we do not know in advance the number of records that are in the file, neither is there any artificial sentinel data. When a file is created, the operating system makes a marker at the end of the data file as the end of file marker. The actual value for the end-of-file marker is system dependent. Therefore, when we write algorithms that require test for end-of-file, we generally use the abbreviation, EOF.

Exercise

1. As it pertains to programming, define the term *algorithm*.

2. Which of the following must be true about algorithm?
   a) It must give correct results most of the times.
   b) It must be precise.
   c) It must be ambiguous.
   d) It must terminate.
   e) It must consist of a finite number of steps.

3. Write pseudocode instruction(s) to carry out each of the following:
   (a) Input a number
   (b) Input two numbers.
   (c) Print "Today is", day
   (d) Display "My country of origin is", country
   (e) Prompt the user to input three numbers from the keyboard, find their sum, difference, product, and quotient.
   (f) Using 5(e) print each value mentioned in the question. Each value output must be appropriately labeled.

4. Airlines in general do not charge airfare for children under 2 years. Children 2 years old, but under 18 years old are charged half price. Adults 65 years or older are charged a 10% reduction. Design a pseudocode algorithm to calculate the total airfare for a family of five people: two children, a one-year-old and a ten-year-old; their mother who is thirty years old; and the children's grandparents, the male is sixty-six years old and his wife who is fifty-nine years old.

5. Given the following scenario, use it to design a decision table.
   The service charge depends on the amount of the check. If the check amount is up to $10.00, the charge is $1.00. If the amount is greater than $10.00 but less than $100.00, the charge is 10% of the amount. If the amount is greater than $100.00, but less than $1,000.00, the charge is $5.00 plus 5% of the amount. If the value is over $1,000.00, the charge is $40.00 plus 1% of the amount. Use the decision table to design a pseudocode solution.

6. Design a pseudocode algorithm to read a positive integer number, N. Following this you are to read N number of positive values, and find their average. Validate each input to make sure that the values being read are positive.

TEST ALGORITHMS FOR CORRECTNESS

Once an algorithm has been established, it should be checked for logic errors. One method that is commonly used is called desk-checking. Desk checking is a manual technique for checking the logic of an algorithm. The computer is not involved in this activity. Instead, the person who is performing the desk checking is effectively acting as the computer, using pencil and paper to record results. Desk checking attempts to confirm that the algorithm works as expected. It also has the benefit of saving time when it comes time to write the program.

In order to carry out desk checking, you must create sample data. This sample data is used to test the algorithm, verifying the order and accuracy of the steps. That is, desk checking concentrates on the data value and the logic of each statement. When carrying out desk checking you should use at least two sets of sample data. Also, have a third party administer the checking, this way that person will be less likely to be influenced by the logic of the algorithm. Be sure that the data that you use are based on the problem requirements, and not on the algorithm.

Desk checking cannot solve all possible errors. For example, it cannot solve spelling errors or syntax errors (violation of programming rules). Desk checking is normally done as a table of rows and columns. The table is called trace table. Each row represents one line in the algorithm solution, and each column represents one value for each of the variables used in the solution.

Example 6

Let us desk check the pseudocode algorithm developed for **Example.1**.

Solution

When doing the checking, the first thing to do is to number each line in the pseudocode, excluding the beginning tag and the ending tag, as shown in **Figure 16**.

```
Find_Total_Cost
1.      Input price1, price2, price3
2.      Total = price1 + price2 + price3
3.      Print "Your total is ", Total
End_Find_Total_Cost
```

Figure 16 Assign line numbers for desk checking

Next, we set up the table, and plug in the values for each input variable, then fill in the value for remaining variables or actions, line by line. See **Figure 17**.

Variables/ Line number	Price1	Price2	Price3	Total	Expected outcome
Data Set 1					
1	10.00	15.50	12.00		37.50
2				**37.50**	
3				Print	
Data Set 2					
1	2.50	20.00	6.50		29.00
2				**29.00**	
3				Print	

Figure 17 Filling in the value for each variable or action line by line.

In **Figure 17** notice that there is an extra column, labeled expected outcome. The values in this column represent the expected results. These values should be recorded in advance in the table, as they will be used to compare with what the algorithm actually produces.

If at the end of a desk check, the actual results differ from the expected results, the solution algorithm probably has logic error. In such a situation it is necessary to re-visit the algorithm and fix whatever the problem is, and desk check it again until you get it right.

Example 7

Let us desk check **Example 2** for finding the area and the perimeter of a rectangle. First assign line number to each line of the pseudocode, as shown in **Figure 18**. As before, select two sets of data, one for each input variable. In my case the first set is 10 and 8; and the second is 5 and 2. Next specify the expected values. In this case the area for the first data set is 80, and the perimeter is 36; and the second is 10 and 14, respectively.

```
Find_Area_and_Perimeter
1.        Prompt user for length
2.        Read length
3.        Prompt user for width
4.        Read width
5.        Area = length * width
6.        Perimeter = 2 * length + 2 * width
7.        Print "The area is ", Area
8.        Print "The perimeter is ", Perimeter
End_Find_Area_and_Perimeter
```

Figure 18 Assign line numbers to the pseudocode algorithm

When building the table, you can combine two or more line numbers in a row, especially when there is a prompt/input situation. See **Figure 19**, lines 1 and 2, and lines 3 and 4, respectively.

Variables/Line number	length	width	Area	Perimeter	Expected area	Expected perimeter
Data Set 1						
1, 2	10					
3, 4		8				
5			10*8 = **80**		80	
6				2*10+2*8 = **36**		36
7			Print			
8				Print		
Data Set 2						
1,2	5					
3,4		2				
5			5*2 = **10**		10	
6				2*5 + 2*2 = **14**		14
7			Print			
8				Print		

Figure 19 Combining multiple line numbers in a single row

Notice that the calculations agree with the expected outcomes.

Example 8

The ABC Manufacturing Company wants you to help convert their manual payroll system to a computer-based system. They know that you are still learning to program, so all they want for now is a program that will calculate and print a payroll report for one employee. The table in **Figure 20** outlines the deduction rates for each employee.

Category of deduction	Rate
National Income Tax deduction	15%
Charitable deduction	1.5%
Union dues	2.5%

Figure 20 Deduction rate table

Each line of input will consist of the employee's id number, the number of hours worked, and the employee's hourly rate of pay. You are to calculate the amount of deduction for each category of deductions, the total deduction and the net pay the employee gets. The employee must get a printed copy of the report, detailing the gross pay, the amount for each deduction, the total deduction, and the net pay. You must also store a copy of the report on a direct-access storage device.

Further, it is known that in the past, two employees, *xxx* and *yyy* worked 10 hours at $5.00 per hour and 20 hours at $10.00 per hour, respectively. Their gross pay, deductions, and net pay are shown in **Figure 21**.

Expected Results	Id	Gross	Tax	Charity	Dues	total Deduction	net Pay
Data set 1	xxx	50.00	7.5	0.75	1.25	9.50	40.50
Data set 2	yyy	200.00	30.00	3.00	5.00	38.00	162.00

Figure 21 Data set for two employees

Things to do:

(a) As a precursor to writing the program, design a pseudocode algorithm.
(b) Desk check the algorithm with the information provided for employee *xxx* and *yyy*.

DEFINING THE PROBLEM

As we did before, underline the key terms in the passage. Look for nouns, descriptive phrases, and action words or phrases. After reading the problem, we observed that the following segment of the passage is most relevant to the solution.

> Each line of input will consist of the employee's id number, the number of hours worked, and the employee's hourly rate of pay. You are to calculate the amount of deduction for each category of deductions, the total deduction, and the net pay the employee gets. The employee must get a printed copy of the report, detailing the gross pay, the amount for each deduction, the total deduction, and the net pay. Must also store a copy of the report on a direct-access storage device.

Based on this analysis, the IPO chart shown in **Figure 22** describes the possible inputs, processes and outputs.

Input	Process	Output
• Id number • Hours worked • Hourly rate	• Input id, Hours worked, Hourly rate • Calculate gross pay • Calculate income tax deduction • Calculate charitable deduction • Calculate union dues • Total the deductions • Calculate net pay • Print • Store	• gross • Tax deduction. • Charity deduction • Union dues • Total deduction • Net pay

Figure 22 IPO chart depicting the solution

When making an IPO chart, use self-explanatory words or phrases, especially in the process column. This will help us intuitively as we attempt to solve the problem. When we have finished making the IPO chart we then design the pseudocode algorithm.

PSEUDOCODE SOLUTION

When making the pseudocode algorithm, use meaningful variable names that match the situation. For instance, instead of using something like *h* for *hours*, use the actual word *hours*. As a matter of fact, hoursWorked (compound word), would even be better. Also, because we will be desk checking the algorithm, we can go right ahead and assign line numbers to the pseudocode as shown in **Figure 23**.

```
Start_Payroll_Report
   1.    Input id, hours, rate
   2.    gross = hours * rate
   3.    tax = gross * 0.15
   4.    charity = gross * 0.015
   5.    dues = gross * 0.025
   6.    deductions = tax + charity + dues
   7.    net = gross – deductions
   8.    Print "Id number = ", id
   9.    Print "Gross ", gross, "Total deduction = ", deductions, "Net pay = ", net
   10.   Print "Income tax = ", tax, "Charity = ", charity, "Union dues = ", dues
   11.   Store "Id number = ", id
   12.   Store "Gross ", gross, "Total deduction = ", deductions, "Net pay = ", net
   13.   Store "Income tax = ", tax, "Charity = ", charity, "Union dues = ", dues
End_Payroll_Report
```

Figure 23 Pseudocode solution with line numbers

DESK CHECKING THE SOLUTION

Let us design a trace table in order to desk check the solution as we did in the previous example. The first row of the table details the variables used in the algorithm and the first column represents the line number of each statement of the algorithm. We will use the two sets of data provided in the problem definition, since the correct result is well known. **Figure 24** and **Figure 25** show for each data set.

	Id	hour	rate	gross	tax	charity	dues	deductions	net
1	xxx	10	5						
2				50.00					
3					50*0.15 = 7.50				
4						50*0.015 = 0.75			
5							50*0.025 = 1.25		
6								7.5+0.75+1.25 = 9.50	
7									50-9.5 = 40.50
8	Print								
9				Print				Print	Print
10					Print	Print	Print		
11	Store								
12				Store				Store	Store
13					Store	Store	Store		

Figure 24 (at left) Desk checking using the first set of values

In the trace table, **Line 1** shows the input, and **Lines 2** through 7 show the calculation for the respective amount. **Lines 8** through **10** indicate what will be printed, and **Lines 11** through **13** specify what will be stored on the DASD.

	Id	hour	rate	gross	tax	charity	dues	totalDeduction	netPay
1	xxx	20	10						
2				200.00					
3					200*0.15 = 30.00				
4						200*0.015 = 3.00			
5							200*0.025 = 5.00		
6								30.0+3.0+5.0 = 38.00	
7									200- 38.0 =162.00
8	Print								
9				Print				Print	Print
10					Print	Print	Print		
11	Store								
12				Store				Store	Store
13					Store	Store	Store		

Figure 25 Desk checking using the second set of values

Exercise

1. What is meant by the term "Desk checking"?
2. What is a trace table?
3. Name one thing that a trace table can detect and one that it cannot detect.
4. Given the following pseudocode algorithm, complete the trace table that follows it.

```
Begin_algorithm
  a. P = 10
  b. Q = 20
  c. R = 30
  d. R = P + Q
  e. Q = 2 * R
  f. Q = Q – R
  g. P = 3 * Q – P – R
  h. Print P, Q, R
End_algorithm
```

	P	Q	R
a	10		
b		20	
c			30
d			
e			
f			
g			
h	Print	Print	Print

5. This question has three activities, namely:
   (a) Write a pseudocode algorithm to read three numbers and find the average of the numbers.
   (b) Make a trace table to verify that the algorithms are correct.

SUMMARY

In this article we learned that after defining the problem we should develop an algorithm solution, and desk check the algorithm for correctness. We generally use pseudocode to describe the algorithms. We also learned how to build decision tables in order to help clearly define the problem.

When desk checking an algorithm you should build a trace table, and use at least two sets of data to check it. You should bear in mind that desk checking does not guarantee finding all the errors, but instead it seeks to detect as many logic errors as possible. Once the desk check is acceptable, you can choose a programming language and start the coding.

Part IV: Java Statements

Part IV: Java Statements

INTRODUCTION

TERMINOLOGIES

Sequence • Selection • Iteration

Java's executable statements are classified as sequence, selection, and iteration. These concepts are now discussed as they play major roles in programming.

Sequence

BY JOSLYN A. SMITH

The order in which statements are executed in programs is determined by the controls to which each statement is subjected. Unless otherwise specified, the execution of a program proceeds in a linear fashion, from the first statement to the last; no statement is skipped, and none is repeated. **Figure 1** shows what happens when statements are executed in sequence. Each statement represented by **S,** is executed in the order in which each is written.

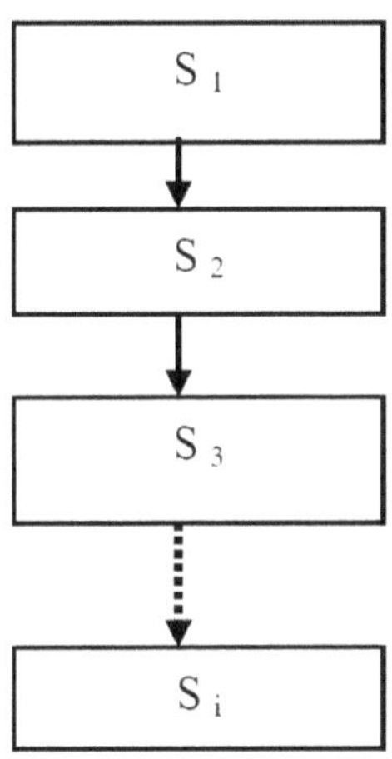

Figure 1 Program statements executed in sequence

The invocation of methods does not constitute altering the flow of control, but rather it is an expansion of the statement call. In this case the statement is expanded by the method definition. If we let **M** represents a method instead of a single statement, as shown in **Figure 2,** then when the method is called, it simply executes its statements, and then re-enters the original linear formation of statements.

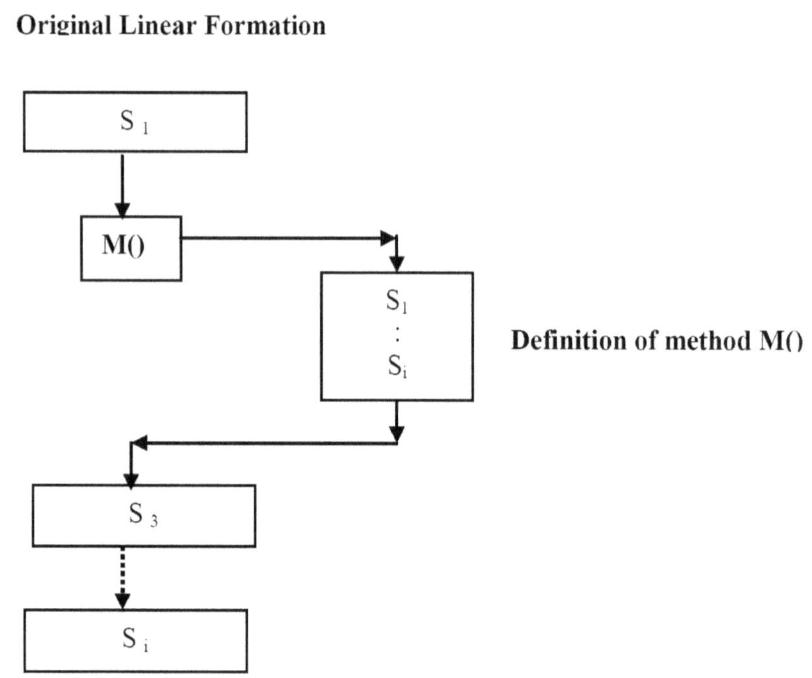

Figure 2 Program statements calls method in sequence

EXAMPLE 1

Suppose a company bought an item for certain amount of money and sells it. Do the following:

a. Define a class called Trade that accepts the name, buying price and selling price of the product.
b. Define accessor methods that returns the value represented by each variable.
c. Include a mutator method that calculates the profit, (assuming profit was made).
d. Provide mutator methods to change the purcha
e. sing price and the selling price of the product.

```
1.  // Test class creates two trade products and calculates their profit
2.  class TestTrade {
3.          public static void main(String arg[]) {
4.              System.out.println("\tABC Trading Co");
5.              System, out. println("_____________________________ ");
6.              Trade tl = new Trade("Chair", 150, 205);
7.              tl.calculateTheProfitO;
8.              display(tl);
9.              Trade t2 = new Trade("Piano", 5500, 7000);
10.             t2.calculateTheProfitO;
11.             display(t2);
12.         }
13.         static void display(Trade t) {
14.              System.out.println("Product:....... " +
            tgetTheNameOfTheProduct());
15.              System.out.println("Purchase price: $" + t.getThePurchasePrice());
16.              System.out.println("Sale price: ....$" + t.getTheSellingPrice());
17.              System, out. println("_____________________________ ");
18.              System.out.println("Proflt:........ $" + t.getTheProfit());
19.              System.out.println("\n");
20.         }
```

Listing 1a Program statements in sequence

In **Listing 1a** Lines **6** through **11** calls constructors and methods in the class Trade. The class Trade is shown in **Listing 1b.**

```
class Trade {
String product;
double price, sell, profit;

Trade(String name, double p, double s) {
        product = name;
        price = p;
        sell = s;
}

void calculateTheProfit() {
    profit = sell - price;
}

String getTheNameOfTheProduct() {
    return product;
}

double getTheProfit() {
    return profit;
}

double getThePurchasePrice(){
    return price;
}

double getTheSellingPrice(){
    return sell;
}

void changeThePurchasePrice(double amount){
    price = amount;
}

void changeTheSellingPrice(double amount){
    sell = amount;
}
}
```

Listing 1b Class Trade

Control structure seeks to alter the flow of program statements within a given piece of code. This is carried out using two control structures—selection and iteration.

Selection

BY JOSLYN A. SMITH

Selection statements are those statements that allow choice. The decision for making a choice is based on the result of a conditional expression. **Figure 3** represents a decision-making process. In this Figure, notice that the result of the conditional expression—representing a decision—is one of the Boolean values, true or false. There are two basic forms of selection statements in Java. These are the if statement and the switch statement.

The **if** statement has two forms, namely, if without an alternate choice, and **if** with alternate choice, symbolized by the keyword else. **Figure 3** shows the format of the if statement.

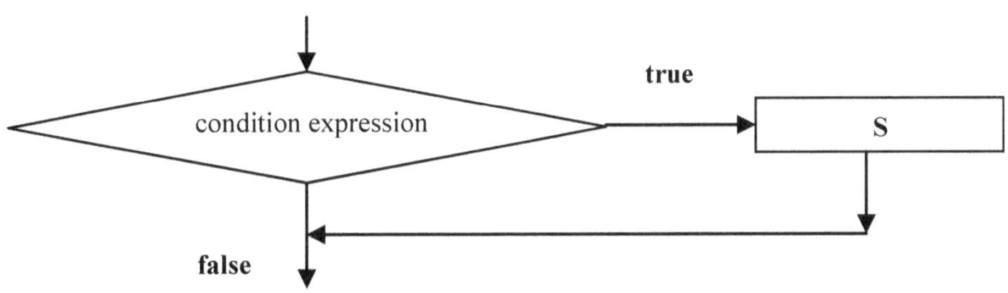

Figure 3 The if statement without alternate choice

The general format of this construct is as follows:

```
if ( conditional expression )
{
    Java statement(s)
}
```

The interpretation of this form of the **if** statement is this, if the conditional expression evaluates to **true**, then the statement or the block of statements that follow the condition will be executed. If the result is false, then the statements or block of statements that follow the condition will be skipped.

The if/else statement has alternative choices as shown in **Figure 4.** The diagram illustrates that whichever of the conditional expressions results in **true**, the associated statement or block is executed, and the rest of the statement is skipped. If none of the conditions yields **true**, then the last block following the last **false** is executed.

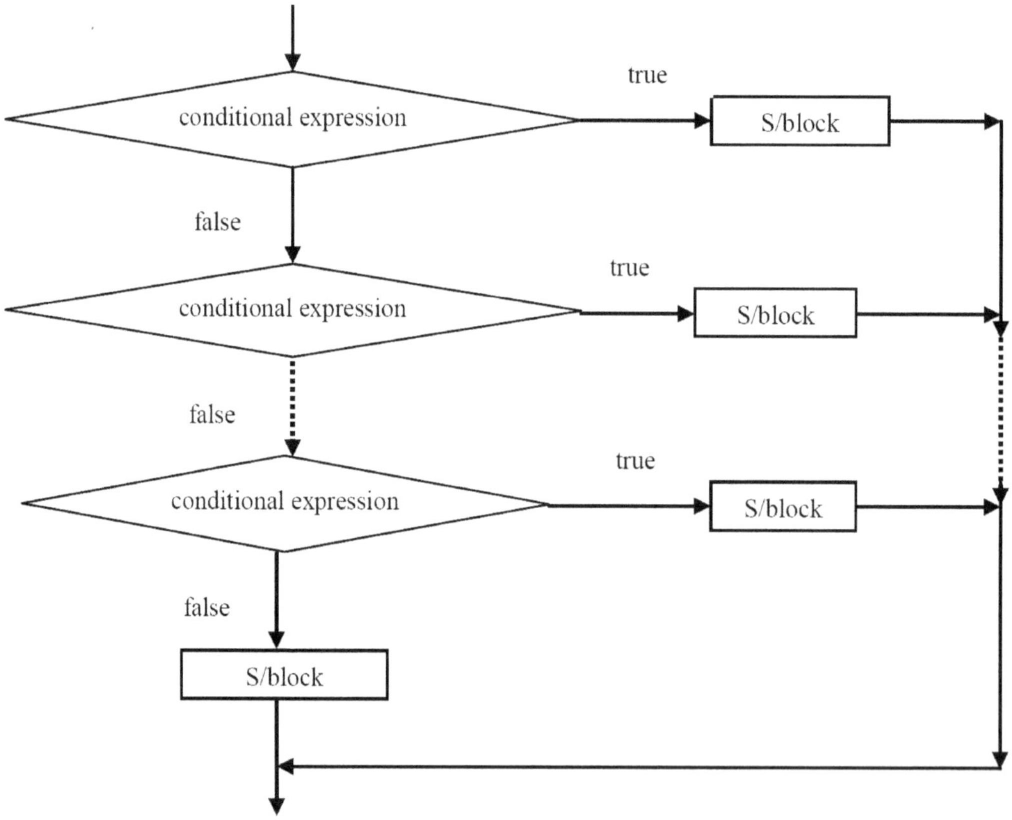

Figure 4 The if/else construct and how it works

The general form of the if/else statement is as follows:

```
if ( condition 1 )
{
        Java statements
}
else if (condition 2 )
{
        Java statements
}
else
{
        Java statements
}
```

EXAMPLE 2

The ABC Company offers scholarships to individuals who are in need of financial assistance. The company advertises the scholarship nationwide. Preferences are given according to the following rules:

- Florida residents get 50% of the fund with no age restriction
- Other US residents get 35% of the fund, but must be 18 to 30 years old
- International students get 15% of the fund, but the applicant must be 18 to 25 years old.

Write a class called **Scholarship** that accepts the name, age, the place of residence, and the amount of money that is to be shared. Include an instance method called **checkEligibility**, that determines the eligibility of each applicant. The class must also provide methods to retrieve each attribute. Write a test class that reports on applicants' eligibility status, including those that are ineligible.

We will use the **if..else** construct to implement these alternative expressions. Against this background it is necessary to maintain the three Boolean variables—**florida, usa, international**—to store the status of an applicant. **Listing 2a** shows the class Scholarship.

```
public class Scholarship
{
    private static final double FL = 0.5, US = 0.35, OTHER =0.15;

    private String name, state;
    private int age;
    private boolean eligible,florida, usa, international;
    private double award, amount;

    public Scholarship(String name, int age, String state, double amount)
    {
        this.name = name;
        this.age = age;
        this, state = state;
        this. amount = amount;
        eligible = true; // We assume that everybody initially is eligible
    }

    public void checkEligibility()
    {
        if(state.equalsIgnoreCase("Florida"))
        {
            florida = true;
            award = amount * FL;
        }
        else if (state.equalsIgnoreCase("USA") && (age >= 18 && <= 30))
        {
            usa = true;
            award = amount * US;
        }
        else if (state.equalsIgnoreCase("International") && (age >= 18 && <= 25))
        {
            international = true;
            award = amount * OTHER;
        }
        else
            eligible = false;
    }
    public boolean isFloridaEligible() { return florida; }
    public boolean isUsaEligible(){ return usa; }
    public boolean isInternationalEligible() { return international;}
    public boolean isEligible() { return eligible; }
    public double getAward() { return award; }
    public String getName() {return name;}
    public int getAge() {return age;}
}
```

Listing 2a Class determines eligibility of individuals

There are several things to observe in **Listing 2a,** namely:

1. The central theme of this class is the use of the **if..else** statement, which is implemented by the method checkEligibility, **Lines 19–38.**
2. **Line** 7 shows the Boolean variables that are used to keep track of the eligibility status of each applicant.
3. The variable called **eligibility** is used to track whether or not any applicant was successful. At the beginning we assume that every applicant is eligible, so we set this variable to **true,** in the constructor **Line 16.** If during the process we find that an applicant is ineligible, we reset the value to **false.** As seen on **Line 37.**
4. The second and third **if..else** statement, each implements logical expression, instead of simply a relational expression.
5. Each **if..else** statement comprises a block with two statements, hence these statements are placed within pairs of curly braces. The last else statement comprises only a single statement. This single statement does not require curly.

```
import Java.util. Scanner;

class TestScholarship
{
    public static void main(String[] arg)
    {
        Scanner read = new Scanner(System.in);
        String name = read.next();
        int age = read.nextInt();
        String residency = read.next();
        int amount = read.nextInt();

        Scholarship s = new Scholarship(name, age, residency, amount);

        s.checkEligibility();

        System.out.println(s.getName() + " is " + s.getAge() + " years old ");

        if(ls.isEligible())
            System.out.println("Applicant is not eligible for scholarship ");
        else
        {
            if(s.isFloridaEligible())
                System.out.println("is a Floridian");
            elseif(s.isUsaEligible())
                System.out.println("is a USA student not from Florida");
            else
                System.out.println("is an international student");
            System.out.println("gets a scholarship of " + nf.format(s.getAward()));
        }
    }
}
```

Figure 2b Generates report using if .. else

In generating the report for each applicant, we must identify the candidate by using once again the **if..else** statement. In this case however, there is something that is different from the former usage. See figure 2b. Inside the first else statement there is an **if..else** statement. You may wonder why. If the applicant is not eligible, then the first print statement is executed. If this is not the case, then the applicant is eligible. This is represented by the else statement. Since the applicant would be eligible, then we must identify which kind it is. It is against this background we need the **if..else** statement within the first else statement.

The **switch** statement is an alternate method for multi-way selection. It is a special case of the **if..else** statement in the sense that it can only test some integral values. This means that the statement cannot test floating-point values or string values. The only values that the switch statement can test are **byte, short, int,** and **char.** It does not accept **long.** The general format of the **switch** statement is

```
switch (selectionVariable)
{
        case value1:
                statement1;
        break;
        case value2:
                statement2;
        break;
          :
          :
        case value1;
                statement1;
        break;
        default:
                statement;
        break;
}
```

With the introduction of the **switch** statement, are four new reserved words: **switch, case, break,** and **default.** Where:

1. The **switch** expression contains the integral value that is to be matched with the **case** label values.
2. The **case** statement provides entry to the statement or set of statements that are to be executed if a match is made. The **case** label must be a constant. Each **case** label must be unique.
3. The **default** statement specifies what must be done if no match is made. It is optional, and may be placed anywhere within the scope of the **switch** statement.
4. The **break** statement terminates the switch statement.

EXAMPLE 3

An Internet service provider has three subscription packages for its customers. The packages are as follows:

> Package A: For $39.95 per month, 100 hours of access are provided free. Additional hours are charged at $0.12 cents per hour. Package B: For $49.95 per month, 250 hours of access are provided free. Additional hours are charged at $0.07 per hour. Package C: For $79.95 per month unlimited access is provided.
>
> Design a class called **InternetServiceProvider** that accepts a character and an integer value, where the character represents the package type and the integer value represents the number of hours used. Include a method that determines the package type and calculate each customer's monthly bill. Note: the number of hours used in a month cannot exceed 720. Also, design a test class to implement the class **TestInternetServiceProvider.**

As a design consideration, identify the following:

- Those values that can be regarded as constants.
- Separate methods that test for extraneous situations, for example, design methods to test specifically any value that could be negative, and any value that could exceed the allowable number of hours in an average thirty-day month.
- A method that is dedicated to determine he charges for each customer. This method uses the **switch** statement exclusively for the purpose of determining the charges. When we treat the solution this way, the overall solution is not cluttered with extraneous ideas.

```
import java.text.NumberFormat;
public class InternetServiceProvider
{
    static final double PACKAGE_A = 39.95, PACKAGE_B = 49.95, PACKAGE_C = 79.95;
    static final int MAX_HOURS = 720;
    int hours;
    char package;
    double charges;
    String message;

    public InternetServiceProvider(char p, int hours) {
        this.hours = hours;
        pakage = p;
    }
    public boolean isGreaterThanZero() { return hours > 0; }
    public Boolean exceed720() { return hours > MAX_HOURS; }
    public void calculateCharges() {
        switch(package)
        {
          case'a':   case A':
                message = "PACKAGE A";
                charges = PACKAGE_A;
                if (minutes > 50) charges = charges + (hours -100) * 0.12;
          break;
          case'b': case'B':
                message = "PACKAGE B";
                charges = PACKAGE_B;
                if (minutes > 100) charges = charges + (hours - 250) * 0.07;
          break;
          case 'c': case 'C:
                message = "PACKAGE C";
                charges = PACKAGE_C;
          break;
          default:
                message = "No such PACKAGE";
                charges = 0
          break;
        }
    }
    public String toString() {
        NumberFormat df = NumberFormat.getCurrencyInstance();
        return "Your package is " + message + "\nYour charge for this month is " + dfformat(charges);
    }
}
```

Listing 3a The class *InternetServiceProvider*.

The use of the switch statement in this exercise places emphasis on the **case** statement. Since someone could input uppercase letters as well as lower case letters, provision is made for both situations by using the case statement as a **logical-OR.** For example, see **Lines 20** and **25,** or **Line 30.**

Listing 3b is a typical test class for the class *TestInternetServiceProvider.* It further makes us of the if..else statement in determining a customer's bill. Notice the use of the nested **if** concept.

```
class TestInternetServiceProvider {
public static void main(String[] arg) {
    InternetServiceProvider t = new InternetServiceProvider('b', 500);
    if(t.isGreaterThanZero())
    {
            if(t.exceed720())
            System.out.println("The number of hours given exceeds the allowable limit");
            else
            {
                t.calculateCharges();
                System.out.println(t.ToString());
            }
    }
    else
        System.out.println("Error: cannot calculate charges");
}
```

Listing 3b Using nested if to determine customer's bill.

Java If and Boolean

NICK PARLANTE

IF STATEMENT

For a program to do anything interesting, it needs if-statements and booleans to control which bits of code to execute. Here is a simple if-statement:

```
if (temperature > 100) {
  System.out.println("Dang, it's hot!");
}
```

The simplest if-statement has two parts—a boolean "test" within parentheses () followed by "body" block of statements within curly braces { }. The test can be any expression that evaluates to a boolean value—**true** or **false**. The if-statement evaluates the test and then runs the body code only if the test is true. If the test is false, the body is skipped.

IF THEN ELSE

Another common form of if-statement adds an "else" clause such as with the code below which prints one message or the other:

```
if (temperature > 100) {
  System.out.println("Too darn hot");
}
else {
  System.out.println("At least it's not more than 100");
}
```

The if/else form is handy for either-or logic, where we want to choose one of two possible actions. The if/else is like a fork in the road. Under the control of the boolean test, one or the other will be taken, but not both. For example, the famous Robert Frost poem is a thinly disguised comment on the importance of the if/else structure:

Two roads diverged in a wood, and I—
I took the one less traveled by,
And that has made all the difference.

JAVA COMPARISON OPERATORS: <, <=, >, >=

The easiest way to get a boolean value (true or false) is using a comparison expression, such as (a < 10). The less-than operator, <, takes two values and evaluates to true if the first is less than the second. So for example, the expression (var < 10) evaluates to the value true if var is less than 10, and false otherwise. The < is an "operator" just like + and *—appearing between two values to compute something. Instead of "var" and "10", the comparison operator < can use any int or double expressions, so for example we could write a comparison expression like (score < (highScore+100)). This comparison will evaluate to true if the score value is less than the (highScore+100) value, and will evaluate to false otherwise.

There are four comparison operators:

- < less-than
- > greater-than
- <= less-or-equal (i.e. ≤)
- >= greater-or-equal (i.e. ≥)

There is overlap between these, since we could use less-than to write something like (aa). It makes no difference to the computer. We will prefer the version which reads most naturally.

NO: 10 < X < 20

It's tempting to write an expression like "10 < X < 20" to see if X is between 10 and 20. That does not work. Each "<" operator must get its own two values. So the correct way to write it is "10<X && X<20".

EQUALITY TEST OPERATORS ==, !=

The == operator tests if two values are the same, so (x == 6) is true if x contains the value 6. The not-equal operator, !=, is the opposite, evaluating to true if the values are different. Typically, you use == and != with primitives such as int and boolean, not with objects like String and Color. With objects, it is most common to use the equals() method to test if two objects represent the same value.

The similarity of == and .equals() can be confusing, so here is a suggested rule: Every value in Java is either a primitive (e.g., int) or an object (e.g., String). Use ==, <, >=, etc., with primitives like int. Use .equals() with objects like String and Color. Since the dereference dot (.) only works with objects, you can remember it this way: if it can take a dot then use .equals() (e.g., a String), otherwise use == (e.g., an int).

It is also possible to use == with objects. In that case, what == does is test if two pointers point to exactly the same object. Such as use of == is a little rare in Java code, and so it's simpler to concentrate on using equals() with objects, and == only with primitives.

BOOLEAN TYPE

The simplest and most common form of boolean expression is the use a < in an if-statement as shown above. However, boolean is a full primitive type in Java, just like int and double. In the boolean type, there are only two possible values: true and false. We can have variables and expressions of type boolean, just has we have variables and expressions of type int and double. A boolean variable is only capable of storing either the value true or the value false. The words true and false are built-in literals in Java that can be used right in the code. As with other types, Java checks the code to make sure that the right type of value goes into each variable:

```
int i = 6;              // ok
boolean a = false;      // ok
boolean b = "hello";    // NO, String and boolean are different
boolean c = "false";    // NO, "false" in quotes is a String!
String s = "false";     // ok
```

BOOLEAN OPERATORS

Just as we have + and * operators that work on int values, we have operators that work on boolean values. Suppose we have boolean expressions b1 and b2, which may be simple boolean variables, or may be boolean expressions such as (score < 100). The "and" operator **&&** takes two boolean values and evaluates to true if both are true. The "or" operator **||** (two vertical bars) takes two boolean values and evaluates to true if one or the other or both are true.

Suppose we have int variables score and temperature, the code below prints "It's hot out and so am I" if the score is 10 or more and temperature is 100 or more. The && is true only if both of the two booleans it connects are true:

```
if ( (score >= 10) && (temperature >= 100) ) {
  System.out.println("It's hot out, and so am I!");
}
```

Suppose we are in a bad mood if our score is less than 5 or the temperature is 32 or below:

```
if ( (score < 5) || (temperature <= 32) ) {
  System.out.println("I'm in a bad mood");
}
```

Finally, the "not" operator **!** (an exclamation mark) goes to the left of a boolean expression and inverts it, changing true to false and false to true. Suppose we want to print something if it is not the case that the score is less than 5, we could write that as:

```
if (!(score < 5)) {
  System.out.println("Score is 5 or more)");
}
```

First, the expression (score < 5) evaluates to true or false, and then the ! inverts the boolean value. The result is that the body runs if the expression (score < 5) is false, which is to say it runs if (score >= 5) is true. (We could equivalently write the if-statement with (score >= 5), but the point was to demonstrate the !).

BOOLEAN RESTAURANT EXAMPLE

Suppose you want to get a table at a hip restaurant, but we are afraid that the Maitre d' is going to say something rude instead of seating you. The variable "style" represents the stylishness of your clothes and the variable "bribe" represents the bribe presented to the Maitre d'. The Maitre d' is satisfied if style is 8 or more and bribe is 5 or more. The Matire'd says "Je n'think so" if they are not satisfied. One way to code this up is to write the "satisfied" expression as a straight translation of the problem statement, and then put a ! in front of it:

```
// Say something mean if not satisfied
if (! ((style>=8) && (bribe>=5)) ) {
  System.out.println("Je n'think so");
}
```

With combinations of !, <, >=, etc., there can be a few different ways to code what amounts to the same thing. As a matter of style, we prefer the code that reads most naturally to express the goal of the code. For example, the following is equivalent to the above, although I find it near impossible to decipher:

```
// Say something mean if not satisfied
if (!(!(style<8) && !(bribe<5))) { ...
```

Here is another equivalent form, which is not so bad ...

```
// Say something mean if not satisfied
if ((style<8) || (bribe<5)) { ...
```

Java also has "bitwise" operators & and | (more rarely used) which are different from && and ||. If your boolean code will not compile, make sure you did not accidentally type a bitwise operator (&) instead of a boolean operator (&&).

BOOLEAN PRECEDENCE

The above examples use parentheses to spell out the order of operations. The boolean not ! has a high precedence—in (!a && b) the ! is evaluated on the a, before the &&. We could add in parenthesis (!(a && b)) to force the && to evaluate before the !. The && operator is higher precedence than ||, so in (a || b && c), the && happens first. There are parallels between the boolean operators and arithmetic: ! is like unary -, && is like *, || is like +. The comparison operators (<, <=, ==, ...) all have higher precedence than && and ||, so without parentheses, comparisons always happen before the && and ||. This is very convenient, since we can use <= to get some booleans, and then && and || to combine the booleans. So our earlier example:

```
if (! ((style>=8) && (bribe>=5))) {
```

works fine without parentheses around the comparisons, since the comparisons have high precedence than && ||:

```
if (! (style>=8 && bribe>=5)) {
```

The not ! has a high precedence (as do all the unary operators), so we need parentheses to force the ! to evaluate after the >= and &&. Remember that all the unary operators, such as !, have a high precedence. To evaluate something before the !, we frequently need to put the something in parentheses like this !(something). For example:

```
if (! i < 10 ) { ... // NO does not work
```

The precedence of the ! is too high, it wants to execute before the <. To fix this, we add parentheses around the (i < 10) so it goes first:

```
if (!(i < 10 )) { ...          // Ok
```

OPPOSITE OF <?

What is the opposite of the expression (score < 100)? That is, an expression that will be true when the first is false, and false when the first is true. The opposite expression is (score >= 100). You might think that the opposite of < is >, but it is not. The opposite of < is >=, and the opposite of > is <=.

BOOLEAN SHORT CIRCUITING

Boolean expressions stop evaluating as soon as the result is clear. This is called "short circuiting". The && short circuits at the first false—then the whole expression must be false. The || short circuits at the first true—then the whole expression must be true. Suppose we have an int i, and we want to check if i is 2 or 3:

```
if (i==2 || i==3) { ...
```

If i is 2, the boolean expression evaluates to true after the i==2 is true. It does not even look at the i==3. Suppose we want to do something if 100.0/i is less than 10. We use short-circuiting to screen out the i==0 case, checking it before the division. If i is 0, the expression short-circuits out before the division:

```
if (i!=0 && (100.0/i < 10.0)) { ...
```

A common use of short-circuiting is to call a method on an object, but only if the pointer to the object is not null. For example, suppose we have a bear pointer which may or may not be null:

```
if (bear!=null && bear.hasCubs() && bear.isMom()) { ...// run!
```

THE TRUTH ABOUT CURLY BRACES { }

If the body of a while-loop or if-statement is made of many statements, then we use curly braces { } to group the statements in the body, as we have seen in many examples. However, if there is only a single statement in such a body, then the curly braces are optional. For example, suppose if score is greater than 100 then we want to set it to 100 and print something. This can be written with curly braces as we usually do:

```
if (score > 100) {
  score = 100;
  System.out.println("Score is 100");
}
```

However, if there is only one statement in the body (say just "score = 100;") then it can be written without the curly braces:

```
// One-statement body written without curly braces
```

```
if (score > 100)
  score = 100;
```

Or, in fact it can be written all on one line:

```
// One-statement body written without curly braces
if (score > 100) score = 100;
```

DIGRESSION—WHY WE USE CURLY BRACES

The no-brace style saves a little typing, and you can do it if you like. However, in our example code we will never do it. The problem is that it can lead to bugs if you later come to add a statement to the body. Suppose we want to add a println() statement to the above code, it's natural to just type it on the next line:

```
if (score > 100)
  score = 100;
  System.out.println("Score is 100");

// BUG, this code compiles fine, but it gives the appearance
// that the println() is controlled by the if, which it is not.
```

Unfortunately, without the curly braces, the code can have a deeply misleading appearance. Above, it appears (due to the misleading indentation) that the println() is under the control of the if-statement, but it is not. The "score = 100;" is controlled by the if-statement, and the println() is just the next statement that is outside of the control of the if-statement. To avoid this situation where the code says one thing, but the indentation and spacing suggests something else, we prefer to write out our if-statements and loops with the curly braces for maximum clarity.

READABILITY

When writing comparisons, there are often different ways to say the same thing. For example, if we want to check if an int score is 100 or more, any of the following will do the same thing:

```
if (score >= 100) { ...          // version 1

if (100 <= score) { ...          // version 2

if (score > 99) { ...            // version 3
```

Though the three versions are effectively the same, as a matter of style we prefer the code that reads as the most natural translation of the goal of the code. In this case, the first is probably the best translation of the idea "score is 100 or more".

NESTED IF-STATEMENT

We can write an if-statement inside the body or else part of another, outer if-statement. The outer if-statement executes first, then proceeds to its body or else code normally. In this case, the code happens to be another if-statement. Suppose we are writing the code for an alarm clock, and the int variable "day" represents the current day with Mon = 1, Tue = 2, … Sun=7. On weekdays the clock tells us to get up, and weekends it tells us to snooze more. On Monday, the clock adds some extra harassment to get us out of bed. The code uses an if-statement to distinguish weekends from weekdays, and inside the "weekday" case there is another if-statement for Mondays:

```
if (day <= 5) {  // 1..5 are weekdays
  System.out.println("Hi ho, hi ho, it's off to school we go …");
  if (day = 1) {  // Something extra for Mon
    System.out.println("It's not the weekend any more!");
  }
} else {          // 6..7, it's the weekend
  System.out.println("Hit the snooze button now!");
}
```

IF-ELSE CHAIN

If we have exactly two choices, we can use the basic if-else structure, but what if there are more than two? We can run a series of if-else together to make a chain, as shown below. Suppose we have a bowling score (300 is perfect, 200 is very good):

```
if (score >= 300) {
  System.out.println("Perfect!");
}
else if (score >= 200) {
  System.out.println("Very good");
}
else if (score >= 50) {
  System.out.println("Good job");
}
else {
  System.out.println("Everyone is good at something.");
  System.out.println("You are good at something else!");
}
```

The if-else chain checks each test, working from top to bottom. The first test that is true runs the corresponding body, and then exits the whole chain. So for the above code, if the score is 250, the program prints "Very good" and exits the chain. The result of the if-else chain is to choose one piece of code from among many. The optional final "else" in the chain does not have an "if" and plays a catch-all role in case all the others are false.

For the design of the bowling code above, notice that the tests must be done in the order shown, working from high to low. Each test relies on the fact that the tests above have been checked already, and were all false. For example, if the chain gets to the (score >= 50) line, we know that (score >= 200) must have been false, and so the score is 199 or less.

USING BOOLEANS DIRECTLY

Suppose you want an if-statement to check if a "num" variable is 3 like this:

```
// suppose num is an int
if (num == 3) {
  ...
```

That code works fine. Suppose instead that you have a boolean variable "isSummer" and you want an if-statement that runs if isSummer is true. Here is one way to write that code:

```
if (isSummer == true) {
  ...
```

That code works ok, but it is a little longer than necessary. It also has a problem if you accidentally type a single "=" instead of "==":

```
if (isSummer = true) {  // BAD bug
  ...
```

Unfortunately, the above code compiles fine. When run, it **assigns** true to isSummer, and then the if-statement always passes since the test is always true. This bug is very hard to spot, since the "=" looks reasonable. A shorter way to write the code, and a good defense against the above bug is to use the boolean variable directly without "==" or anything, like this

```
if (isSummer) {
  ...
```

Or for not isSummer, just:

```
if (!isSummer) {
  ...
```

Code that uses the boolean variable directly like that is nice and short.

BOOLEAN METHODS

One useful sort of method for a class is one that tests if some condition is true or not about the receiver object. One convention is that such methods begin with the word "is" or "has". For example, a Car object might implement an isOutOfGas() method which returns true if the car is out of gas or false otherwise. In general, the client can use boolean messages to check for various true/false conditions of the receiver. For example a Bear class might have an isMother() method which is true if the bear is a mother, and a hasCubs() method which is true if the bear has cubs with it:

```
public class Bear {
  ...
 // Returns true if the bear is a mother bear
 public boolean isMother() { ...

 // Returns true if the bear has cubs with it
 public boolean hasCubs() { ...
```

Now suppose we are writing the meetBear() code for a Backpacker, used when the Backpacker meets a bear in the woods:

```
// Code for when we meet a bear in the woods
 void meetBear(Bear bear) {
  System.out.println("Oh look, a bear.");

  if (bear.isMother()) {
   System.out.println("Hi mom!");
  }

  if (bear.hasCubs()) {
   System.out.println("Hi cute little bears!");
  }
```

```
  if (bear.isMother() && bear.hasCubs()) {
    System.out.println("Oh @#$@#$!, Run!");
  }

}
```

Another way to write the mother if-statement uses "== true" like this:

```
if (bear.isMother() == true) {
  System.out.println("Hi mom!");
}
```

That code will work fine, but it is not the best style. The "== true" adds nothing, since the if-statement itself already checks if the test is true. Therefore, it is better to write it the direct way:

```
if (bear.isMother()) {
  System.out.println("Hi mom!");
}
```

WRITING A BOOLEAN METHOD

Writing a method that returns a boolean is just like writing any method that returns value, but ultimately we are just returning either true or false. For example, suppose we are writing code for a hybrid-electric car. The car class as instance variables that track the amount of gasoline and battery charge: myGasoline (in the range 0..100), and myBatteries (also 0..100). Suppose the Car class implements an isLow() message that returns true if the car is low on fuels. It returns true if the sum of the gasoline level and the battery level is less than 10. The isLow() message is used by the dashboard to decide to light the "low fuel" light. What does the code for isLow() look like? Here is one way to write it:

```
public class Car {
  private int myGasoline;
  private int myBattery;

   ...
  // Returns true if we are low on fuels
  public boolean isLow() {
    if ((myGasoline + myBattery) < 10) {
      return true;
    }
    else {
```

```
      return false;
    }
  }
}
```

The above code will work fine. It has a boolean test checking for low fuels, and depending on that it runs either "return true;" or "return false;". But there is a better way. We can cut out the if-statement middle-man. Notice that the boolean in the if-test (true or false) happens to be the same as the value we want to return. If the test value is true, we return true. If the test value is false, we return false. So you can just return the test value directly! In the short version below, we compute the desired boolean value with the expression "((myGasoline+myBattery) < 10)", and just return that value (which at runtime will either be the value true or the value false, depending on the gasoline and battery levels):

```
public boolean isLow() {
  // Compute (true or false) if we are low,
  // and return that boolean value directly.
  return ((myGasoline + myBattery) < 10);
```

Writing the method the long way is not terrible style (i.e. we won't mark off for it!), but it's nice to be comfortable enough with boolean values to write it the short way.

BOOLEAN LOGIC EXAMPLES

```
/*
 * Do we go on a second date with someone?
 * The given chemistry is in the range 0..100 and isSchool
 * is true if it is during the school year. The answer is yes if chemistry is
 * 60 or more, or 40 or more not in the school year.
 */
public void secondDate(int chemistry, boolean isSchool) {
 if (chemistry>=60 || (!isSchool && chemistry>=40)) {
   System.out.println("Sure!");
 }
 else {
   System.out.println("I don't want to spoil our friendship");
 }
}

/*
 * Returns true if the person gets into Stanford.
```

```
* Given gpa = 0 ...4.0, isGates = child of Bill Gates,
* isDarth = associated with Darth Vader.
* To get in: must not be associated with Darth Vader at all
* Gpa must be over 3.95
* Or gpa over 1.0 if child of Bill Gates
*/
public boolean getIntoStanford(double gpa, boolean isGates, boolean isVader) {
  if (!isVader && (gpa>=3.95 || (gpa>=1.0 && isGates))) {
    return true;
  }
  else {
    return false;
  }
}


// Variant, where we return the boolean directly
public boolean getIntoStanford2(double gpa, boolean isGates, boolean isVader) {
  return (!isVader && (gpa>=3.95 || (gpa>=1.0 && isGates)));
}


// Variant, where we use an if-return for the darth case.
// I think maybe this one is the best—the one big expression is
// a bit hard to follow, this version makes it more obvious.
public boolean getIntoStanford3(double gpa, boolean isGates, boolean isVader) {
  if (isVader) {    // no way, it'a  deal killer!
    return false;
  }

  // Otherwise just use gpa and isGates
  return (gpa>=3.95 || (gpa>=1.0 && isGates));
}
```

BOOLEAN PUZZLES

These are little puzzles based on reading boolean code. I have used questions like these to write CS exams.

```
// For all values of num and bool. what does this print?
public void test1(int num, boolean bool) {
  if (num >= 90 || !bool) {
```

```
    System.out.println("A");
  }
  else {
    System.out.println("B");
  }
}


// For all values of num and bool, what does this print?
// Note: deciphering this is hard, harder than most
// code-writing problems, but it's a good way to
// exercise your logic skills. I can only figure it
// out by making a little chart of the possible values.
public void test2(int num, boolean bool) {
  if (num >= 90 && bool) {
    System.out.println("Tic");
  }
  else if (num >= 20) {
    System.out.println("Tac");
  }
  else {
    System.out.println("Toe");
  }
}
```

PUZZLE ANSWERS

test1:

	bool	
	true	false
num >=90	A	A
num < 90	B	A

test2:

	bool	
	true	false
num >= 90	Tic	Tac
20<=num<90	Tac	Tac

num < 20 Toe Toe

DOUBLES VS. ==

One odd case of == is that you should not use == or != with doubles, since the intrinsic little error term on every double value throws off the operation of ==. For example, summing up 1/10, 100 times may not exactly == 10.0. To compare two doubles, subtract one from the other, and then see if the difference is very small:

```
// suppose we have doubles d1 and d2
// We use the Math.abs() standard method that computes
// absolute value

// check if d1 and d2 are essentially equal
// (if the absolute value of their difference is less
//  than 1e-6 (i.e. 0.000001)
if (Math.abs(d1 - d2) <= 1e-6) { ...
```

Iteration

BY JOSLYN A. SMITH

Iterative statements, commonly called loops, cause a program to repeat certain statements or block of statements. The statements or block of statements is referred to as the loop body. The construct uses conditional expression to determine if the loop is to continue to execute, or to terminate. There are three forms of iterative statements—**while, do/while,** and **for.** Only the **while** and the **for** statement will be discussed. Whatever the **do/while** statement can do, the **while** statement can accomplish the same.

Figure 4 shows the general form of the while statement. The while statement specifies that the conditional expression must be tested at the beginning of the loop. If the conditional expression is initially false, then the loop body is skipped.

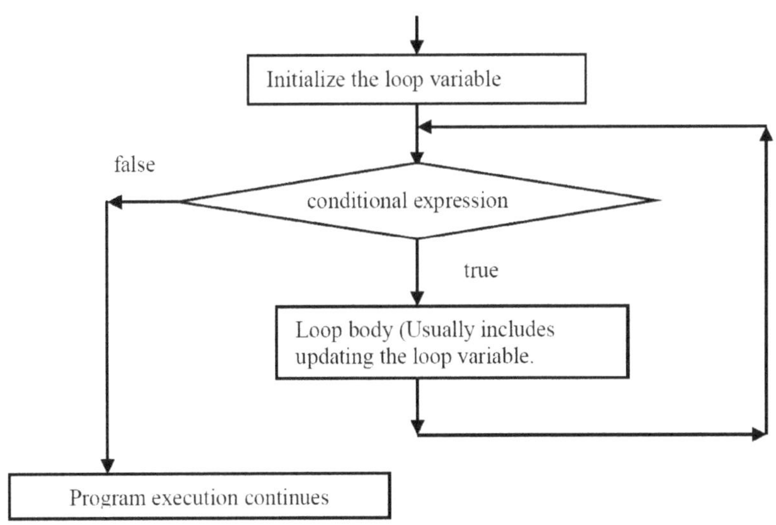

Figure 4 shows a representation of the while loop

EXAMPLE 4

The XYZ School wants to carry its grade 10 students on a trip. The cost of the trip is $5,000.00. The school has only thirty days in which to collect the funds in order to go on the trip. Design a class called **SchoolContribution** to create a contribution account to which each day's total contribution is added. The program should give a list of the daily contributions and a statement whether or not the target was met.

Analysis

For the class **SchoolContribution** we can identify the following:

- Constants
- TARGET—the amount of money to be made - $5000.00
- MAX_DAYS—number of days in which to meet target - 30
- Variables
- day—the day that contribution is made.
- totalContribution—the amount collected at the close of each day.
- Constructor
- The initial amount of money collected is zero.
- Methods
- addContribution—accepts a contribution, adds it to total contribution, and
- updates the count for number of days.
- Boolean methods—**hasMoreTime()** and **hasNotMadeTarget()** allow the loop to continue if target is not met within the 30 days. That is, the target is not met if the amount collected is below the targeted amount and the number of days is less than 30. The following conditional expressions represent each of the methods, respectively.

  day <= MAX_DAYS and **totalAmount < TARGET**

- Boolean method **metTarget()—**tells us if the target was met. That is, after 30 days, was the target met. This is answered by the following conditional expression.

  day >= MAX_DAYS && totalContribution < TARGET

This is less obvious, but it is necessary to know, in order to print the output. See **Listing 4a.**

```
import Java. text.NumberFormat;
public class SchoolContribution
{
        static final byte DAYS  = 30;
        static final float TARGET = 5000;
        intday;
        double totalContribution;
        String s;
        NumberFormat df;

        public SchoolContribution()
        {
                totalContribution = ();
                day = ();
                s = "Day \tDaily Contribution\tTotal Contribution\n";
                df = NumberFormat.getCurrencyInstance();
        }

        public void addContribution(double amount)
        {
                totalContribution = totalContribution + amount;
                day = day+1;
                s = s + day+"\t     " + df.format(amount);
                s = s + "\t\t     " + df.format(totalContribution) + "\n";
        }

        public boolean hasNotMadeTarget () { return totalContribution < TARGET; }
        public boolean hasMoreTime() { return day < MAX_DAYS; }
        public boolean metTarget () {
              return day <= MAX_DAYS && totalContribution >= TARGET; }
        public String toString() { return s; }
}
```

Listing 4a. The class Contribution.

The test class, **TestContribution,** shown in **Listing 4b** does the following:

- Creates an empty contribution account.
- Continuously checks if the target has been met. It uses the result from the method *didNotMakeTarget()* to control the loop after a day's contribution has been made.
- Prints the result after the loop is exited. The if statement on Line 12 uses the result from the Boolean method *isInadequate()* to print the result.

```
1.      import javax.swing.JOptionPane;
2.      public class TestContribution
3.      {
4.      public static void main(String[] arg)
5-      {
6.          SchoolContribution s = new SchoolContribution();
7.          while (s. hasNotMadeTarget() && s.hasMoreTime())
8.          {
9.              s.addContribution(Double.parseDouble(
10.             JOptionPane.showInputDialog("Make contribution")));
11.         }
12.
13.         if (s. metTarget ())
14.             System.out.println(s);
15.         else
16.             System.out.println("We did not make the target" + "\nSorry we cannot go on the trip\n" + s);
17.     }
18. }
```

Listing 4b. The test class TestContribution.

The **for** statement, like the **while** statement, is a looping construct that continually executes a section of code, if a given condition is true. When the condition becomes false the section of code is skipped, and the next statement following it is executed. The general format of the **for** statement is as follows:

for *(datatype id—initialValue; conditional_expression; adjust_id) statements;*

The **for** loop is a single executable statement consisting of two major parts—loop heading, following the keyword **for,** and the loop body. The loop heading is enclosed within the pair of parentheses and consists of three parts, each separated from the other by a semi-colon.

- The first expression—*data_type id = initial*—constitutes the declaration and initialization of the control variable for the loop.
- The second expression—*conditional_expression*—constitutes the condition under which the loop iterates. Any valid conditional expression is acceptable.

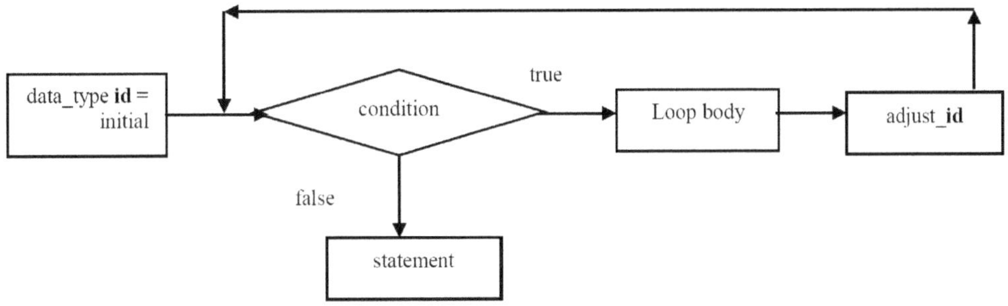

- The third expression—*adjust_id*—updates the value of the loop variable.

The loop body constitutes the statement or statement block to be executed. The loop body executes only if the conditional expression is true, other than that the **`for`** loop terminates. **Figure 6** shows a diagram of the **`for`** loop.

Figure 5 shows a representation of the for loop

EXAMPLE 5

A palindrome is a set of data values that is identical to its reverse. For example the word **MADAM** is a palindrome; the number **123454321** is a palindrome; likewise **aaabbaaaabbaaa.** Design a class called Palindrome that accepts a string and determines if the string is a palindrome.

To determine if a sequence of characters is a palindrome do the following:

- Compare the first and last character in the sequence. If they are the same,
- Compare the second character and the second to the last character in the sequence.
- Continue the process in similar manner. If all items match, then the string is a palindrome.
- Conversely, at the first mismatch occurrence, then the string is not a palindrome.

- **Listing 5a** shows the use of the **for** statement on **Line 17.**

```
1.  public class Palindrome
2.  {
3.          private String word;
4.          private boolean palindrome;
5.          private int index, halfIndex;
6.
7.          public Palindrome(String s)
8.          {
9.              word = s;
10.             index = s.length();
11.             palindrome = true;
12.             halfIndex = index/2;
13.         }
14.
15.         boolean isPalindrome()
16.         {
17.                 for (int i = 0; i < halfIndex && palindrome; i++)
18.                     if (word.charAt(i) != word.charAt(index - i - 1))
19.                         palindrome = false;
20.                 return palindrome;
21.         }
22. }
```

Listing 5a class *Palindrome* accepts the string and checks if it is a palindrome.

In **Listing 5a** we assume that the string is a palindrome, by using the Boolean variable **palindrome = true.** See **Line 19.** Instead of traversing the entire string in one direction, we halve the index so that we can compare values at the corresponding ends as described above. If any two characters at corresponding ends are not the same, then the variable palindrome is set to false and the *for* loop terminates. As we said earlier, the conditional expression in a *for* loop can be any valid Boolean expression. For instance, the conditional expression **for** this for loop is a logical expression—i < halfIndex &&palindrome**.**

Listing 5b shows the test class.

```
public class TestPalindrome
{
        public static void main(String[] arg)
        {
            Palindrome p  =  new Palindrome(" aaabbaaaabbaaa");
            System.out.println(p.isPalindrome());
            }
    }
```

Listing 5b the test class TestPalindrome.

Java While and For Loops

BY NICK PARLANTE

JAVA LOOP

With loops, you get to leverage the power in the computer. Working with computers, you quickly learn that they lack any sort of insight to solve problems on their own. On the other hand, the computer is happy to execute the code we specify a million times over, which is its own sort of power. Loops are the way to do this.

A while loop has a boolean test and a body containing statements, like this

```
int count = 0;
while (count < 100) {  // test: boolean test within (..)
  System.out.println("count:" + count);  // body: statements within {..}
  count = count + 1;
}
System.out.println("all done!");
```

An if-statement looks at the test one time and then maybe executes the body once. The while-loop extends this idea, executing the body again and again, checking the test each time. The while-loop follows these steps:

1. Check if the test is true or false. If false, the loop "exits" and does not execute the body. If the test is true, continue with step 2.
2. Execute the body statements, starting at the top and proceeding down through them all.
3. Go back to step 1 and check the test again. If it is true, run the body again. Each time the body finishes, "loop around" and check the test again. Each run of the body is called an "iteration" of the loop.

Eventually the test is false, the loop exits, and the program continues with the line after the while-loop. For example, the above while-loop prints:

```
count:0
count:1
count:2
count:3
...
count:98
count:99
all done!
```

The count variable starts at 0, and increases by 1 on each iteration. On the 100th iteration of the loop body, the body prints "99" and then increases count to 100. The program loops back to the top and checks the test (count < 100) again. On all previous checks, the test was true. This time the test is false, and the loop exits without executing the body. We use while-loops to execute some code until some condition is satisfied.

HOW TO WRITE A WHILE LOOP

To write a while-loop, we think about three parts ...

- **test**—a boolean test of what should be true before each iteration. Or put another way, the test is the "green light" condition that says that each iteration can go ahead. (The phrase "green light" is a good mnemonic for what the test does.) Eventually, the test should become false and the loop can exit. Think about the precondition that describes the state before each iteration runs—how are things arranged, what is true? (Also known as an "invariant".) In the above example, the test (count < 100) means that each iteration can proceed, so long as (count < 100) is true.
- **work**—code in the body that does something for each iteration such as printing or drawing something. Some loops do not have any identifiable work in the body. In the above example, the work is the println() that prints something out for each iteration.
- **increment**—code in the body that advances things so we are closer to making the test false. At the end of the body, the code will loop around to the top of the body. Sometimes, some cleanup is required at the end of the body to set things up for the next iteration. In the above example, the line "count = count + 1;" accomplishes the increment. That can also be written as "count++;".

WHILE-LOOP EXAMPLE

Here's a while loop example that uses a loop to see how many times you can divide a number by 2:

```
// Given a num, returns how many times can we divide it by 2 to get down to 1.
int count2Div(int num) {
  int count = 0;   // count how many divisions we've done
  while (num >= 1) {
    num = num / 2;
    count++;
  }
  return count;
}
```

ZERO-LOOP ITERATIONS

Since the while-loop checks the test before every iteration, it is possible for the body to not run even once:

```
int count = 100;
while (count < 100) {        // the test is false the very first time
  count = count + 1                    // this line never runs
}
```

INFINITE LOOP

The most famous sort of bug you can get with loops is an "infinite loop", where through some mis-arrangement, running the loop body fails to get any closer to making the test false. Typically, this comes down to some sort of logical disconnect between the body and the test. For example, suppose the body fails to make the count bigger by accident:

```
int count = 0;
while (count < 100) {
  System.out.println("count:" + count);
  count = count * 1;                         // OOPS, does not change count
}
```

Or suppose we forget to put in the count line entirely, so the loop just spins in place with count stuck at zero:

```
int count = 0;
while (count < 100) {
  System.out.println("count:" + count);
  // OOPS, forget to put in a line that changes count at all
}
```

Prints when run:

```
count:0
count:0
count:0
count:0
 ...
--never stops--
```

In some cases, we want the code to run on and on without stopping. In that case, we might write an infinite loop on purpose by giving **true** as the test:

```
while (true) {                  // deliberate infinite loop
   ...
   ...
}
```

Many computer people like to think of themselves as part of a whimsical field that does not take itself too seriously compared to more established disciplines. For example, Apple Computer headquarters is located on "1 Infinite Loop, Cupertino CA".

LOOP AND A HALF - "BREAK"

Sometimes, the computation we want does not fit into the tidy while-test-body structure. For example, suppose we want to do operations A, B, C and D, but the natural place for the test is after B and before C. So the sequence we want is A, B, test, C, D. It's awkward to use the while loop as shown so far to solve this sort of problem. To position the test wherever we want, not just at the top, we will use the "break" statement, shown in the example below.

For example, suppose we have a Frog object that responds to dive() and float() methods that move the frog around in a pond. The frog also responds to an isSunny() method that returns true if the frog is in the sun. We want to write a "find sun" loop that does this float, check if there is sun. If there is sun, we're done. Otherwise, dive and try the cycle again. So the sequence is float, sun check, dive, float, sun check, dive, ... until the sun check returns true. The key feature here is that the test does not naturally fit at the top of the loop. Instead the test most cleanly goes in the middle of the loop.

The code for this problem demonstrates uses an while-break structure. An if statement in the middle of the while loop checks for the exit condition. If the exit condition is true, the code calls "break" which exits the while loop immediately:

```
// suppose we have a variable "frog"
while (true) {                          // use "true" as test -- exit is handled by the if-break below
```

```
  frog.float();

  // Exit using if-break
  // Check for exit condition, and if true call break
  if (frog.isSunny()) {
    break;// this exits the loop
  }

  frog.dive();
}
// The break exits the loop, leading to this line
```

With the while-break, we have the power of a while loop, but now we can position the test anywhere we want instead of just at the top. In fact, a standard while loop of this form:

```
while (test) {
  body
}
```

Is equivalent to a while-break loop where the break is positioned at the very top:

```
while (true) {
  if (!(test)) {
    break;
  }
  body
}
```

As a matter of good coding style, we would not write a loop using while-break unless there was no other way. The standard while loop is shorter, more readable, and can express what we want 90% of the time. We use the while-break version where necessary to deal with cases where the test does not go at the top.

Notice that the normal while loop test is a “green light” condition—if it is true, the loop continues; if it is false the loop exits. With a while-break, the test is the opposite. The while-break test is a “red light” condition. If it is true, the loop exits.

FOR-LOOPS

The for-loop is a variant of the while-loop, specialized to deal with a particular looping problem. The for-loop is specialized for the case where we want to step a variable through a series of values. For example, the following for-loop steps the variable “i” through the values 0, 1, 2, …99:

```
for (int i=0; i<100; i++) {
  System.out.println("i:" + i);
    }
```

This loop prints:

```
i:0
i:1
i:2
i:3
i:4
 …
i:99
```

The for-loop has four parts—init, test, increment, and body—separated by semi-colons (;)

```
for ( init ; test ; increment ) {
  body
}
```

The for-loop is used specifically to step a variable through a sequence of values, such as 0, 1, 2, 3,.. 99. In fact, most for-loops adhere to that pattern so closely, that they will look similar to the 0..99 for-loop code above.

The for-loop follows four steps:

1. Init

The init code runs once to set things up at the very start of the loop. Typically, this looks like "int i = 0", declaring a variable to use for the counting, and setting its start value. The variable exists only within the loop (down through the } of the body).

It is idiomatic to use the variable name "i" for a counter variable. Although we avoid single-letter variable names for general-purpose storage, this use of "i" is standard in a for-loop like this. Indeed, this pattern is so standard that other programmers would likely be a little confused if you used a variable name other than "i" in a for-loop. The convention extends to using the names "j", and "k" for loop variables if "i" is already in use. Never use lowercase L "l", since it looks just like the digit one "1" in many fonts.

2. Test

The boolean test is evaluated. If it is true the loop body will execute (green light, just like a while-loop). Typically, the test is a boolean expression such as "i<100", showing what should be true for the loop to continue.

3. Loop-body

If the test was true, the body runs once. The body is a series of statements, just like in a while-loop. The loop body will very often make some use of the loop variable, such as "i" in this example.

4. Increment

Finally, the increment code executes just after the body, and then the program loops back to the test, (step 2). The increment advances the state of things in preparation for the next iteration. The increment code advances the state, and then the test (2) looks at the state. Eventually, we advance the state so far that the test is false and the loop exits. This is analogous to the "increment" idea in the while-loop. In the while-loop, the increment is just a conceptual goal, but in the for-loop, the increment has its own slot in the syntax. When writing a for-loop, we are less likely to forget to do the increment, since the syntax has an explicit slot for it.

In this case, the increment is "i++" which increments the variable "i" by one. Since "i" is the common variable choice for a for-loop, it is very common for the increment to be "i++". It is idiomatic to write the increment as "i++" as opposed to the similar "i = i + 1".

FOR-LOOP EXAMPLES

The examples below demonstrate use the basic for-loop structure and change the init, test, and increment to get all sorts of different series: 0, 1, 2, … 98, 99 -or- 5, 10, 15,..90, 95, 100 -or- 100, 98, 96, … 2, 0.

```
/*
 Classic for-loop counting up from 0 to 99
 0, 1, 2, 3, … 99
-init int i = 0
-test i<100
-increment i++
*/
for (int i=0; i<100; i++) {
  System.out.println(i);
}

/*
 For-loop to print the values
 0, 2, 4, 6, .. 98
 -increment by i+=2, instead of i++
  (same as i = i + 2)
*/
for (int i=0; i<100; i+=2) {
  System.out.println(i);
```

```
}

/*
 For-loop from 99 down to 0
 99, 98, 97, … 0
 -init i=99
 -test i>=0
 -increment i--
*/
for (int i=99; i>=0; i--) {
  System.out.println(i);
}

/*
 For-loop from 0 to 100 by 5's
 0, 5, 10, 15, .. 100
 -test i<=100
 -increment i+=5
*/
for (int i=0; i<=100; i+=5) {
  System.out.println(i);
}
```

TEST STYLE < VS. <=

In the for-loop test, we can choose between < and <=—which is the better way to write it? If the for-loop stops at 1 less than some nice round value, such as stopping at 99, then it's better to write the test using < and the nice round value—"i < 100"—instead of the equivalent "i <= 99". If the loop goes up to and includes the nice round value, then write the loop with <=. So a loop up to and including the value 100 would use the test "i <= 100" instead of the equivalent "i < 101".

FOR VS. WHILE LOOPS

The for-loop can actually be understood as equivalent to a while-loop version, like this

```
init
while (test) {
  body
  increment
}
```

So for example, we could write the standard 0 … 99 loop like this, although for real code we would prefer the for-loop in this problem:

```
int i = 0;
while (i<100) {
  System.out.println(i);
  i++;
}
```

As a matter of style, if we are solving a series-of-values 0, 1, 2, 3, … 100 type problem, then the for-loop is preferable. That's exactly what it does. If the looping problem does not fit into the series-of-values pattern, then the standard while-loop is best.

LOOP WITH 2 EXIT TESTS

When writing a loop that looks for something, we often have two exit conditions. Suppose as a sort of James Bond example, we have a Vault object with something locked up inside of it, and it responds to a tryCode(int code) message that returns true if that code number opens the vault. The codes are between 0 and 1 million. We want to write a method findCode() that takes a vault, tries all the codes, and returns the first code that opens the vault, or -1 if no code opened the vault. The best way to write this is with the standard for-loop on the outside to iterate the range 0 … 1 million, and then inside the loop use an if-statement to check for additional exit conditions.

```
public int findCode(Vault vault) {
  for (int i=0; i<=1000000; i++) {
    if (vault.tryCode(i)) {
      // found the code!
      return(i);
    }
  }
  return(-1);  // if we get here, we did not find the code
}
```

So in this case, reaching 1 million is one exit condition, and tryCode() returning true is the other.

ONLY TEST AT THE TOP

The while loop checks the test, runs the body, checks the test, runs the body, … and so on until the test is false. The test is only checked once for each iteration, just before the body runs. The test is not checked while the body runs, although the English phrasing "while (count < 100) { …" can give the false impression that the test is checked continuously. Suppose we have the loop:

```
count = 0;
while (count < 100) {
  count = count + 10;
  count = count - 10;
  count = count + 1;
}
```

This loop changes count up and down inside the loop. For example, at some point we imagine that the line "count = count + 10" will make the test (count < 100) false. However, that will not exit the loop, because the test is not checked at that time. The test is only checked at the very top of the loop, just before each run of the body. So in this strange example, there will be times that count is greater than 100, and the loop will continue to run, exiting only when count is >= 100 at the top of the loop.

Java String

BY NICK PARLANTE

The Java String object contains a sequence char values (pronounced "car"). A char represents a single character, such as 'a' or 'Z' or 'μ' or '∑'. A char value is written in Java code using single quotes (') as shown here. Java supports the unicode character set, so we are no limited to just roman A-Z characters. The char type is a simple primitive type, very similar to int, so use simple = to copy char values, and == and != to compare char values. Rather than dealing with individual characters, you mostly deal with sequences of characters stored in a Java String object.

A string holds a sequence of characters, such as the string "Hello" or the string "It was the best of times. It was the worst of times.". A string can store a single word or the text of an entire book. Java's built in **String** class has many powerful and convenient features to operate on string data. Each String object stores a sequence of chars, such as "Hello", and implements methods that operate on those chars. We can create a String object the usual way with the "new" operator:

```
String str = new String("Hello");
```

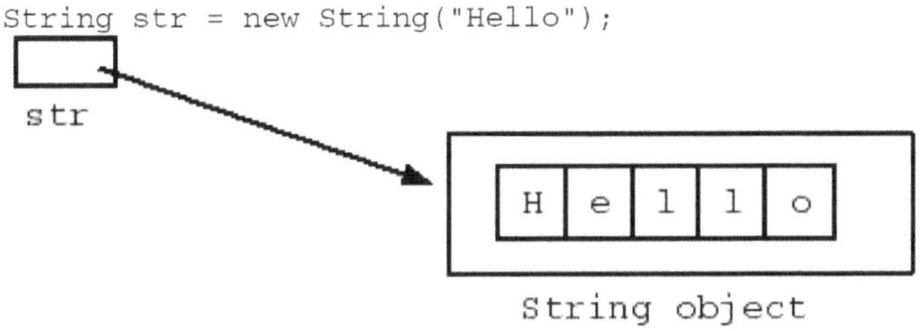

Strings are so common in Java code that there is a special syntax to create them. You can create a String object simply by writing the desired text within double quotes "like this". The shorter version of the code below creates a new String object exactly as above.

String str = "Hello";

It's valid to create a string made of zero characters—the quotes are right next to each other with nothing in between. This is known as the "empty string".

String empty = ""; // creates an empty string (zero chars)

The empty string is a valid string object, and the many of the operations described below work correctly on the empty string where it makes sense.

Special Characters

What if we want to create a string with a double quote (") in it? Java uses backslash (\) "escape" codes to insert special chars in a string, such as \" to get a double quote. Many computer languages use these same special backslash escape codes.

- \" -- a double quote char
- \t -- a tab char
- \n -- a newline char (the common end-of-line char, like the return key on the keyboard)
- \r -- a carriage return (a less common end-of-line char)
- \\ -- a backslash char

Testing a Character

The **Character** class has static utility methods that work on a single char:

- Character.isLetter(ch) -- true if the char is an alphabetic letter, a-z or the analogous in other alphabets
- Character.isDigit(ch) -- true if the char is a decimal digit 0-9
- Character.isWhitespace(ch) -- true if the char is a space, tab, newline, etc.
- Character.isLetterOrDigit(ch) -- true if the char is a letter or digit
- Character.isUpperCase(ch)/isLowerCase(ch) -- true if the char is upper/lower case
- Character.toUpperCase(ch)/Character.toLowerCase(ch) -- return the upper/lower case version of a char
- Character.toString(ch) -- return a string made of the single char

String Concatenation +

When used between two int values, the + operator does addition. When used between two or more strings, the + operator appends the strings together to form a new, bigger string.

String start = "Hi";
String end = "coffee time!";

String result = start + " it's " + end; // result is "Hi it's coffee time!"

In computer science, the verb "concatenate" is used for this situation -- appending sequences together to make one big sequence. This special feature of the + operator also works when a string is combined with a primitive such as an int or double or char. The int or double value is automatically converted to string form, and then the strings are appended together. This feature of the + is very a convenient way to mix int and double values into a string:

int donutCount = 123;
char end = '!';

String result = "I ate " + donutCount + " donuts" + end; // "I ate 123 donuts!"

String Immutable Style

Java string objects use the "immutable" style, which means that once a string object is created, its data never changes. For example, notice that the above uses of + concatenation do not change existing strings. Instead, the + creates and returns new strings, leaving the originals intact. As we explain the many string methods below, notice that no method changes an existing string. The immutable style is popular since it keeps things simple.

Basic String Methods

The Java String class has many useful methods.

- int length() -- length() returns the number of chars in the receiver string. The empty string "" returns a length of 0.
- String a = "Hello";
- int len = a.length(); // len is 5
- String toLowerCase() -- toLowerCase() returns a new string which is a lowercase copy of the receiver string. Does not change the receiver.
- String a = "Hello";
- String b = a.toLowerCase(); // b is "hello"

- String toUpperCase() -- toUpperCase() is like toLowerCase(), but returns an all uppercase copy of the receiver string. Does not change the receiver.
- String a = "Hello"
- String b = a.toUpperCase(); // b is "HELLO"
- String trim() -- trim() returns a copy of the receiver but with whitespace chars (like space, tab, newline) removed from the start and end of the String. Does not remove whitespace everywhere, just at the ends. Does not change the receiver.
- String a = " Hello There ";
- String b = a.trim(); // b is "Hello There"

Using Basic String Methods

Methods like trim() and toLowerCase() always return new string objects to use; they never change the receiver string object (this is the core of "immutable" style -- the receiver object never changes). For example, the code below does not work:

```
String word = "  hello  ";
word.trim(); // ERROR, this does not change word
// word is still "  hello  ";
```

When calling trim() (or any other string method) we must use the result returned by the method, assigning into a new variable with = for example:

```
String word = "  hello  ";
String trimmed = word.trim(); // Ok, trimmed is "hello"
```

If we do not care about keeping the old value of the string, we can use = to assign the new value right into the old variable:

```
String word = "  hello  ";
word = word.trim(); // Ok, word is "hello" (after the assignment)
```

This works fine. The trim() method returns a new string ("hello") and we store it into our variable, forgetting about the old string.

String Comparison

Given two string objects, use the equals() method to check if they contain the same characters. In Java, you typically use the equals() method to compare two objects—strings are just an example of that rule. The == operator is similar but is used most often to compare primitives such as int and char. In general, use equals() to compare objects, and use == to compare primitives. Unfortunately, using == with string objects will compile fine, but at runtime it will not actually compare the strings (the == checks if the two pointers point to the same object). It's easy to accidentally use == with objects instead of equals(), so it is a common error. The equals() method follows the pointers to the two String objects and compares them char by char to see if they are the same. This is sometimes called a "deep" comparison—following the pointers and looking at the actual objects. The comparison is "case-sensitive" meaning that the char 'A' is considered to be different from the char 'a'.

```
String a = "hello";
String b = "there";

// Correct -- use the .equals() method
if (a.equals("hello")) {
  System.out.println("a is \"hello\"");
}

// NO NO NO -- do not use == with Strings
if (a == "hello") {
  System.out.println("oops");
}

// a.equals(b) -> false
// b.equals("there") -> true
// b.equals("There") -> false
// b.equalsIgnoreCase("THERE") -> true
```

There is a variant of equals() called equalsIgnoreCase() that compares two strings, ignoring uppercase/lowercase differences. If you want to ignore uppercase/lowercase differences in your application, another solution is to covert all strings to, say, lowercase with toLowerCase() when they come into the system.

String also includes the handy startsWith()/endsWith() methods that test if one string matches the start or end of another:

```
String str = "hello";
str.endsWith("llo") -> true
str.startsWith("he") -> true
str.startsWith("hx") -> false
str.startsWith("") -> true (note, empty string is true)
```

String Comparison Ordering

The string compareTo(String other) methods compares the receiver string object against passed in string, returning a negative int if the receiver is less, 0 if the strings are the same, and a positive int if the receiver is greater. For example comparing the string "apple" to other strings:

```
String a = "apple";
a.compareTo("zebra") --> -1
a.compareTo("apple")  -->  0
a.compareTo("aaa")  -->  +1
```

The example shows a return values of -1/+1. However, in reality, compareTo() can returns a more complex int value reflecting the first char where the strings differ, but the sign of the returned int will be -1/0/+1 as shown here.

There is also a compareToIgnoreCase() comparison method that ignores uppercase/lowercase differences.

String Index Numbers

The chars in a String are each identified by an index number, from 0 .. length-1. The leftmost char is at index 0, the next at index 1, and so on, like this:

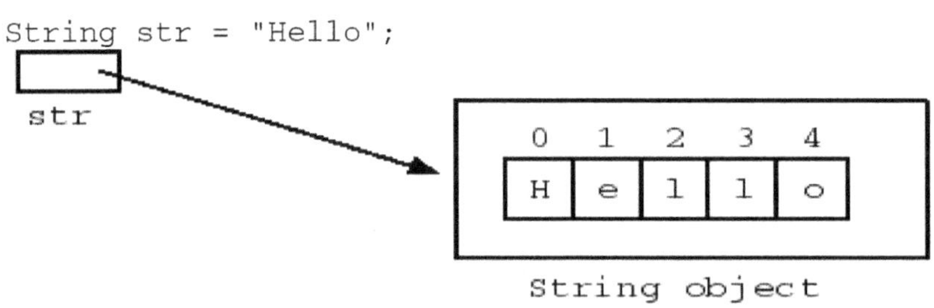

This "zero based" indexing style is very common in computer science for identifying elements in a collection. The method charAt(int index) returns an individual char from inside a string (see also the substring() method below). The valid index numbers are in the range 0..length-1. Using an index number outside of that range will raise a runtime exception and stop the program at that point.

```
String string = "hello";
char a = string.charAt(0);  // a is 'h'
char b = string.charAt(4);  // b is 'o'
char c = string.charAt(string.length() - 1);  // same as above line
char d = string.charAt(99);  // ERROR, index out of bounds
```

String Substring

The substring() method is a way of picking out a sub-part of string. It uses index numbers to identify the part of the string you want. The simplest version of substring() takes a single int index value and returns a new string made of the chars starting at that index and extending through the end of the string:

```
String string = "hello";
String a = string.substring(2);  // a is "llo"
String b = string.substring(3);  // b is "lo"
```

The more complex substring(int start, int end) method takes both start and end index numbers, returning a string of the chars between start and one before end:

```
String string = "Hello";
String a = string.substring(2, 4);  // a is "ll" (not "llo")
String b = string.substring(0, 3);  // b is "Hel"
```

Remember that substring() goes up to but does not include the end index. The length of the result is (end - start). It's easy to make off-by-one errors with index numbers in any algorithm. Make a little drawing of a sample string with its index numbers to get your code exactly right.

String indexOf()

The indexOf() method searches inside the receiver string for a "target" string. The indexOf() method returns the index number where the target string is first found (searching left to right), or -1 if the target is not found.

- int indexOf(String target) -- searches for the target string in the receiver. Returns the index where the target is found, or -1 if not found.

The indexOf() search is case-sensitive—upper and lowercase letters must match exactly.

```
String string = "Here there everywhere";

int a = string.indexOf("there");  // a is 5
int b = string.indexOf("er");     // b is 1
int c = string.indexOf("eR");     // c is -1, "eR" is not found
```

String indexOf() Other Versions

There are a few different versions of indexOf() that are more powerful than the basic version:

- int indexOf(String target, int fromIndex)—this indexOf() searches left-to-right for the target as usual, but starts the search at the given fromIndex (see code example below). The fromIndex does not actually need to be valid. If it is negative, the search happens from the start of the string. If the fromIndex is greater than the string length, then -1 will be returned. Here is an example that calls indexOf() in a loop to find all the "OOP" in string—note how the fromIndex is used to iterate over the whole string:
- void findOOP(String str) {
- int start = 0;
- while (true) {
-   int found = str.indexOf("OOP", start);
-   if (found == -1) break;
-   System.out.println("Found OOP at:" + found);
-   start = found + 2; // move start up for next iteration
- }
- }
- int lastIndexof(String target)—lastIndexOf() does the search right-left starting at the end of the receiver string
- int lastIndexof(String target, int fromIndex)—this lastIndexOf() does the search starting at the given index and working towards 0 (leftwards) in the receiver string
- int indexOf(char ch)—indexOf() version that searches for a single target char instead of a target string.

String Parsing

"Parsing" is the process of taking a string from a file or the network or the user, and processing it to extract the information we want. A common strategy is to use a few calls to indexOf() to figure out the index numbers of something interesting inside the string. Then use substring() to pull out the desired part of the string. After processing the data, we can use + to reassemble the parts to make a new string.

Suppose we have a string that contains some text with a pair parenthesis somewhere inside of it, like this: "It was hot (darn hot!) I'm telling you". Suppose we want to fix the string so that the part in parenthesis is in all upper case. We can use two calls to indexOf() to find the '(' and ')', and substring to extract the text. Example code:

```
String string = "It was hot (so hot!) I'm telling you.";
int left = string.indexOf("(");
int right = string.indexOf(")");

// pull out the text inside the parens
String sub = string.substring(left+1, right); // sub is "so hot!"

sub = sub.toUpperCase(); // sub is "SO HOT!"

// Put together a new string
```

```
String result =
  string.substring(0, left+1) +   // It was hot (
  sub +                           // SO HOT!
  string.substring(right);        // ) I'm telling you.

// result is "It was hot (SO HOT!) I'm telling you."
```

STRING CODE EXAMPLES

Example 1

Given a string, returns a string made of repetitions of that string. This code demonstrates using + to assemble a larger string in a loop:

```
public String repeat(String string, int count) {
  String result = "";
  for (int i=0; i<count; i++) {
    result = result + string;
  }
  return result;
}
```

Example2

Given a string, returns how many '!' chars it contains. This code demonstrates using a for loop, calling length() and charAt() to look at all the chars in a string:

```
public String countExclaim(String string) {
  int count = 0;
  for (int i=0; i<string.length(); i++) {
    if (string.charAt(i) == '!') count++;
  }
  return count;
}
```

Example 3

Given a string where the string "OOP" appears at least two times, find the first and last OOP in the whole string. Return the text from between the two OOP. Demonstrates using indexOf() and substring():

```
public String oopPair(String string) {
  int start = string.indexOf("OOP");
  int end = string.lastIndexOf("OOP");
  return string.substring(start+1, end);
}
```

Example 4

Suppose you have a string like this:"Once there was a woman name:angelina: and a man name:tony: and their freind name:jane: and …" Inside of a long text there are little "name:" sections. Write code to find and print all the names. Demonstrates a more complex use of indexOf() and substring() in a loop to parse a string:

```
public void printNames(String string) {
  int i = 0;
  while (true) {
    int found = string.indexOf("name:", i);
    if (found == -1) break;
    int start = found + 5; // start of actual name
    int end = string.indexOf(":", start);
    System.out.println(string.substring(start, end));
    i = end + 1;  // advance i to start the next iteration
  }
}
```

Part V: Exception and Exception Handling

Exceptions in Java

BY BILL VENNERS

Exceptions are the customary way in Java to indicate to a calling method that an abnormal condition has occurred. This article is a companion piece to this month's Design Techniques installment, which discusses how to use exceptions appropriately in your programs and designs. Look to this companion article for a tutorial on the nuts and bolts of what exceptions are and how they work in the Java language and virtual machine.

When a method encounters an abnormal condition (an exception condition) that it can't handle itself, it may throw an exception. Throwing an exception is like throwing a beeping, flashing red ball to indicate there is a problem that can't be handled where it occurred. Somewhere, you hope, this ball will be caught and the problem will be dealt with. Exceptions are caught by handlers positioned along the thread's method invocation stack. If the calling method isn't prepared to catch the exception, it throws the exception up to its calling method, and so on. If one of the threads of your program throws an exception that isn't caught by any method along the method invocation stack, that thread will expire. When you program in Java, you must position catchers (the exception handlers) strategically, so your program will catch and handle all exceptions from which you want your program to recover.

EXCEPTION CLASSES

In Java, exceptions are objects. When you throw an exception, you throw an object. You can't throw just any object as an exception, however—only those objects whose classes descend from Throwable. Throwable serves as the base class for an entire family of classes, declared in java.lang, that your program can instantiate and throw. A small part of this family is shown in Figure 1.

As you can see in Figure 1, Throwable has two direct subclasses, Exception and Error. Exceptions (members of the Exception family) are thrown to signal abnormal conditions that can often be handled by some catcher, though it's possible they may not be caught and therefore could result in a dead thread. Errors (members of the Error family) are usually thrown for more serious problems, such as OutOfMemoryError, that may not be so easy to handle. In general, code you write should throw only exceptions, not errors. Errors are usually thrown by the methods of the Java API, or by the Java virtual machine itself.

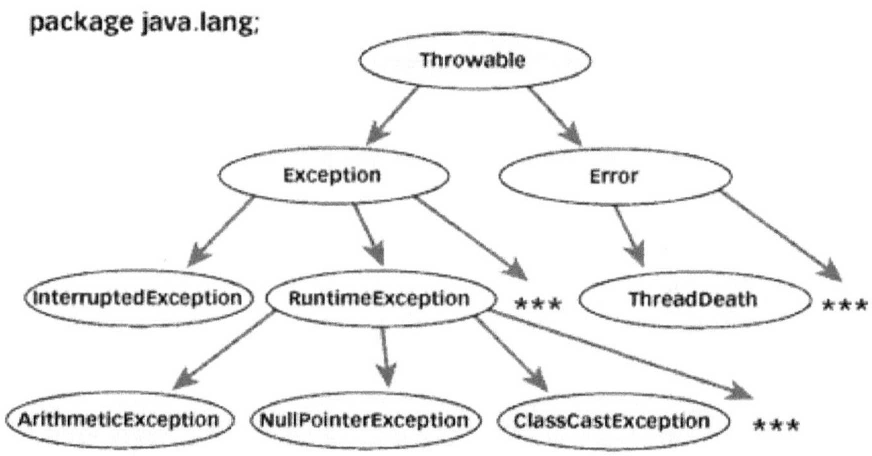

Figure 1. A partial view of the Throwable family

In addition to throwing objects whose classes are declared in java.lang, you can throw objects of your own design. To create your own class of throwable objects, you need only declare it as a subclass of some member of the Throwable family. In general, however, the throwable classes you define should extend class Exception. They should be "exceptions." The reasoning behind this rule will be explained later in this article.

Whether you use an existing exception class from java.lang or create one of your own depends upon the situation. In some cases, a class from java.lang will do just fine. For example, if one of your methods is invoked with an invalid argument, you could throw IllegalArgumentException, a subclass of RuntimeException in java.lang.

Other times, however, you will want to convey more information about the abnormal condition than a class from java.lang will allow. Usually, the class of the exception object itself indicates the type of abnormal condition that was encountered. For example, if a thrown exception object has class IllegalArgumentException, that indicates someone passed an illegal argument to a method. Sometimes you will want to indicate that a method encountered an abnormal condition that isn't represented by a class in the Throwable family of java.lang.

As an example, imagine you are writing a Java program that simulates a customer of a virtual café drinking a cup of coffee. Consider the exceptional conditions that might occur while the customer sips. The class hierarchy of exceptions shown in Figure 2 represents a few possibilities.

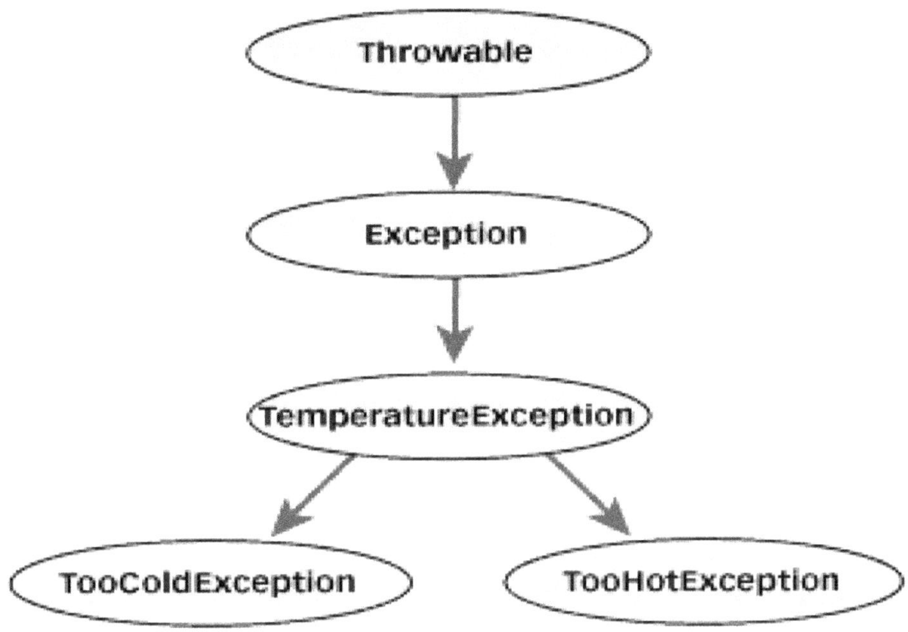

Figure 2. Exception hierarchy for coffee sipping

If the customer discovers, with dismay, that the coffee is cold, your program could throw a TooColdException. On the other hand, if the customer discovers that the coffee is overly hot, your program could throw a TooHotException. These conditions could be exceptions because they are (hopefully) not the normal situation in your café. (Exceptional conditions are not necessarily rare, just outside the normal flow of events.) The code for your new exception classes might look like this

```
// In Source Packet in file except/ex1/TemperatureException.java
class TemperatureException extends Exception {
}
// In Source Packet in file except/ex1/TooColdException.java
class TooColdException extends TemperatureException {
}
// In Source Packet in file except/ex1/TooHotException.java
class TooHotException extends TemperatureException {
}
```

This family of classes, the TemperatureException family, declares three new types of exceptions for your program to throw. Note that each exception indicate's by its class the kind of abnormal condition that would cause it to be thrown: TemperatureException indicates some kind of problem with temperature; TooColdException indicates something was too cold; and TooHotException indicates something was too hot. Note also that TemperatureException extends Exception—not Throwable, Error, or any other class declared in java.lang.

THROWING EXCEPTIONS

To throw an exception, you simply use the throw keyword with an object reference, as in:

```
throw new TooColdException();
```

The type of the reference must be Throwable or one of its subclasses.

The following code shows how a class that represents the customer, class VirtualPerson, might throw exceptions if the coffee didn't meet the customer's temperature preferences. Note that Java also has a throws keyword in addition to the throw keyword. Only throw can be used to throw an exception. The meaning of throws will be explained later in this article.

```
// In Source Packet in file except/ex1/VirtualPerson.java
class VirtualPerson {
  private static final int tooCold = 65;
  private static final int tooHot = 85;
  public void drinkCoffee(CoffeeCup cup) throws
    TooColdException, TooHotException {
    int temperature = cup.getTemperature();
    if (temperature <= tooCold) {
      throw new TooColdException();
    }
    else if (temperature >= tooHot) {
      throw new TooHotException();
    }
    //...
  }
  //...
}
// In Source Packet in file except/ex1/CoffeeCup.java
class CoffeeCup {
  // 75 degrees Celsius: the best temperature for coffee
  private int temperature = 75;
  public void setTemperature(int val) {
    temperature = val;
  }
  public int getTemperature() {
```

```
        return temperature;
    }
    //...
}
```

CATCHING EXCEPTIONS

To catch an exception in Java, you write a `try` block with one or more catch clauses. Each catch clause specifies one exception type that it is prepared to handle. The try block places a fence around a bit of code that is under the watchful eye of the associated catchers. If the bit of code delimited by the try block throws an exception, the associated catch clauses will be examined by the Java virtual machine. If the virtual machine finds a catch clause that is prepared to handle the thrown exception, the program continues execution starting with the first statement of that catch clause.

As an example, consider a program that requires one argument on the command line, a string that can be parsed into an integer. When you have a String and want an int, you can invoke the parseInt() method of the Integer class. If the string you pass represents an integer, parseInt() will return the value. If the string doesn't represent an integer, parseInt() throws NumberFormatException. Here is how you might parse an int from a command-line argument:

```
// In Source Packet in file except/ex1/Example1.java
class Example1 {
    public static void main(String[] args) {
        int temperature = 0;
        if (args.length > 0) {
            try {
                temperature = Integer.parseInt(args[0]);
            }
            catch(NumberFormatException e) {
                System.out.println(
                    "Must enter integer as first argument.");
                return;
            }
        }
        else {
            System.out.println(
                "Must enter temperature as first argument.");
            return;
        }
        // Create a new coffee cup and set the temperature of
        // its coffee.
```

```
        CoffeeCup cup = new CoffeeCup();
        cup.setTemperature(temperature);
        // Create and serve a virtual customer.
        VirtualPerson cust = new VirtualPerson();
        VirtualCafe.serveCustomer(cust, cup);
    }
}
```

Here, the invocation of parseInt() sits inside a try block. Attached to the try block is a catch clause that catches NumberFormatException:

```
catch(NumberFormatException e) {
    System.out.println(
        "Must enter integer as first argument.");
    return;
}
```

The lowercase character e is a reference to the thrown (and caught) NumberFormatException object. This reference could have been used inside the catch clause, although in this case it isn't. (Examples of catch clauses that use the reference are shown later in this article.)

If the user types Harumph as the first argument to the Example1 program, parseInt() will throw a NumberFormatException exception and the catch clause will catch it. The program will print:

```
Must enter integer as first argument.
```

Although the above example had only one catch clause, you can have many catch clauses associated with a single try block. Here's an example:

```
// In Source Packet in file except/ex1/VirtualCafe.java
class VirtualCafe {
    public static void serveCustomer(VirtualPerson cust,
        CoffeeCup cup) {
        try {
            cust.drinkCoffee(cup);
            System.out.println("Coffee is just right.");
        }
        catch (TooColdException e) {
            System.out.println("Coffee is too cold.");
            // Deal with an irate customer ...
        }
```

```
        catch (TooHotException e) {
            System.out.println("Coffee is too hot.");
            // Deal with an irate customer ...
        }
    }
}
```

If any code inside a try block throws an exception, its catch clauses are examined in their order of appearance in the source file. For example, if the try block in the above example throws an exception, the catch clause for TooColdException will be examined first, then the catch clause for TooHotException. During this examination process, the first catch clause encountered that handles the thrown object's class gets to "catch" the exception. The ordering of catch-clause examination matters because it is possible that multiple catch clauses of a try block could handle the same exception.

Catch clauses indicate the type of abnormal condition they handle by the type of exception reference they declare. In the example above, the catch clauses declare exception type TooColdException and TooHotException. Had a single catch clause declared a TemperatureException, a thrown TooColdException or TooHotException still would have been caught, because TemperatureException is the superclass of both these classes. In the object-oriented way of thinking, a TooColdException is a TemperatureException, therefore, a catch clause for TemperatureException also will catch a thrown TooColdException. An example of this is shown below:

```
// In Source Packet in file except/ex2/VirtualCafe.java
class VirtualCafe {
    public static void serveCustomer(VirtualPerson cust,
        CoffeeCup cup) {
        try {
            cust.drinkCoffee(cup);
            System.out.println("Coffee is just right.");
        }
        catch (TemperatureException e) {
            // This catches TooColdException, TooHotException,
            // as well as TemperatureException.
            System.out.println("Coffee is too cold or too hot.");
            // Deal with an irate customer ...
        }
    }
}
```

Multiple catch clauses could handle the same exception because you may, for example, declare two catch clauses, one for TooColdException and another for TemperatureException. In this case, however, you must place the catch clause for TooColdException above the one for TemperatureException, or the source file won't compile.

If a catch clause for TemperatureException could be declared before a catch clause for TooColdException, the first catch clause would catch all TooColdExceptions, leaving nothing for the second catch clause to do. The second catch clause would never be reached. The general rule is subclass catch clauses must precede superclass catch clauses. Here's an example of both orders, only one of which compiles:

```
// In Source Packet in file except/ex3/VirtualCafe.java
class VirtualCafe {
   public static void serveCustomer(VirtualPerson cust,
      CoffeeCup cup) {
      try {
         cust.drinkCoffee(cup);
         System.out.println("Coffee is just right.");
      }
      catch (TemperatureException e) {
         // This catches TooColdException, TooHotException,
         // as well as TemperatureException.
         System.out.println("Coffee is too cold or too hot.");
         // Deal with an irate customer ...
      }
      // THIS WON'T COMPILE, BECAUSE THIS catch clause
      // WILL NEVER BE REACHED.
      catch (TooColdException e) {
         System.out.println("Coffee is too cold.");
      }
   }
}
// In Source Packet in file except/ex4/VirtualCafe.java
// This class compiles fine.
class VirtualCafe {
   public static void serveCustomer(VirtualPerson cust,
      CoffeeCup cup) {
      try {
         cust.drinkCoffee(cup);
         System.out.println("Coffee is just right.");
      }
      catch (TooColdException e) {
         System.out.println("Coffee is too cold.");
         // Deal with an irate customer ...
      }
      catch (TemperatureException e) {
```

```
            // This catches TooHotException as well
            // as TemperatureException.
            System.out.println(
                "There's temperature trouble in this coffee.");
            // Deal with an irate customer ...
        }
    }
}
```

EMBEDDING INFORMATION IN AN EXCEPTION OBJECT

When you throw an exception, you are performing a kind of structured go-to from the place in your program where an abnormal condition was detected to a place where it can be handled. The Java virtual machine uses the class of the exception object you throw to decide which catch clause, if any, should be allowed to handle the exception. But an exception doesn't just transfer control from one part of your program to another, it also transmits information. Because the exception is a full-fledged object that you can define yourself, you can embed information about the abnormal condition in the object before you throw it. The catch clause can then get the information by querying the exception object directly.

The Exception class allows you to specify a String detail message that can be retrieved by invoking getMessage() on the exception object. When you define an exception class of your own, you can give client programmers the option of specifying a detail message like this:

```
// In Source Packet in file except/ex5/UnusualTasteException.java
class UnusualTasteException extends Exception {
    UnusualTasteException() {
    }
    UnusualTasteException(String msg) {
        super(msg);
    }
}
```

Given the above declaration of UnusualTasteException, client programmers could create an instance in one of two ways:

1. new UnusualTasteException()
2. new UnusualTasteException("This coffee tastes like tea.")

A catch clause can then query the object for a detail string, like this \

```
// In Source Packet in file except/ex5/VirtualCafe.java
class VirtualCafe {
    public static void serveCustomer(VirtualPerson cust,
        CoffeeCup cup) {
        try {
            cust.drinkCoffee(cup);
            System.out.println("Coffee tastes just right.");
        }
        catch (UnusualTasteException e) {
            System.out.println(
                "Customer is complaining of an unusual taste.");
            String s = e.getMessage();
            if (s != null) {
                System.out.println(s);
            }
            // Deal with an unhappy customer ...
        }
    }
}
```

When you need to embed more information into an exception object than you can represent with a String, you can add data and access methods to your exception class. For example, you could define the temperature exception classes like this:

```
// In Source Packet in file except/ex6/TemperatureException.java
abstract class TemperatureException extends Exception {
    private int temperature; // in Celsius
    public TemperatureException(int temperature) {
        this.temperature = temperature;
    }
    public int getTemperature() {
        return temperature;
    }
}
// In Source Packet in file except/ex6/TooColdException.java
class TooColdException extends TemperatureException {
    public TooColdException(int temperature) {
        super(temperature);
    }
```

```
}
// In Source Packet in file except/ex6/TooHotException.java
class TooHotException extends TemperatureException {
    public TooHotException(int temperature) {
        super(temperature);
    }
}
```

Given a TemperatureException family as defined above, catch clauses can query the exception object to find out the precise temperature that caused the problem. The temperature field of the exception object must be set when the object is created, as in:

```
// In Source Packet in file except/ex6/VirtualPerson.java
class VirtualPerson {
    private static final int tooCold = 65;
    private static final int tooHot = 85;
    public void drinkCoffee(CoffeeCup cup) throws
        TooColdException, TooHotException {
        int temperature = cup.getTemperature();
        if (temperature <= tooCold) {
            throw new TooColdException(temperature);
        }
        else if (temperature >= tooHot) {
            throw new TooHotException(temperature);
        }
        // ...
    }
    // ...
}
```

Wherever the exception is caught, the catch clause can easily determine the actual temperature of the coffee and act accordingly, as in:

```
// In Source Packet in file except/ex6/VirtualCafe.java
class VirtualCafe {
    public static void serveCustomer(VirtualPerson cust,
        CoffeeCup cup) {
        try {
            cust.drinkCoffee(cup);
            System.out.println("Coffee is just right.");
```

```
        }
        catch (TooColdException e) {
            int temperature = e.getTemperature();
            System.out.println("Coffee temperature is "
                + temperature + " degrees Celsius.");
            if (temperature > 55 && temperature <= 65) {
                System.out.println("Coffee is cooling off.");
                // Add more hot coffee ...
            }
            else if (temperature > 0 && temperature <= 55) {
                System.out.println("Coffee is too cold.");
                // Give customer a new cup of coffee with the
                // proper temperature ...
            }
            else if (temperature <= 0) {
                System.out.println("Coffee is frozen.");
                // Deal with an irate customer ...
            }
        }
        catch (TooHotException e) {
            int temperature = e.getTemperature();
            System.out.println("Coffee temperature is "
                + temperature + " degrees Celsius.");
            if (temperature >= 85 && temperature < 100) {
                System.out.println("Coffee is too hot.");
                // Ask customer to let it cool a few minutes ...
            }
            else if (temperature >= 100 && temperature < 2000) {
                System.out.println(
                    "Both coffee and customer are steamed.");
                // Deal with an irate customer ...
            }
            else if (temperature >= 2000) {
                System.out.println(
                    "The coffee is plasma.");
                // Deal with a very irate customer ...
            }
        }
    }
}
```

The program could deal with the temperature problem differently depending upon the coffee's actual temperature. If the coffee is just a little cold, the program could add more hot coffee to the cup. If the coffee is so cold that the customer's lips were instantly frozen to the cup, alternative measures could be taken.

EXCEPTIONS AND THE METHOD INVOCATION STACK

Code inside a `try` block is in a sense surrounded by the catch clauses associated with the try block. When an exception is thrown, the surrounding catch clauses are examined in inside-out order. You can nest try blocks inside try blocks, in effect building up more and more layers of catch clauses that surround the code. When a method is invoked from within a try block, the catch clauses associated with that try block surround the code in the *invoked* method as well. If that method has try blocks and catch clauses, they are added as inner surrounding layers. What this means is that an exception may be thrown far up the method invocation stack before landing in a catch clause that can handle it.

As an example, consider the following exception classes, which are simpler versions of exceptions introduced in examples above:

```
// In Source Packet in file except/ex7/TemperatureException.java
class TemperatureException extends Exception {
}
// In Source Packet in file except/ex7/TooColdException.java
class TooColdException extends TemperatureException {
}
// In Source Packet in file except/ex7/TooHotException.java
class TooHotException extends TemperatureException {
}
// In Source Packet in file except/ex7/UnusualTasteException.java
class UnusualTasteException extends Exception {
}
```

When the drinkCoffee() method of class VirtualPerson is invoked, it throws one of these four exceptions, chosen at random:

```
// In Source Packet in file except/ex7/VirtualPerson.java
class VirtualPerson {
   public void drinkCoffee(CoffeeCup cup) throws TooColdException,
      TemperatureException, UnusualTasteException {
      try {
         int i = (int) (Math.random() * 4.0);
         switch (i) {
         case 0:
```

```
            throw new TooHotException();
        case 1:
            throw new TooColdException();
        case 2:
            throw new UnusualTasteException();
        default:
            throw new TemperatureException();
        }
    }
    catch (TooHotException e) {
        System.out.println("This coffee is too hot.");
        // Customer will wait until it cools to an
        // acceptable temperature.
    }
  }
  // ...
}
```

If variable i in the drinkCoffee() method above happens to be set to a value of 0 the switch statement will instantiate and throw a TooHotException. Because the switch statement itself is enclosed within a try block that has a catch clause for TooHotException, execution continues at that catch clause. The program prints out:

This coffee is too hot.

If variable i in the drinkCoffee() method above happens to be set to the value of 1, the switch statement will instantiate and throw a TooColdException. When this exception is thrown, the Java virtual machine will first check the catch clauses of the try block that surrounds the switch statement. In this case, however, no catch clause matches the thrown exception.

Because the TooColdException is not caught by the drinkCoffee() method, the Java virtual machine throws the exception up the method invocation stack to the method that invoked drinkCoffee(). As used here, a *method invocation stack* (or *call stack*) is a list of the methods that have been invoked by a thread, starting with the first method the thread invoked and ending with the current method. A method invocation stack shows the path of method invocations a thread took to arrive at the current method.

A graphical representation of the method invocation stack for drinkCoffee() is shown in Figure 3. In this figure, the method invocation stack is shown on the right and the corresponding Java stack is shown on the left. The *Java stack* is where methods keep their state inside the Java virtual machine. Each method gets a *stack frame* (or *frame*), which is pushed onto the stack when the method is invoked and popped from the stack when the method completes. The frame is an area in memory that contains the method's local variables, parameters, return value, and other information needed by the Java virtual machine to execute the method. In Figure 3, the stack is shown growing downwards. The top of the stack is at the bottom of the picture.

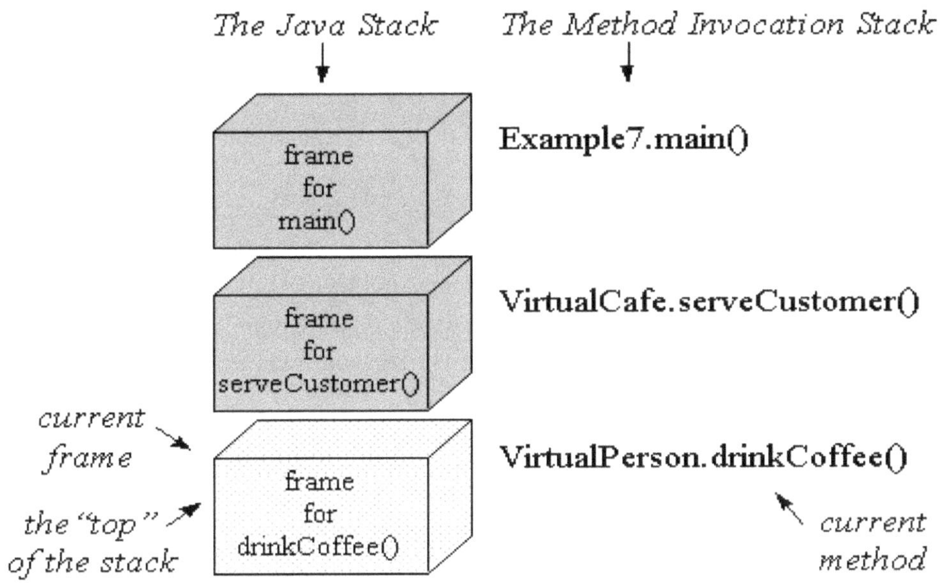

Figure 3. The method invocation stack for `drinkCoffee()`

When a method completes by executing a return statement, or by successfully executing the last statement in a method declared as void, it is said to *complete normally*. The Java virtual machine pops the returning method's stack frame, and continues executing just after the method invocation in the calling method. The calling method becomes the *current method* and its stack frame becomes the *current frame*.

When a method throws an exception that it doesn't catch itself, it is said to *complete abruptly*. Methods do not return a value when they complete abruptly, though they do pass along an exception object.

For example, when the drinkCoffee() method throws a TooColdException, it completes abruptly. Because the exception isn't caught by drinkCoffee(), the Java virtual machine pops drinkCoffee()'s stack frame. It then examines the next method up the invocation stack, in this case the serveCustomer() method of VirtualCafe, to see if it has a catch clause prepared to handle the exception.

Here's the code for VirtualCafe:

```
// In Source Packet in file except/ex7/VirtualCafe.java
class VirtualCafe {
  public static void serveCustomer(VirtualPerson cust,
    CoffeeCup cup)throws TemperatureException,
    UnusualTasteException {
    try {
      cust.drinkCoffee(cup);
    }
```

```
        catch (TooColdException e) {
            System.out.println("This coffee is too cold.");
            // Add more hot coffee ...
        }
    }
}
```

The serveCustomer() method above does indeed surround its invocation of drinkCoffee() with a try block that has an attached catch clause for TooColdException. So the exception stops here. The Java virtual machine makes the serveCustomer() method's stack frame current and continues execution at the first statement inside the catch clause. The program prints out:

```
This coffee is too cold.
```

If variable i in the drinkCoffee() method above happens to be set to the value of 2, the switch statement will instantiate and throw an UnusualTasteException. When this exception is thrown, the Java virtual machine will first check the catch clauses of the try block that surrounds the switch statement. In this case, no catch clause matches the thrown exception. The virtual machine will then pop drinkCoffee()'s stack frame and examine the serveCustomer() method. But in serveCustomer(), no catch clause attached to the try block matches the thrown exception either. The virtual machine will therefore pop serveCustomer()'s stack frame and examine the next method up the invocation stack: the main() method of class Example7.

Here's the code for Example7:

```
// In Source Packet in file except/ex7/Example7.java
class Example7 {
    public static void main(String[] args)
        throws TemperatureException {
        // Create a new coffee cup.
        CoffeeCup cup = new CoffeeCup();
        // Create and serve a virtual customer.
        try {
            VirtualPerson cust = new VirtualPerson();
            VirtualCafe.serveCustomer(cust, cup);
        }
        catch (UnusualTasteException e) {
            System.out.println("This coffee has an unusual taste.");
        }
    }
}
```

This main() method was farsighted enough to surround its invocation of serveCustomer() with a try block that includes a catch clause for UnusualTasteException. Thus, the Java virtual machine will make the main() method's stack frame current and will continue execution at the first statement in the catch clause. The program will print:

```
This coffee has an unusual taste.
```

In the UnusualTasteException case, both drinkCoffee() and serveCoffee() methods completed abruptly. The Java virtual machine popped two frames from the Java stack, stopping its popping only when it reached the main() method.

The last case in this example occurs if the variable i in the drinkCoffee() method gets set to a value greater than 2. In this case, the switch statement will instantiate and throw a TemperatureException. When this exception is thrown, the Java virtual machine will go through its usual procedure of examining methods for catch clauses and popping frames for methods that can't handle the exception. The virtual machine will examine drinkCoffee(), pop its frame, examine serveCustomer(), pop its frame, examine main(), and pop its frame. At this point, however, the virtual machine has run out of frames. It can't go any further up the method invocation stack because main() was the first method invoked by the thread.

Because none of the methods on the invocation stack is prepared to handle the TemperatureException, the exception is "uncaught." It will be handled by a default handler and result in the death of the thread. Because this is the main thread of the Example7 application and the application didn't fire off any other threads that are still running when the main thread dies, the application terminates. (A dead thread doesn't always cause the death of its application, only when a dying thread is the last "non-daemon" thread running inside the application.) In most Java runtime environments, the default handler for an uncaught exception will print out a stack trace when a thread dies. For example, the java program from JDK 1.1.1 prints the following when the main thread of Example7 dies due to an uncaught TemperatureException:

```
TemperatureException
    at VirtualPerson.drinkCoffee(VirtualPerson.java:20)
    at VirtualCafe.serveCustomer(VirtualCafe.java:9)
    at Example7.main(Example7.java:12)
```

THE THROWS CLAUSE

As you may have guessed from the examples above, the Java language requires that a method declare in a throws clause the exceptions that it may throw. A method's throws clause indicates to client programmers what exceptions they may have to deal with when they invoke the method.

For example, the drinkCoffee() method of class VirtualPerson, shown below, declares three exceptions in its throws clause: TooColdException, TemperatureException, and Unusual Taste Exception. These are the three exceptions that the method throws but doesn't catch. The method also may throw TooHotException, but this exception doesn't appear in the throws clause because drinkCoffee() catches and handles it internally. Only exceptions that will cause a method to complete abruptly should appear in its throws clause.

```
// In Source Packet in file except/ex7/VirtualPerson.java
class VirtualPerson {
   public void drinkCoffee(CoffeeCup cup) throws TooColdException,
      TemperatureException, UnusualTasteException {
      try {
         int i = (int) (Math.random() * 4.0);
         switch (i) {
         case 0:
            throw new TooHotException();
         case 1:
            throw new TooColdException();
         case 2:
            throw new UnusualTasteException();
         default:
            throw new TemperatureException();
         }
      }
      catch (TooHotException e) {
         System.out.println("This coffee is too hot.");
         // Customer will wait until it cools to an
         // acceptable temperature.
      }
   }
   // ...
}
```

In the drinkCoffee() method above, each exception declared in the throws clause is explicitly thrown by the method via a throw statement. This is one of two ways a method can complete abruptly. The other way is by invoking another method that completes abruptly.

An example of this is VirtualCafe's serveCustomer() method, shown below, that invokes VirtualPerson's drinkCoffee() method. The serveCustomer() method contains no throw statements, but it does declare two exceptions in its throws clause: TemperatureException and UnusualTasteException. These are two of three exceptions that may be thrown by drinkCoffee(), which serveCustomer() invokes. The third exception, TooColdException, doesn't appear in the throws clause because serveCustomer() catches and handles it internally. Only those exceptions that will cause the serveCustomer() method to complete abruptly appear in its throws clause.

```
// In Source Packet in file except/ex7/VirtualCafe.java
class VirtualCafe {
    public static void serveCustomer(VirtualPerson cust,
        CoffeeCup cup)throws TemperatureException,
        UnusualTasteException {
        try {
            cust.drinkCoffee(cup);
        }
        catch (TooColdException e) {
            System.out.println("This coffee is too cold.");
            // Add more hot coffee ...
        }
    }
}
```

Although a throws clause lists exceptions that may cause a method to complete abruptly, the list is not necessarily complete. Not everything that can be thrown by a method need be put in a throws clause.

CHECKED VS. UNCHECKED EXCEPTIONS

There are two kinds of exceptions in Java, *checked* and *unchecked*, and only checked exceptions need appear in `throws` clauses. The general rule is, any checked exceptions that may be thrown in a method must either be caught or declared in the method's `throws` clause. Checked exceptions are so called because both the Java compiler and the Java virtual machine check to make sure this rule is obeyed.

Whether or not an exception is "checked" is determined by its position in the hierarchy of throwable classes. Figure 4 shows that some parts of the `Throwable` family tree contain checked exceptions while other parts contain unchecked exceptions. To create a new checked exception, you simply extend another checked exception. All throwables that are subclasses of `Exception`, but not subclasses of `RuntimeException` are checked exceptions.

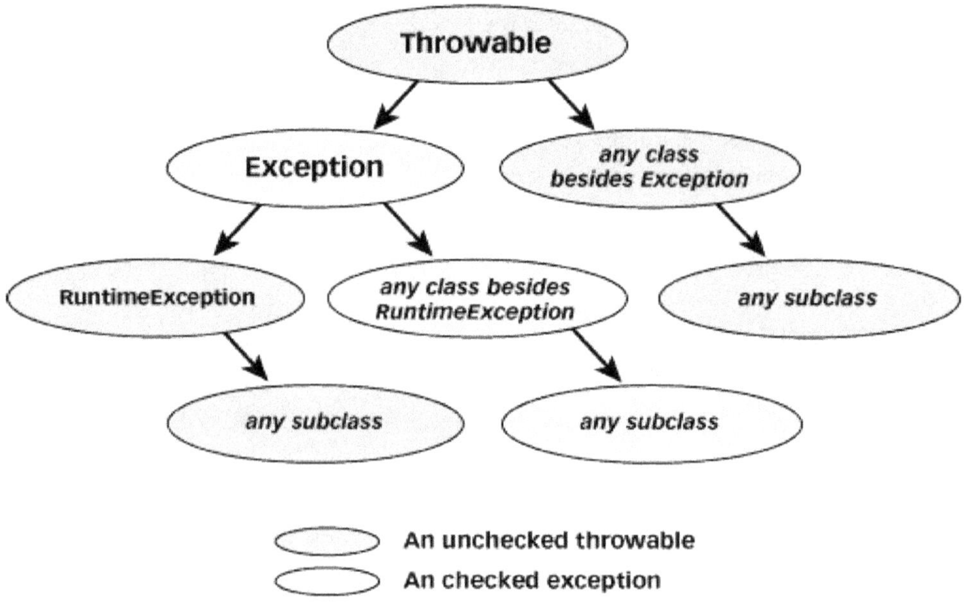

Figure 4. Checked and unchecked throwables

The conceptual difference between checked and unchecked exceptions is that checked exceptions signal abnormal conditions that you want client programmers to deal with. For instance, because the drinkCoffee() method allocates memory with the new operator, it could potentially complete abruptly by throwing an OutOfMemoryError. This is not a checked exception, because it's not a subclass of Exception. It's a subclass of Error. Conceptually, OutOfMemoryError isn't a checked exception because you don't want client programmers to have to deal directly with the fact that drinkCoffee() could complete abruptly due to low memory.

When you place an exception in a throws clause, it *forces* client programmers who invoke your method to deal with the exception, either by catching it or by declaring it in their own throws clause. If they don't deal with the exception in one of these two ways, their classes won't compile. For example, because the drinkCoffee() method declares three exceptions in its throws clause, the serveCustomer() method, which invokes drinkCoffee(), has to deal with those three exceptions. In this case, serveCustomer() catches one exception, TooColdException, but not the other two. If serveCustomer() hadn't declared in its throws clause the other two exceptions, TemperatureException and UnusualTasteException, the VirtualCafe class would not have compiled.

Most unchecked throwables declared in java.lang (subclasses of Error and RuntimeException) are problems that would be detected by the Java virtual machine. Errors usually signal abnormal conditions that you wouldn't want a program to handle. Problems with linking, such as NoClassDefFoundError, or memory, such as StackOverflowError, could happen just about anywhere in a program. In the rare cases in which they happen, it is usually reasonable that the thread terminate.

Although most runtime exceptions (members of the RuntimeException family) also are thrown by the Java virtual machine itself, they usually are more an indication of software bugs. Problems with arrays, such as ArrayIndexOutOfBoundsException, or passed parameters, such as IllegalArgumentException, also could happen just about anywhere in a program. When exceptions like these are thrown, you'll want to fix the bugs that caused them to be thrown. You won't, however, want to force client programmers to wrap every invocation of a method that uses arrays with a catch clause for ArrayIndexOutOfBoundsException.

You can throw and catch unchecked exceptions just like checked exceptions, but the Java Language Specification advises against throwing errors. It is intended that errors be thrown only by the Java runtime. You may, however, reasonably throw runtime exceptions. You can throw a runtime exception declared in java.lang or declare your own subclasses of RuntimeException.

To decide whether to throw a checked exception or an unchecked runtime exception, you must look at the abnormal condition you are signalling. If you are throwing an exception to indicate an improper use of your class, you are signalling a software bug. The class of exception you throw probably should descend from RuntimeException, which will make it unchecked. Otherwise, if you are throwing an exception to indicate not a software bug but an abnormal condition that client programmers should deal with every time they use your method, your exception should be checked.

THE FINALLY CLAUSE

Once a Java virtual machine has begun to execute a block of code—the statements between two matching curly braces—it can exit that block in any of several ways. It could, for example, simply execute past the closing curly brace. It could encounter a break, continue, or return statement that causes it to jump out of the block from somewhere in the middle. Or, if an exception is thrown that isn't caught inside the block, it could exit the block while searching for a catch clause.

Given that a block can be exited in many ways, it is important to be able to ensure that something happens upon exiting a block, no matter how the block is exited. For example, if you open a file in a method, you may want to ensure the file gets closed no matter how the method completes. In Java, you express such a desire with a finally clause.

To use a finally clause, you simply: (1) Enclose the code that has multiple exit points in a try block; and (2) place the code that must be executed when the try block is exited in a finally clause.

Here's an example:

```
try {
   // Block of code with multiple exit points
}
finally {
   // Block of code that must always be executed when the try block
   // is exited, no matter how the try block is exited
}
```

At least one clause, either catch or finally, must be associated with each try block. If you have both catch clauses and a finally clause with the same try block, you must put the finally clause after all the catch clauses, as in:

```
// In Source Packet in file except/ex8/VirtualPerson.java
class VirtualPerson {
    public void drinkCoffee(CoffeeCup cup) {
        try {
            int i = (int) (Math.random() * 4.0);
            switch (i) {
            case 0:
                throw new TooHotException();
            case 1:
                throw new TooColdException();
            case 2:
                throw new UnusualTasteException();
            default:
                System.out.println("This coffee is great!");
            }
        }
        catch (TooHotException e) {
            System.out.println("This coffee is too hot.");
        }
        catch (TooColdException e) {
            System.out.println("This coffee is too cold.");
        }
        catch (UnusualTasteException e) {
            System.out.println("This coffee is too strong.");
        }
        finally {
            System.out.println("Can I please have another cup?");
        }
    }
    // ...
}
```

If during execution of the code within a try block, an exception is thrown that is handled by a catch clause associated with the try block, the finally clause will be executed after the catch clause. For example, if a TooColdException exception is thrown during execution of the try block above, the program would print the following:

```
This coffee is too cold.
Can I please have another cup?
```

If an exception is thrown that is *not* handled by a catch clause associated with the try block, the finally clause is still executed. The Java virtual machine will execute the code of the finally clause before it continues searching elsewhere for an appropriate catch clause. There is no way to leave a try block without executing the code of its finally clause.

You can do anything inside a finally clause that you can do elsewhere, including executing break, continue, or return statements, or throwing exceptions. Such actions inside a finally clause, however, can have some surprising effects. For example, consider a finally clause that is entered because of an uncaught exception. If the finally clause executes a return, the method would complete normally via the return, not abruptly by throwing the exception. The exception would have in effect been handled by the finally clause instead of a catch clause.

As another example, consider a finally clause that is entered because a return true; statement was executed inside the try block. If the finally clause executes a return false; statement, the method will return false.

CONCLUSION

Java goes to great lengths to help you deal with error conditions. Java's exception mechanisms give you a structured way to perform a go-to from the place where an error occurs to the code that knows how to handle the error. These mechanisms also enable you to *force* client programmers (those who use your code by calling your methods) to deal with the possibility of an error condition encountered by your code. But Java's mechanisms do not force you to design your programs to take advantage of these capabilities. In the end, if you want your programs to handle error conditions in a structured, methodical way, you must use the exception mechanisms correctly.

ABOUT THE AUTHOR

Bill Venners has been writing software professionally for 12 years. Based in Silicon Valley, he provides software consulting and training services under the name Artima Software Company. Over the years he has developed software for the consumer electronics, education, semiconductor, and life insurance industries. He has programmed in many languages on many platforms: assembly language on various microprocessors, C on Unix, C++ on Windows, Java on the Web. He is author of the book: Inside the Java Virtual Machine, published by McGraw-Hill.

The Essence of OOP Using Java, Exception Handling

BY RICHARD G. BALDWIN

PREVIEW

This lesson explains Exception Handling in Java. The discussion includes the following topics:

- What is an exception?
- How do you throw and catch exceptions?
- What do you do with an exception once you have caught it?
- How do you make use of the exception class hierarchy provided by the Java development environment?

This lesson will cover many of the details having to do with exception handling in Java. By the end of the lesson, you should know that the use of exception handling is not optional in Java, and you should have a pretty good idea how to use exception handling in a beneficial way.

DISCUSSION AND SAMPLE CODE

Introduction

Stated simply, the exception-handling capability of Java makes it possible for you to:
Monitor for exceptional conditions within your program
Transfer control to special exception-handling code *(which you design)* if an exceptional condition occurs

The Basic Concept

This is accomplished using the keywords: **try**, **catch**, **throw**, **throws**, and **finally**. The basic concept is as follows:

- You **try** to execute the statements contained within a block of code. *(A block of code is a group of one or more statements surrounded by braces.)*
- If you detect an exceptional condition within that block, you **throw** an exception object of a specific type.
- You **catch** and process the exception object using code that you have designed.
- You optionally execute a block of code, designated by **finally**, which needs to be executed whether or not an exception occurs. *(Code in the **finally** block is normally used to perform some type of cleanup.)*

Exceptions in Code Written by Others

There are also situations where you don't write the code to **throw** the exception object, but an exceptional condition that occurs in code written by someone else transfers control to exception-handling code that you write.

For example, the **read** method of the **InputStream** class throws an exception of type **IOException** if an exception occurs while the **read** method is executing. In this case, you are responsible only for the code in the **catch** block and optionally for the code in the **finally** block.

> *(This is the reason that you must surround the invocation of* System.in.read() *with a* try *block followed by a* catch *block, or optionally declare that your method* throws *an exception of type* IOException.*)*

Exception Hierarchy, An Overview

When an exceptional condition causes an exception to be *thrown*, that exception is represented by an object instantiated from the class named **Throwable** or one of its subclasses.
Here is part of what Sun has to say about the **Throwable** class:

> *"The* Throwable *class is the superclass of all errors and exceptions in the Java language. Only objects that are instances of this class (or one of its subclasses) are thrown by the Java Virtual Machine or can be thrown by the Java* throw *statement. Similarly, only this class or one of its subclasses can be the argument type in a* catch *clause."*

Sun goes on to say:

> *"Instances of two subclasses,* Error *and* Exception, *are conventionally used to indicate that exceptional situations have occurred. Typically, these instances are freshly created in the context of the exceptional situation so as to include relevant information (such as stack trace data)."*

The Error and Exception Classes

The virtual machine and many different methods in many different classes throw *exceptions* and *errors*. I will have quite a lot more to say about the classes named **Error** and **Exception** later in this lesson.

Defining Your Own Exception Types

You may have concluded from the Sun quotation given above that you can define and **throw** exception objects of your own design, and if you did, that is a correct conclusion. *(Your new class must extend **Throwable** or one of its subclasses.)*

The Difference Between Error and Exception

As mentioned above, the **Throwable** class has two subclasses:

- **Error**
- **Exception**

What is an Error?

What is the difference between an **Error** and an **Exception**? Paraphrasing David Flanagan and his excellent series of books entitled Java in a Nutshell, an **Error** indicates that a non-recoverable error has occurred that should not be caught. Errors usually cause the Java virtual machine to display a message and exit.
Sun says the same thing in a slightly different way:

> *"An **Error** is a subclass of **Throwable** that indicates serious problems that a reasonable application should not try to catch. Most such errors are abnormal conditions."*

For example, one of the subclasses of **Error** is named **VirtualMachineError**. This error is *"Thrown to indicate that the Java Virtual Machine is broken or has run out of resources necessary for it to continue operating."*

What is an Exception?

Paraphrasing Flanagan again, an **Exception** indicates an abnormal condition that must be properly handled to prevent program termination.
Sun explains it this way:

> *"The class **Exception** and its subclasses are a form of **Throwable** that indicates conditions that a reasonable application might want to catch."*

As of JDK 1.4.0, there are more than fifty known subclasses of the **Exception** class. Many of these subclasses themselves have numerous subclasses, so there is quite a lot of material that you need to become familiar with.

The Runtimeexception Class

One subclass of **Exception** is the class named **RuntimeException** As of JDK 1.4.0, this class has about 30 subclasses, many which are further subclassed. The class named **RuntimeException** is a very important class.

Unchecked Exceptions

The **RuntimeException** class, and its subclasses, are important not so much for what they do, but for what they don't do. I will refer to exceptions instantiated from **RuntimeException** and its subclasses as *unchecked* exceptions.

Basically, an unchecked exception is a type of exception that you can optionally handle, or ignore. If you elect to ignore the possibility of an unchecked exception, and one occurs, your program will terminate as a result. If you elect to handle an unchecked exception and one occurs, the result will depend on the code that you have written to handle the exception.

Checked Exceptions

All exceptions instantiated from the **Exception** class, or from subclasses of **Exception** other than **RuntimeException** and its subclasses must either be

- Handled with a **try** block followed by a **catch** block, or
- Declared in a **throws** clause of any method that can throw them

In other words, checked exceptions *cannot be ignored* when you write the code in your methods. According to Flanagan, the exception classes in this category represent routine abnormal conditions that should be anticipated and caught to prevent program termination.

Checked by the Compiler

Your code must anticipate and either handle or declare checked exceptions. Otherwise, your program won't compile. *(These are exception types that are checked by the compiler.)*

Throwable Constructors and Methods

As mentioned above, all errors and exceptions are subclasses of the **Throwable** class. As of JDK 1.4.0, the **Throwable** class provides four constructors and about a dozen methods. The four constructors are shown in Figure 1.

```
Throwable()
Throwable(String message)
Throwable(String message,
       Throwable cause)
Throwable(Throwable cause)
```

Figure 1

The first two constructors have been in Java for a very long time. Basically, these two constructors allow you to construct an exception object with, or without a **String** message encapsulated in the object.

New to JDK 1.4

The last two constructors are new in JDK 1.4.0. These two constructors are provided to support the *cause facility.* The *cause facility* is new in release 1.4. It is also known as the *chained exception* facility. *(I won't cover this facility in this lesson. Rather, I plan to cover it in a series of lessons that I am developing having to do with the myriad of new features in JDK 1.4.)*

Methods of the Throwable Class

Figure 2 shows some of the methods of the **Throwable** class. *(I omitted some of the methods introduced in JDK 1.4 for the reasons given above.)*

```
fillInStackTrace()
getStackTrace()
printStackTrace().
setStackTrace(StackTraceElement[]
                 stackTrace)
getLocalizedMessage()
getMessage()
toString()
```

Figure 2

The StackTrace

The first four methods in Figure 2 deal with the *StackTrace*. In case you are unfamiliar with the term *StackTrace,* this is a list of the methods executed in sequence that led to the exception. *(This is what you typically see on the screen when your program aborts with a runtime error that hasn't been handled.)*

Messages

The two methods dealing with messages provide access to a **String** message that may be encapsulated in the exception object. The **getMessage** class simply returns the message that was encapsulated when the object was instantiated. *(If no message was encapsulated, this method returns null.)*

The **getLocalizedMessage** method is a little more complicated to use. According to Sun, *"Subclasses may override this method in order to produce a locale-specific message."*

The toString Method

The **toString** method is inherited from the **Object** class and overridden in the exception subclass to *"return a short description of the* ***Throwable****"*.

Inherited Methods

All exception objects inherit the methods of the **Throwable** class, which are listed in Figure 2. Thus, any of these methods may be invoked by the code in the **catch** block in its attempt to successfully handle the exception.

For example, exceptions may have a message encapsulated in the exception object, which can be accessed using the **getMessage** method. You can use this to display a message describing the error or exception.

You can also use other methods of the **Throwable** class to:

- Display a stack trace showing where the exception or error occurred
- Produce a **String** representation of the exception object

So, What is an Exception?

According to the online book entitled The Java Tutorial by Campione and Walrath:

> *"The term exception is shorthand for the phrase 'exceptional event'.. It can be defined as follows: Definition: An exception is an event that occurs during the execution of a program that disrupts the normal flow of instructions."*

When an exceptional condition occurs within a method, the method may instantiate an exception object and hand it off to the runtime system to deal with it. This is accomplished using the **throw** keyword. *(This is called throwing an exception.)*

To be useful, the exception object should probably contain information about the exception, including its type and the state of the program when the exception occurred.

Handling the Exception

At that point, the runtime system becomes responsible for finding a block of code designed to handle the exception.

The runtime system begins its search with the method in which the exception occurred and searches backwards through the call stack until it finds a method that contains an *appropriate* exception handler *(catch block).*

An exception handler is *appropriate* if the type of the exception thrown is the same as the type of exception handled by the handler, or is a subclass of the type of exception handled by the handler.

Thus, the requirement to handle an exception that has been thrown progresses up through the call stack until an appropriate handler is found to handle the exception. If no appropriate handler is found, the runtime system and the program terminate.

> *((If you have ever had a program terminate with a* ***NullPointerExceptio****n, then you know how program termination works.).*

According to the jargon, the exception handler that is chosen is said to *catch the exception.*

Advantages of Using Exception Handling

According to Campione and Walrath, exception handling provides the following advantages over "traditional" error management techniques:

- Separating Error Handling Code from "Regular" Code
- Propagating Errors Up the Call Stack
- Grouping Error Types and Error Differentiation

Separating Error Handling Code from Regular Code

I don't plan to discuss these advantages in detail. Rather, I will simply refer you to The Java Tutorial and other good books where you can read their discussions. However, I will comment briefly.

Campione and Walrath provide a good illustration where they show how a simple program having about six lines of code get "bloated" into about 29 lines of very confusing code through the use of traditional error management techniques. Not only does the program suffer bloat, the logical flow of the original program gets lost in the clutter of the modified program.

They then show how to accomplish the same error management using exception handling. Although the version with exception handling contains about seventeen lines of code, it is orderly and easy to understand. The additional lines of code do not cause the original logic of the program to get lost.

You Must Still do the Hard Work

However, the use of exception handling does not spare you from the hard work of detecting, reporting, and handling errors. What it does is provide a means to separate the details of what to do when something out of the ordinary happens from the normal logical flow of the program code.

Propagating Exceptions Up the Call Stack

Sometimes it is desirable to propagate exception handling up the call stack and let the corrective action be taken at a higher level.

For example, you might provide a class with methods that implement a *stack*. One of the methods of your class might be to *pop* an element off the stack.

What should your program do if a using program attempts to pop an element off an empty stack? That decision might best be left to the user of your stack class, and you might simply propagate the notification up to the calling method and let that method take the corrective action.

Grouping Exception Types

When an exception is thrown, an object of one of the exception classes is passed as a parameter. Objects are instances of classes, and classes fall into an inheritance hierarchy in Java. Therefore, a natural hierarchy can be created, which causes exceptions to be grouped in logical ways.

For example, going back to the stack example, you might create an exception class that applies to all exceptional conditions associated with an object of your stack class. Then you might extend that class into other classes that pertain to specific exceptional conditions, such as *push* exceptions, *pop* exceptions, and *initialization* exceptions.

When your code throws an exception object of a specific type, that object can be caught by an exception handler designed either to:

- Catch on the basis of a group of exceptions, or
- Catch on the basis of a subgroup of that group, or
- Catch on the basis of one of the specialized exceptions.

In other words, an exception handler can catch exceptions of the class specified by the type of its parameter, or can catch exceptions of any subclass of the class specified by the type of its parameter.

More Detailed Information on Exception Handling

As explained earlier, except for **Throwable** objects of type **Error** and for **Throwable.Exception** objects of type **RuntimeException**, Java programs must either *handle* or *declare* all **Exception** objects that are thrown. Otherwise, the compiler will refuse to compile the program.

In other words, all exceptions other than those specified above are *checked* by the compiler, and the compiler will refuse to compile the program if the exceptions aren't handled or declared. As a result, exceptions other than those specified above are often referred to as *checked* exceptions.

Catching an Exception

Just to make certain that we are using the same terminology, a method *catches* an exception by providing an exception handler whose parameter type is appropriate for that type of exception object. *(I will more or less use the terms **catch** block and exception handler interchangeably.)*

The type of the parameter in the **catch** block must be the class from which the exception was instantiated, or a superclass of that class that resides somewhere between that class and the **Throwable** class in the inheritance hierarchy.

Declaring an Exception

If the code in a method can throw a checked exception, and the method does not provide an exception handler for the type of exception object thrown, the method must *declare* that it can throw that exception. The **throws** keyword is used in the method declaration to declare that it **throws** an exception of a particular type.

Any checked exception that can be thrown by a method is part of the method's programming interface *(see the* read *method of the InputStream class, which throws* IOException, *for example).* Users of a method must know about the exceptions that a method can throw in order to be able to handle them. Thus, you must declare the exceptions that the method can throw in the method signature.

Checked Exceptions

Checked exceptions are all exception objects instantiated from subclasses of the **Exception** class other than those of the **RuntimeException** class.

Exceptions of all **Exception** subclasses other than **RuntimeException** are checked by the compiler and will result in compiler errors if they are neither *caught* nor *declared.*

You will learn how you can create your own exception classes later. Whether your exception objects become checked or not depends on the class that you extend when you define your exception class.

(If you extend a checked exception class, your new exception type will be a checked exception. Otherwise, it will not be a checked exception.)

Exceptions that Can Be Thrown within the Scope of a Method

The exceptions that can be thrown within the scope of a method include not only exceptions which are thrown by code written into the method, but also includes exceptions thrown by methods called by that method, or methods called by those methods, etc..

According to Campione and Walrath,

> *"This ... includes any exception that can be thrown while the flow of control remains within the method. Thus, this ... includes both exceptions that are thrown directly by the method with Java's throw statement, and exceptions that are thrown indirectly by the method through calls to other methods."*

Sample Programs

Now it's time to take a look at some sample code designed to deal with exceptions of the types delivered with the JDK. Initially I won't include exception classes that are designed for custom purposes. However, I will deal with exceptions of those types later in the lesson.

The first three sample programs will illustrate the successive stages of dealing with checked exceptions by either catching or declaring those exceptions.

Sample Program with No Exception Handling Code

The first sample program shown in Listing 1 neither catches nor declares the **InterruptedException** which can be thrown by the **sleep** method of the **Thread** classA possible InterruptedException

```
/*File Excep11.java
Copyright 2002, R.G.Baldwin
Tested using JDK 1.4.0 under Win2000
**************************************/
import java.lang.Thread;

class Excep11{
  public static void main(
                    String[] args){
    Excep11 obj = new Excep11();
    obj.myMethod();
  }//end main
  //--------------------------------//

  void myMethod(){
    Thread.currentThread().sleep(1000);
  }//end myMethod
}//end class Excep11
```

Listing 1

A Possible Interruptedexception

The code in the **main** method of Listing 1 invokes the method named **myMethod**. The method named **myMethod** invokes the method named **sleep** of the **Thread** class. The method named **sleep** declares that it throws **InterruptedException**.

InterruptedException is a checked exception. The program illustrates the failure to either catch or declare **InterruptedException** in the method named **myMethod**.

As a result, this program won't compile. The compiler error is similar to that shown in Figure 3. Note the caret in the last line that points to the point where the compiler detected the problem.

```
unreported exception
java.lang.InterruptedException;
must be caught or declared to be thrown
   Thread.currentThread().sleep(1000);
                  ^
```

Figure 3

As you can see, the compiler detected a problem where the **sleep** method was called, because the method named **myMethod** failed to deal properly with an exception that can be thrown by the **sleep** method.

Sample Program that Fixes One Compiler Error

The next version of the program, shown in Listing 2, fixes the problem identified with the call to the **sleep** method, by declaring the exception in the signature for the method named **myMethod**. The declaration of the exception of type **InterruptedException** is highlighted in boldface in Listing 2

```
/*File Excep12.java
Copyright 2002, R.G.Baldwin
Tested using JDK 1.4.0 under Win2000
**************************************/
import java.lang.Thread;

class Excep12{
  public static void main(
                    String[] args){
    Excep12 obj = new Excep12();
    obj.myMethod();
  }//end main
  //-------------------------------//

  void myMethod()
          throws InterruptedException{
    Thread.currentThread().sleep(1000);
  }//end myMethod
}//end class Excep12
```

Listing 2

Another Possible Interruptedexception

As was the case in the previous program, this program also illustrates a failure to catch or declare an **InterruptedException**. However, in this case, the problem has moved up one level in the call stack relative to the problem with the program in Listing 1.

This program also fails to compile, producing a compiler error similar to that shown in Figure 4. Note that the caret indicates that the problem is associated with the call to **myMethod**.

```
unreported exception
java.lang.InterruptedException;
must be caught or declared to be thrown
    obj.myMethod();
       ^
```

Figure 4

Didn't Solve the Problem

Simply declaring a checked exception doesn't solve the problem. Ultimately, the exception must be handled if the compiler problem is to be solved.

*(Note, however, that it is possible to declare that the **main** method throws a checked exception, which will cause the compiler to ignore it and allow your program to compile.)*

The program in Listing 2 eliminated the compiler error identified with the call to the method named **sleep**. This was accomplished by declaring that the method named **myMethod** *throws InterruptedException*. However, this simply passed the exception up the call stack to the next higher-level method in the stack. This didn't solve the problem, it simply handed it off to another method to solve.

The problem still exists, and is now identified with the call to **myMethod** where it will have to be handled in order to make the compiler error go away.

Sample Program that Fixes the Remaining Compiler Error

The version of the program shown in Listing 3 fixes the remaining compiler error. This program illustrates both declaring and handling a checked exception. This program compiles and runs successfully.

```
/*File Excep13.java
Copyright 2002, R.G.Baldwin

Tested using JDK 1.4.0 under Win2000
**************************************/
import java.lang.Thread;

class Excep13{
  public static void main(
                 String[] args){
    Excep13 obj = new Excep13();
    try{//begin try block
      obj.myMethod();
    }catch(InterruptedException e){
      System.out.println(
            "Handle exception here");
    }//end catch block
  }//end main
  //-------------------------------//

  void myMethod()
        throws InterruptedException{
    Thread.currentThread().sleep(1000);
  }//end myMethod
}//end class Excep13
```

Listing 3

The Solution to the Problem

This solution to the problem is accomplished by surrounding the call to **myMethod** with a **try** block, which is followed immediately by an *appropriate* **catch** block. In this case, an appropriate **catch** block is one whose parameter type is either **InterruptedException**, or a superclass of **InterruptedException**.

(Note, however, that the superclass cannot be higher than the ***Throwable*** *class in the inheritance hierarchy.)*

The myMethod Method Declares the Exception

As in the previous version, the method named **myMethod** declares the exception and passes it up the call stack to the method from which it was called.

The Main Method Handles the Exception

In the new version shown in Listing 3, the **main** method provides a **try** block with an *appropriate* **catch** block for dealing with the problem *(although it doesn't actually deal with it in any significant way).* This can be interpreted as follows:

- Try to execute the code within the **try** block.
- If an exception occurs, search for a **catch** block that matches the type of object thrown by the exception.
- If such a **catch** block can be found, immediately transfer control to the catch block without executing any of the remaining code in the **try** block. *(For simplicity, this program didn't have any remaining code. Some later sample programs will illustrate code being skipped due to the occurrence of an exception.)*

Not a Method Call

Note that this transfer of control is not a method call. It is an unconditional transfer of control. There is no *return* from a catch block.

Matching Catch Block was Found

In this case, there was a matching **catch** block to receive control. In the event that an **InterruptedException** is thrown, the program would execute the statement within the body of the **catch** block, and then transfer control to the code following the final **catch** block in the group of **catch** blocks *(in this case, there was only one* ***catch*** *block).*

No Output is Produced

It is unlikely that you will see any output when you run this program, because it is unlikely that an **InterruptedException** will be thrown. *(I didn't provide any code that will cause such an exception to occur.)*

A Sample Program that Throws an Exception

Now let's look at the sample program in Listing 4, which throws an exception and deals with it. This program illustrates the implementation of exception handling using the try/catch block structure.

```
/*File Excep14.java
Copyright 2002, R. G. Baldwin

Tested with JDK 1.4.0 under Win2000
**************************************/

class Excep14{
  public static void main(
                  String[] args){
    try{
      for(int cnt = 2; cnt >-1; cnt--){
        System.out.println(
             "Running. Quotient is: "
                        + 6/cnt);
      }//end for-loop
    }//end try block
    catch(ArithmeticException e){
      System.out.println(
            "Exception message is:  "
            + e.getMessage()
            + "\nStacktrace shows:");
      e.printStackTrace();
      System.out.println(
        "String representation is\n " +
                  e.toString());
      System.out.println(
         "Put corrective action here");
    }//end catch block
    System.out.println(
              "Out of catch block");
  }//end main

}//end class Excep14
```

Listing 4

Keeping it Simple

I try to keep my sample programs as simple as possible, introducing the minimum amount of complexity necessary to illustrate the main point of the program. It is easy to write a *really simple* program that throws an unchecked **ArithmeticException**. Therefore, the program in Listing 4 was written to throw an **ArithmeticException**. This was accomplished by trying to perform an integer divide by zero.

The Try/Catch Structure is the Same ...

It is important to note that the *try/catch* structure illustrated in Listing 4 would be the same whether the exception is checked or unchecked. The main difference is that you are not required by the compiler to handle unchecked exceptions and you are required by the compiler to either handle or declare checked exceptions.

Throwing an ArithmeticException

The code in Listing 4 executes a simple counting loop inside a **try** block. During each iteration, the counting loop divides the integer 6 by the value of the counter. When the value of the counter goes to zero, the runtime system tries to perform an integer divide by zero operation, which causes it to throw an **ArithmeticException**.

Transfer Control Immediately

At that point, control is transferred directly to the **catch** block that follows the **try** block. This is an *appropriate* **catch** block because the type of parameter declared for the **catch** block is **ArithmeticException**. It matches the type of the object that is thrown.

> *(It would also be appropriate if the declared type of the parameter were a superclass of* ***ArithmeticException****, up to and including the class named* ***Throwable****.* ***Throwable*** *is a direct subclass of* ***Object****. If you were to declare the parameter type for the* ***catch*** *block as* ***Object****, the compiler would produce an incompatible type error.)*

Invoking Methods Inside the Catch Block

Once control enters the **catch** block, three of the methods of the **Throwable** class are invoked to cause information about the situation to be displayed on the screen. The output produced by the program is similar to that shown in Figure 5.

```
Running. Quotient is: 3
Running. Quotient is: 6
Exception message is:  / by zero
Stacktrace shows:
java.lang.ArithmeticException:
 / by zero
  at Excep14.main(Excep14.java:35)
String representation is
 java.lang.ArithmeticException:
 / by zero
Put corrective action here
Out of catch block
```

Figure 5

Key Things to Note

The key things to note about the program in Listing 5 are

- The code to be protected is contained in a **try** block.
- The **try** block is followed immediately by an appropriate **catch** block.
- When an exception is thrown within the **try** block, control is transferred immediately to the **catch** block with the matching or appropriate parameter type.
- Although the code in the **catch** block simply displays the current state of the program, it could contain code that attempts to rectify the problem.
- Once the code in the **catch** block finishes executing, control is passed to the next executable statement following the **catch** block, which in this program is a print statement.

Doesn't Attempt to Rectify the Problem

This program doesn't attempt to show how an actual program might recover from an exception of this sort. However, it is clear that *(rather than experiencing automatic and unconditional termination)* the program remains in control, and in some cases, recovery might be possible.

This sample program illustrates **try** and **catch**. The use of **finally**, will be discussed and illustrated later.

A Nuisance Problem Explained

While we are at it, I would be remiss in failing to mention a nuisance problem associated with exception handling.

As you may recall, the scope of a variable in Java is limited to the block of code in which it is declared. A block is determined by enclosing code within a pair of matching braces: { ...}.

Since a pair of braces is required to define a **try** block, the scope of any variables or objects declared inside the **try** block is limited to the **try** block.

While this is not an insurmountable problem, it may require you to modify your programming style in ways that you find distasteful. In particular, if you need to access a variable both within and outside the **try** block, you must declare it before entering the **try** block.

The Process in More Detail

Now that you have seen some sample programs to help you visualize the process, let's discuss the process in more detail.

The Try Block

According to Campione and Walrath,

> *"The first step in writing any exception handler is putting the Java statements within which an exception can occur into a try block. The try block is said to govern the statements enclosed within it and defines the scope of any exception handlers (established by subsequent catch blocks) associated with it."*

Note that the terminology being used by Campione and Walrath treats the **catch block** as the *"exception handler"* and treats the **try** block as something that precedes one or more exception handlers. I don't disagree with their terminology. I mention it only for the purpose of avoiding confusion over terminology.

The Syntax of a Try Block

The general syntax of a **try** block, as you saw in the previous program, has the keyword **try** followed by one or more statements enclosed in a pair of matching braces, as shown in Figure 6.

```
try{
  //java statements
}//end try block
```

Figure 6

Single Statement and Multiple Exceptions

You may have more than one statement that can throw one or more exceptions and you will need to deal with all of them.

You could put each such statement that might throw exceptions within its own **try** block and provide separate exception handlers for each **try** block.

> *(Note that some statements, particularly those that invoke other methods, could potentially throw many different types of exceptions.)*

Thus a **try** block consisting of a single statement might require many different exception handlers or **catch** blocks following it.

Multiple Statements and Multiple Exceptions

You could put all or several of the statements that might throw exceptions within a single **try** block and associate multiple exception handlers with it. There are a number of practical issues involved here, and only you can decide in any particular instance which approach would be best.

The Catch Blocks Must Follow the Try Block

However you decide to do it, the exception handlers associated with a **try** block must be placed immediately following their associated *try* block. If an exception occurs within the **try** block, that exception is handled by the appropriate exception handler associated with the **try** block. If there is no appropriate exception handler associated with the **try** block, the system attempts to find an appropriate exception handler in the next method up the call stack.

A **try** block must be accompanied by at least one **catch** block *(or one **finally** block).* Otherwise, a compiler error that reads something like *'try' without 'catch' or 'finally'* will occur.

The Catch Block(s)

Continuing with what Campione and Walrath have to say:

> *"Next, you associate exception handlers with a try block by providing one or more catch blocks directly after the try block."*

There can be no intervening code between the end of the **try** block and the beginning of the first **catch** block, and no intervening code between **catch** blocks.

Syntax of a Catch Block

The general form of a **catch** block is shown in Figure 7.

```
catch(ThrowableObjectType paramName){
  //Java statements to handle the
  // exception
}//end catch block
```

Figure 7

The declaration for the **catch** block requires a single argument as shown. The syntax for the argument declaration is the same as an argument declaration for a method.

Argument Type Specifies Type of Matching Exception Object

The argument type declares the type of exception object that a particular **catch** block can handle. The type must be **Throwable**, or a subclass of the **Throwable** class discussed earlier.

A Parameter Provides the Local Name

Also, as in a method declaration, there is a parameter, which is the name by which the handler can refer to the exception object. For example, in an earlier program, I used statements such as **e.getMessage()**to access an instance method of an exception object caught by the exception handler. In that case, the name of the parameter was **e**.

You access the instance variables and methods of exception objects the same way that you access the instance variables and methods of other objects.

Proper Order of Catch Blocks

According to Campione and Walrath:

> *"The catch block contains a series of legal Java statements. These statements are executed if and when the exception handler is invoked. The runtime system invokes the exception handler when the handler is the first one in the call stack whose type matches that of the exception thrown."*

Therefore, the order of your exception handlers is very important, particularly if you have some handlers, which are further up the exception hierarchy than others.

Those handlers that are designed to handle exception types furthermost from the root of the hierarchy tree *(**Throwable**)* should be placed first in the list of exception handlers.

Otherwise, an exception handler designed to handle a specific type of object may be preempted by another handler whose exception type is a superclass of that type, if the superclass exception handler appears earlier in the list of exception handlers.

Catching Multiple Exception Types with one Handler

Exception handlers that you write may be more or less specialized. In addition to writing handlers for very specialized exception objects, the Java language allows you to write general exception handlers that handle multiple types of exceptions.

Java exceptions are **Throwable** objects *(instances of the **Throwable** class or a subclass of the **Throwable** class).*

The Java standard library contains numerous classes that are subclasses of **Throwable** and thus build a hierarchy of **Throwable** classes.

According to Campione and Walrath:

> *"Your exception handler can be written to handle any class that inherits from **Throwable**. If you write a handler for a "leaf" class (a class with no subclasses), you've written a specialized handler: it will only handle exceptions of that specific type. If you write a handler for a "node" class (a class with subclasses), you've written a general handler: it will handle any exception whose type is the node class or any of its subclasses."*

You Have a Choice

Therefore, when writing exception handlers, you have a choice. You can write a handler whose exception type corresponds to a node in the inheritance hierarchy, and it will be appropriate to **catch** exceptions of that type, or any subclass of that type.

Alternately, you can write a handler whose exception type corresponds to a *leaf,* in which case, it will be appropriate to **catch** exceptions of that type only.

And finally, you can mix and match, writing some exception handlers whose type corresponds to a node, and other exception handlers whose type corresponds to a leaf. In all cases, however, be sure to position your exception handlers in reverse subclass order, with the furthermost subclass from the root appearing first, and the root class appearing last.

The Finally Block

And finally *(no pun intended),* Campione and Walrath tell us:

> *"Java's finally block provides a mechanism that allows your method to clean up after itself regardless of what happens within the try block. Use the finally block to close files or release other system resources."*

To elaborate, the **finally** block can be used to provide a mechanism for cleaning up open files, etc.., before allowing control to be passed to a different part of the program. You accomplish this by writing the cleanup code within a **finally** block.

Code in Finally Block is Always Executed

It is important to remember that the runtime system always executes the code within the **finally** block regardless of what happens within the **try** block.

If no exceptions are thrown, none of the code in **catch** blocks is executed, but the code in the **finally** block is executed.

If an exception is thrown and the code in an exception handler is executed, once the execution of that code is complete, control is passed to the **finally** block and the code in the **finally** block is executed.

*(There is one important exception to the above. If the code in the **catch** block terminates the program by executing **System.exit(0)**, the code in the **finally** block will not be executed.)*

The Power of the Finally Block

The sample program shown in Listing 5 illustrates the power of the **finally** block.

```
/*File Excep15.java
Copyright 2002, R. G. Baldwin

Tested with JDK 1.4.0 under Win2000
**************************************/

class Excep15{
  public static void main(
                    String[] args){
    new Excep15().aMethod();
  }//end main
  //--------------------------------//

  void aMethod(){
    try{
      int x = 5/0;
    }//end try block
    catch(ArithmeticException e){
      System.out.println(
      "In catch, terminating aMethod");
      return;
    }//end catch block

    finally{
      System.out.println(
          "Executing finally block");
    }//end finally block

    System.out.println(
             "Out of catch block");
  }//end aMethod

}//end class Excep15
```

Listing 5

Execute Return Statement in Catch Block

The code in Listing 5 forces an **ArithmeticException** by attempting to do an integer divide by zero. Control is immediately transferred to the matching **catch** block, which prints a message and then executes a **return** statement.

Normally, execution of a **return** statement terminates the method immediately. In this case, however, before the method terminates and returns control to the calling method, the code in the **finally** block is executed. Then control is transferred to the **main** method, which called this method in the first place.

Figure 8 shows the output produced by this program.

```
In catch, terminating aMethod
Executing finally block
```

Figure 8

This program demonstrates that the **finally** block really does have the final word.

Declaring Exceptions Thrown by a Method

Sometimes it is better to handle exceptions in the method in which they are detected, and sometimes it is better to pass them up the call stack and let another method handle them.

In order to pass exceptions up the call stack, you must *declare* them in your method signature.

To *declare* that a method throws one or more exceptions, you add a **throws** clause to the method signature for the method. The **throws** clause is composed of the **throws** keyword followed by a comma-separated list of all the exceptions thrown by that method.

The **throws** clause goes after the method name and argument list and before the curly bracket that defines the scope of the method.

Figure 9 shows the syntax for declaring that a method **throws** four different types of exceptions.

```
void myMethod() throws
       InterruptedException,
       MyException,
       HerException,
       UrException
{
  //method code
}//end myMethod()
```

Figure 9

Assuming that these are checked exceptions, any method calling this method would be required to either handle these exception types, or continue passing them up the call stack. Eventually, some method must handle them or the program won't compile.

*(Note however that while it might not represent good programming practice, it is allowable to declare that the **main** method **throws** exceptions. This is a way to avoid handling checked exceptions and still get your program to compile.)*

The Throw Keyword

Before your code can **catch** an exception, some Java code must **throw** one. The exception can be thrown by code that you write, or by code that you are using that was written by someone else.

Regardless of who wrote the code that throws the exception, it's always thrown with the Java **throw** keyword. At least that is true for exceptions that are thrown by code written in the Java language.

*(Exceptions such as **ArithmeticException** are also thrown by the runtime system, which is probably not written using Java source code.)*

A Single Argument is Required

When formed into a statement, the **throw** keyword requires a single argument, which must be a reference to an object instantiated from the **Throwable** class, or any subclass of the **Throwable** class. Figure 10 shows an example of such a statement.

```
throw new myThrowableClass("Message");
```

Figure 10

If you attempt to throw an object that is not instantiated from **Throwable** or one of its subclasses, the compiler will refuse to compile your program.

Defining Your Own Exception Classes

Now you know how to write exception handlers for those exception objects that are thrown by the runtime system, and thrown by methods in the standard class library.

It is also possible for you to define your own exception classes, and to cause objects of those classes to be thrown whenever an exception occurs. In this case, you get to decide just what constitutes an exceptional condition.

For example, you could write a data-processing application that processes integer data obtained via a TCP/IP link from another computer. If the specification for the program indicates that the integer value 10 should never be received, you could use an occurrence of the integer value 10 to cause an exception object of your own design to be thrown.

Choosing the Exception Type to Throw

Before throwing an exception, you must decide on its type. Basically, you have two choices in this regard:

- Use an exception class written by someone else, such as the myriad of exception classes defined in the Java standard library.
- Define an exception class of your own.

An Important Question

So, an important question is, when should you define your own exception classes and when should you use classes that are already available. Because this is only one of many design issues, I'm not going to try to give you a ready answer to the question. However, I will refer you to The Java Tutorial by Campione and Walrath where you will find a checklist to help you make this decision.

Choosing a Superclass to Extend

If you decide to define your own exception class, it must be a subclass of **Throwable**. You must decide which class you will extend.

The two existing subclasses of **Throwable** are **Exception** and **Error**. Given the earlier description of **Error** and its subclasses, it is not likely that your exceptions would fit the **Error** category. *(In concept, errors are reserved for serious hard errors that occur deep within the system.)*

Checked or Unchecked Exception

Therefore, your new class should probably be a subclass of **Exception**. If you make it a subclass of **RuntimeException**, it won't be a checked exception. If you make it a subclass of **Exception**, but not a subclass of **RuntimeException**, it will be a checked exception.

Only you can decide how far down the **Exception** hierarchy you want to go before creating a new branch of exception classes that are unique to your application.

Naming Conventions

Many Java programmers append the word **Exception** to the end of all class names that are subclasses of **Exception**, and append the word **Error** to the end of all class names that are subclasses of **Error**.

One More Sample Program

Let's wrap up this lesson with one more sample program named **Excep16**. We will define our own exception class in this program. Then we will **throw**, **catch and** process an exception object instantiated from that class.

Discuss in Fragments

This program is a little longer than the previous programs, so I will break it down and discuss it in fragments. A complete listing of the program is shown in Listing 10.

The class definition shown in Listing 6 is used to construct a custom exception object that encapsulates a message. Note that this class extends **Exception**. *(Therefore, it is a checked exception.)*

```
class MyException extends Exception{
  MyException(String message){//constr
    super(message);
  }//end constructor
}//end MyException class
```

Listing 6

The constructor for this class receives an incoming **String** message parameter and passes it to the constructor for the superclass. This makes the message available for access by the **getMessage** method invoked in the catch block.

The Try Block

Listing 7 shows the beginning of the **main** method, including the entire **try** block

```
class Excep16{//controlling class
  public static void main(
                    String[] args){
    try{
      for(int cnt = 0; cnt < 5; cnt++){
        //Throw a custom exception, and
        // pass  message when cnt == 3
        if(cnt == 3) throw
                new MyException("3");
        //Transfer control before
        // processing for cnt == 3
        System.out.println(
          "Processing data for cnt = "
                          + cnt);
      }//end for-loop
    }//end try block
```

Listing 7

The **main** method executes a **for** loop *(inside the **try** block)* that guarantees that the variable named **cnt** will reach a value of 3 after a couple of iterations.

Once during each iteration, *(until the value of **cnt** reaches 3)* a print statement inside the **for** loop displays the value of **cnt**. This results in the output shown in Figure 11.

```
Processing data for cnt = 0
Processing data for cnt = 1
Processing data for cnt = 2
```

Figure 11

What Happens When cnt Equals 3?

However, when the value of **cnt** equals 3, the **throw** statement highlighted in boldface in Listing 7 is executed. This causes control to transfer immediately to the matching **catch** block following the **try** block *(see Listing 8)*. During this iteration, the print statement following the **throw** statement is not executed. Therefore, the output never shows a value for **cnt** greater than 2, as shown in Figure 11.

The Catch Block

Listing 8 shows a **catch** block whose type matches the type of exception thrown in Listing 7.

```
  catch(MyException e){
    System.out.println(
          "In exception handler, "
             + "get the message\n"
               + e.getMessage());
  }//end catch block
```

Listing 8

When the **throw** statement is executed in Listing 7, control is transferred immediately to the **catch** block in Listing 8. No further code is executed within the **try** block.

A reference to the object instantiated as the argument to the **throw** keyword in Listing 7 is passed as a parameter to the **catch** block. That reference is known locally by the name **e** inside the **catch** block.

Using the Incoming Parameter

The code in the **catch** block invokes the method named **getMessage** *(inherited from the **Throwable** class)* on the incoming parameter and displays that message on the screen. This produces the output shown in Figure 12.

```
In exception handler, get the message
3
```

Figure 12

When the Catch Block Finishes Execution ...

When the code in the **catch** block has completed execution, control is transferred to the first executable statement following the **catch** block as shown in Listing 9.

```
    System.out.println(
      "Out of catch block");
  }//end main
}//end class Excep16
```

Listing 9

That executable statement is a print statement that produces the output shown in Figure 13.

```
Out of catch block
```

Figure 13

A complete listing of the program is shown in Listing 10.

```
/*File Excep16.java
Copyright 2002, R. G. Baldwin
Illustrates defining, throwing,
catching, and processing a custom
exception object that contains a
message.

Tested using JDK 1.4.0 under Win 2000

The output is:

Processing data for cnt = 0

Processing data for cnt = 1
Processing data for cnt = 2
In exception handler, get the message
3
Out of catch block
**************************************/

//The following class is used to
// construct a customized exception
// object containing a message
class MyException extends Exception{
  MyException(String message){//constr
    super(message);
  }//end constructor
}//end MyException class
//===================================//
class Excep16{//controlling class
  public static void main(
                    String[] args){
    try{
      for(int cnt = 0; cnt < 5; cnt++){
       //Throw a custom exception, and
        // pass  message when cnt == 3
        if(cnt == 3) throw
              new MyException("3");
        //Transfer control before
        // processing for cnt == 3
```

```
    System.out.println(
      "Processing data for cnt = "
                    + cnt);
  }//end for-loop
 }//end try block
 catch(MyException e){
  System.out.println(
       "In exception handler, "
         + "get the message\n"
          + e.getMessage());
 }//end catch block
 //-------------------------------//

 System.out.println(
  "Out of catch block");
}//end main
```

Listing 10

SUMMARY

This lesson has covered many of the details having to do with exception handling in Java. By now, you should know that the use of exception handling is not optional in Java, and you should have a pretty good idea how to use exception handling in a beneficial way.

Along the way, the discussion has included the following topics:

- What is an exception?
- How do you throw and catch exceptions?
- What do you do with an exception once you have caught it?
- How do you make use of the exception class hierarchy provided by the Java development environment?

WHAT'S NEXT?

For the time being, that completes the miniseries entitled *"The Essence of OOP using Java."* I may decide to come back later and add some lessons on inner classes and other similar topics, but it will probably be a while before I get around to that. In the meantime, I sincerely hope that you have enjoyed this miniseries, and have found the lessons useful in your continuing effort to learn and understand OOP as implemented using Java.

ABOUT THE AUTHOR

Richard Baldwin *is a college professor (at Austin Community College in Austin, Texas) and private consultant whose primary focus is a combination of Java, C#, and XML. In addition to the many platform and/or language independent benefits of Java and C# applications, he believes that a combination of Java, C#, and XML will become the primary driving force in the delivery of structured information on the Web.*

Richard has participated in numerous consulting projects, and he frequently provides onsite training at the high-tech companies located in and around Austin, Texas. He is the author of Baldwin's Programming Tutorials, *which has gained a worldwide following among experienced and aspiring programmers. He has also published articles in JavaPro magazine.*

Richard holds an MSEE degree from Southern Methodist University and has many years of experience in the application of computer technology to real-world problems.

Part VI:
Data Structure and Algorithms

Part VI: Data Structures and Algorithms

INTRODUCTION

The concept, data structure is a particular way of storing, organizing and manipulating data in a computer. The end result is more efficient programming and efficient use of the hardware components such as memory and external storage.

Data structures are used in almost every program or software system. There are different kinds of data structures that are suited to different kinds of applications. There are those that are described as general purpose data structures, and those that are highly specialized to specific tasks. Two of those most frequently use general purpose data structures are:

Array – a fixed size structure that stores data a contiguously in memory. All the data elements must be of the same data type. That is, either primitive types or reference types.

ArrayList – variable size array. In Java, all the data that are to be stored must be strictly objects.

Some highly specialized ones are:

Stack – used by compilers in evaluating expressions such as matching of parentheses that may be found in arithmetic expressions.

Queues – used by operating to sequence jobs such as files that are waiting on the printer to be printed.

Linked List - used to organize data in specific way in memory. Items can easily be added to the end, or beginning, or even the middle. Similarly, data can be removed just as easily.

B-trees - are particularly well-suited for implementation of databases.

Hash tables – used in compilers to look up identifiers.

This section focuses on the following types of data structures: arrays, the class ArrayList, the class Stack, queue, and linked list.

Just as we have data structure, we also have algorithms – the step by step process to getting something done. Every computer program uses algorithm to solve problems. There are different kinds of algorithms for different kinds of problem, and different kinds of data structures. This section focuses on two kinds of algorithms that deal data structure – searching and sorting.

There are some basic but frequently used algorithms for manipulating data stored in an array. These algorithms are so important that some programming languages including Java make them a standard part of their definition. On the other hand, from a pedagogical point of view they are so important that every scholar studying computer science should understand them from first principle and be able to code them in exercises. The ranges of applications are:

Print array values in reverse order of how they were stored.
Sum the values in a numeric array
Find the average of the values
List all of the reading above or below the average.
Find the standard deviation of a set of values.
Find the highest or the lowest value in a set of stored values
Search the array for a specific value.
Sort the values in ascending or descending order.

The concept of searching and sorting play vitals a role from the early inception of computer science. A high percentage of computer time is spent on these two activities. These concepts are so important that although a large collection has been developed over the years, they are still being critiqued and researched continually.

Arrays

INTRODUCTION

OBJECTIVES

After reading this article you will:

- Understand what arrays are
- Know the reasons for using arrays
- Understand how to declare, create, and manipulate arrays
- Learn to use arrays of objects
- Learn to use multi-dimensional arrays

TERMINOLOGIES

Array • Instantiating arrays • Initializing arrays • Multi-dimensional array

Arrays vs. the class ArrayList

BY JOSLYN A. SMITH

OBJECTIVES

- To be able to define what arrays are.
- To understand the purpose of using arrays.
- To be able to create one-dimensional and two-dimensional arrays.
- To be able manipulate one-dimensional and two-dimensional numeric arrays.
- To become familiar with arrays of objects including strings.
- To become familiar with the class called ArrayList.
- To know the advantage of using ArrayList over Arrays.

ARRAYS

An array is a data structure that stores homogeneous values in memory. Each element, as the data is called, is placed contiguously to the next. Arrays are useful because you store data as a collection, and use just one variable name to refer to them, instead of having to store data with common attributes using different variables names. This is quite convenient, especially if there is a lot of data. Individual variables make the program cumbersome. In addition, it is more efficient for a program to access and process the data in an array, than it would, using many separate variable names.

Arrays are objects in Java. They are created just like any other object. They can be used to store primitive data values as well as reference type objects. In the case of primitive types, all elements in that array must be of the specified type, such as **int** values. Similarly, in the case of the reference type, all elements must be of the same reference type, such as **String** values. Every array object has an instance variable called **length**, which is used to specify the size of the array; i.e., the number of elements the array is made to hold.

DECLARING ONE-DIMENSIONAL ARRAY VARIABLES

In order to use an array in a program, you must first declare a variable that will reference the array. That is, you must specify the name of the variable that will be used to reference the array, and the type of data values that the array is expected to store. The format for declaring a one-dimensional array is:

```
data_type arr[];        or        data_type [] arr;
```

Where **data_type** is any valid data type, whether it is primitive type or reference type, and **arr** is the name of the array variable. The pair of square bracket symbols denotes the construct for a linear (one dimensional) array. Notice that the order of placing the array operator [] is commutative.

Example 1 - Declaring One-Dimensional Arrays

- int numbers[];
- String str[];
- byte[] someBytes;
- char [] consonants;
- Student s[];

In the last example, the name Student represents a user defined class with fields. The above declarations signal an intention to create an array. That is, the array itself has not yet been created; it is only the reference variable that has been declared. The blob in **Figure 1** depicts the array reference variable called **numbers**.

int numbers[];

Figure 1 - Reference address for integer array called numbers.

No use can be made of a declaration other than to create the array object. Any attempt to use the variable before the array is created will generate syntax error. In **Listing 1, Line 5** shows the declaration of the array reference variable, and **Line 6** shows an attempt to print information from it.

```
1. class ArrayDeclaration
2. {
3.     public static void main(String[] arg)
4.     {
5.         int numbers[];
6.         System.out.println(numbers);
7.     }
8. }
```

Listing 1- Declaring and attempting to use an array reference variable

Figure 2 shows the compiler error generated because of **Line 6**.

```
------------------- Configuration: j2sdk1.4.1_03 <Default> --------------------
C:\listing1 \ArrayDeclaration.java:6: variable numbers might not have
been initialized
System.out.println( numbers);
                    ^
1 error
```

Figure.2 - Compilation error, caused by attempting to use reference variable

CREATING ONE-DIMENSIONAL ARRAYSA

As was mentioned, before you can use an array reference variable you must first create the array. If an array already exists, assign the variable to it. In this case, both array variables must be of the same type. The format for creating a one-dimensional array is as follows:

```
data_type []arr = new data_type[number_of_cells]:
or
data_type arr[] = new data_type[number_of_cells];
```

Example 2 - Creating One-Dimensional Arrays

- int x[] = new int[10];
- String str[] = new String[10];
- byte []someBytes = new byte[10];
- char [] consonants = new char [10];
- Student s[] = new Student [10];

Each of the above statements creates an array of ten contiguously placed memory storage. However, only one type of data can be stored in each of the arrays. Once the array is created, then values can be assigned to each cell. The following are valid assignments for each of the arrays in **Example 2.**

- x[2] = 95;
- str[8] = "Hello there";
- someBytes[5] = 120;
- consonants[0] = 'b';
- s[4] = new Student ("John Doe", " 000-00-2x00" , 85);

ARRAY INDICES VS ARRAY VALUES

The cells in a linear array are numbered by the operating system. The numbering scheme begins with the first cell labeled **0**, the second **1**, the third **2**, and so on. Each of these numbers is referred to as an index of the array. **Figure 3** illustrates the indexing scheme of a linear array of size 10.

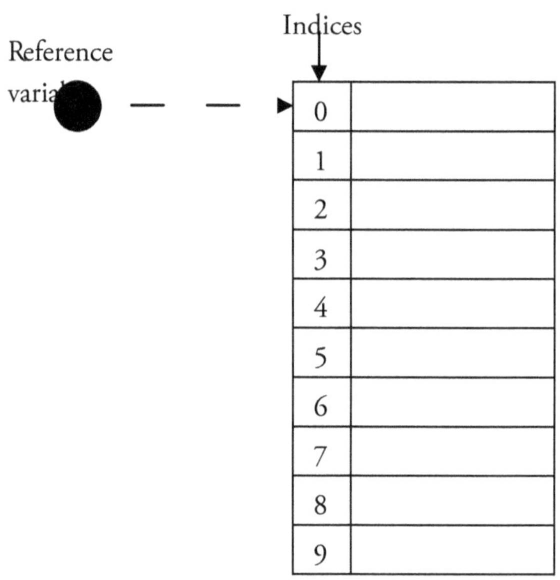

Figure 3 - An array of size 10

In **Figure 3,** each number represents the index for each position in the array. The cells to the right represent the space to hold the data value. Note that if an array has **n** cells, the range of the indices is **0** thru **n-1**. Also, notice that although the whole array is referenced by its name, it is the array operator [] that is used to access the individual cells, hence the individual elements.

CREATING AND INITIALIZING A ONE DIMENSIONAL ARRAYS

Java provides an alternate way of declaring, constructing, and initializing arrays. The construct for a one-dimensional array is as follows:

data_type [] arrayName = {<individual

When using this construct you must observe the following:

- Each numeric data value must be separated by a comma.
- Character values must be placed within a pair of single quotation marks, and each must be separated by comma.
- String values must be placed within a pair of double quotation marks, and each must be separated by a comma.
- Boolean values are not quoted; they are simply separated by commas.
- Objects are not quoted; they are separated by commas.

Example 3 - Creating and Initializing One-Dimensional Arrays

1. Create array of 10 consecutive even numbers beginning with the number two.
   int evens[] = { 2, 4, 6, 8, 10, 12, 14, 16, 18, 20};
2. Create an array of all the vowels.
   char [] vowels = { 'a', 'e', 'i', 'o', 'u'};
3. Create an array of the set of character escape sequences. Character escape sequences must be placed within single quotation marks.
   char [] escape = { '\n', '\r', '\b, '\t', '\\', '\"', '\"};
4. Create an array of menu items, using the following strings: File, Edit, Insert, and Help.
   String [] menu = { "File", "Edit", "Insert", "Help"};
5. Create an array of three objects of type Person, assuming there is a class Student that accepts the student's name, id, and grade.
   Student[] s = { new Student("John Brown", "00-11-22", 80),
   new Student("Mary Henry", "55-55-55", 90),
   new Student("Berris Hammond", 13-56-78", 78)}

ACCESSING THE ELEMENTS OF ONE DIMENSIONAL ARRAYS

You can directly assign and re-assigned values in an array. The general format for assigning values is as follows:

arr[i] = value;

Where:

- **arr** is the name of the array
- **i** is the index of the array, and
- **value** represents the data that is being assigned to that cell.

For instance, using the array called **even**, we could re-assign the fifth cell with the value 100 this way:

```
evens[4] = 100;
```

In array **s** of type Student, suppose the student's name was Johnny Browne, instead of the current spelling. We could replace the object the following way:

```
s[0] = new Student("Johnny Browne", "00-11-22", 80);
```

In all cases you must ensure that the index you specify is within the limits of the array (0 thru n-1); where n represents the size of the array.

EXAMPLE 4 - ARRAY APPLICATIONS

Define a class called BinaryDigits that converts an integer value into its binary equivalence.
Solution

- The class receives an integer value that represents the number to be converted to binary.
- Define a method that decomposes the number into its binary form.
- Return the binary value.

The algorithm for converting an integer into binary is as follows:

1. Use the long division method to divide the original number by 2, and
   i. Record the remainder
   i. Set the number to the quotient of the division.
2. Repeat step **1** until the new production of the number is zero
3. Write the result, by listing the remainders in the reverse order of how they were stored. That is, starting with the last value and ending with the first.

Let us test the algorithm with the number **53**.

∞ 53 ÷ 2 = 26, remainder 1 ---> first digit to be generated
∞ 26 ÷ 2 = 13, remainder 0
∞ 13 ÷ 2 = 6, remainder 1
∞ 6÷ 2 = 3, remainder 0
∞ 3÷ 2 = 1, remainder 1
∞ 1÷ 2 = 0, remainder 1 ---> The last digit to be generated

Hence the binary equivalence of **53** is **110101**

Listing 2 shows the class BinaryDigits that converts positive integers their binary equivalence.

```
1.  class BinaryDigits
2.  {
3.      int binary[], x, theNumber, index;
4.      static final int MAX = 32;
5.
6.      BinaryDigits(int x)
7.      {
8.          binary = new int[MAX];
9.          this.x = x;
10.         theNumber = x;
11.     }
12.     void makeBinaryDigits()
13.     {
14.          while (x > 0 && index < MAX)
15.          {
16.              int remainder = x % 2;
17.              binary[index] = remainder;
18.              x = x/2;
19.              index = index + 1;
20.          }
21.     }
22.     public String toString()
23.     {
24.             String s = "The number " + theNumber + " = ";
25.             for (int i = MAX -1; i >= 0; i --)
26.                 s = s + binary[i];
27.                 return's + "in binary";
28.     }
29. }
```

Listing 2 - Class BinaryDigits

In **Listing 2**, **Line 3** shows the declaration of the array variable, called binary. This variable will be used to reference the array of binary digits. **Line 8** shows how the constructor creates the array. Notice that we use 32 as the size of the array, because an **int** value requires four bytes (32 bits) of storage.

Based on the algorithm, we must repeatedly divide the quotient of the number by 2, and store the remainders in the array. In this case a remainder is either 0 or 1. **Line 16** shows how the remainders are calculated (using the modulus operator); and **Line 17** shows how each remainder is stored in the array. The new quotient is generated as shown in **Line 18**. Each time through the loop the index variable is updated by 1, as shown in **Line 19**. The loop stops when either the new quotient is zero, or when the index exceeds the array size.

The result is generated by the for loop in the toString method. Notice the loop must be traversed in the reverse order of how the data was stored, that is, from the last element down to the first. Each time through the loop a digit is extracted from the ith position of the array. **Figure 4** shows binary equivalence of **53**.

The number 53 = 00000000000000000000000000110101 in binary

Figure 4 - The binary equivalence of the decimal number 53

Listing 3 shows a typical test class. It simply creates a BinaryDigit object with the number 53, calls the method makeBinaryDigits, and displays the result.

```
class TestBinaryDigits
{
    public static void main(String[] arg)
    {
        BinaryDigits b = new
        BinaryDigits(53);
        b.makeBinaryDigits();
        System.out.println(b.toString());
    }
}
```

Listing 3 - Test class TestBinaryDigits

Example 5 - Creating Arrays of Objects

As we have stated, arrays can store reference types also. For example, let's say a teacher wants to store the test scores for a set of students, and from the data stored, generate reports such as letter grades for valid scores. In this scenario each student along with his/her test scores represents an object. With this in mind, we can develop a class that represents the object for each student. Each object that is created will be stored in an array. Let us design a class called Student, and let us limit the kind of information to the name, id number, test scores, average grade for each student, average grade of each test, and the class average.

Listing 4 shows the class called Student that represents the scenario. The constructor accepts the name, id number, and numeric grade of the individual student. The mutator method called calculateGrade(), determines if the score is a valid one. If it determines that the score is valid then it goes on to calculate the appropriate letter grade, otherwise it sets the boolean variable, valid, to **false**, and no calculation is performed.

```
public class Student
{
    String name, id;
    char grade;
    byte score;
    boolean valid;

    Student(String name, String id, byte score)
    {
        this.name = name;
        this.id = id;
        this.score = score;
        valid = true;
        grade = '-';
    }
    public void calculateGrade()
    {
        if (score <  0 || score > 100)
            valid = false;
        else if (score > 90 )
            grade = 'A';
        else if (score > 80 )
            grade = 'B';
        else if (score > 70 )
            grade = 'C';
        else grade = 'F';
    }
    public char getGrade(){return grade;}
    public String getName(){return name;}
    public  String getId (){return id;}
    public byte getScore(){return score;}
    public boolean validScore(){return valid;}
    public String getInvalidScore(){ return score + " , invald number, it is out of range"; }
    public String getValidScore(){return score + " , valid score, the individual is "; }
}
```

Listing 4 - lass Student

Listing 5 shows a typical test class. First it gets a number that represents the number of Student object to be stored. See **Line 10**. Line **11** uses that number to create the size array. **Lines 19** thru **26** simply read the data from the keyboard. As each set of data values is read, it is used to create the Student object. See **Line 28**. This object is then stored in the ith position of the array. So, indeed arrays can store objects. **Line 29** calls the method calculateGrade() to calculate the letter grade if possible. The method called display, simply displays the requisite information for the array.

```
Enter number of students  --> 3
Enter lastname  --> Small
Enter lastname  --> Kendell
Enter id --> 1000
Enter grade (0  - 100) --> 90
Enter lastname  --> Henry
Enter lastname  --> Berris
Enter id --> 2000
Enter grade (0  - 100) --> -60
Enter lastname  --> Browne
Enter lastname  --> Yvette
Enter id --> 3000
Enter grade (0  - 100) --> 78
90 , valid score, the individual is Small Kendell the grade is B
-60 , invald number, it is out of range
78 , valid score, the individual is Browne Yvette the grade is C
```

Figure 5 - Input and output from the program

MULTI-DIMENSIONAL ARRAYS

Java like many other programming languages makes provision for multi-dimensional arrays. The general format for multi-dimensional arrays is as follows:

```
data_type arr [ ][ ][ ].....
```

Where **data_type** represents the kind of data that the array will store; **arr**, represents the name of the array; and the pairs of square brackets represent the dimension of the array. The most commonly used arrays are one-dimensional, two-dimensional, and three-dimensional. Higher dimensional arrays are less frequently used. Only two-dimensional arrays will be discussed in this section.

```
import java.util.Scanner;

public class School
{
   public static void main(String[] arg)
   {
       Scanner scan = new Scanner(System.in);
       System.out.print("Enter number of students  --> ");

       final byte MAX = scan.nextByte();
       Student s[] = new Student[MAX];
       loadArray(s, scan);
       display(s);
   }
   public static void loadArray  (Student s[], Scanner scan)
   {
       for (int i = 0; i < s.length; i++)
       {
           System.out.print("Enter lastname  --> ");
           String lastname = scan.next();
           System.out.print("Enter lastname  --> ");
           String firstname = scan.next();
           System.out.print("Enter id  --> ");
           String id = scan.next();
           System.out.print("Enter grade (0  - 100) --> ");
           byte score = scan.nextByte();

           s[i] = new Student(lastname + " " + firstname, id, score);
           s[i].calculateGrade();
       }
   }
   public static void display(Student s[])
   {
       for (int i = 0; i < s.length; i ++)
       {
           if (!s[i].validScore())
               System.out.println(s[i].getInvalidScore());
           else
           {
               System.out.println(s[i].getInvalidScore());
               System.out.println(s[i].getInvalidScore());
           {
       {
   {
}
```

Listing 5- Test class School

TWO-DIMENSIONAL ARRAYS

A two-dimensional array is an array of references. Each of the references points to a linear array of values. For example, **Figure 6** is an array of four references; each reference points to a linear array of three values. This construct represents what is called a 4 by 3 array. That is, 4 rows by 3 columns.

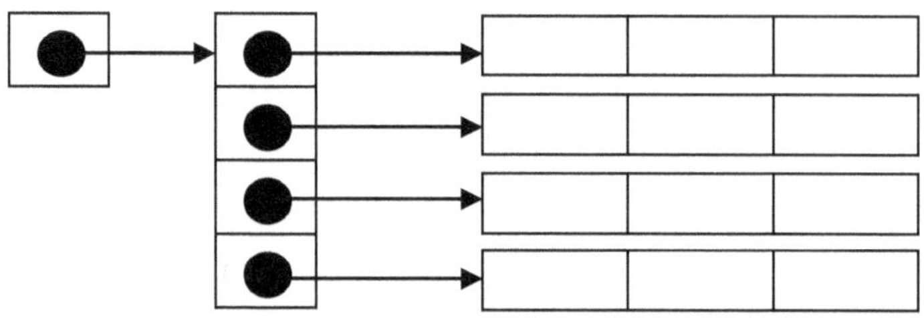

Figure 6 - A 4 x 3 array

Example 6 – Declaring Two-Dimensional Arrays

The format for declaring a two-dimensional array satisfies any of the following three formats:

```
data_type [][] arr;        data_type [] arr[];        data_type
```

Let us create a 4 by 3 array to store integers. To create this 4 by 3 array we first have to declare the array variable, and then create the array. Let us call this array **numbers**. To declare it we would write:

At this point, only the reference address for the array is allocated:

The following statement creates the array:

```
number = new int[4][3];
```

This statement has the effect of creating the array as shown in **Figure 7**. Because the array is an integer array, the compiler loads each cell with the default value for integer variables; in this case zero.

Example 7 - Calculating Averages

Consider the following situation. Write a program that:

1. Tabulates the test scores for a set of students.
2. Finds the average score for each student.
3. Finds the average score for each test
4. Finds the class average for all tests, and for all the students.

Let us use the data shown in **Figure 8** to illustrate the point.

Student	Test 1	Test 2	Test 3
1000-1	80	70	100
1000-2	75	80	80
1000-3	60	90	80
1000-4	80	80	60

Figure 8 - Table of students' test scores

From the data given in **Figure 6**, and the requirements listed above, we will design an array large enough to store the test scores, the average for each student, the average for each test, and the class average. In this case we will use a two-dimensional array of size 5 rows by 4 columns. See **Figure 9**.

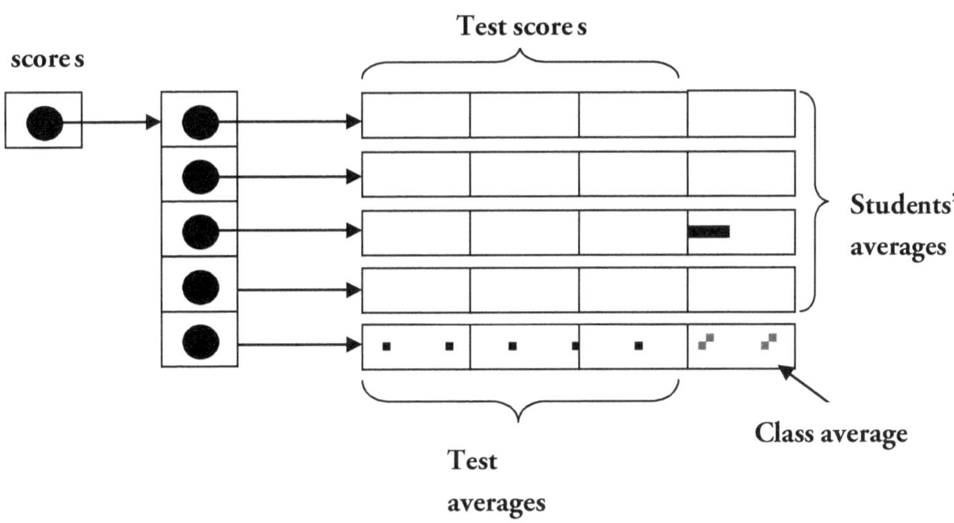

Figure 9 - The 5 by 4 integer array called scores

In addition to the two-dimensional array, we also need to create a one dimensional array to store the id number of each student. The id numbers will be stored as strings for two reasons – firstly, they usually are not used in calculations, and secondly, they sometimes come with characters other than digits. The last cell in this array will have no student id, but instead it will be used as a label for averages.

Listing 6 shows the complete test class that creates the arrays and loads the arrays. Focus will be on the declaration, creation, and manipulation of the two-dimensional array. **Line 14** for example, shows how the two-dimensional array is declared and created. That is,

```
14. double scores[][] = new double[ROWS][COLUMNS];
```

Two-dimensional arrays are almost always processed using nested for loops. The two index variables are often referred to as *i* and *j*, though any other name would be as good. The first index, *i*, refers to the ith row of the array, and the second index, *j*, refers to the jth column of the array.

Once the arrays have been created, it is now time to load them with values. **Lines 30** thru **39** show how both arrays are loaded. The for loop of **Lines 30** excludes the last row of the array. This is indicated by the expression, **i < scores.length-1**. Similarly, the last column is excluded, as indicated by, **j < scores[i].length-1**. These cells are reserved for the rows and columns averages, respectively.

```
30. for (int i = 0; i < scores.length-1; i++)
31. {
32.     System.out.print("Enter id for student " + (i+1) + "--> ");
33.     student[i] = scan.next();
34.     for (int j = 0; j < scores[i].length-1; j++)
35.     {
36.         System.out.print("Enter score " + (j+1) + "---> ");
37.         arr[i][j] = scan.nextDouble();
38.     }
39. }
```

Line 33 shows how the array called student, stores the id number for each of the individuals. **Line 37** shows how the test scores are stored in the cells of each row. The inner loop controls the reading of the scores for each cell of each of the rows. **Listing 6** shows the complete definition for the class Test2DArray.

```
import java.util.Scanner;

class Test2DArray
{
    public static void main(String[] arg)
    {
        Scanner scan =  new Scanner(System.in);
        System.out.print("Enter the number of rows  ---> ");
        final int ROWS = scan.nextInt();
        System.out.print("Enter the number of columns  ---> ");
        final int COLUMNS = scan.nextInt();

        String student[] = new String[ROWS];
        double scores [][] = new
        double[ROWS][COLUMNS];

        loadArray( scores , student, scan);
        StudentScore s = new StudentScore(  scores , student);

        System.out.println(" \n.... Original array .....");
        s.print();
        s.average_row();
        System.out.println(" \n.... Average row  .....");
        s.print();
        s.average_col umn();
        System.out.println(" \n.... Average column .....");
        s.print();
    }
    static void loadArray(  double [][]scores , String student[],
    Scanner scan)
    {
        for (int i = 0; i < scores.length  -1; i++)
        {
            System.out.print("Enter id for student " + (i+1) +
            "--> ");
            student[i] = scan.next() ;
            for (int j = 0; j < scores[i].length  -1; j++)
            {
                System.out.print("Enter score " + (j+1) + "---> ");
                arr[i][j] = scan.nextInt();
            }
        }
        student[scores.length-1] = "Avg";

    }
}
```

Listing6 – Creating and loading arrays

Now that the arrays are loaded, it is time to manipulate them. There are basically three operations that we will perform on the data – display the arrays as a table of values, calculate the students' average on all three tests (average the rows), and calculate the test averages on all the tests (average the columns). We will implement these operations independently of the test class, by developing a class called StudentScore. Apart from a constructor the class defines three mutator methods – display(), average_row() and average_column(). See **Listing 7.**

```
class StudentScore
{
    double score[][];
    String student[];

    StudentScore( double arr[][], String student[])
    {
        score = arr;
        this.student = student;
    }
    void display ()
    {
        System.out.printf("%4s %14s %5s  %5s %5s%n", "Id", "Test 1", "Test 2",
        "Test 3", "Avg");
        for (int i = 0; i < score.length; i++)
        {
            System.out.printf("%8s", student[i]);
            for (int j = 0; j < score[i].length; j++)
                System.out.printf("%8d", score[i][j]);
            System.out.printf("%n");
        }
    }
    void average_row()
    {
        for (int i = 0; i < score.length; i++)
        {
            double sum = 0;
            int length =  score[i].length;
            for (int j = 0; j < length -1; j++)
                sum = sum + score[i][j];
            score[i][length -1] = sum/(length-1);
        }
    }
    void average_col umn()
    {
        int cols = sco re[0].length;
        double tavge = 0;
        for (int j = 0; j < cols -1; j++)
        {
            int i = 0;
            double sum = 0;
            while (i < score.length)
            {
                sum = sum + score[i][j];
                i++;
            }
            score[i-1][j] = sum/cols;
            tavge = tavge + score[i-1][j-1];
        }
        score[score.length-1][cols-1] = tavge/(cols-1);
    }
}
```

Listing7 - Class StudentScore

First we look at the method called display, in particular **Lines 14** thru **20**. In this segment of code, the for loop of Line **14** controls the row references of the two-dimensional array, and **Line 17** controls the individual cells in the ith row. See the expression **j < score[i].length**, where the index *i*, represents the ith row (the ith student). The scores are extracted from the array, denoted by the expression **score[i][j]**). Notice also that for each row reference the student's identification number is displayed, as shown in **Line 16.**

```
14. for (int i = 0; i < score.length; i++)
15. {
16.     System.out.printf("%8s", student[i]);
17.     for (int j = 0; j < score[i].length; j++)
18.         System.out.printf("%8.0f", score[i]
            [j]);
19.     System.out.printf("%n");
20. }
```

The method average_row first sums the test scores, one student at a time. See **Lines 28** and **29**. After each student's scores are added, the average is taken. This average is then assigned to the last position in that row. See **Line 30**. Notice that the last cell in the ith row always has indices pair **(i-1, length-1).**

```
24. for (int i = 0; i < score.length ; i++)
25. {
26.     double sum = 0;
27.     int length =  score[i].length;
28.     for (int j = 0; j < length-1; j++)
29.         sum = sum + score[i][j];
30.     score[i-1][length-1] = sum/(length-1);
31. }
```

The method average_column does two things – first, it finds the average for each test, and then finds the class average for all tests. See **Lines 35** thru **49**. In this piece of code we start with the column index. See **Line 37**. Using the row index we now visit every cell in that column, and sum those values. See the while loop, **Lines 41** thru **45**. The average is calculated when the while loop terminates. This value is then assigned to the last cell of that column. Notice that the indices for the last cell in each column are denoted by the index pair (**i-1, j**). Within the for loop the individual test averages are summed in the variable called, tavge. See **Line 47**. After all test averages have been calculated, the class average is calculated and is assigned to the very last cell in the array. The last cell is denoted by the index pair (**score.length-1, cols-1**). See **Line 49**.

```
int cols = score[0].length;
double tavge = 0;
for (int j = 0; j < cols; j++)
{
     int i = 0;
     double sum = 0;
     while (i < score.length)
     {
          sum = sum + score[i][j];
          i++;
     }
     score[i-1][j] = sum/cols;
     tavge = tavge +  score[i-1][j];
}
score[score.length-1][cols-1] = tavge/cols;
```

Figure 10 shows the output from this program, using the data in **Figure 8**.

```
General Output
Enter the number of rows ---> 5
Enter the number of columns ---> 4
Enter id for student 1--> 1000-1
Enter score 1---> 80
Enter score 2---> 70
Enter score 3---> 100
Enter id for student 2--> 1000-2
Enter score 1---> 75
Enter score 2---> 80
Enter score 3---> 80
Enter id for student 3--> 1000-3
Enter score 1---> 60
Enter score 2---> 90
Enter score 3---> 80
Enter id for student 4--> 1000-4
Enter score 1---> 80
Enter score 2---> 80
Enter score 3---> 60

.... Original array .....
  Id          Test 1 Test 2  Test 3    Avg
  1000-1        80      70     100       0
  1000-2        75      80      80       0
  1000-3        60      90      80       0
  1000-4        80      80      60       0
     Avg         0       0       0       0

.... Average row    .....
  Id          Test 1 Test 2  Test 3    Avg
  1000-1        80      70     100      83
  1000-2        75      80      80      78
  1000-3        60      90      80      77
  1000-4        80      80      60      73
     Avg         0       0       0       0

.... Average column .....
  Id          Test 1 Test 2  Test 3    Avg
  1000-1        80      70     100      83
  1000-2        75      80      80      78
  1000-3        60      90      80      77
  1000-4        80      80      60      73
     Avg        74      80      80      78
```

Figure 10 - Output using the data of Figure 6

THE CLASS ARRAYLIST

One of the disadvantages of arrays is that after the array is created, its size cannot be changed. It can neither grow nor shrink, which means that you must know in advance how many elements you want to store before creating it. Sometimes this is not always the case; you may not know until run time exactly how large an array you need. For instance, in a classroom situation the teacher will know the exact number of students in a class, so an array would be appropriate. However, in the case of commercial banking, it cannot be ascertained in advance how many people will become customer of the bank, or how many customers might close their accounts with the bank. To handle this latter situation, Java defines a class called **ArrayList** to handle any unexpected growth or shrinkage of a list. This means that the list adjusts its size dynamically during runtime.

Unlike arrays, ArrayLists are created with an initial size. The default initial capacity of an ArrayList is 10. When this size is exceeded, the list capacity is automatically enlarged. On the other hand, when objects are removed, the array may be shrunken. As with arrays, ArrayList uses index to access the list. The index begins at zero. Unlike arrays, ArrayList can store homogeneous as well as heterogeneous objects. Primitive types are not permitted. Java 1.5 and later versions allow you to restrict the type of object to be stored. **Figure 11** shows the constructors and some frequently used methods of the ArrayList class.

Constructors	Purpose
ArrayList( )	Builds an empty array list.
ArrayList(Collection c)	Builds an array list that is initialized with the elements of the collection c
ArrayList(int capacity)	Builds an array list that has the specified initial capacity.
Frequently used methods	Purpose
boolean add(E e)	Appends the specified element to the list
void clear()	Removes all of the elements from this list.
E get(int index)	Returns the element at the specified position in this list.
boolean isEmpty()	Returns `true` if this list contains no elements
E remove(int index)	Removes the element at the specified position in this list.
boolean remove(Object o)	Removes the first occurrence of the specified element from this list, if it is present.
`E set(int index, E element)`	Replaces the element at the specified position in this list with the specified element.
int size()	Returns the number of elements in this list.

Figure 11 - Constructors and some frequently used methods

Example 7 - Some ArrayList Operations

The following example serves to demonstrate the using of some of the methods in the class ArrayList. It shows how to append, insert, replace, and remove objects from the list. It also shows that the data to be stored are all objects, including user-defined classes. **Listing 8** shows a user-defined class called Person. This class will be used in this example.

```
class Person
{
    private String name;
    private int age;

    Person(String name, int age)
    {
        this.name = name;
        this.age = age;
    }

    public String toString() { return name + " age " + age ; }
}
```

Listing 8 -User defined class Person

Listing 9 shows a class called CheckArrayList. It creates an ArrayList object that can store just about any type of object. This is denoted by the type shown within the pairs of angle brackets. See **Line 7**.

```
import java.util.ArrayList;

class CheckArrayList
{
    public static void main(String[] arg)
    {
        ArrayList <Object> list = new ArrayList <Object> ();

        list.add("World");
        display(list);
        list.add(0, "Hello");
        display(list);
        list.add(1, 'C');
        display(list);
        list.add(new Character('P'));
        display(list);
        System.out.pr intln("\nRemove the object " + list.remove(3) );
        display(list);
        list.add(new Integer(25));
        display(list);
        list.add(100.0);
        display(list);
        list.add(3, new Person("Boris Gardener", 69));
        display(list);
        list.set(0, new Person("Bill Henry", 26));
        display(list);
    }
    static void display(ArrayList list)
    {
        System.out.println(" \nThe size of the list is " + list.size());
        for (int i = 0; i < list.size(); i++)
        {
            Object o = list.get(i);
            if( o instanceof String )
                System.out.println("Object position " + i + "  " + (String)  o + " is a string " );
            else if (o instanceof Integer)
                System.out.println("Object position " + i + "  " + (Integer)o + " is an integer " );
            else if (o instanceof Double)
                System.out.println("Object position " + i + "  " + (Double)o + " is a double " );
            else if (o instanceof Character)
                System.out.println("Object position " + i + "  " + (Character)o + " is an character " );
            else if (o instanceof Person)
                System.out.println("Object position " + i + "  " + (Person)o + " is a person " );
        }
    }
}
```

Listing9 - The class CheckArrayList

Figure 12 shows the output generated from the program. In **Listing 10**, **Line 9** places the first object in the list. When the list is displayed (**Line 10**) its size is 1, and the string object **World** is stored in the first position, 0. **Line 11** has the effect of inserting a new object at the first location, thereby repositioning the first object to the second position, 1. When the list is displayed you will notice that there are two elements in the list, and that they are in their respective position as described.

Line 13 has the similar effect as **Line 11**, except that the data 'C' is a primitive type. However, before it is added to the list, it is first converted to an object of type Character inside the method. This construct works for **Java 1.5** and later versions.

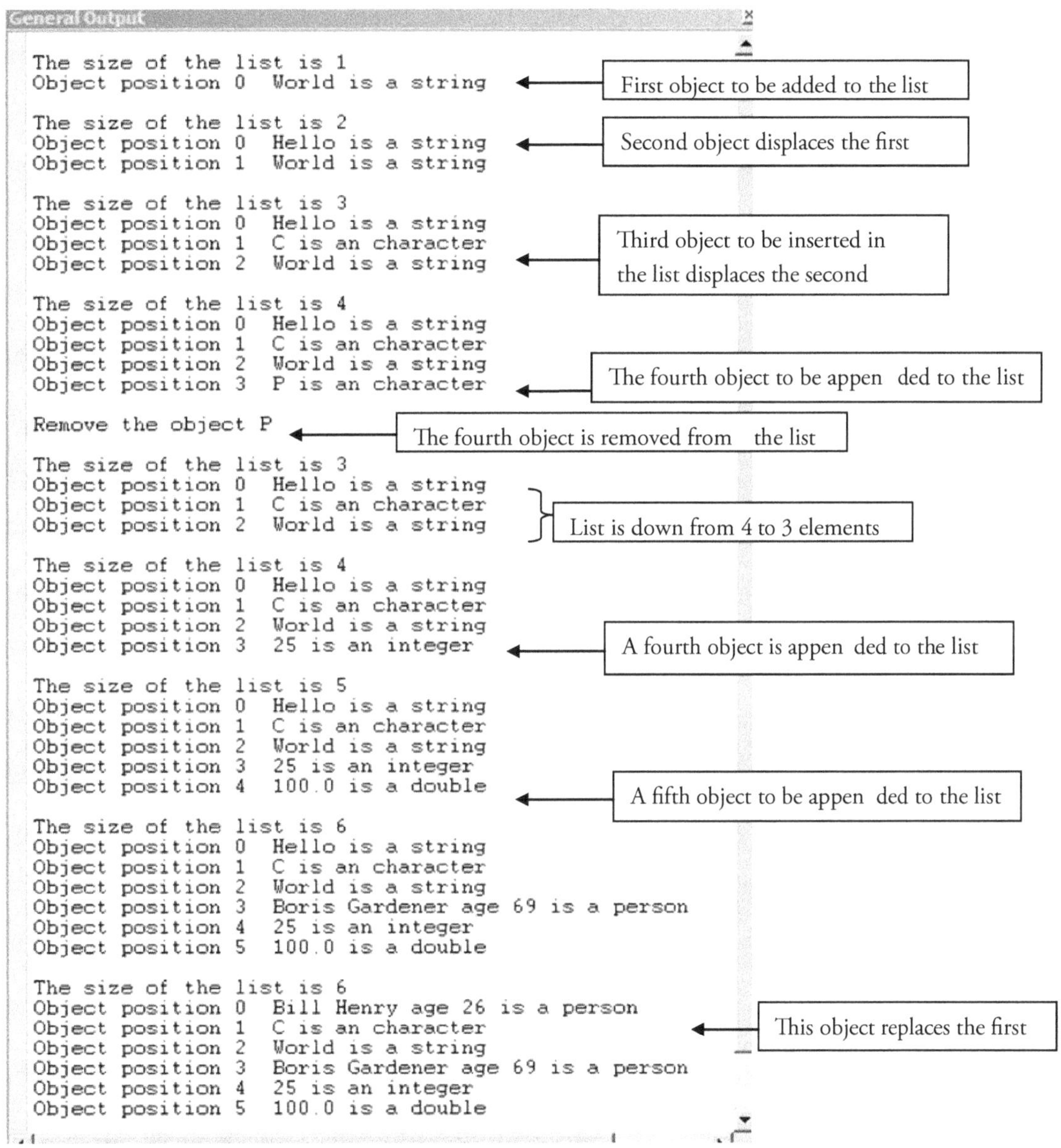

Figure 12 - The output from the programam

Line 15 appends the character object '**P**' to the list. This addition increases the size of the list by 1, to 4. **Line 17** removes the fourth element from the list, which happens to be the last element added. The list size is reduced to 3. **Line 19** has similar effect as **Line 15**; and **Line 21** has similar effect as **Line 13**, except that in this case the object is appended to the list. With these two additions, the list now has 5 elements.

As was stated, ArrayList can store heterogeneous objects. In **Line 23** the object of the user defined class Person is created and is inserted in the fourth position in the list. Hence it displaces the objects that were occupying the third and fourth position in the list, respectively. At this point the list has 6 elements. In **Line 25** the new Person object replaces the object in the first position in the list. The replaced object is completely gone. Notice that the size of the list is still 6.

When a list has different types of object we must identify the respective object in order to get correct information. Java provides an operator called **instanceof**. This operator enables us to identify objects according to their type. See the **if/else** statement, **Lines 34** thru **42**.

SUMMARY

Arrays store groups of data items, all of which must be of the same type. Once the array is created, its size cannot be changed. Declaring an array does not create one, it merely creates the reference variable that will point to the actual array when it is created. Java implements one-dimensional as well as multi-dimensional arrays.

Arrays have two major disadvantages – they are fixed size, and they can store only one kind of data. These restrictions are relaxed with the concept of a variable length array data structure called ArrayList. With ArrayList, it size grows and shrinks dynamically. In addition, it can store any form of object.

Java Arrays and Loops

BY NICK PARLANTE

An "array" is a way to store a collection of "elements". Arrays use square brackets [ ] for their syntax. Each array is declared with a type that indicates the type of element that it stores, like this: the "int[]" type is an array of int elements, a "String[]" type is an array of string elements. Arrays are allocated in the heap with the "new" operator and accessed through pointers (just like objects). The following line declares a variable "values" that can point to an int array. The code does not allocate the array yet:

```
int[] values;     // declare an int array variable "values"
```

The expression "new int[100]" allocates a new array in the heap, sized to hold 100 int values.:

```
values = new int[100];     // allocate the array, store the pointer
```

In the heap, the array is a block of memory made of all the elements together. Each element in the array is identified by a zero-based index number: 0, 1, 2, ... and so on. An attempt to access an index outside the 0..length-1 range will fail with a runtime exception. When first created, all of the elements in the array are set to zero. So the memory drawing for the code above looks like:

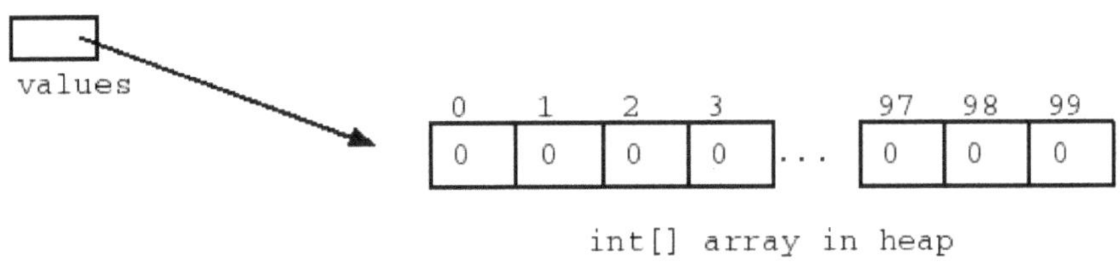

Arrays use square brackets as a convenient syntax to refer to individual elements: "values[2]" is the element at index 2 within the "values" array. This square bracket syntax is an easy way to get or set any particular element in the array. Here is a longer example that declares an array variable, allocates the array with "new", and then uses the [ ] syntax to access particular elements:

```
int[] values;          // declare in array variable

values = new int[100];// allocate the array (initially all zero)

values[0] = 4;                  // store a 4 into element 0
values[1] = 8;                  // store an 8 into element 1

// read ints out of values[0] and values[1], do
// some math, store result into values[2]
values[2] = 2*values[0] + values[1];

// store a 13 into the last element in the array
values[99] = 13;
```

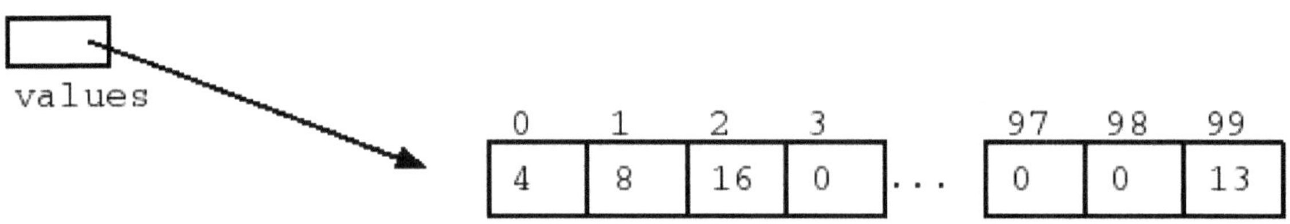

The length of an array is set when it is created with "new" and that length never changes for the lifetime of the array. In contrast, Java Lists can grow and shrink over time—this is a big feature that Lists have that arrays do not. The length of an array can be accessed as a special ".length" attribute. For example, with the above "values" array, we can access the size of the array as "values.length". It is common to use a 0 ...length-1 for-loop to iterate over all the elements in array:

```
int[] values = new int[100];
// Loop over all the elements in the values array
for (int i=0; i<values.length; i++) {
  // Do something with values[i], such as print it
  System.out.println( values[i] );
}
```

Note that the syntax to access the length is just "values.length", not "values.length()". Why do we need .length? Don't we know how big the array is from when we created it—length 100 or whatever? The answer is that .length is useful, since it allows us to write a method that takes an array parameter, where the array is of any size. For example, the method computeSum() below takes an int[] array argument, and computes the sum of the ints in the array:

```
public int computeSum(int[] nums) {
  int sum = 0;
  for (int i=0; i<nums.length; i++) {
    sum = sum + nums[i];
  }
  return sum;
}
```

Since the code uses the .length of the array passed in, it will work for any size array that we pass in.

EXAMPLE ARRAY CODE

Here is code that iterates over a non-empty array to find the index of the smallest element:

```
int findSmallest(int[] values) {

  int minIndex = 0;  // start with 0th element as min
  for (int i=1; i<values.length; i++) {
    if (values[i] < values[minIndex]) {
      minIndex = i;
    }
  }
  return minIndex;
}
```

OBJECT ARRAY CODE

Suppose we have an Account class that has a constructor with zero arguments. Here's some example code that allocates an array of 100 Account objects:

```
Account[] accounts;

// 1. allocate the array (initially all the pointers are null)
accounts = new Account[100];

// 2. allocate 100 Account objects, and store their pointers in the array
```

```
for (int i=0; i<accounts.length; i++) {
  accounts[i] = new Account();
}

// 3. call a method on one of the accounts in the array
account[0].deposit(100);
```

ARRAY LITERALS

There's a special syntax to specify an array and its elements right in the code using curly braces { … }. This is called an "array constant" or an "array literal". This is a very convenient if you know what all the elements are at compile time.

```
String[] words = new String[]{ "hello", "foo", "bar" };
int[] squares = new int[] { 1, 4, 9, 16 };
```

ARRAY CODE PATTERNS

A "pattern" or "idiom" is a phrase or section of code that we see or use often since it solves a common problem. With arrays, there are a few very common patterns for iterating over the elements in an array. You want to be familiar with these basic patterns since many array problems can be solved with variations and combinations of these basic patterns.

1. FOR-ALL LOOP

The "for-all" or "for-each" loop, as we have already seen, is a very common idiom for arrays. The goal is to iterate over all the elements from 0 to length-1, doing some operation once for each element.

```
// For-All
// Do something for every element
public void forAll(int[] nums) {
  for (int i=0; i<nums.length; i++) {
    System.out.println( nums[i] );
  }
    }
```

We can change the init/test/increment in the for-loop to iterate through the elements backwards, from length-1 down to 0.

```
// For-All variant
// Go through the elements backwards
// by adjusting the for-loop
public void forAllBackwards(int[] nums) {
  for (int i = nums.length-1; i>=0; i--) {
    System.out.println( nums[i] );
  }
}
```

With this sort of code, we have to be careful with the exact specification of the for-loop to hit the right elements in the array. It's easy to be off-by-one—for example, the backwards loop above has to init i to "length-1" instead of "length" to start with the last element. The test should be "i>=0" instead of "i>0" to include the 0th element. Oftentimes in loop and array problems, getting these "edge" cases correct is the trickiest part. When writing a loop, look at the code and think how it will behave for the very first and very last elements. If it works for those, it will most likely work for all the elements in between. In Java, if the running code tries to access an index that is too big or too small to fit in the array, the program will get an ArrayOutOfBounds exception on that line. Other examples of for-all operations that look at every element in the array include: sum up the int values in an array, call a method on every object in an array, count the number of times a particular value appears in an array.

2. SEARCH LOOP

Another common problem is searching through all the elements in an array to find a particular "target" value. The code is basically the standard for-all loop with an if-statement inside looking at each element. The example code below takes array and target arguments and searches through the array for an element that is the same as the target. The method returns the index where the target appears in the array, or -1 if the target does not appear in the array.

In the loop, an if-statement checks if each element is the same as the target value. If the test is true we have found the target and can stop looking. In the example below, the if-statement uses a "return" to exit the loop and method immediately when a matching element is found. Another solution might use a "break". The point is, once the target is found, we do not need to keep iterating the loop.

How do we know if the target does not appear in the array? This requires a little logic. The search-loop looks at every element in the array, tests each one, and exits the method when a match is found. Therefore, the only way the program can get to the line just after the search-loop is if none of the elements matched. Therefore, the code just after the search-loop only runs when no elements match. In this example, the "return -1;" will run in the case that none of the elements matched.

```
// Search
// Searches through the given array looking
// for the given target. Returns the index number
```

```
// of the target if found, or -1 otherwise.
// (classic search-loop example)
public int search(int[] nums, int target) {
  // Look at every element
  for (int i=0; i<nums.length; i++) {
    if (nums[i] == target) {
      return i; // return the index where the target is found
    }
  }

  // If we get here, the target was not in the array
  return -1;
}
```

For search problems, we generally write the loop in the standard way to go through all the elements, and then add if/break/return logic inside the loop to react to each element. As a matter of style, the search-loop solves two problems. It must iterate over all the elements, and it must figure out if the target is found or not. One of those problems – iterating over all the elements—is just the standard for-all problem, and we are happy to use the standard pattern code to handle it. Or put another way, if part of a problem is common and part is unique, use standard code for the common part and add in code for the unique part. The strength of standard code is, after all, that it is familiar and easy to use, so we use it where we can.

What would it mean to disregard the above advice? We could make up a while-loop that mixes together the logic of the for-all and the search into one:

```
// Another way to write search that combines
// the "end of array" and "found" logic in one
// while loop. As a matter of style, we prefer
// the above version that uses the standard
// for-all loop.
public int searchNotAsGood(int[] nums, int target) {
  int i = 0;
  while (i<nums.length && nums[i]!=target) {
    i++;
  }
  // get here either because we found it, or hit end of array
  if (i==nums.length) {
    return -1;
  }
  else {
    return i;
```

```
  }
}
```

The above loop works, but I think it is not as good as the earlier version that uses the standard for-all loop. The beauty of the for-all idiom is that it is easy to write, easy to read, and hard to get wrong. We should take advantage of that clarity where we can.

HEADS/TAILS ARRAY LOOP EXAMPLE

Here is a more complex search loop problem. Given the results of a series of heads/tails coin tosses as a boolean[] array (true=heads, false=tails), figure out if there were ever 10 heads in a row. This is essentially the search problem again: we go through the array looking for a something, stopping if we find it:

```
// Given an array of booleans representing a series
// of coin tosses (true=heads, false=tails),
// returns true if the array contains anywhere within it
// a string of 10 heads in a row.
// (example of a search loop)
public boolean searchHeads(boolean[] heads) {
  int streak = 0;     // count the streak of heads in a row

  for (int i=0; i<heads.length; i++) {
    if (heads[i]) {  // heads : increment streak
      streak++;
      if (streak == 10) {
        return true;  // found it!
      }
    }
    else {           // tails : streak is broken
      streak = 0;
    }
  }

  // If we get here, there was no streak of 10
  return false;
}
```

3. MIN/MAX LOOP

A Max or Min loop searches through all the elements looking for an element that is the most or least among all the elements according to some metric. The max-loop differs from the search-loop since the max-loop must look at every element, while the search-loop can exit as soon as it finds a match.

The basic idea with the max-loop is to keep a local variable that stores max-so-far as we go through the loop, and each element is compared to the max-so-far. If an element is larger than the max-so-far, its value becomes the new max-so-far. At the end of the loop, we have looked at every element and remembered the largest.

What should the initial value of max-so-far be before we look at anything? One possibility is to just use the first value from the array. Although probably not the largest in the array, it will be compared to every element by the time the loop is done, so it's a fine starting candidate.

```
// Find-Max
// Given a non-empty array of ints, returns
// the largest int value found in the array.
// (does not work with empty arrays)
public int findMax(int[] nums) {
  int maxSoFar = nums[0];  // use nums[0] as the max to start

  // Look at every element, starting at 1
  for (int i=1; i<nums.length; i++) {
    if (nums[i] > maxSoFar) {
      maxSoFar = nums[i];
    }
  }
  return maxSoFar;
}
```

A slightly different strategy is to use an extremely small value as the initial max-so-far, such as the constant Integer.MIN_VALUE which is the most negative possible int value, about -2 billion.

```
// Find-Max variant
// Use very small number, Integer.MIN_VALUE,
// as the initial max value.
public int findMax2(int[] nums) {
  int maxSoFar = Integer.MIN_VALUE;  // about -2 billion

  // Look at every element
  for (int i=0; i<nums.length; i++) {
    if (nums[i] > maxSoFar) {
      maxSoFar = nums[i];
```

```
    }
  }

  return maxSoFar;
}
```

Finding a max or min value in an array does not make sense if the array is empty (length of zero)—there are no elements, so the question of which element is biggest does not make sense. Sometimes, a method will stipulate that empty arrays may not be passed in and the method does not promise to behave correctly given an empty array. The burden is on the caller not to pass in an empty array. Sometimes, the method may back up this stipulation by actually detecting an "illegal" argument and rai

sing a descriptive exception, such as the IllegalArgumentException. How do the two versions of findMax() above behave if passed an empty array? (The first will crash with an ArrayOutOfBounds exception. The second will return the value -2 billion.) A final variant of find-max returns the index of the max element in the array, rather than the value of the max element. The easiest solution is probably to use two local variables—one for the max value and one for the index.

```
// Find-Max variant—rather than finding the max value, find the
// *index* of the max value
public int findMaxIndex(int[] nums) {
  int maxIndex = 0;  // say the 0th element is the biggest
  int maxValue = nums[0];

  // Look at every element, starting at 1
  for (int i=1; i<nums.length; i++) {
    if (nums[i] > maxValue) {
      maxIndex = i;
      maxValue = nums[maxIndex];
    }
  }
  return maxIndex;
}
```

Binary Search

INTRODUCTION

OBJECTIVES

After reading this article you will learn:

- What is binary search
- Variations of the binary search

TERMINOLOGIES

Binary search • Overflow • Recursive binary search

Binary Search

BY FRED SWARTZ

DIVIDE IN HALF

A fast way to search a sorted array is to use a *binary search.* The idea is to look at the element in the middle. If the key is equal to that, the search is finished. If the key is less than the middle element, do a binary search on the first half. If it's greater, do a binary search of the second half.

PERFORMANCE

The advantage of a binary search over a linear search is astounding for large numbers. For an array of a million elements, binary search, O(log N), will find the target element with a worst case of only 20 comparisons. Linear search, O(N), on average will take 500,000 comparisons to find the element. Probably the only faster kind of search uses hashing, a topic that isn't covered in these notes.

This performance comes at a price—the array must be sorted first. Because sorting isn't a fast operation, O(N log N), it may not be worth the effort to sort when there are only a few searches.

EXAMPLE

```
//============================================================= binarySearch
/** Binary search of sorted array.  Negative value on search failure.
 *  The upperbound index is not included in the search.
 *  This is to be consistent with the way Java in general expresses ranges.
 *  The performance is O(log N).
 *  @param sorted Array of sorted values to be searched.
 *  @param first Index of first element to serach, sorted[first].
 *  @param upto  Index of last element to search, sorted[upto-1].
 *  @param key   Value that is being looked for.
 *  @return      Returns index of the first match, or or -insertion_position
 *               -1 if key is not in the array. This value can easily be
 *               transformed into the position to insert it.
 */
public static int binarySearch(int[] sorted, int first, int upto, int key) {

    while (first < upto) {
        int mid = (first + upto) / 2;  // Compute mid point.
        if (key < sorted[mid]) {
            upto = mid;     // repeat search in bottom half.
        } else if (key > sorted[mid]) {
            first = mid + 1;  // Repeat search in top half.
        } else {
            return mid;     // Found it. return position
        }
    }
    return -(first + 1);    // Failed to find key
}
```

Style violation? Note: this code violates the advice of not altering method parameters. The reason is that it can under some circumstances make the code less readable. In this case, however, the code would probably be less readable by introducing two extra local variables.

COMPUTING THE MIDPOINT

There are two common ways to compute the index of the middle element. The most common way is to add the lowest and highest and divide by two. For example,

```
int mid = (first + last) + 2;
```

Overflow. This works well, or at least has worked well, until recently. The problem appeared when memories, and arrays, got very large. For the first time the sum of two array indexes, an intermediate value in the computation, can overflow the size of an int. Computing the midpoint by adding the two and then dividing doesn't work. **Reordering the expression avoids overflow.** The solution is to rewrite the expression so that no intermediate value overflows the size of an int. This is easy to do using the following.

```
int mid = first + (last - first) / 2;
```

For most programs the difference between the two computations will never be seen because it will only appear with very large arrays.

VARIATION ON BINARY SEARCH

The following method shows another version of a binary search method: (1) it compares elements of a string array (so comparisons use the compareTo() method), and (2) it sorts the entire array so fewer parameters are supplied, and therefore local variables are declared to take their place.

```
public static int binarySearch(String[] sorted, String key) {
    int first = 0;
    int upto  = sorted.length;

    while (first < upto) {
        int mid = (first + upto) / 2;  // Compute mid point.
        if (key.compareTo(sorted[mid]) < 0) {
            upto = mid;        // repeat search in bottom half.
        } else if (key.compareTo(sorted[mid]) > 0) {
            first = mid + 1;   // Repeat search in top half.
        } else {
            return mid;        // Found it. return position
        }
    }
    return -(first + 1);       // Failed to find key
}
```

Bubble Sorts

INTRODUCTION

OBJECTIVES

After reading this article you will learn:

- What bubble sort is
- Variations of the bubble sort

TERMINOLOGIES

Bubble sort • exchange

Bubble Sorts

BY FRED SWARTZ

People like bubble sorts—could it be the name? One nice aspect of bubble sorts is that they can quit early if the elements are almost sorted.

NOTE: As always, it's better if you don't write your own sorts. Java has better sort methods in java.util.Arrays.sort(...) and java.util.collections.sort(...). But sorts are excellent practice, and are a technique that all students are expected to understand to some extent.

BUBBLE SORT—FIXED NUMBER OF PASSES

This version of bubble sort makes a fixed number of passes (length of the array -1). Each inner loop is one shorter than the previous one.

```
public static void bubbleSort1(int[] x) {
    int n = x.length;
    for (int pass=1; pass < n; pass++) {  // count how many times
        // This next loop becomes shorter and shorter
        for (int i=0; i < n-pass; i++) {
            if (x[i] > x[i+1]) {
                // exchange elements
                int temp = x[i];  x[i] = x[i+1];  x[i+1] = temp;
            }
        }
    }
}
```

Bubble Sort—Stop When No Exchanges

This version of bubble sort continues making passes over the array as long as there were any exchanges. If the array is already sorted, this sort will stop after only one pass.

```
public static void bubbleSort2(int[] x) {
    boolean doMore = true;
    while (doMore) {
        doMore = false;  // assume this is last pass over array
        for (int i=0; i<x.length-1; i++) {
            if (x[i] > x[i+1]) {
               // exchange elements
               int temp = x[i];  x[i] = x[i+1];  x[i+1] = temp;
               doMore = true;  // after an exchange, must look again
            }
        }
    }
}
```

Bubble Sort—Stop When No Exchanges, Shorter Range Each Time

This version of bubble sort combines ideas from the previous versions. It stops when there are no more exchanges, and it also sorts a smaller range each time.

```
public static void bubbleSort3(int[] x) {
    int n = x.length;
    boolean doMore = true;

     while (doMore) {
         n--;
         doMore = false;  // assume this is our last pass over the array
         for (int i=0; i<n; i++) {
             if (x[i] > x[i+1]) {
                 // exchange elements
                 int temp = x[i];  x[i] = x[i+1];  x[i+1] = temp;
                 doMore = true;  // after an exchange, must look again
             }
         }
     }
  }//end method bubbleSort3
```

Bubble Sort—Sort Only Necessary Range

After a pass on bubble sort, it's only necessary to sort from just below the first exchange to just after the last exchange, because everything that wasn't exchanged must be in the correct order. This version of bubble sort remembers the lowest and highest locations where there was an exchange, and sorts only that part of the array. Although it is a little more complicated, it is more efficient than the other bubble sorts.

```
public static void bubbleSort4(int[] x) {
    int newLowest = 0;            // index of first comparison
    int newHighest = x.length-1;  // index of last comparison

    while (newLowest < newHighest) {
        int highest = newHighest;
        int lowest  = newLowest;
        newLowest = x.length;    // start higher than any legal index
        for (int i=lowest; i<highest; i++) {
            if (x[i] > x[i+1]) {
               // exchange elements
               int temp = x[i];  x[i] = x[i+1];  x[i+1] = temp;
               if (i<newLowest) {
                   newLowest = i-1;
                   if (newLowest < 0) {
                       newLowest = 0;
                   }
               } else if (i>newHighest) {
                   newHighest = i+1;
               }
            }
        }
    }
}//end method bubbleSort4
```

Other Bubble Sorts

Note that the part of the array that is completely sorted grows at only one end of the array. The ability to quit early is not symmetrical. The extreme values move all the way to the end in one direction, but only one place in the other direction. The algorithm can be improved by "bubbling" in opposite directions on alternate passes. This is left as an exercise.

Introduction to Stack

INTRODUCTION

OBJECTIVES

1. To understand the concept of a stack as it pertains to computer science
2. Be able to list several programming exercises where stack would be applicable
3. To understand and appreciate through one example how stack can be utilized in programming

TERMINOLOGIES

Stack • Arithmetic expression • Reverse Polish Notation (RPN) • Postfix • Infix • Pop • Push

Introduction to Stack

BY JOSLYN A. SMITH

The concept of stack is one of the most useful concepts in computer science. This section describes the concept, and shows through one example how valuable it is in solving some computer problems.

In programming, a stack is a special type of linear data structure in which items are added at one end of the list, and items are removed in the reverse order from that in which they are added. That is, the most recently added item is the first one removed. This data structure is also called *last-in, first-out (LIFO).* You can think of a stack just like a stack of cards, or like a stack of trays in a tray holder in a cafeteria.
There are five stack operations:

- **push**—Adding an item to a stack.
- **pop**—Removing the topmost element from a stack.
- **peek**—Looking at the topmost element, but do not remove it.
- **empty**—Checking if the stack has any elements.
- **search**—Traverse the stack to look for a particular element.

There are some calculators that use the concept of reverse Polish notation to evaluate arithmetic expressions, or simply carry out calculations. Calculators that use reverse Polish notation use a stack structure to store their values. An arithmetic expression can be represented in prefix, postfix or infix notations. Conversion from one form of the expression to another form requires the use of a stack. All compilers use stack to parse the syntax of expressions, program blocks, and program statements, before translating the code into low-level code.

Stack can be implemented in one of three ways – array based, linked list based, or simply using the class Stack found in the java.util package. Array implementation has a drawback. Since the size of the array must be fixed at compilation time, the stack runs the possibility of overflowing. We will use the Java defined class Stack in this section. **Figure 1** shows an outline of the constructor and methods in the class Stack as defined by Java.

```
public class Stack
{
    •   Stack() –Constructor – when the stack is first created, It has no element
    •   boolean empty() – Test if the stack is empty
    •   Object peek() - Looks at the object at the top of this stack without removing it from the stack.
    •   Object pop() - Removes the object at the top of this stack and returns that object .
    •   Object push(Object item)- Pushes an item onto the top of this stack.
    •   int search(Object o) Returns the 1-based position where an object is on this stack.
}
```

Figure 1 The class Stack

EXAMPLE: EVALUATE ARITHMETIC EXPRESSIONS

As was stated earlier, the concept of stack is extremely important in computer science and is used in a wide variety of problems. In this example we will write a program that can be used to evaluate ordinary arithmetic expressions that contains left and right parentheses, and any of the four arithmetic operators (+, -, *, /). For example, **3 * (10 – 4) + (20 / 2 – 5)**

Solution

This example requires three distinct steps, namely:

1. Verify that the infix arithmetic expression (the original expression), that may contain regular parentheses, **is properly formed as far as parentheses are concerned.**
2. If the parenthesized expression is properly formed, convert the expression from the infix state to its equivalent postfix state, called Reverse Polish Notation (RPN) named after the Polish Mathematician J. Lukasiewics.
3. Evaluate the postfix expression.

STEP 1: VERIFY THE EXPRESSION

Given an arithmetic expression, called an infix expression, to verify that it is properly formed as far as parentheses are concerned, do the following:

- Create an empty stack to hold **left parenthesis ONLY.**
- Scanned the arithmetic expression from left to right, one character at a time.

- While there are more characters in the arithmetic expression

  {

  - If the character just read is a left parenthesis '(', push it on to the stack.
  - However, if the character is a right parenthesis, ')' visit the stack and pop the top element, which should only be a left parenthesis, from off the stack. If the symbol is not a left parenthesis then we are in problem; or if there is no left parenthesis on the stack we will also have problem. In either case the program will terminate abnormally.
  - If it is any other character, skip it.

  }
- When the expression is exhausted, visit the stack. If the stack contains any element at the end of reading the arithmetic expression, then the expression was not properly formed, **as far as parentheses are concerned**.

Using the above algorithm, let us trace the behavior of the stack with the following expression.

"(3 * (10 – 4) + (20 / 2 – 5)) + 5"

Figure 2 shows a trace of the above arithmetic expression.

Input	**Analyze input**	Action	**State of Stack**
Read token	(: left parenthesis	push	(
Read token	3 : number	skip	(
Read token	* : arithmetic operator	skip	(
Read token	(: left parenthesis	push	((
Read token	10 : number	skip	((
Read token	- : arithmetic operator	skip	((
Read token	4 : number	skip	((
Read token	) : right parenthesis	pop	(
Read token	+ : arithmetic operator	skip	(
Read token	(: left parenthesis	push	((
Read token	20 : number	skip	((
Read token	/ : arithmetic operator	skip	((
Read token	2 : number	skip	((
Read token	- : arithmetic operator	skip	((
Read token	5 : number	skip	((
Read token	) : right parenthesis	pop	(
Read token	) : right parenthesis	pop	

Read token	+ : arithmetic operator	skip	
Read token	5 : number	skip	
Read token	End of input	No action	Stack is empty

Figure 2 A trace to determine if parentheses are properly nested.

In **Listing 1** the class **Arithmetic** is based on the above algorithm. All it does is to determine if the parentheses are nested properly. If the expression is invalid otherwise, this algorithm would never know.

In designing class **Line 6** shows the stack variable needed to store left parentheses alone. The stack will be re-used, so instead of declaring it to store any particular type, it is designed to store any kind of object. To a lesser extent we need to know the length of the expression so as to loop through the expression. Against this background the need for the integer variable, length.

In **Listing 1, Lines 30** and **33** use the constants of **LEFT_NORMAL**: and **RIGHT_NORMAL**, respectively. The definitions of these constants are found in the interface called Constants. Their types are char, and are designed to store the character values, left parenthesis, (, and right parenthesis,). See **Listing 2.** It can be expected that this interface will grow as we add more constants such as +, -, *, and /.

The method **isBalance** simply loops through the expression, one character at a time. As it extracts each character, see Line 26, it uses the switch statement, Line 28, to determine what the character is. Line 30 checks if the character is a left parenthesis. If it is, then that parenthesis is placed on the stack, Line 31.. Because the class Stack was designed to store objects, then we have to use the wrapper class Character to create a character object before storing it.

If the character is a right parenthesis, then visit the stack and remove the topmost element. Notice that the test is done on Line 33, and the removal is carried on Line 34. In addition, nothing is required to be done with the character, therefore it is not stored in any variable. Also, nothing is mentioned of any other character. Hence the default statement makes no mention of them.

To remove an element from the stack, as seen on Line 34, we run the risk of popping an empty stack. A condition of the kind is called underflow. If an underflow situation occurs, the program would terminate abnormally. To avoid this from happening, we wrap this section of code with the try-catch (exception), looking for **EmptyStackException**. In the case of an exception occurring, the variable fail would be set to true, Line 45, and the loop terminates.

The if/else statement on Line 48 simply returns the state of the variable fail.

```
import java.util.EmptyStackException;
import java.util.Stack;

public class Arithmetic
{
    private Stack<Object> stk;
    private String expression;
    private int length;

    public Arithmetic(String expression)
    {
        stk = new Stack<Object>();
        this.expression = expression;
        this.length = expression.length();
    }

    boolean isBalance()
    {
        int index = 0;
        boolean fail = false;

        try
        {
            while (index < length && !fail)
            {
                char ch = expression.charAt(index);

                switch (ch)
                {
                    case Constants.LEFT_NORMAL:
                        stk.push(new Character(ch));
                    break;
                    case Constants.RIGHT_NORMAL:
                        stk.pop();
                    break;
                    default:
                        // Skip all other token
                    break;
                }//end of swtich
                index++;
            }//end of while
        }//end of try
        catch (EmptyStackException e)
        {
            fail = true;
        }

        if (stk.empty() && !fail)
            return true;
        else
            return false;
    }
}
```

Listing 1 Class checks if parentheses are balanced

Listing 2 shows the interface Constants. At present it has only two fields, the left parenthesis and right parenthesis. It is expected to grow to include other values.

```
public interface Constants
{
        public static final char LEFT_NORMAL = '(';
        public static final char RIGHT_NORMAL = ')';
}
```

Listing 2 shows interface called Constants.

The test class, TestArithmeticExpression shown in Listing 3, defines a string array, s, with eight infix expressions. See Lines 5 thru 11. The program loops through the array, Line 16, and creates an Arithmetic object with each of them. Each object calls the method isBalance for it to determine if the parentheses in each expression are nested properly. The absence of parentheses also signifies proper nesting.

```
1.  class TestArithmeticExpression
2.  {
3.        public static void main(String[] arg)
4.        {
5.              String s[] = { "5 + ) * ( 2",
6.                             "2 + 3 * 5",
7.                             "( 2 + 3 ) * 5 ",
8.                             "( 5 + 10 ) / ( ( 15 - 20 ) + 25 )",
9.                             "10 + 5  20",
10.                            "( 3 * ( 10 - 4 ) + ( 20 / 2 - 5 ) ) + 5",
11.                            "( 3 * ( 10 - 4 ) + ( 20 / 2 - 5 ) + 5"
12.                          };
13.
14.       for (int i = 0; i < s.length; i++)
15.       {
16.                 Arithmetic a = new Arithmetic(s[i]);
17.                 if (a.isBalance())
18.                       System.out.println(s[i] + " is valid - with respect to parentheses\n");
19.                 else
20.                       System.out.println(s[i] + " is invalid - with respect to parentheses\n");
21.       }
22.       }
23. }
```

Listing 3 Test class TestArithmeticExpression

The output from this segment of the program is shown in **Figure 3**. Notice that the first expression, **5 +) * (2** on Line 5, although it has equal number of right parentheses as left parentheses, the expression is deemed invalid.

If you notice the output carefully, the first line says that an empty stack has been encountered. The reason is that the first time it encountered a closing parenthesis, there were no open parentheses on the stack, and hence empty stack exception has been triggered.

```
General Output
--------------------Configuration: <Default>--------------------
java.util.EmptyStackException
5 + ) * ( 2 is invalid - with respect to parentheses

2 + 3 * 5 is valid - with respect to parentheses

( 2 + 3 ) * 5  is valid - with respect to parentheses

( 5 + 10 ) / ( ( 15 - 20 ) + 25 ) is valid - with respect to parentheses

10 + 5 20 is valid - with respect to parentheses

( 3 * ( 10 - 4 ) + ( 20 / 2 - 5 ) ) + 5 is valid - with respect to parentheses

( 3 * ( 10 - 4 ) + ( 20 / 2 - 5 ) + 5 is invalid - with respect to parentheses
```

Figure 3 Output shows the expression which are valid from those which are invalid.

STEP 2: CONVERT INFIX EXPRESSION TO POSTFIX

Given that an arithmetic expression is properly formed with respect to parentheses, do the following:

- Create an empty stack to hold any arithmetic operators and left parenthesis, **ONLY**.
- A string to contain the postfix expression—the output from this conversion.
- Scan the arithmetic expression from left to right.
- While there are more tokens in the arithmetic expression,

Figure 4 uses the following expression to explain the algorithm: **"(3 * (10 – 4) + (20 / 2 – 5)) + 5"**

Each character is scanned from left to right as an input. This input is analyzed as specified by the algorithm, and the requisite action is taken. At each stage, the state of the stack as well as the output string is shown. Recall that the stack is needed to store left parentheses and operators alone; no other token is allowed.

Input	Analyze input	Action	State of stack	Output string
Read (	Left parenthesis	push	(	
Read 3	Operand	Write to output string	(	3
Read *	Operator, stack top has (	push	(*	3
Read (	Left parenthesis	push	(* (	3

Read 10	Operand	Write to output string	(* (	3 10
Read -	Operator, stack top has (	push	(* (-	3 10
Read 4	Operand	Write to output string	(* (-	3 10 4
Read)	Right parenthesis	Pop everything down to first left parenthesis. Write each element except the parenthesis to the output string	(* ((*	3 10 4 - 3 10 4 -
Read +	Operand, stack top has higher precedence	• Pop and write to the output string • Push the new element onto stack	((+	3 10 4 - *
Read (	Left parenthesis	push	(+ (	3 10 4 - *
Read 20	Operand	Write to output string	(+ (	3 10 4 - * 20
Read /	Operator, stack top has (	push	(+ (/	3 10 4 - * 20
Read 2	Operand	Write to output string	(+ (/	3 10 4 - * 20 2
Read -	Operator, stack top has higher precedence	• Pop and write to the output string • Push the new element onto stack	(+ ((+ (-	3 10 4 - * 20 2 /
Read 5	Operand	Write to output string	(+ (-	3 10 4 - * 20 2 / 5
Read)	Right parenthesis	• Pop everything down to first left parenthesis. • Write each element except the parenthesis to the output string	(+ ((+	3 10 4 - * 20 2 / 5 -
Read)	Right parenthesis	• Pop everything down to first left parenthesis. • Write each element except the parenthesis to the output string	(Empty stack	3 10 4 - * 20 2 / 5 - +
Read +	Operator	Stack is empty, push	+	3 10 4 - * 20 2 / 5 - +
Read 5	Operand	Write to output string	+	3 10 4 - * 20 2 / 5 - + 5
Read	End of input	Remove everything from the stack to the output string	Stack is empty	3 10 4 - * 20 2 / 5 - + 5 +

Figure 4 Understanding the algorithm using the string stated above.

Listing 4 shows the method convert2Postfix. This method first tokenizes the expression, using the Scanner class. Other classes such as th**e StringTokenizer** class would do as well. The method loops through the expression and extracts the tokens from the string. A token can either be placed on the stack or on the output string called **postfix**. We will re-use the stack, this time it will store left parentheses and operands (the numbers).

Before we start the analysis we should know that at this point the stack is empty, because in order for this method to be called, the expression would have to be valid. If the expression is to be valid then the stack would have to be empty, as a condition of step 1.

As the tokens are encountered, **Line 67** calls the method **isNumber** with the token as parameter. The method attempts to parse the token to an **int** value. If the token cannot be parsed, the method throws a number format exception. This means that the string is not a number. If the string is a number then it is appended to the output string, postfix. A space character is also appended as a separator for the next token, if any. This ends **Bullet # 1**.

```
56. // Convert the infix expression to postfix
57. void convert2Postfix()
58. {
59.         Scanner scan = new Scanner(expression);
60.         char current;
61.         boolean fail = false;
62.
63.         while (scan.hasNext() && !fail)
64.         {
65.             String token = scan.next();
66.
67.             if (isNumber(token)) // Bullet # 1
68.                 postfix = postfix + token + Constants.A_SPACE;
69.             else
70.             {
71.                 current = token.charAt(0);
72.                 if (isParentheses(current)) // Bullet # 2
73.                 {
74.                     if (stk.empty() || (current == Constants.LEFT_NORMAL)
75.                     {
76.                         stk.push(new Character(current));
77.                     }
78.                     else if (current == Constants.RIGHT_NORMAL)
79.                     {
80.                         try
81.                         {
82.                             Character topmost = (Character) stk.pop();
83.                             char top = Character.valueOf(topmost); //get the topmost value on the stack
84.
85.                             while (top != Constants.LEFT_NORMAL)
86.                             {
87.                                 postfix = postfix + top + Constants.A_SPACE; //put it on output string
88.                                 top = (Character) stk.pop();
89.                             }
90.                         }
91.                         catch (EmptyStackException e)
92.                         {
93.                             fail = true;
94.                         }
95.                     }
96.                 } // End bullet # 2
```

Listing 4 method convert2Postfix converts the infix expression to postfix.

In **Bullet # 2**, if the token is not a number, then it has to be either a left parenthesis, a right parenthesis, or one of the four arithmetic operators: **+, -, *, or /. Line 71** extracts that character and **Line 72** begins examining it. If the character is any of the two parentheses, method **isParentheses, then determine if it is a LEFT_NORMAL**, or, if the stack is empty. In either case, push the token on the stack, **Line 76.** On the other hand, if the token is a closed parenthesis **RIGHT_NORMAL (Line 78)**, visit the stack, retrieve the topmost element. Turning to the stack, as long as that token is not a **LEFT_NORMAL** element, keep removing each element from the stack and place them on the postfix string. If and when a left parenthesis is encountered it is removed from the stack; neither it nor the right parenthesis is appended to the output string, postfix. It is possible for the operation pop to cause empty stack exception; against this background it is necessary to protect the operation with the exception handler, **EmptyStackException.**

Listing 5 shows what happens if the token read is an operator, **Bullet # 3.**

```
98.                 else if (iOperator(current)) // Bullet # 3
99.                 {
100.                    if (stk.empty())
101.                    {
102.                        stk.push(new Character(current));
103.                    }
104.                    else
105.                    {
106.                        try
107.                        {
108.                            char top = (Character) stk.peek();
109.
110.                            boolean higher = hasHigherPrecedence(top, current);
111.
112.                            while (top != Constants.LEFT_NORMAL && higher)
113.                            {
114.                                postfix = postfix + stk.pop() + Constants.A_SPACE;
115.                                top = (Character) stk.peek();
116.                            }
117.                            stk.push(new Character(current));
118.                        }
119.                        catch (EmptyStackException e)
120.                        {
121.                            stk.push(new Character(current));
122.                        }
123.                    }
124.                }
125.            }
126.        }
127.        try
128.        {
129.            while (!stk.empty()) // Bullet # 4
130.            {
131.                postfix = postfix + stk.pop() + Constants.A_SPACE;
132.            }
133.        }
134.        catch (EmptyStackException e)
135.        {
136.            e.printStackTrace();
137.        }
138.    }// End convert 2 postFix
```

Listing 5 If token is an operator.

According to **Bullet # 3**, if the token is an operator, and the stack is empty, then we simply push it onto the stack. See **Lines 97** through **101**. If on the other hand, it is an operator, then compare the current operator with the one on the top of the stack, **Line 109**, to determine their precedence. As long as the one on the top of the stack is not a left parenthesis, and that it has higher precedence than the current one, remove the topmost one and place it on the output string. This narrative is articulated on **Lines 109** through **116**. Again, the stack may throw EmptyStackException, so we plan for it. If **EmptyStackException** is encountered, then the current token must be placed on the stack. See **Line 121**. This section ends **Bullet #3**.

According **Bullet #4**, any remaining token on the stack must be removed and be appended to the postfix string. This is shown on **Lines 129** through **133**. Again, as a reminder, it is necessary to protect the operation with **EmptyStackException** handling. **Listing 6** shows the definition of the methods: **isNumber**, **isParentheses**, and **isOperator**.

```
// Determine if the token is an integer
boolean isNumber(String s)
{
   boolean number = true;

   try
   {
      Integer.parseInt(s);
   }
   catch(NumberFormatException e)
   {
      number = false;
   }
   return number;
}

// Determine if character read is a left or right parenthesis
boolean isParentheses(char ch)
{
return((ch == Constants.LEFT_NORMAL) || (ch ==Constants.RIGHT_NORMAL));
}

// Determine if the token is one of the four arithemtic operators
boolean isOperator(char ch)
{
   boolean operator;
   switch(ch)
   {
         case Constants.MULTIPLICATION:
         case Constants.DIVISION:
         case Constants.ADDITION:
         case Constants.SUBTRACTION:
            operator = true;
         break;
         default:
            operator = false;
         break;
   }
   return operator;
}
```

Listing 6 Supporting methods isNumber, isParentheses, and isOperator.

The Boolean method **hasHigherPrecedence** shown in **Listing 8** determines whether or not the operator on the top of the stack has higher precedence than the current one that was read from the input string.

The accessor methods sizeIsOne, getResult, and getPostfixExpression shown in Figure simply return respective values that will be needed by the third module of the program.

```
// Determine which token has higher precedence
boolean hasHigherPrecedence(char top, char current)
{
    boolean higher;

    switch(top)
    {
        case Constants.MULTIPLICATION:
        case Constants.DIVISION:
            switch(current)
            {
                case Constants.ADDITION:
                case Constants.SUBTRACTION:
                    higher = true;
                break;
                default:
                    higher = false;
                break;
            }
        break;
        default:
            higher = false;
        break;
    }
    return higher;
}
```

Listing 7 Method hasPrecedence

```
boolean sizeIsOne()
{
    return (stk.size() == 1);
}

int getResult()
{
    Integer i = (Integer)stk.pop();
    return i.intValue();
}

// return the post fix string
String getPostfixExpression()
{
    return postfix;
}
```

Listing 8 accessor methods

```
public interface Constants
{
      public static final char LEFT_NORMAL = '(';
      public static final char RIGHT_NORMAL = ')';

      public static final String A_SPACE = " ";

      public static final char MULTIPLICATION = '*';
      public static final char DIVISION = '/';
      public static final char ADDITION = '+';
      public static final char SUBTRACTION = '-';
}
```

Listing 9 The expanded definition of the interface

Listing 10 shows the new version of the test class. The if/else statement determines whether or not an expression gets converted. Expressions that do not have balanced parentheses are excluded. In the output shown in **Figure 5**, you will see that the first expression was not converted because empty stack exception had occurred. This happens because the first parenthesis encountered was a right parenthesis. According to the algorithm the pop operation was performed. At this time the stack was empty, so popping it caused the exception to be raised.

```
class TestArithmeticExpression
{
      public static void main(String[] arg)
      {
            String s[] = { "5 + ) * ( 2",
                              "2 + 3 * 5",
                              "( 2 + 3 ) * 5 ",
                              "( 5 + 10 ) / ( ( 15 - 20 ) + 25 )",
                              "10 + 5 20",
                              "( 3 * ( 10 - 4 ) + ( 20 / 2 - 5 ) ) + 5",
                              "( 3 * ( 10 - 4 ) + ( 20 / 2 - 5 ) + 5"
                           };

            for (int i = 0; i < s.length; i++)
            {
                  Arithmetic a = new Arithmetic(s[i]);
                  if (a.isBalance())
                  {
                        System.out.println(s[i] + " is valid - with respect to parentheses);
                        a.convert2Postfix();
                        System.out.println("The postfix string is: " + a.getPostfixExpression() + “\n”);
                  }
                  else
                  System.out.println(s[i] + " is invalid - with respect to parentheses\n");
            }
      }
}
```

Listing 10 Modified test class

The output generated from the method **convert2Postfix** is shown in **Figure 5.** Notice that all the original input strings, except the first one, have been converted to their respective postfix representation. Looking ahead, the string **10 + 5 20**, although it is converted, it will not yield any arithmetic sense. This module however, would not know of this, because it was not its purpose to make this determination.

STEP 3: EVALUATE THE POSTFIX EXPRESSION

- Initialize an empty stack.
  While there are more tokens in the postfix string
  {
    - If the token is an operand, push it onto the stack.
    - If the token is an operator
      {
      - Pop the two topmost values from the stack, and store them in the order **t1**, the topmost, and **t2** the second value.
      - Calculate the partial result in the following order **t2 operator t1**
      - Push the result of this calculation onto the stack.
        - NOTE: If the stack does not have two operands, a malformed postfix expression has occurred, and evaluation should be terminated.

      }

  }
- When the end of the input string is encountered, the result of the expression is popped from the stack. If the stack has more than one operand remaining, the result is unreliable.

In implementing this program we assume that all operations are carried out as integer operations. Also to keep things simple, place at least one blank space between each token in the input string.

Listing 11 shows the method **evaluateRPM** which actually evaluates the expression. This method simply loops through the postfix expression and extracts each token one at a time. By now you should know that the only kinds of token that are in the postfix expression are operators and operands. The method **convert2RPN** in the second step had eliminated all parentheses.

The algorithm loops through the expression. When it encounters an operand, it places that operand onto the stack. See **Line 220**. When an operator is observed, the stack is visited twice in succession. The two topmost elements are removed in the order **x1** and **x2**. See **Lines 228** and **231**, respectively. Because these elements are integer objects, we use the method **inValue** to extract their **int** value.

It is important to remember that the operations, subtraction and division are not commutative. That is **a ÷ b ≠ b ÷ a**. Similarly, **a – b ≠ b – a**. Therefore when carrying out the calculations, they must be carried out in the order, **x2 operator x1**. See **Lines**

- **237**: (t2 + t1)
- **239**: (t2 - t1)

- **242**: (t2 * t1), and
- **246**: (t2 / t1)

Because each value is a primitive type, we must convert it to its integer object in order to store it in the stack; hence statement like: **stk.push(new Integer(t2 + t1));**

Figure 5 Each expression, except the first is converted to its equivalent postfix notation

```
General Output
--------------------Configuration: <Default>--------------------
java.util.EmptyStackException
5 + ) * ( 2 is invalid - with respect to parentheses

2 + 3 * 5 is valid - with respect to parentheses
The postfix string is: 2 3 5 * +

( 2 + 3 ) * 5  is valid - with respect to parentheses
The postfix string is: 2 3 + 5 *

( 5 + 10 ) / ( ( 15 - 20 ) + 25 ) is valid - with respect to parentheses
The postfix string is: 5 10 + 15 20 - 25 + /

10 + 5 20 is valid - with respect to parentheses
The postfix string is: 10 5 20 +

( 3 * ( 10 - 4 ) + ( 20 / 2 - 5 ) ) + 5 is valid - with respect to parentheses
The postfix string is: 3 10 4 - * 20 2 / 5 - + 5 +

( 3 * ( 10 - 4 ) + ( 20 / 2 - 5 ) + 5 is invalid - with respect to parentheses
```

It is possible for the operation pop to cause empty stack exception; as such we protect the operation with the exception handler, **EmptyStackException**. Also, the operation division could cause division by zero, hence we protect the operation with the exception handler, **ArithmeticException.**

```
// Evaluate RPN
void evaluateRPN()
{
  stk.clear();
  Scanner scan = new Scanner(postfix);
  char current;

  while (scan.hasNext())
  {
        String token = scan.next();

        if (isNumber(token))
            stk.push(new Integer(token));
        else
        {
            current = token.charAt(0);
            if (isOperator(current))
            {
                try
                {
                    Integer x1 = (Integer)stk.pop();
                    int t1 = x1.intValue();

                    Integer x2 = (Integer) stk.pop();
                    int t2 = x2.intValue();

                    switch (current)
                    {
                        case Constants.ADDITION:
                            stk.push(new Integer(t2 + t1));
                        break;
                        case Constants.SUBTRACTION:
                            stk.push(new Integer(t2 - t1));
                        break;
                        case Constants.MULTIPLICATION:
                            stk.push(new Integer(t2 * t1));
                        break;
                        case Constants.DIVISION:
                            stk.push(new Integer(t2 / t1));
                        break;
                        default:
                        break;
                    }
                }
                catch (EmptyStackException e)
                {
                    e.printStackTrace();
                }
                catch (ArithmeticException e)
                    System.out.println(e.toString());
                    result = "divde by zero - error.";
                result = "divde by zero - error.";
                }
                catch(NumberFormatException e)
                {

                }
            }
        }
  }
}
```

Listing 11 method evaluateRPN (at left)

```
1.  class TestArithmeticExpression
2.  {
3.      public static void main(String[] arg)
4.      {
5.          String s[] = { "5 + ) * ( 2",
6.                         "2 + 3 * 5",
7.                         "( 2 + 3 ) * 5 ",
8.                         "( 5 + 10 ) / ( ( 15 - 20 ) + 25
9.                         "10 + 5 20",
10.                        "( 3 * ( 10 - 4 ) + ( 20 / 2 - 5
11.                        "( 3 * ( 10 - 4 ) + ( 20 / 2 - 5
12.                      };
13.
14.         for (int i = 0; i < s.length; i++)
15.         {
16.             Arithmetic a = new Arithmetic(s[i]);
17.             if (a.isBalance())
18.             {
19.                 System.out.println(s[i] + " is valid - with respect to parentheses");
20.                 a.convert2Postfix();
21.                 System.out.println("The postfix string is: " + a.getPostfixExpression());
22.                 a.evaluateRPN();
23.                 if (a.sizeIsOne())
24.                     System.out.println("The result is: " + a.getResult() + "\n");
25.                 else
26.                     System.out.println("The result is indeterminate\n");
27.             }
28.             else
29.                 System.out.println(s[i] + " is invalid - with respect to parentheses\n");
30.         }
31.     }
32. }
```

Listing 12 The complete test class

Listing 12 shows the complete test class. Notice that line 23 checks to make sure that no extraneous result is printed. That is, when the input is exhausted, if more than one element or no element is left on the stack, the result is unreliable. This further means that the original arithmetic expression was not written correctly in the first place

Figure 6 shows the output for each valid expression.

```
General Output
5 + ) * ( 2 is invalid - with respect to parentheses

2 + 3 * 5 is valid - with respect to parentheses
The postfix string is: 2 3 5 * +
The result is: 17

( 2 + 3 ) * 5  is valid - with respect to parentheses
The postfix string is: 2 3 + 5 *
The result is: 25

( 5 + 10 ) / ( ( 15 - 20 ) + 25 ) is valid - with respect to parentheses
The postfix string is: 5 10 + 15 20 - 25 + /
The result is: 0

10 + 5 20 is valid - with respect to parentheses
The postfix string is: 10 5 20 +
The result is indeterminate

( 3 * ( 10 - 4 ) + ( 20 / 2 - 5 ) ) + 5 is valid - with respect to parentheses
The postfix string is: 3 10 4 - * 20 2 / 5 - + 5 +
The result is: 28

( 3 * ( 10 - 4 ) + ( 20 / 2 - 5 ) + 5 is invalid - with respect to parentheses
```

Figure 6 The complete output

An Introduction to Linear Linked List

BY JOSLYN A. SMITH

OBJECTIVE

To learn how to:

- Create a list
- Traverse a list
- Insert items in a list
- Remove items from a list.

TERMINOLOGIES

Linked List • node • traverse • null

INTRODUCTION

Linked list is one of the fundamental data structures used in programming. A list is a finite sequence of elements where insertion of elements occurs at any point and anytime in the list. Also, deletion of elements can take place from any point in the list and at anytime. Linked list does not carry index like array or ArrayList. Hence, whether it is inserting, deleting, or traversing the list, indexing of nodes is not a requirement.

CHARACTERISTICS OF LINKED LIST

A linked list consists of a set of elements called nodes. Each node is connected to the next by address rather than by index. The first node in a list is referenced by a variable described as the header address. The last node connects to no succeeding node, so it is assigned the **null** address, indicating the end of the list. **Figure 1** shows a linked list of four nodes.

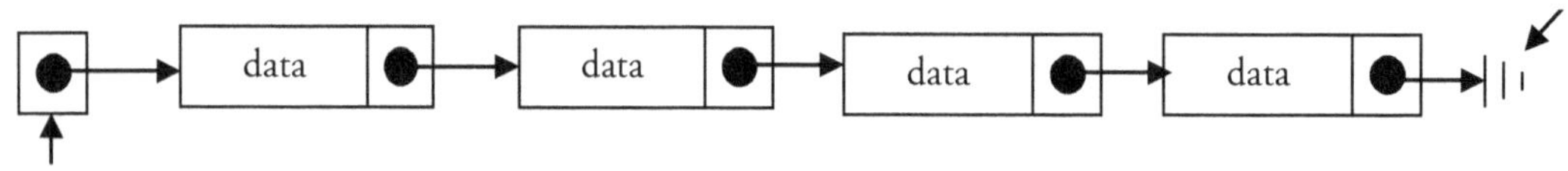

Figure 1 - A Linked List of four nodes.

There are different forms of linked list, such as singly-list (called linear list), doubly-list, multiply linked list and circular linked list. Only linear linked list will be discussed in this article.

In a linear list, a node is comprised of two components. One of the components stores the data, and the other stores the address of its succeeding node. The component that stores the address is called the link field. See **Figure 2**.

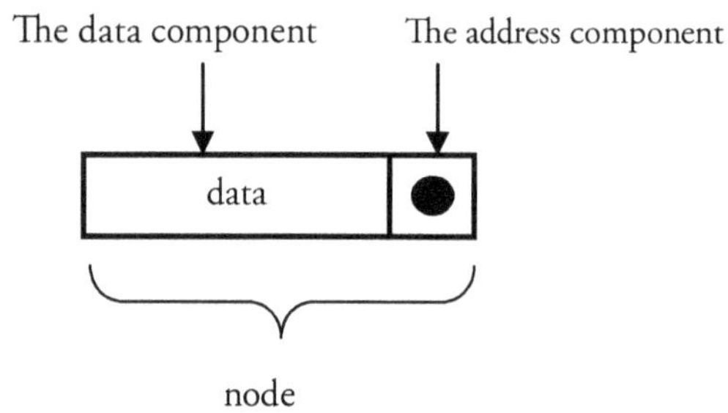

Figure 2 - A node

Figure 3 shows a list consisting of a single node. This node is referenced by the variable called **list**. The part that stores the data we will call **data** for now. Later we will add meaning to it. The address part we will call **next**, any other variable name is just as good. At this point the link field **next** contains the null address, signifying the end of the list. To refer to the data component of the node we say list dot data, written as **list•data**; and to refer to the link field, **next**, we say list dot next, written as **list•next**. The statement **list•next = null** assigns the null address to the link field variable.

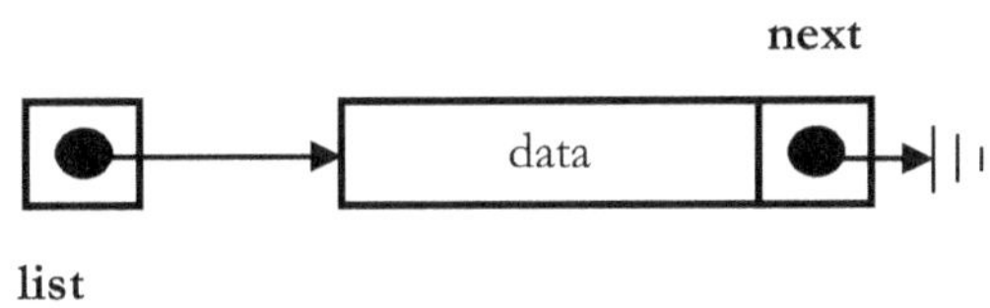

Figure 3 - A Linear Linked List containing one node.

The statement **list = null** abandons the list, by disconnecting the header reference from the list. See **Figure 4**. In this context there is no way of re-connecting the list with the header reference.

Figure 4 An abandoned list

In a linked list data structure, the header reference and the link reference are of the same type. Hence, linked list are referred to as self referencing data structure. This kind of data structure leads to more complex linked list implementations such as stacks, queues, and binary trees.

REPRESENTING LINKED IN LIST JAVA

Java defines a class called **LinkedList**, an implementation of the **List** interface. Its immediate super class is **AbstractSequentialList**, which implements the interface. We will not use this class; instead we will design and construct a linked list, in order to have a better understanding of it.

Let us design a node class called **Node.java**. This class will have two fields: the data field represented by a string variable; and a link field represented by the variable **next**. See **Listing 1**. **Figure 5** shows a pictorial representation of the code.

```
1.  class Node
2.  {
a.        String data;
b.        Node next;
3.  }
```

Listing 1 - The class Node

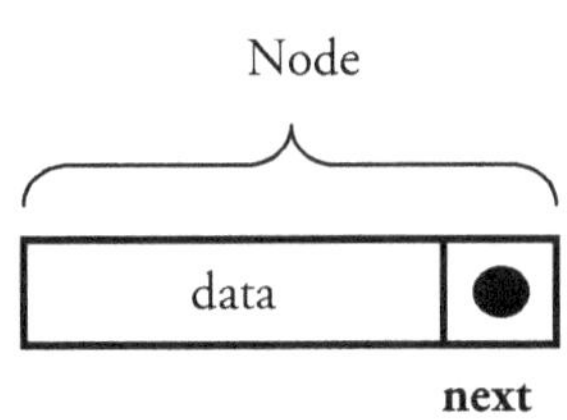

Figure 5 – Representation of the class Node

Listing 2 shows how the constructor initializes each of the fields. Notice that the linked field, **next**, points to no node. It is assigned the null address, as indicated by **Line 9**. **Figure 6** shows a pictorial representation of the class.

```
class Node
{
        String data;
        Node next;

        Node(String s)
        {
                data = s;
                next = null;
        }
}
```

Listing 2 - Constructor initializes the

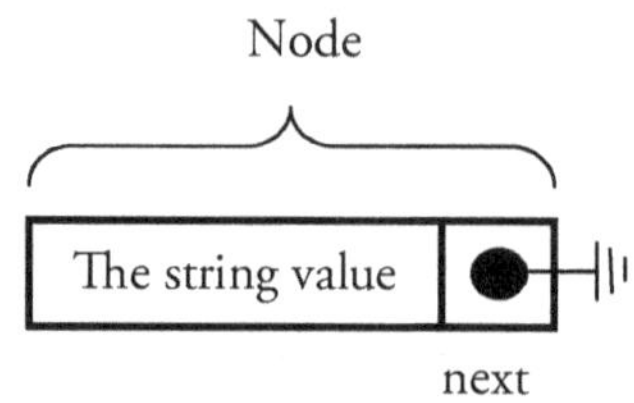

Figure 6 - Representation of the initialized

We will now create an empty list. To create an empty list necessitates implementing a class that will be used to create and maintain the list. Let us call this class **LinkedNode**. **Listing 3** shows a partial definition of the class.

```
1.  class LinkedNode
2.  {
3.          Node list;
4.
5.          LinkNode()
6.          {
7.                  list = null;
8.          }
9.  }
```

Listing 3 - Partial definition of the class LinkedNode

Line 3 of the code declares a reference variable of type **Node,** called **list**. This variable will serve to point to the beginning or head of the list. **Figure 7** shows a pictorial representation of the variable.

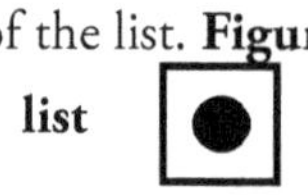

Figure 7 - Reference variable list **of type Node**

The code in **Line 7** creates an empty list. See **Figure 8** shows a pictorial representation of the list. Next we will define an accessor method that will serve to determine if the list is empty. See **Listing 4**, **Line 9**.

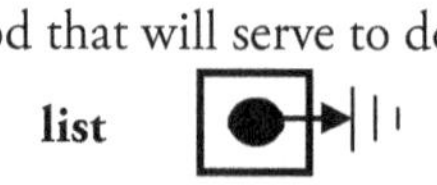

Figure 8 - The variable list **is assigned the null address**

We now define a method called prepend, that adds a node at the beginning of the list. See **Listing 5**.

```
1.  class LinkNode
2.  {
3.        Node list;
4.
5.        LinkNode()
6.        {
7.              list = null;
8.        }
9.
10.       boolean isEmpty()
11.       {
12.              return list == null;
13.       }
14.
15.       void prepend(String s)
16.       {
17.             Node temp = new Node(s);
18.             temp.next = list;
19.             list = temp;
20.       }
21. }
```

Listing 5 - Includes the method prepend

Figures 10 through 12 show the state of the list when a node is inserted at the front of the list

a) Line 7 creates an empty list , as shown in **Figure 9**

a) Line 7 creates an empty list , as shown in Figure 9

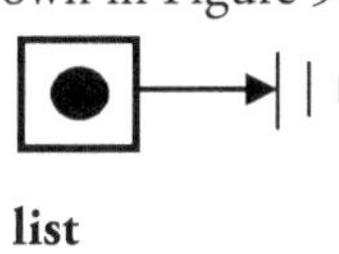

Figure 9 – An empty list

b) **Line 17** creates a new node using the string value it gets, and sets the link field to null. See **Figure 10**

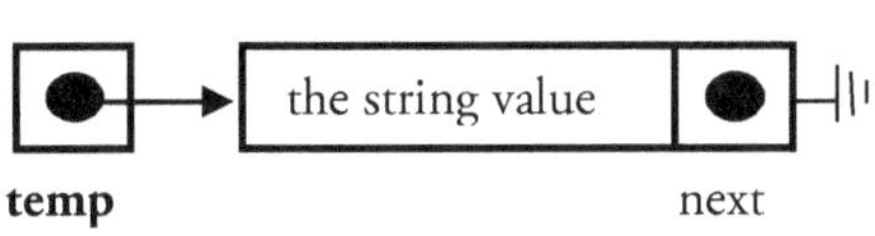

Figure 10 - A new node created

c) **Line 18** points the link field of the recent node, to the reference variable list. See **Figure 11.**

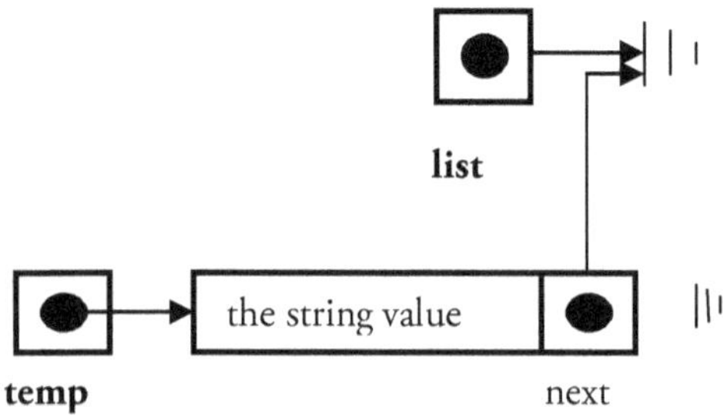

Figure 11 – Link field points to the null address

d) **Line 19** – The variable list points to the node being referenced by the variable temp, thereby making the variable list pointing to the head of the list. **See Figure 12**

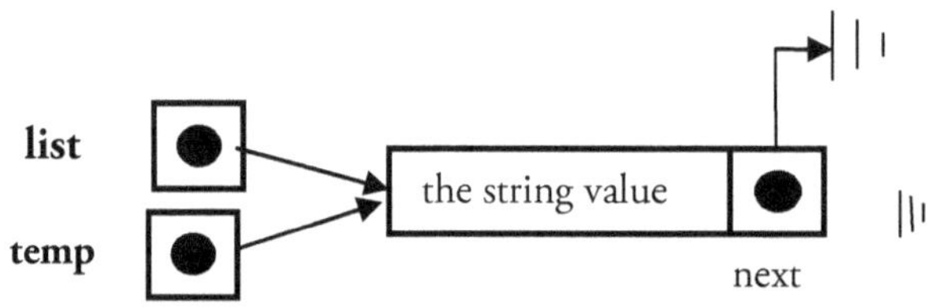

Figure 12 – The variable list is pointing at the beginning of the list

To append a node to a list requires traversing the list, visiting every node, starting from the first to the last, skipping none. That is, loop through the list and update the reference field for each node visited. When traversing a linked list never use the original reference variable that points to the beginning of list; rather, get an auxiliary reference variable to do that task. In this example we declare and initialize an auxiliary reference variable as follows:

ListNode current = list;

Figure 13 shows the effect of this statement. That is, the variable current, points to the first node of the list.

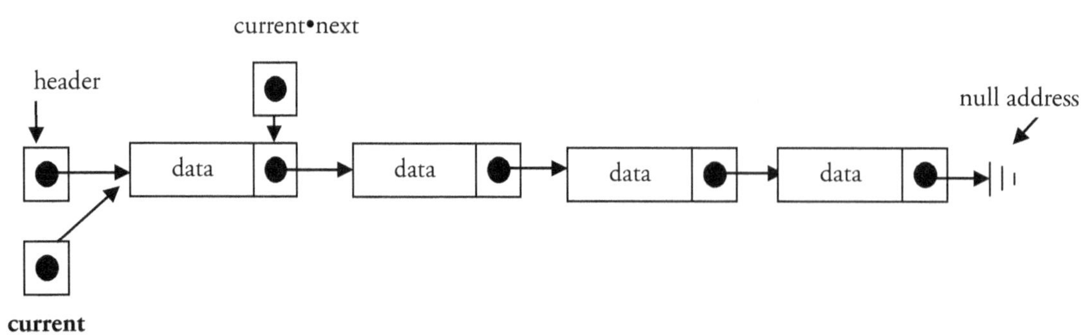

Figure 13- Reference variable current **points to the head of the list.**

In **Figure 13**, the address component of the first node (**current.next**) points to the second node in the list. In order for the reference, current to visit the second node, it must point to the node to which **current.next** is pointing. The required code for this statement is:

```
current = current.next;
```

Figure 14 shows the effect of the above statement.

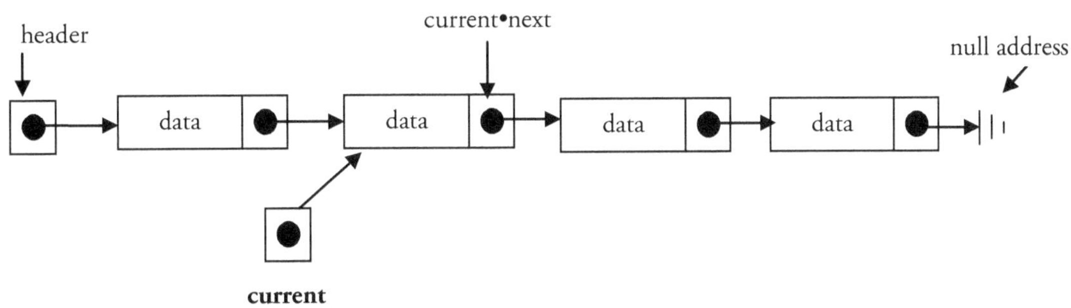

Figure 14 - current = current.next;

If we repeat the statement a second time, then the reference variable current will now be pointing to the third node. In addition to traversing the list, you must determine when **current.next** is pointing to null. When it is determined, divert **current.next** from pointing to null, and let it point to the new node that **temp** is pointing to. See **Figure 15**.

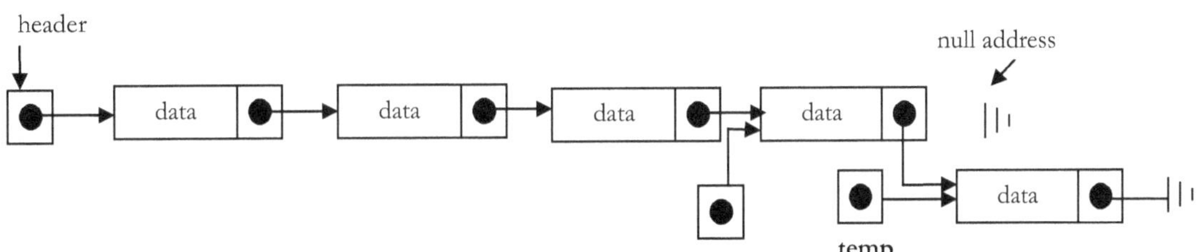

Figure 15 - New node temp is appended to the list

In **Listing 6**, the method append places the new node, which is being pointing to by temp, at the end of the list.

```
1.  class LinkNode
2.  {
3.      Node list;
4.
5.      LinkNode() { list = null; }
6.
7.      boolean isEmpty() { return list ==  null; }
8.
9.      void prepend(String s)
10.     {
11.         Node temp = new Node(s);
12.         temp.next = list;
13.         list = temp;
14.     }
15.
16.     void append(String s)
17.     {
18.         Node temp = new Node(s);
19.
20.         if (isEmpty())
21.             list = temp;
22.         else
23.         {
24.             Node current = list;
25.             try
26.             {
27.                 while (current.next != null)
28.                     current = current.next;
29.             }
30.             catch(NullPointerException e)
31.             {
32.                 e.printStackTrace();
33.             }
34.             current.next = temp;
35.         }
36.     }
37. }
```

Listing 6 - shows the code for appending a node to the list.

As shown in **Listing 6**:

- The method accepts a string value as the string, and uses the string to create a new temporary node reference by the variable temp. See **Line 18**.
- If the list is empty, then this new node will be the first in the list. See **Lines 20** and **21**.
- If the list is not empty, declare an auxiliary reference, and let this auxillary reference point to the beginning of the list. See **Line 24**.
- Use the auxiliary reference to traverse the list, looking for when **current.next** points to the null address. See **Lines 27** and **28**.

- As soon as we know when **current.next** is pointing to the null address, change its direction, and let it point to the new node instead. See **Line 34**.

Traversing a linked list has the potential of encountering null pointer. Against this background, enclose this portion of the code with the exception handler, **NullPointerException**.

You can insert a node anywhere in the list. Usually we use this method to maintain an ordered list. You can also delete a node just about any point in the list. This property requires traversing the list, looking for a given node. When the node is found, re-arrange the reference fields so as to eliminate that node. We will use an example to illustrate these two situations.

EXAMPLE

Librarians get books from time to time. Formally, when a librarian gets a book, the title would be recorded manually in alphabetical order. This means frequent re-writing of the list. Write a program such that as a book is received, it is automatically placed in the right sequence. From time to time books become obsolete. When a book becomes obsolete it is removed the collection. The program must take this into consideration also.

Use the concept of linked list to implement this idea, by designing the following classes:

- Book - this class the holds the title of book.
- BookNode – this class creates the node of information and its link field.
- BookList – this class creates and maintains the linked list of book titles in alphabetically order, and.
- Library – this is the test class that co-ordinate the activities of the other classes.

Solution

The solution to this problem runs parallel to the properties of linked list outlined above. The data in this case is referring to books. A book as we know has several attributes: title, ISBN, pages, price, author, etc. To keep things relatively simple we define the class book with a single field, the title. In addition we provide an accessor method to return the title of the book. See **Listing 7**.

```
class Book //  This class contains the information
{
        String title;

        Book(String t)
        {
                title = t;
        }

        public String getTitle()
        {
                return title;
        }
}
```

Listing 7 - class Book

The class BookNode is the most important of the four classes. It is used to store the data was well as the reference to the succeeding node. The data field is an object of type Book, and the link field we will call next. Notice that the link field is of the type BookNode. The book field is initialized the usual way; however, the link field is assigned the null address. This makes this node potentially the last node in the list. See Listing 8

```
class BookNode // Creates book node objects
{
        Book book;
        BookNode next;

        BookNode(Book b)
        {
                book = b;
                next = null;
        }

        Book getBook() {return book;}

        BookNode getNextNode(){return next;}

        void setNode(BookNode b){ next = b;}
}
```

Listing 8 - The class BookNode

The problem requires that the titles are to be arranged alphabetically. This means finding the proper place to insert the title. To search for the proper place requires traversing the list and comparing the title of the new book with the title of each book visited in the list.

As before, traversal of the list requires an auxiliary reference. If the data in the new node is alphabetically rank less than the data in the current node of the list, then the position is found. At this point, place the new node in the list. See **Figure 16**. As can be seen, the value of **temp.data** is less than the value at **current.data**. So we have found the right position to place the node. That is, the new node must fall between the node containing the letter **M** and the node containing the letter **P**. This solution has one problem. We cannot reference the node containing the letter **M**, since there is no reference pointing to it.

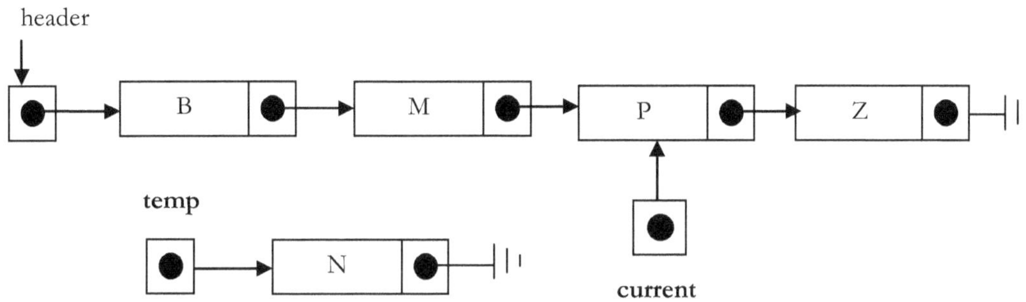

Figure 16 - Traversing the list to find proper place

To fix this problem, a second auxiliary reference is required. This reference will be made to trail the reference, **current**. When the position is found we re-arrange the references to include the new node. We will call this new reference, **back**. This reference must be set to the node being pointed to by the reference current, before advancing current to its successor node. That is:

1. Set back to point to current. The requisite code is, **back = current**, and
2. Advance current to point to its successor. That is, (**current = current.next**)

See **Figure 17**.

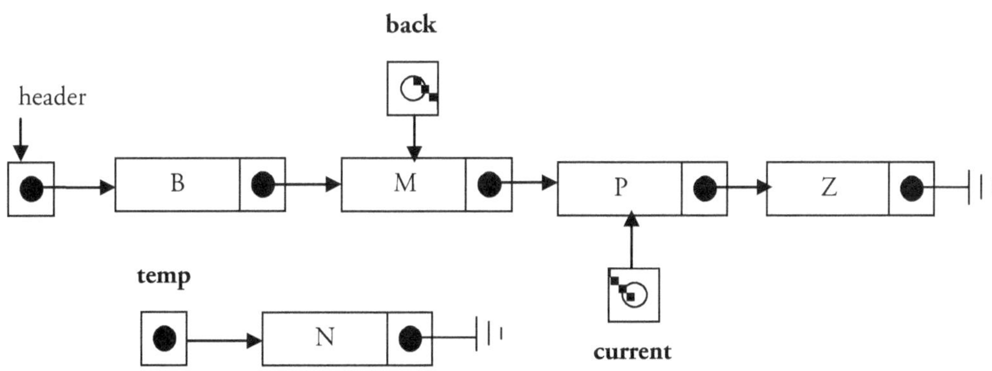

Figure 17- Introduction of new reference variable back

Once we have these variables in place, it is only a matter of re-arranging them to accommodate the new node. The two required actions are:

1. Set **temp•next** to to point to **current.** That is, **temp•next = current**, and
2. Set back.next to point to temp. That is, **back•next = temp**.

The bold arrows in **Figure 18** show the re-arrangement of the references.

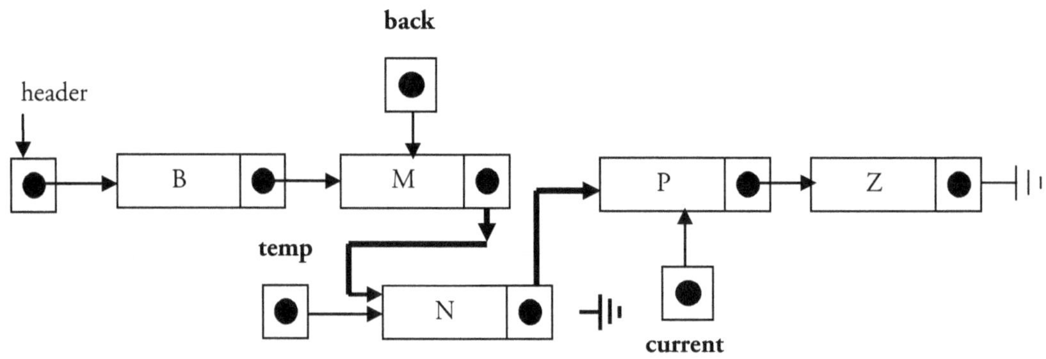

Figure 18- Placing temp node in list

Initially the reference back must be set to null. If after traversing the list back is still null, then this new node must be placed at the head of the list. On the other hand, if after the list is traversed you did not find a place to insert it, and back is not null, then the new node must be placed at the end of the list.
The class BookList does the following:

1. Declares the reference variable **list**, of type BookNode. See **Listing 9**, **Line 3**.
2. The constructor creates an empty list, by initializing the reference to null. See **Line** 7.

This variable will be used to point to the beginning of the list at all times. If we need to traverse the list, use an auxiliary reference to do so.

```
1.  class BookList
2.  {
3.      private BookNode list;
4.
5.      BookList()
6.      {
7.          list = null;
8.      }
9.  }
```

Listing 9 - class BookList creates an empty list

Listing 10 shows the method **insert** that inserts a node in its proper position in the list. The method receives the book object **b**, and uses it to create a book node object, that is referenced by the variable called **temp**.

```
10.   void insert(Book b)
11.   {
12.       try
13.       {
14.           BookNode temp = new BookNode(b);
15.
16.           BookNode current = list; //  Auxillary node points to the head of the list
17.           BookNode back = null; // This reference will trail current
18.           boolean found = false;
19.
20.           while (current != null && !found)
21.               if (temp.book.getTitle().compareTo(current.book.getTitle()) < 0)
22.                   found = true;
23.               else
24.               {
25.                   back = current; // Save the current position in the list
26.                   current =  current.getNextNode(); // Advance to the next book node in the list
27.               }
28.
29.           temp.setNode(current);
30.
31.           if (back == null)
32.               list = temp;
33.           else
34.               back.setNode(temp);
35.       }
36.       catch(NullPointerException e){
37.           e.printStackTrace();
38.       }
39.   }
```

Listing 10 - The method insert places a node in its proper position in the list

In preparation to traverse the list we introduce the two auxiliary reference variables, one that will traverse the list, and the other that will trail this current reference that is traversing the list. See **Lines 16** and **17**. Both variables are necessary in order to position the new node in its proper place. In addition, we declare and initialize a Boolean variable called **found** to false. This variable will alert us when we have found the position to place the node. See **Line 18**.

The heart of this method is the while loop. The condition to continue looping is that the list should not be exhausted; neither should the position be found. This is represented by the conditional expression in **Line 20**.

current != null && !found

The **if** statement on **Line 21** compares both titles. As soon as the condition is true, the loop is terminated. If not, set the reference **back** to the reference **current**, then move the reference **current** to the succeeding node pointed to by **current.next**. See **Lines 25** and **26**.

When the while loop is exited re-organize the references. First, let the **temp•next** point to where **current** is pointing. See **Line 29**. Now, depending on the state of back, we will know how to position the node. That is, if **back** is still null, then it means that the new node must be at the front of list. If back is not null, then the new node must fall between the two nodes – back and current. Hence we let **back•next** point to **temp**. See **Lines 31** thru **34**.

The problem requires us to be able to remove a node from the list at anytime. To remove a node, requires knowing the title of the book. First we search for the title, using similar principle to the insert method. Once the node is located, re-arrange the references so that the particular node is excluded. See **Listing 11**.

```
47. void remove(String title)
48. {
49.     try
50.     {
51.         BookNode back = null,
52.         current = list;
53.         boolean found = false;
54.
55.         while (current != null && !found)
56.             if (current.book.getTitle().compareToIgnoreCase(title) == 0)
57.                 found = true;
58.             else
59.             {
60.                 back = current;
61.                 current = current.getNextNode(); //current = current.next;
62.             }
63.
64.         if (found)
65.         {
66.             back.setNode(current.getNextNode()); // back.next = current.next;
67.             current.setNode(null);               // current.next = null;
68.         }
69.     }
70.     catch(NullPointerException e)
71.     {
72.         e.printStackTrace();
73.     }
74. }
```

Listing 11 - The method removes a node from the list.

As stated earlier, the remove method is similar to the insert method. The first change is the conditional expression of the **if** statement. Instead of testing for the inequality less than (<) we test for the equality (==). That is:

if (current.book.getTitle().compareToIgnoreCase(title) == 0

There are two actions that must be taken after exiting the loop:

1. The reference **back.next** must point where the reference of **current.next** is pointing. See **Line 66.**
2. The reference **current.next** must be assigned null, in order to drop the node from the list. See **Line 67**.

Figure 19 shows the re-arrangement of the nodes.

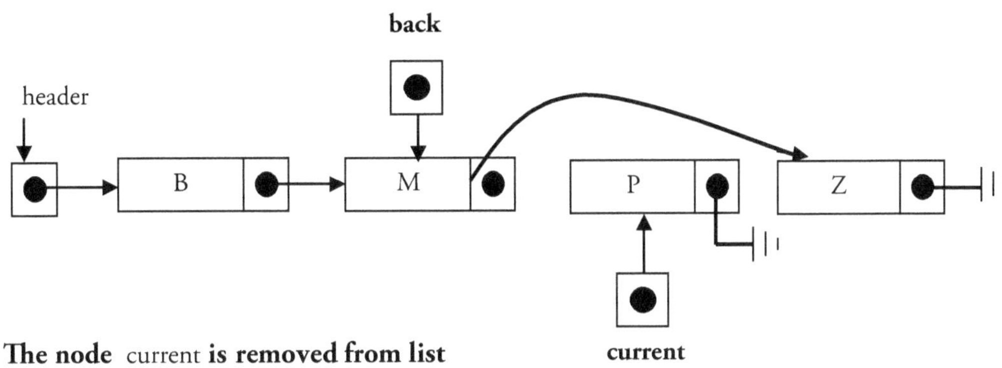

Figure 19 The node current **is removed from list**

Finally, **Listing 12** shows the definition of the **toString** method. This method traverses the list and extracts the title from each node in the list. The titles are appended to the string called result. The string is returned for printing.

```
/*
  * This method traverses the list and extracts the title from    the
     linked list of nodes. They are appended to a string.
    The string is returned for printing.
*/

public String toString()
{
      String result = "";

      BookNode current = list;

      while (current != null)
      {
            result += current.book.getTitle() + " \ n";
            current = current.next;
      }
      return result;
}
```

Listing 12 - Method that displays the list.

Listing 13 shows the test class called Library. This class creates an empty BookList object, and then adds four book objects to the list. After displaying the list of books, it removes a book from the list and displays the list again. In both cases this procedure maintains the book titles alphabetically.

```
class Library
{
        public static void main(String[] arg)
        {
              // Create a book list object.
              BookList books = new BookList();

              // Create book nodes and add them to the list.
              books.insert(new Book("Danger on the Waters"));
              books.insert(new Book("Paradise Lost"));
              books.insert(new Book("Building Bridges"));
              books.insert(new Book("Hall Mark of Fame"));

              // Print  the original list
              System.out.println("\ nOriginal List");
              System.out.println(books);

              // Remove a book
              books.remove("Hall Mark of Fame");

              // Print new list
              System.out.println("\ nNew List");
              System.out.println(books);
        }
}
```

Listing 13 - The test class Library

Figure 20 shows the output generated from the program

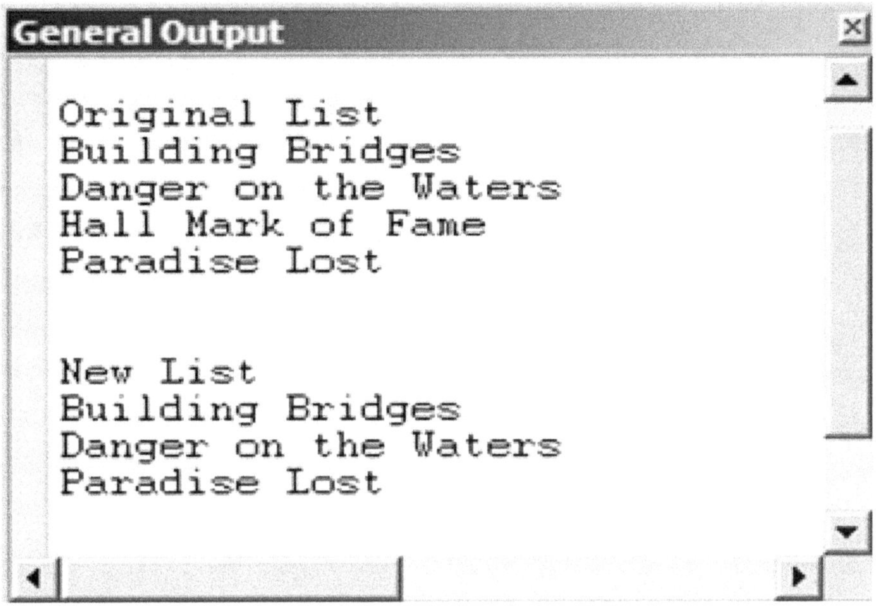

Figure 20 – List of titles alphabetically

SUMMARY

Linked list is one of the simplest but most commonly used data structures in programming. Linear linked list is fundamental to other complex abstract data structures such as stacks, queues, circular list, and binary trees, and multiply linked lists. Linked lists allow insertion and removal of nodes at any point in the list without disturbing the data from its position. This is a major advantage over arrays and ArrayList.

Linked Lists, Recursion

- Pointers and pointer notation
- Linked data representations
- A linked-list animation applet
- The SimpleList ADT
- A linked-list implementation of the List ADT

POINTERS

The concept of pointers is a central theme in data structures. Java implements pointers implicitly through reference-type variables. Recall that all non-primitive variables in Java are references to objects. For example, the statement

Point coord1 = new Point(25, 50);

declares and instantiates a new Point object. The variable coord1 is a reference (i.e., implicit pointer) to the object.

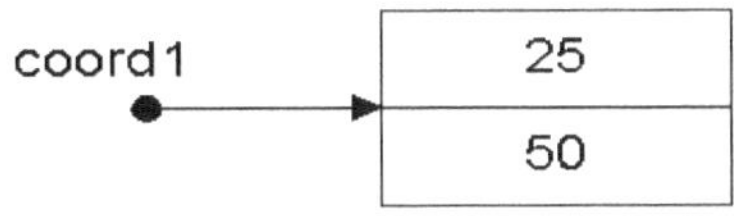

The above illustration is an example of pointer diagramming notation, which we shall use extensively throughout the course. This notation only shows the instance variables in an object and not the methods.

If we now declare and instantiate another Point object, then we will have two reference variables and two objects, as shown below.

```
Point coord2 = new Point();
coord2.x = coord1.y;
coord2.y = coord1.x;
```

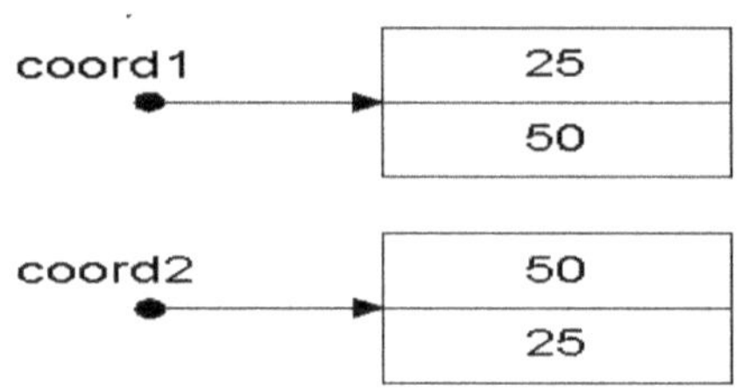

Assigning a reference variable to refer to another merely causes the reference value to point to the target object. coord1 = coord2;

Note that the above operation does not create a new Point object. The original object (25,50) is no longer referenced by any variable and will eventually be reclaimed by the garbage collector.

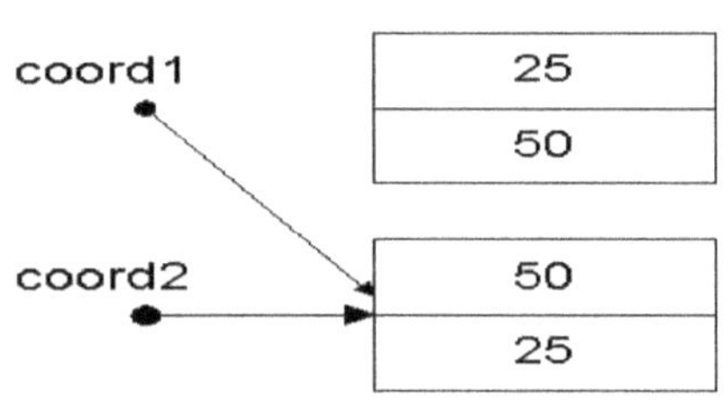

LINKED LISTS

- Store a collection of elements non-contiguously.
- Allow insertion or deletion of items anywhere in the collection with only a constant (i.e., Q (1)) amount of data movement.
- Are dynamic data structures whose size can be arbitrarily modified? In contrast, arrays are static data structures whose size cannot be changed.
- Can be either ordered (i.e., positioned according to ascending or descending order) or unordered.
- Can be used to implement many abstract data types:
- stacks
- queues
- deques
- sequences

- priority queues
- others

LINKED-LIST NODE

A linked list is constructed from a collection of self-referential nodes which may be defined as follows:

```
class SLNode {
private Object element; // element stored in this node
private SLNode next; // reference to the next node in the list
:
}
```

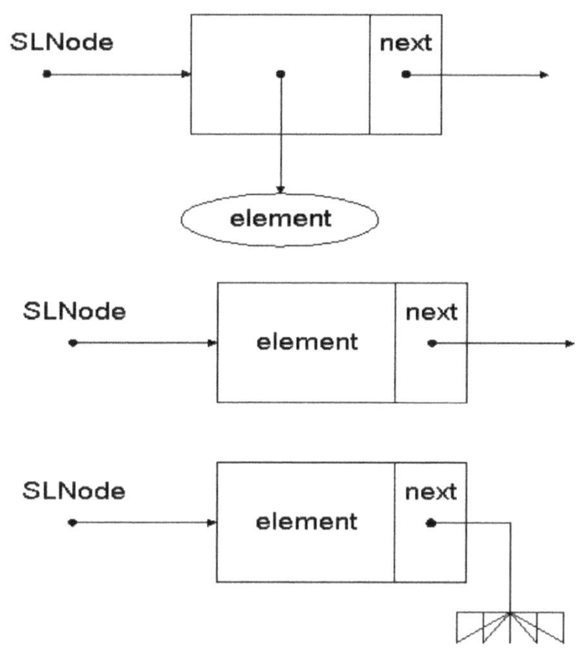

SLNode Constructors and Methods

A SLNode object can be created to point to the next object in the list.

```
public SLNode(Object e, SLNode n) { //# create a node given element and next
element = e;
next = n;
}
```

An alternative constructor has only one argument for the item; the next field is set to null.

```
public SLNode(Object element)
{
this.element = element;
this.next = null; //optional
}
```

An update method allows modification of the next field.

```
public void setNext(SLNode newNext)
{
    next = newNext;
}
```

Another update method allows modification of the element field.

```
public void setElement(Object newElem) { element = newElem; }
```

An access method returns the value of the next reference.

```
public SLNode getNext() { return next; }
```

Another access method returns the object stored in the element field.

```
public Object getElement() { return element; }
```

Building a Linked List from SLNode Objects

```
SLNode myNode = new SLNode("MD");
```

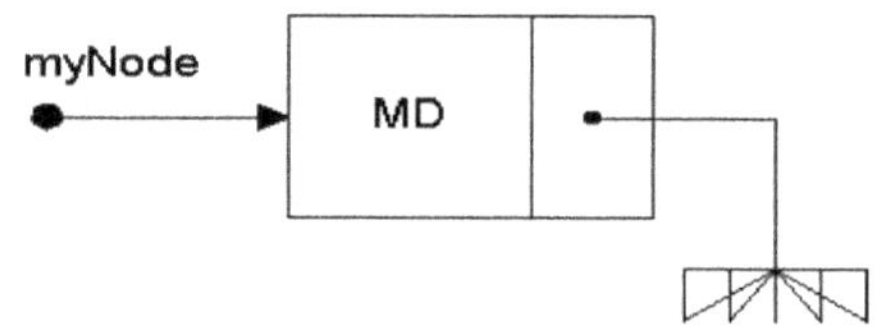


```
myNode.setNext(new ListNode("VA"));
```

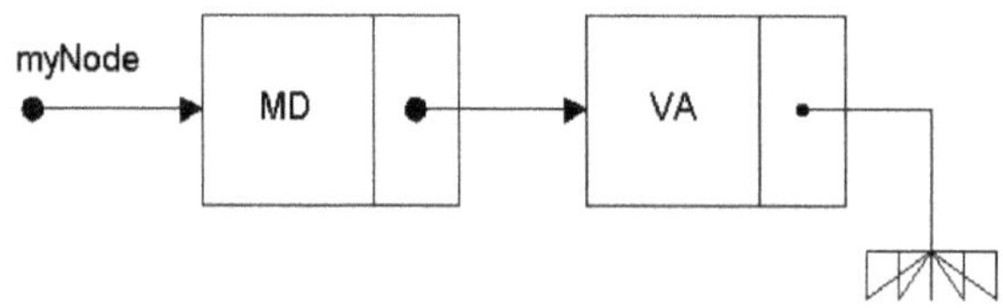

myNode.getNext().setNext(new ListNode("DC"));

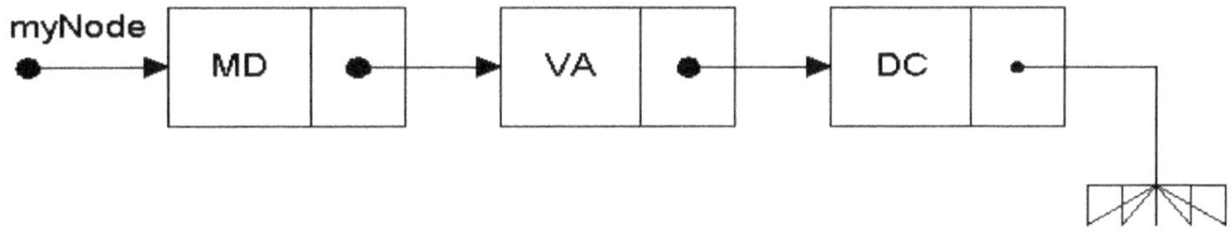

We could have built the same list with a single command.
ListNode myNode = new ListNode("MD", new ListNode("VA", new ListNode("DC")));

Linked-List Animation

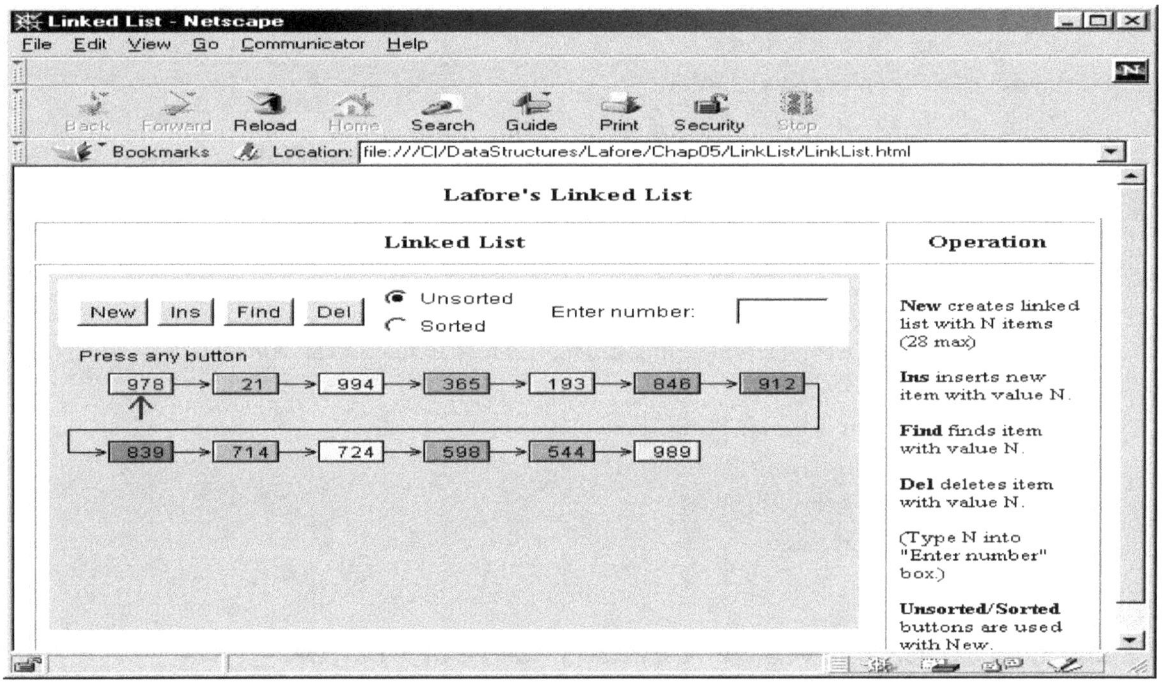

ABSTRACT DATA TYPES (ADTS)

- An abstract data type (ADT) is a collection of data and the particular operations allowed on them.
- An ADT is considered abstract because the operations performed on it are separated from the underlying implementation.
- Most data-structure ADTs can be implemented using either a contiguous (array-based) or linked-data representation.

- An ADT hides the implementation of a data structure behind a well-defined interface.

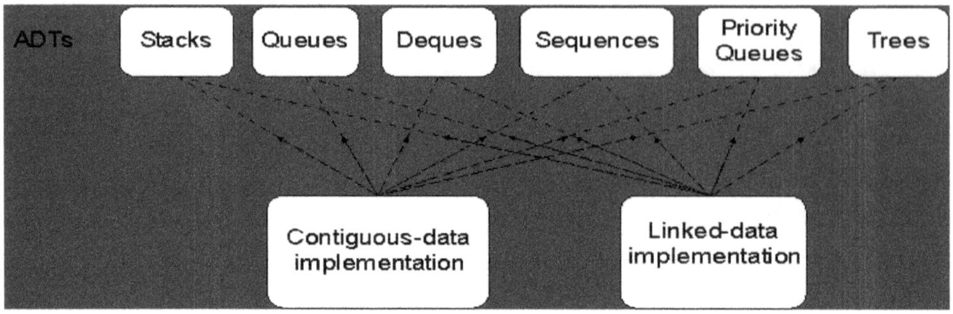

SCOPE

Today we concentrate on

- Understanding what a linked list is
- Fundamental operations on a linked list
- Defining the SimpleList ADT using a Java interface
- Implementing the SimpleList ADT using a linked list

Topics to be covered later in the course

- A more comprehensive "Sequence" ADT.
- Detailed performance comparison of linked-data versus contiguous-data representations of the Sequence and other ADTs.
- Functional operations: what is a list used for.
- Ordering of the list items (sorted? unsorted?).
- How to efficiently search a list.
- How to efficiently sort a list.

CONSIDER CONSEQUENCE OF "OBVIOUS" IMPLEMENTATION

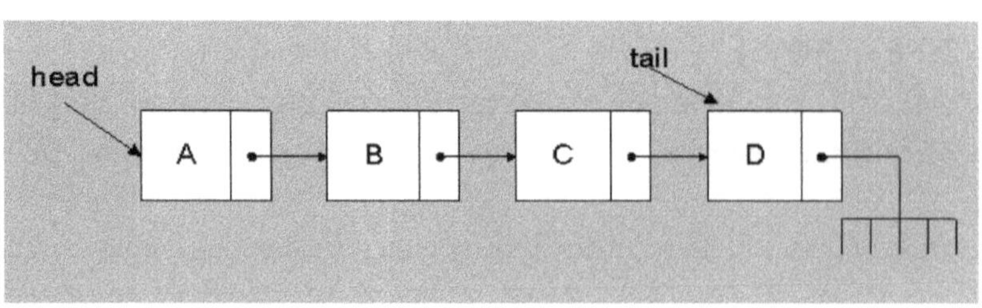

Removal from Head

tmp <--- head
head <--- head.getNext()
elem <--- tmp.getElement()
tmp.setNext(null)
return elem

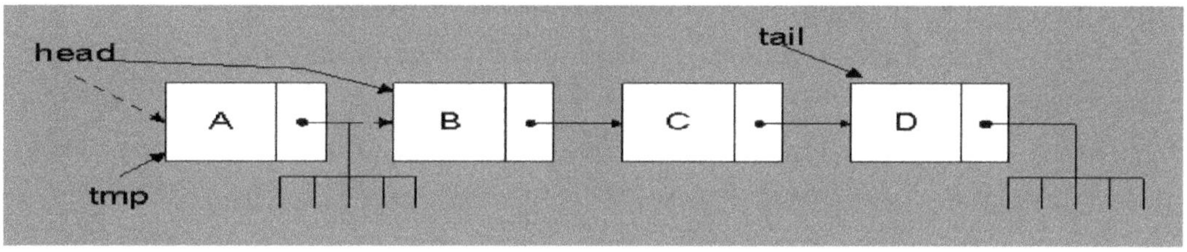

Insertion at Head

newNode.setNext(head)
head <--- newNode

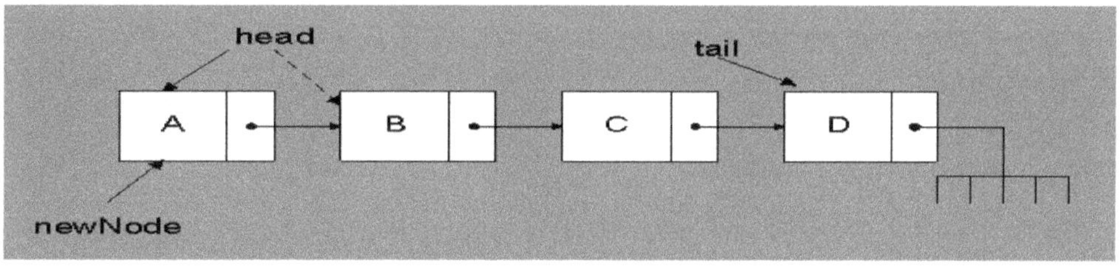

Insertion at Tail

tail.setNext(newNode)
tail <--- tail.getNext()
tail.setNext(null)

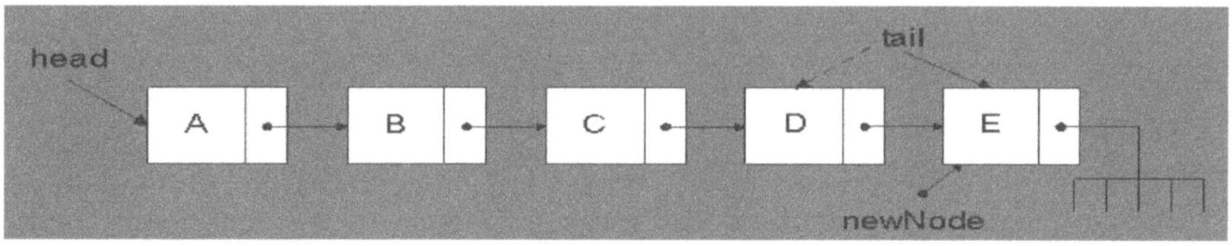

Deletion from Tail

Can't be done without incurring $O(n)$ operations.

THE NEED FOR A SENTINEL NODE

Consider inserting at the position prior to the current node.

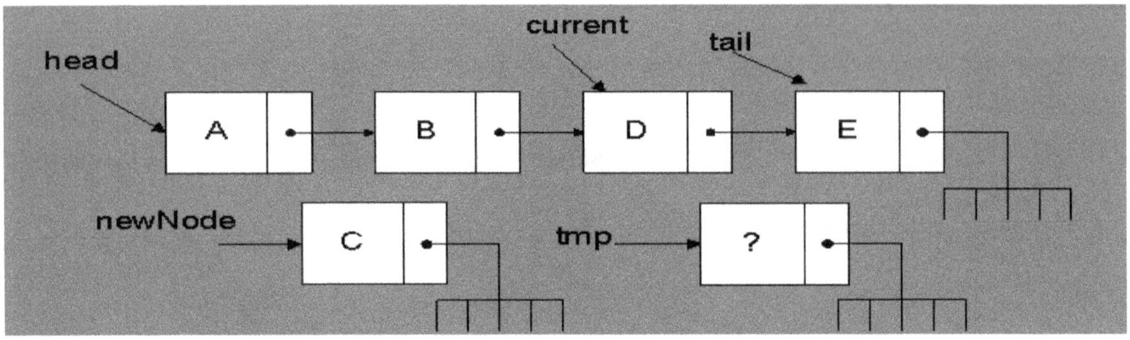

We would either have to traverse the list up to current or create a new temporary node in which the contents of current are copied. The latter solution is O(1) so we can opt for it.

```
tmp.setElement(current.getElement());
tmp.setNext(current.getNext());
current.setElement(newNode.getElement());
current.setNext(tmp);
```

But what if we wanted to delete the last node?

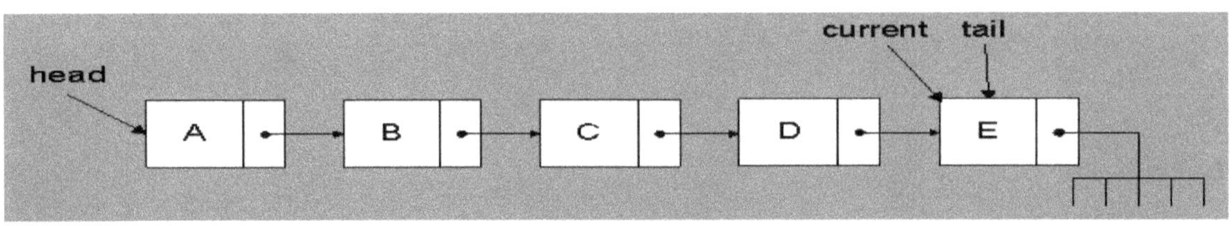

In this case, there is no way to avoid traversing the entire list, since we need to make a change to the node storing "D".

So we adopt the convention that "precursor" points to the node prior to current. The insertion point is in front of current and beyond precursor.

But this new convention leads to problems when removing the first element in the list, inserting in front of the first element in the list, and lists of one or fewer elements.

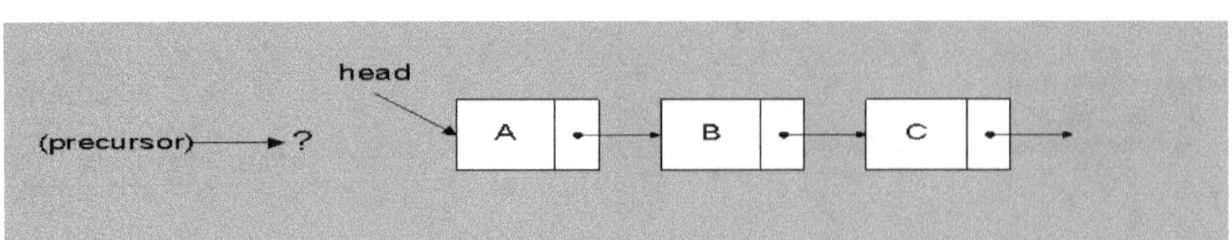

The solution is to use a *sentinel*, or header node.

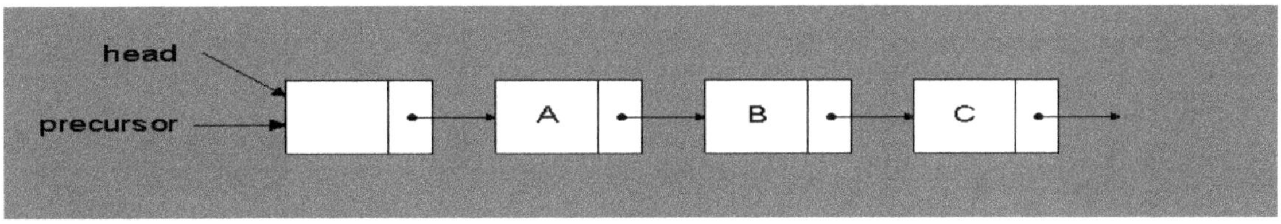

LINKED-LIST IMPLEMENTATION OF SIMPLELIST ADT

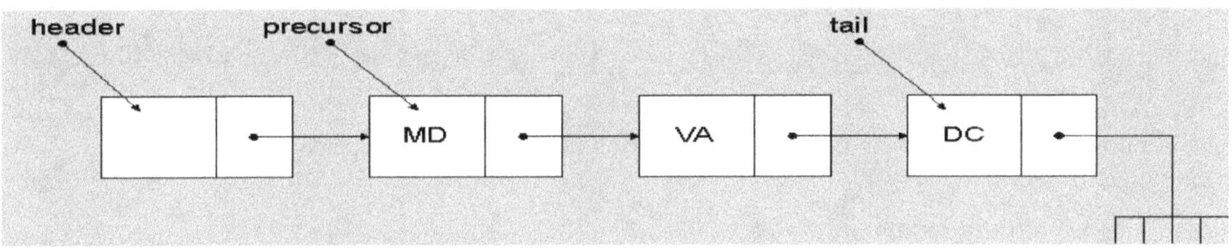

Store header, tail, and current references to point to front of list, end of list, and current position, respectively.

```
public class LinkedSimpleList implements SimpleList
{
// Instance variables:
    SLNode header, precursor, tail;
:::}
```

Two features of the implementation are subtle and require elaboration. The precursor reference actually points to the node *prior* to the target node, rather than the target node itself. This use of precursor avoids expensive deletions at the end of the list ($O(n)$ if current points to target node). All data movements are Q (1). The other feature is the use of an empty header or *sentinel* node. When precursor points to the previous node, insertions and deletions at the front of the list become an annoying special case. The sentinel node avoids this problem by providing a previous node for all cases. We shall see other examples of sentinel nodes later. The initial state of the linked list is empty.

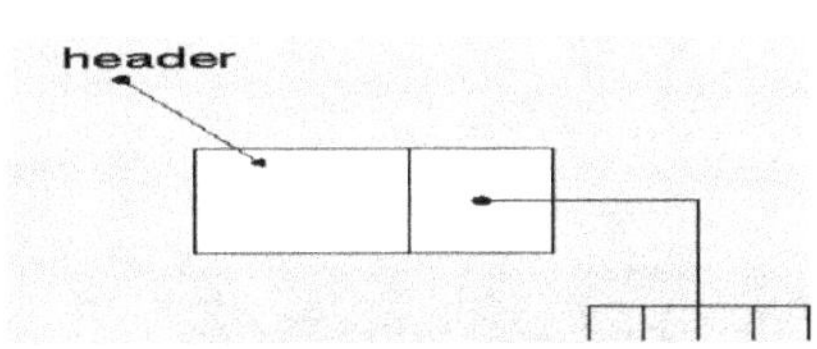

INSERTING AND APPENDING NODES TO A LINKED LIST

We insert new nodes at the position between precursor and precursor.next. Insertion is thus a simple splice and can be applied to any position.

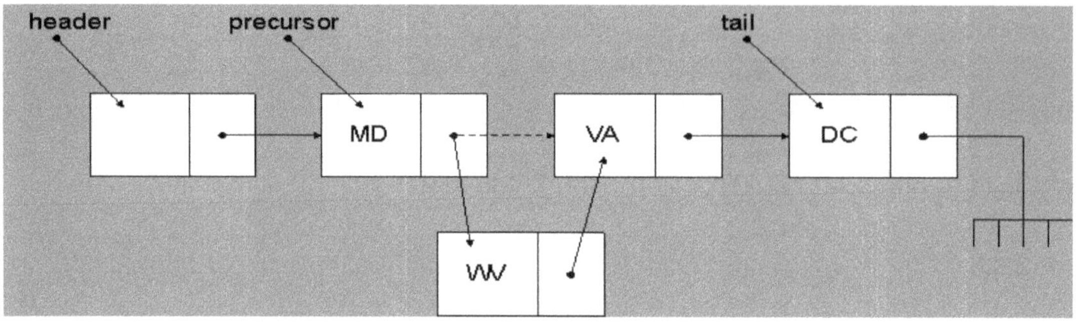


```
public void insert(Object newElem) throws BoundaryViolationException
{
    if (precursor == null )
        throw new BoundaryViolationException( "Linked list insertion error" );
    else
    {
        SLNode newNode = new SLNode(newElem, precursor.getNext());
        precursor.setNext(newNode);
        if (precursor == tail)
        tail = precursor.getNext();
    }
}
```

The append() method appends a new SLNode to the end of the linked list, i.e., at tail.next.

```
public void append(Object newElem)
{
    SLNode newNode = new SLNode(newElem);
    tail.setNext(newNode);
    tail = newNode;
}
```

REMOVING AND RETRIEVING ITEMS

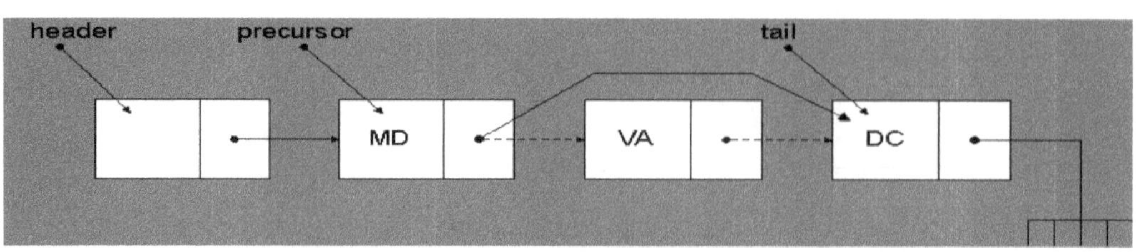

Basic deletion is a bypass in the linked list. We assume that precursor.next points to the node to be removed.

```
//-----------------------------------------------------------
// Removes the SLNode at the current position, i.e., at
// precursor.next. Returns the object that was stored in the node
// that was removed.
public Object remove() throws BoundaryViolationException
{
        if(!isInList())
        {
              throw new BoundaryViolationException(
              "Linked list error removing current node");
        }
        else
        {
        Object retElem = precursor.getNext().getElement();
        if(tail == precursor.getNext()) tail = precursor;
        precursor.setNext(precursor.getNext().getNext());
        return retElem;
        }
}
```

METHODS FOR CLASS LINKEDSIMPLELIST

```
//-----------------------------------------------------------
// Returns the object stored at the current position, precursor.next.
public Object getCur() throws BoundaryViolationException
{
        if (!isInList())
        {
              throw new BoundaryViolationException(
              "Error getting current elem");
        }
        else
        {
              Object retElem = precursor.getNext().getElement();
              return retElem;
        }
}
```

```
//-----------------------------------------------------------
// Copies the formal parameter elem to the SLNode at the current
// position, precursor.next. Throws a BoundaryViolationException if
// the current position does not refer to a non-null node.
public void setCur(Object elem) throws BoundaryViolationException
{
        if (!isInList())
        {
              throw new BoundaryViolationException(
              "Error getting current elem");
        }
        else
        {
                precursor.getNext().setElement(elem);
        }
}

//-----------------------------------------------------------
// Resets the linked list to the initial state.

public void clear()
{
       header.setNext(null);
       precursor = tail = header;
}

//-----------------------------------------------------------
// Sets the precursor position to point to the first node in the list.
// Since precursor points to the node prior to the current node,
// it is set to point to the heaser node.
public void setFirst()
{
     precursor = header;
}

//-----------------------------------------------------------
// Assigns the current position to the last node in the list. As such,
// precursor is set to point to the node prior to tail.
public void setLast()
{
         if(!isEmpty())
```

```
        {
            if(!isInList())
                precursor = header;
            while(precursor.getNext() != tail) advance();
        }
}
//----------------------------------------------------------
// Sets precursor to point to tail. Afterwards, isInList will return
// false because the current position, precursor.next, will be null.
// This method may be useful for the purpose of appending new nodes
// to the list in conjunction with the insert method. However, this
// method should probably be avoided, since a separate append method
// has been provided.
public void setTail()
{
      precursor = tail;
}
//----------------------------------------------------------
// Advances the precursor position by one elem. Throws a
// BoundaryViolationException if the current position is outside
// the boundaries of the list.
public void advance() throws BoundaryViolationException
{
        if(!isInList())
        {
            throw new BoundaryViolationException("Error advancing linked list");
        }
        else
            precursor = precursor.getNext();
}

//----------------------------------------------------------
// Returns the number of elems in the list.
// Is this method efficient?
public int length()
{
      SLNode tmp;
      int count = 0;
      tmp = header.getNext();
      while(tmp != null)
      {
```

```
            count++;
            tmp = tmp.getNext();
        }
        return count;
    }
    //-----------------------------------------------------------
    // Returns true is the list has no elements, true if it has at least
    // one element.
    public boolean isEmpty()
    {
         return (header.getNext() == null);
    }

    //-----------------------------------------------------------
    // Returns true if the current position is a valid position in the
    // list.
    public boolean isInList()
    {
        return ((precursor != null) && (precursor.getNext() != null));
    }

    // Prints all objects in the list to standard output.
    public void print()
    {
        for(setFirst();isInList();advance())
        System.out.println(getCur());
```

LINKED LISTS: DISCUSSION

- We could have chosen many other implementations of a linked list.
- The header reference could have pointed to the actual first node on the list.
- A current node could have pointed to the actual target node (as opposed to using a precursor node).
- We can also implement the SimpleList ADT using an array. One disadvantage of an array is that arbitrary insertions and deletions may require $O(n)$ data movement operations, which are expensive in practice.
- We can also implement the SimpleList ADT using a doubly linked list.
- The important thing to remember is that the user of the software should not have to be concerned with the implementation you choose.

RECURSION

- Recursive methods in Java
- Recursion and mathematical induction

- Dangers of recursion
- Infinite regress
- Redundant calculations
- Mutual recursion
- Divide-and-conquer recursion
- The "Towers of Hanoi" puzzle

WHAT IS RECURSION?

A recursive definition is one that is defined in terms of itself. It must include a base case so that the recursion will eventually end.

RECURSION IN MATHEMATICS

Many mathematical functions have recursive definitions. Consider the factorial (!) operation on non-negative integers.

To illustrate,

$$n! = \begin{cases} 1, & n \le 1 \\ n(n-1)!, & n > 1 \end{cases}$$

$$\begin{aligned} 5! &= 5(4!) \\ &= 5(4(3!)) \\ &= 5(4(3(2!))) \\ &= 5(4(3(2(1!)))) \\ &= 5(4(3(2(1)))) \\ &= 5(4(3(2))) \\ &= 5(4(6)) \\ &= 5(24) \\ &= 120 \end{aligned}$$

RECURSIVE METHODS IN JAVA

Java methods may be recursively defined; that is, a Java method may contain one or more calls to itself. The programmer should be aware that every method call, recursive or otherwise, has certain overhead operations associated with it. When a method is invoked, information about that method (such as its actual parameters, local variables, and return value) are placed on the Java Virtual Machine *method stack*, also known as the *Java stack, virtual stack* or *activation record*. As such, recursive methods are often more expensive than their iterative equivalents. Recursion is nonetheless a useful programming tool and is encountered frequently in data structures and algorithms. Later in the course, we shall encounter highly effective algorithms for searching and sorting that make use of recursion.

Recursive Factorial Method

```
int factorial(int n)
{
  if(n < 1) // base case
    return 1;
  else
    return n * factorial(n-1); // recursive call
}
```

Iterative Factorial Method

```
int factorial(int n)
{
  int result = 1;
  for(int m = n; m > 0; m--)
    result *= m;
  return result;
}
```

RECURSIVE CALL TRACE, FACTORIAL METHOD

Call traces help us understand the recursive process and analyze the complexity of recursive algorithms. Since each node of the factorial method's call trace is $O(1)$, the recursive invocation of factorial(n) is $O(n)$.

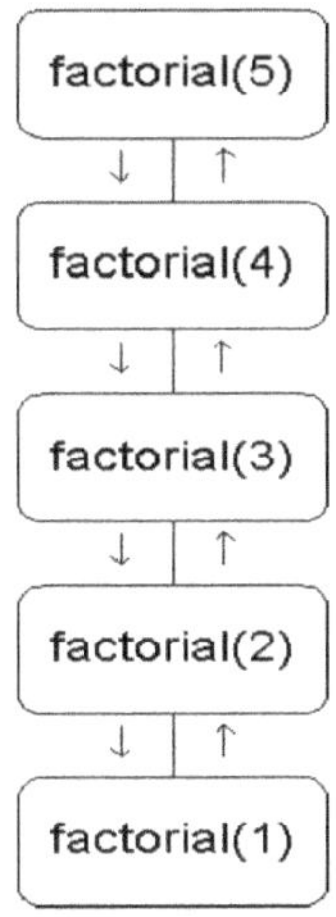

RECURSION AND MATHEMATICAL INDUCTION

Recall proofs by induction:

1. Show that the theorem is true for the smallest case. This can usually be done by inspection.
   ===> *basis*
2. Show that if the theorem is true for the basis cases, it can be extended to include the next case. If the theorem is true for the case $k=n-1$, show that it is true for the case $k=n$.
   ===> *Inductive hypothesis* assumes that the theorem is true for the case $k=n-1$.

Similarity with recursive programming :

1. The *base case* of a recursive method is the case that can be solved without a recursive call.
2. For the general (non-base) case, $k=n$, we assume that the recursive method works for $k=n-1$.

Recursion is the programming equivalent of induction.

DANGERS OF RECURSION: INFINITE REGRESS

Consider the following poorly designed implementation of the factorial method:

```
int factorial(int n)
{
   System.out.println("factorial("+n+") called");
   if(n == 1)
      return 1;
   else
      return n * factorial(n-1);
}
```

What if we called this method with an argument of 0? We would see the following console output.

```
factorial(0) called
factorial(-1) called
factorial(-2) called
:
factorial(-9999) called
```

... and so on, until a stack overflow occurs. This phenomenon is known as *infinite regress* and is a real danger of recursive programming. To avoid infinite regress, follow these two rules.

1. Take special care to ensure that the base case is properly implemented.
2. Make sure that each subsequent recursive call represents progress toward the base case.

DANGERS OF RECURSION: REDUNDANT CALCULATIONS

Consider the Fibonacci number sequence, defined as

$$F_n = \begin{cases} 0, & n = 0 \\ 1, & n = 1 \\ F_{n-1} + F_{n-2}, & n \geq 2 \end{cases}$$

The sequence {0,1,1,2,3,5,8,13 ...} where n is a non-negative integer. A method to generate Fibonacci numbers can be implemented recursively.

```
public static int fib(int n)
{
if(n <= 1) return n; //base case
else return fib(n-1) + fib(n-2);
}
```

Consider now the call trace for n=5.

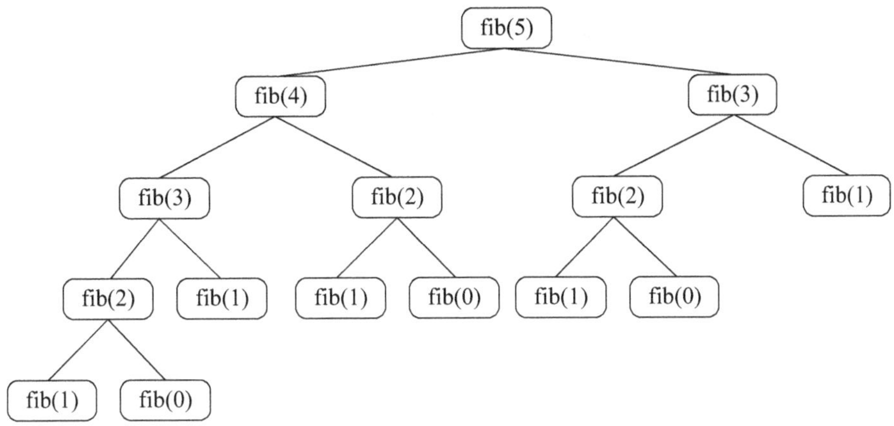

Note the redundant calculations: 3 calls to fib(0), 5 calls to fib(1), and so on. Each recursive call does more and more redundant work, resulting in exponential growth.

MUTUAL RECURSION

So far we have only considered recursive methods that call themselves. Another type of recursion involves methods that cyclically call each other. This is known as cyclical or mutual recursion. In the following example, methods A and B are mutually recursive.

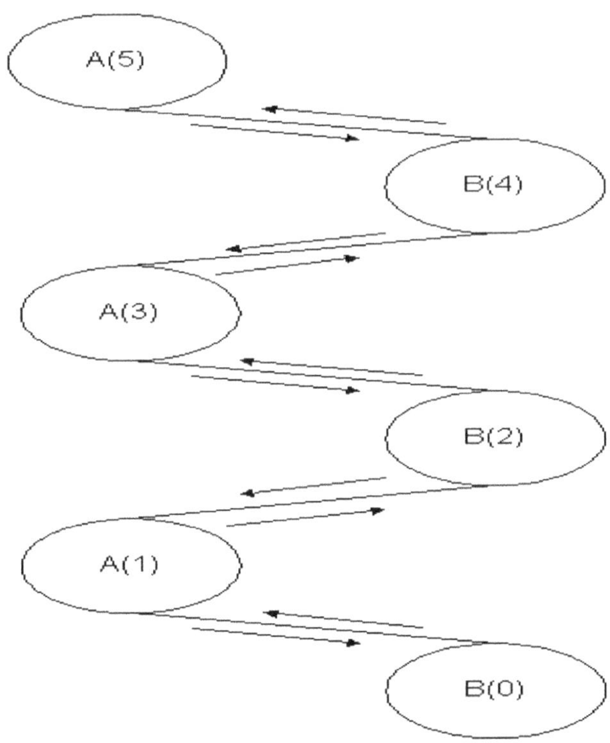


```
void A(int n)
{
 if (n <= 0) return;
 n--;
 B(n);
}

void B(int n)
{
 if (n <= 0) returnl
 n--;
 A(n);
}
```

DIVIDE-AND-CONQUER RECURSION

One of the more effective uses of recursion is through a class of algorithms known as *divide and conquer.*

Divide—Smaller problems (subproblems) are solved recursively (except, of course, for the base case).

Conquer—The solution to the original problem is then formed from solutions to the subproblems.

- Divide-and-conquer algorithms generally contain at least two recursive calls in the method.
- The smaller recursive subproblems must be disjoint (i.e., non-overlapping) in order for the approach to be considered divide-and-conquer.

The following is a divide-and-conquer method for computing the sum of squares of all integers between *m* and *n*, i.e.,

$$\sum_{i=m}^{n} i^2$$

```
int ssq(int m, int n)
{
  if(m > n) return –1; // error condition
  else if (m == n) return m*m;
  else
  {
    int middle = (m+n)/2;
    return ssq(m,middle) + ssq(middle+1,n);
  }
}
```

RECURSION CALL TRACE FOR SSQ METHOD

- The two numbers inside the nodes are *m* and *n*.
- The number above a node is its return value.

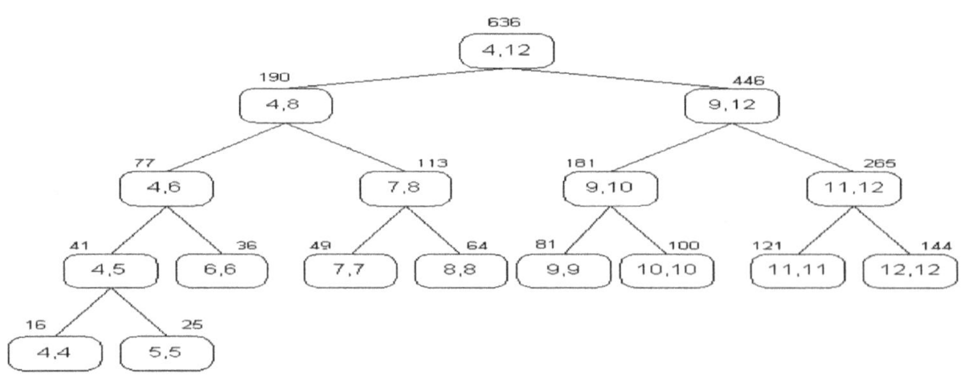

TOWERS OF HANOI

At a remote temple somewhere in Asia, a group of monks is working to move 64 disks from the leftmost peg (peg A) to the rightmost peg (peg C). After all 64 disks have been moved, the universe will dissolve! When will this happen if each disk takes 1 second to move?

Rules of the puzzle:

- Larger disks may not be placed on top of smaller disks.
- Only one disk may be moved at a time.

10-disk illustration

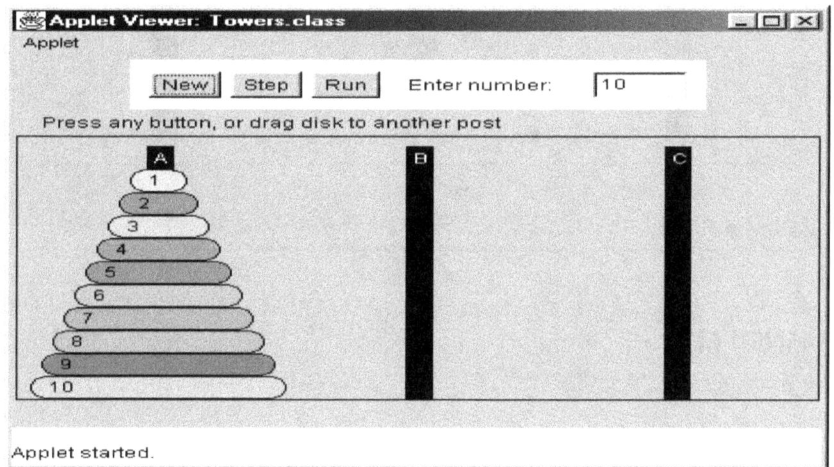

TOWERS OF HANOI (2)

Consider the n=4 subproblem.

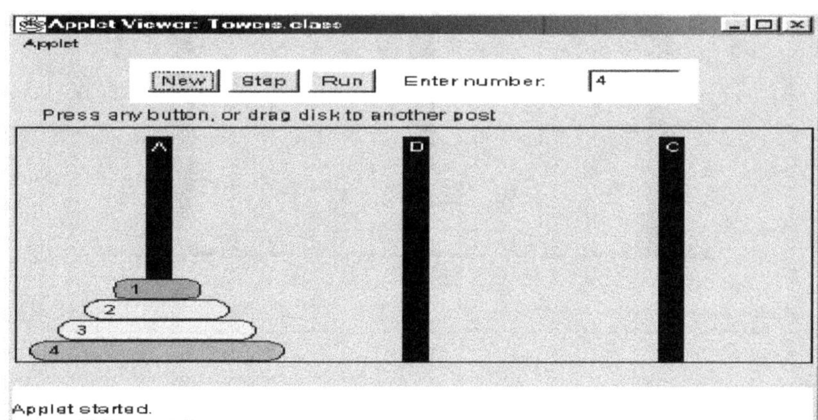

Step 1: move 3 disks f rom peg A to peg B

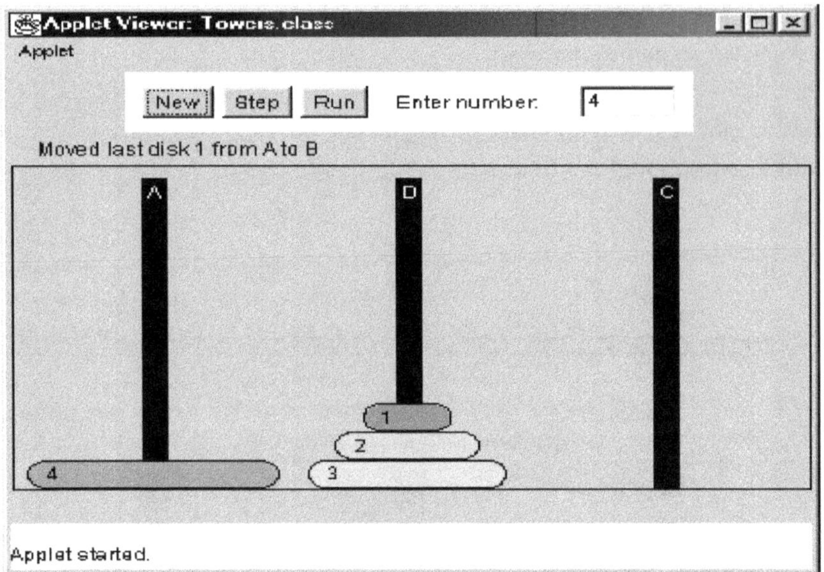

TOWERS OF HANOI (3)

Step 2: move 1 disk from peg A to peg C

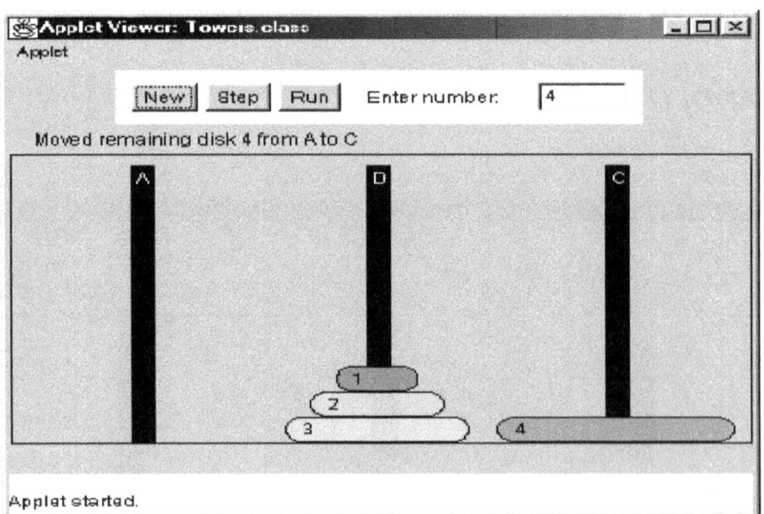

Step 3: move 3 disks from peg B to peg C

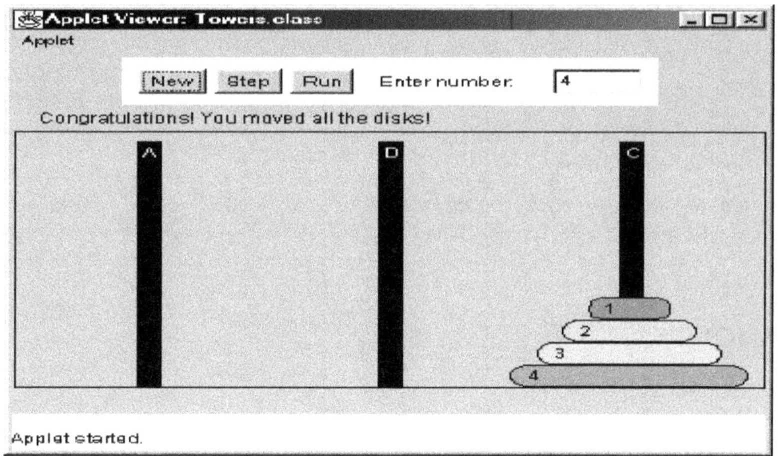

TOWERS OF HANOI (4)

```
public static void tower(int n, char start, char finish, char spare)
{
  if (n<=1)
    System.out.println("Moving a disk from peg " + start +" to peg " +
                    finish);
  else
  {
    tower(n-1,start,spare,finish);
    System.out.println("Moving a disk from peg " + start +" to peg " +
                      finish);
   tower(n-1,spare,finish,start);
  }
}
```

Note that the solution to this problem is a divide-and-conquer algorithm. Calling the above method with n=4, i.e., tower(4,'A','C','B') yields the following result.

Moving a disk from peg A to peg B
Moving a disk from peg A to peg C
Moving a disk from peg B to peg C
Moving a disk from peg A to peg B
Moving a disk from peg C to peg A
Moving a disk from peg C to peg B
Moving a disk from peg A to peg B
Moving a disk from peg A to peg C
Moving a disk from peg B to peg C

Moving a disk from peg B to peg A
Moving a disk from peg C to peg A
Moving a disk from peg B to peg C
Moving a disk from peg A to peg B
Moving a disk from peg A to peg C
Moving a disk from peg B to peg C

TOWERS OF HANOI (5)

Call trace for n=4:
numbers inside nodes are *n, start, finish*

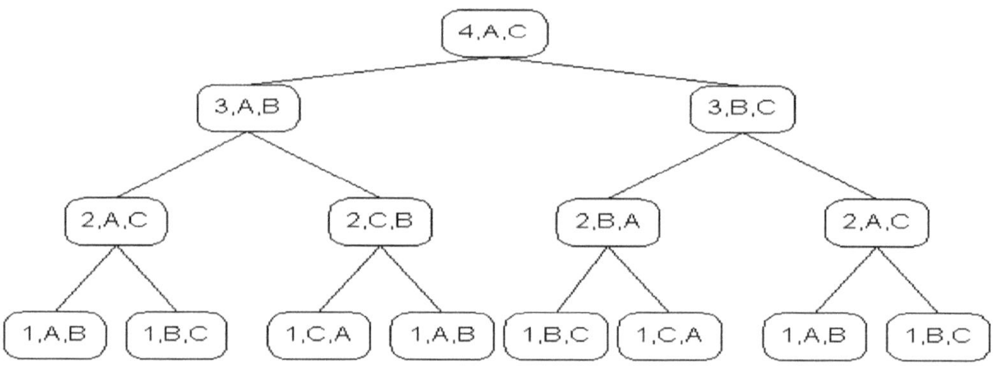

Number of moves = 1 + 2 + 4 + 8.

For general n, number of moves = $\sum_{k=0}^{n-1} 2^k = 2^n - 1$.
===> $O(2^n)$ complexity

For n=64, number of moves = 2^{64}-1 or 1.844×10^{19}.
Recall that one move takes one second.
===> Time left in universe = 1.844×10^{19} seconds = 5.85×10^{11} years.
Astronomers estimate the present age of the universe to be 20 billion (2×10^{10}) years.

PART VII: Files and Streams

Part VII: Files and Streams

INTRODUCTION

TERMINOLOGIES

- Input and output • I/O operations • File
- Character streams • Byte stream • Buffered I/O streams
- Object serialization • Random Access Files • Formatted Text I/O

Java programs support input/output operations through the concept of streams. A stream is an abstraction that either produces or consumes data. Streams are linked to a physical device by the Java I/O system. All streams behave in the same manner because they inherit many of their methods from their respective super class. The Java package called **java.io** can be divided into three broad categories of classes:

The File - The **File** class represents a filename. That is, instances of the **File** class represent the name of a file or directory on the host file system. This class details the characteristics of a file, such as the name and path of a file, whether the file can be read from or written to, or whether the name represents a directory of an ordinary data file. It cannot be used for reading and writing.

Character stream classes - These classes allow the program to read data as characters from input streams, and to write data as characters to the output stream.

The Byte stream classes - These classes allow the program to read data as bytes from input streams, and to write data as bytes to the output stream.

There are some other classes that do not fit into either of these set of classes, because they are not inherited from any of the classes in this package. Two of the more frequently used ones are the classes **StreamTokenizer** and **RandomAccessFile.**

StreamTokenizer - This class takes an input stream and parses it into individual sets of data, each called a token. The tokens are read one at a time. The parsing process is controlled by a table and a number of flags that can be set to various states. The class recognizes different kinds of tokens such as: identifiers, numbers, quoted strings, and various comment styles. This class does not permit the writing of data to it.

RandomAccessFile - This class supports both reading data from a random access file and writing of data also to a random access file. It uses a kind of indexing mechanism called the file pointer to access positions in the data file.

The standard **in** input stream is used by the program to read character data from the keyboard. By default **in** is a **buffered** input stream. This means that input from the keyboard is kept in a buffer until the program reads it. This stream can be used in conjunction with the class called Scanner to read other format of data.

The following article **Java Programming Input & Output (I/O)** will elaborates on the class File, and on the different types of streams.

Java Programming

INPUT & OUTPUT (I/O)

JDK has two sets of IO packages: the Standard IO (`java.io`) (since JDK 1.0) and the New IO (`java.nio`) (introduced in JDK 1.4). In addition, JDK 1.5 introduced the formatted text-IO via new classes `Scanner`/`Formatter` and `printf()`.

CLASS JAVA.IO.FILE

The class `java.io.File` can represent either a *file* or a *directory*.

It also maintains two system-dependent properties, for you to write programs that are portable:

- Directory Separator: Windows systems use backslash '`\`' (e.g., "`c:\jdk\bin\java.exe`"), while Unixes use forward slash '`/`' (e.g., "`/usr/jdk/bin/java.exe`"). This system-dependent property is maintained in the static field `File.separator` (as `String`) or `File.separatorChar`. (They failed to follow the naming convention for constants, which was adopted in JDK 1.2.)
- Path Separator: Windows use semi-colon '`;`' to separate paths (or directories) white Unixes use colon '`:`'. This system-dependent value can be retrieved from static field `File.pathSeparator` (as `String`) or `File.pathSeparatorChar`.

The commonly used constructor in `java.io.File` is (not throwing `FileNotFoundException`?!):

public File(String fileOrDirName)

For example,

File file = new File("in.txt");

For applications that you intend to distribute as Jar files, you should use URL class to reference resources, as it can reference disk file as well as Jar'ed file , for example,

java.net.URL url = this.getClass().getResource("icon.png");

The commonly-used methods are:

```
public boolean exists()       // tests if the file/directory exists.
public boolean isDirectory()  // tests if this instance is a directory.
public boolean isFile()       // tests if this instance is a file.
public boolean canRead()      // tests if the file readable.
public boolean canWrite()     // tests if the file writeable.
public long length()          // returns the length of the file.
public boolean delete()       // deletes the file or directory.
public void deleteOnExit()    // deletes the file or directory when the program terminates.
public boolean renameTo(File dest) // renames the file
public boolean mkdir()        // create this directory.
```

For a directory, the following methods can be used to list its contents:

```
// List the contents of a directory
public String[] list()
public File[] listFiles()
// List with a filename filter
public String[] list(FilenameFilter filter)
public File[] listFiles(FilenameFilter filter)
public File[] listFiles(FileFilter filter)
```

Example 1: Recursively list the contents of a directory (similar to Unix's "`ls -r`" command).

```
// Recursively list the contents of a directory
import java.io.File;
public class ListDirectoryRecusive {
   public static void main(String[] args) {
```

```
        File dir = new File("d:\\bin\\test");
        listRecursive(dir);
    }

    public static void listRecursive(File dir) {
        if (dir.isDirectory()) {
            File[] items = dir.listFiles();
            for (File item : items) {
                System.out.println(item.getAbsoluteFile());
                if (item.isDirectory()) listRecursive(item);
            }
        }
    }
}
```

Example 2: Filename filter

```
// List all the files end with ".java"
import java.io.File;
import java.io.FilenameFilter;
public class ListDirectoryWFilter {
    public static void main(String[] args) {
        File dir = new File(".");     // current working directory
        if (dir.isDirectory()) {
            String[] files = dir.list(new FilenameFilter() {
                public boolean accept(File dir, String file) {
                    return file.endsWith(".java");
                }
            });    // an anonymous inner class as FilenameFilter
            for (String file : files) {
                System.out.println(file);
            }
        }
    }
}
```

The interface `java.io.FilenameFilter` declares one abstract method:

```
public boolean accept(File dirname, String filename)
```

where *dirname* and *filename* are the directory name and filename respectively. The `list()` method does a *callback* to `accept()` for each of the file/sub-directory produced. You can specify your filtering criteria to the *dirname* and *filename* in `accept()`. Those files/sub-directories that result in a `false` return will be excluded.

IO OPERATIONS IN STANDARD IO PACKAGE (JAVA.IO)

Programs read inputs from data sources (e.g., keyboard, file, network, or another program) and write outputs to data sinks (e.g., console, file, network, or another program). Inputs and outputs in Java are handled by the so-called stream. A stream is a sequential and continuous one-way flow of information (just like water or oil flows through the pipe). It is important to mention that Java does not differentiate between the various types of data sources or sinks (e.g., file or network). They are all treated as a sequential flow of data. The input and output streams can be established from/to any data source/sink, such as files, network, keyboard/console or another program. The Java program receives data from data source by opening an input stream, and sends data to data sink by opening an output stream. All Java I/O streams are one-way (except the RandomAccessFile, which will be covered later). If your program needs to perform both input and output, you have to open two separate streams - an input stream and an output stream.

IO operations involved three steps:

1. Open an input/output stream associated with a physical device (e.g., file, network, console/keyboard), by constructing an appropriate IO-stream object.
2. Read from the opened input stream until "end-of-stream" encountered, or write to the opened output stream (optionally flush the buffered output).
3. Close the input/output stream.

Java's IO operations are more complicated than C/C++, as Java uses 16-bit character set (instead of 8-bit character set). As a consequence, it needs to differentiate between byte-based IO and character-based IO.

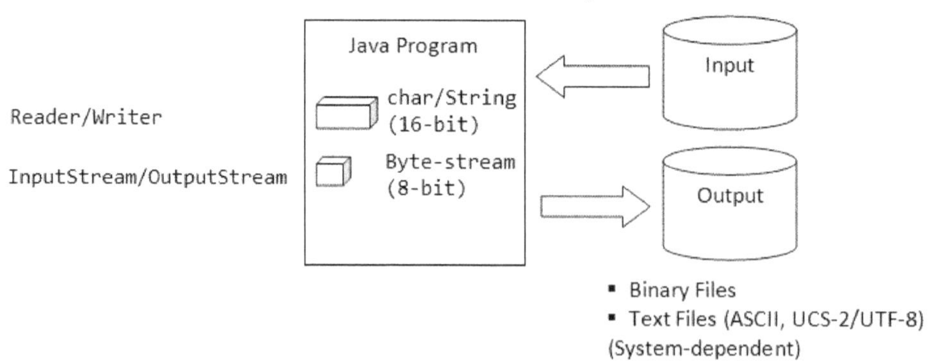

BYTE-BASED IO & BYTE STREAMS

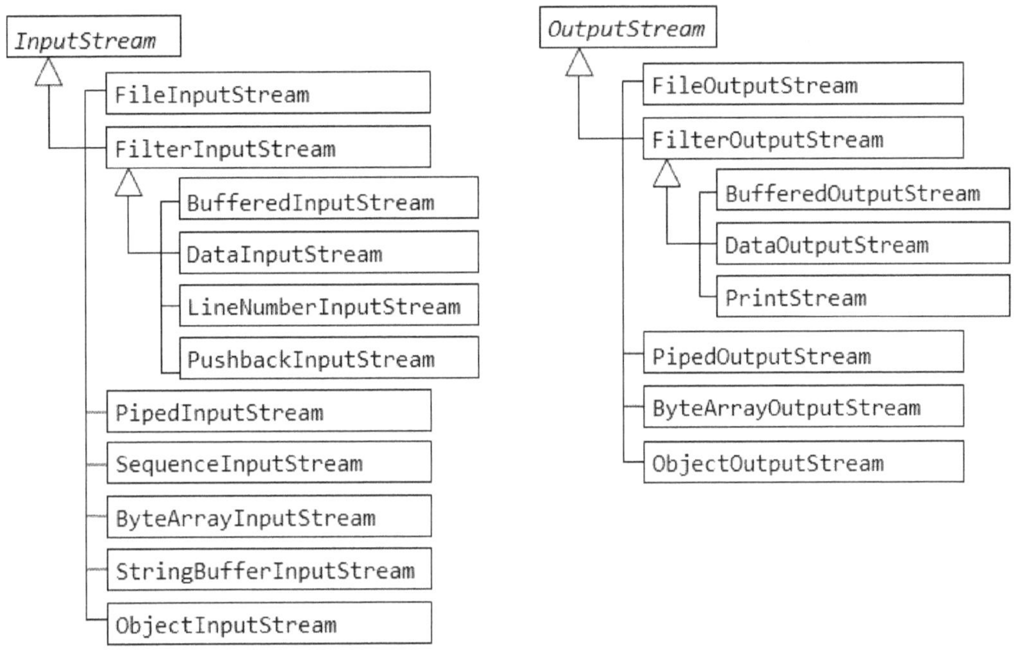

Byte streams can be used to read or write bytes serially from an external device. All the byte streams are derived from the abstract superclass `InputStream` and `OutputStream`, as illustrated in the above class diagram.

The abstract superclass `InputStream` declares an abstract method `read()` to read one data-byte from the input source, and convert the unsigned byte value (of 0 to 255) to an `int`. The `read()` method will *block* until a byte is available, an I/O error occurs, or the "end of stream" is reached. It returns -1 if for "end of stream", and throws an `IOException` if it encounters an I/O error.

```
public abstract int read() throws IOException  // read one data-byte from the
input stream
```

Two variations of `read()` methods are implemented in the `InputStream` for reading a block of bytes into a byte-array buffer. It returns the number of bytes read, or -1 if "end-of-stream" encounters.

```
// Read "length" number of bytes, store in bytesBuffer array starting from index
offset.
public int read(byte[] bytesBuffer, int offset, int length) throws IOException
// Same as read(bytesBuffer, 0, bytesBuffer.length)
public int read(byte[] bytesBuffer) throws IOException
```

Similar to the input counterpart, the abstract superclass `OutputStream` declares an abstract method `write()` to write a data-byte to the output sink. The least significant byte of the `int` argument is written out; while the upper 3 bytes are discarded.

```
public void abstract void write(int unsignedByte) throws IOException  // write
one data-byte to the output stream
```

Similar to the `read()`, two variations of the `write()` method to write a block of bytes from a byte-array buffer are implemented:

```
// Write "length" number of bytes, from the bytesBuffer array starting from
index offset.
public void write(byte[] bytesBuffer, int offset, int length) throws IOException
// Same as write(bytesBuffer, 0, bytesBuffer.length)
public void write(byte[] bytesBuffer) throws IOException
```

Both the `InputStream` and the `OutputStream` provides a `close()` method to close the stream, which performs the necessary clean-up operations as well as frees the system resources. (Although it is not absolutely necessary to close the IO streams explicitly, as the garbage collector will do the job, it is probably a good practice to do it to free up the system resources immediately when the streams are no longer needed.)

```
public void close() throws IOException  // close the opened Stream
```

In addition, the `OutputStream` provides a `flush()` method to flush the remaining bytes from the output buffer.

```
public void flush() throws IOException  // Flush the output
```

`InputStream` and `OutputStream` are abstract classes that cannot be instantiated. You need to choose an appropriate concrete implementation subclass (such as `FileInputStream` and `FileOutputStream`) to establish a connection to a physical device (such as file, network, keyboard/console).

LAYERED (OR CHAINED) IO STREAMS

The IO streams are often layered or chained with other IO steams, for purposes such as buffering, filtering or format conversion. For example, we can layer a `BufferedInputStream` to a `FileInputStream` for buffered input, and stack a `DataInputStream` in front for formatted data input, as illustrated in the following diagram.

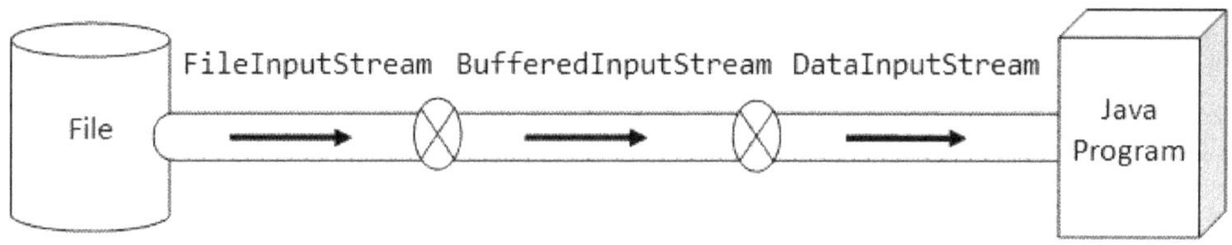

FILE IO STREAMS - FILEINPUTSTREAM & FILEOUTPUTSTREAM

FileInputStream and FileOutputStream are concrete implementation to the abstract class of InputStream and OutputStream, to support File IO.

BUFFERED IO STREAMS - BUFFEREDINPUTSTREAM & BUFFEREDOUTPUTSTREAM

The InputStream and OutputStream is designed to read/write a single byte of data, which is grossly inefficient. Buffering is commonly applied to speed up the IO operations.

To chain the streams together, simply pass an instance of one stream into the constructor of another stream. For example, the following codes chain a `FileInputStream` to a `BufferedInputStream`, and finally, a `DataInputStream`:

```
FileInputStream fin = new FileInputStream("in.dat");
BufferedInputStream bin = new BufferedInputStream(fin);
DataInputStream din = new DataInputStream(bin);
// or
DataInputStream in = new DataInputStream(
                        new BufferedInputStream(
                           new FileInputStream("in.dat")));
```

Example 1: Copying a file without Buffering

```
import java.io.*;
public class FileCopyNoBuffer {
   public static void main(String[] args) {
      File fileIn;
      FileInputStream in = null;
      FileOutputStream out = null;
      long startTime, elapsedTime;  // for speed benchmarking

      try {
         fileIn = new File("test-in.jpg");
```

```
            System.out.println("File size is " + fileIn.length() + " bytes");
            in = new FileInputStream(fileIn);
            out = new FileOutputStream("test-out.jpg");

            startTime = System.nanoTime();
            int byteRead;
            // Read a unsigned byte (0-255) and padded to 32-bit int
            while ((byteRead = in.read()) != -1) {
               // Write the least significant byte, drop the upper 3 bytes
               out.write(byteRead);
            }
            elapsedTime = System.nanoTime() - startTime;
            System.out.println("Elapsed Time is " + (elapsedTime / 1000000.0) + " msec");
         } catch (IOException ex) {
            ex.printStackTrace();
         } finally {       // always close the streams
            try {
               if (in != null) in.close();
               if (out != null) out.close();
            } catch (IOException ex) { ex.printStackTrace(); }
         }
   }
}
File size is 417455 bytes
Elapsed Time is 3781.500581 msec
```

The first example copies a file by reading a byte from an input file and writing it to the output file. It uses `FileInputStream` and `FileOutputStream` directly without buffer. Notice that most the IO methods "throws" `IOException`, which must be caught by the program or declared to be thrown to the calling method. The method `close()` is often called inside the "`finally`" clause. However, method `close()` also throws an `IOException`, and therefore must be enclosed inside a nested try-catch block (which makes the codes a little ugly).

I used `System.nanoTime()`, which is new in JDK 1.5, for a more accurate measure of the elapsed time, instead of the legacy and not-so-precise `System.currentTimeMillis()`.

The output shows that it took about 4 seconds to copy a 400KB file.

Example 2: Copying a file with a Programmer-Managed Buffer

```
import java.io.*;
```

```
public class FileCopyUserBuffer {

   public static void main(String[] args) {

      File fileIn;

      FileInputStream in = null;

      FileOutputStream out = null;

      long startTime, elapsedTime;  // for speed benchmarking


      try {

         fileIn = new File("test-in.jpg");

         System.out.println("File size is " + fileIn.length() + " bytes");

         in = new FileInputStream(fileIn);

         out = new FileOutputStream("test-out.jpg");

         startTime = System.nanoTime();

         byte[] byteBuf = new byte[4096];    // 4K buffer

         int numBytesRead;

         while ((numBytesRead = in.read(byteBuf)) != -1) {

            out.write(byteBuf, 0, numBytesRead);

         }

         elapsedTime = System.nanoTime() - startTime;

         System.out.println("Elapsed Time is " + (elapsedTime / 1000000.0) +
" msec");
```

```
        } catch (IOException ex) {
            ex.printStackTrace();
        } finally {             // always close the streams
            try {
                if (in != null) in.close();
                if (out != null) out.close();
            } catch (IOException ex) { ex.printStackTrace(); }
        }
    }
}
```

```
File size is 417455 bytes
Elapsed Time is 2.938921 msec
```

This example again uses `FileInputStream` and `FileOutputStream` directly. However, instead of reading/writing one byte at a time, it reads/writes a 4KB block. This program took only 3 millisecond - a more than 1000 times speed-up compared with the previous example.

Below are the elapsed times for the various buffer size (Warning: The timing depends on many factors, your processor speed, OS, RAM size, etc.):

- 0.5 KB: 13.8 msec
- 1 KB: 6.9 msec
- 2 KB: 4.6 msec
- 4 KB: 2.9 msec
- 8 KB: 2.0 msec
- 16 KB: 1.76 msec
- 32 KB: 1.58 msec
- 64 KB: 1.33 msec
- 128 KB: 2.03 msec
- 256 KB: 1.74 msec

- 512 KB (larger than file size): 6.13 msec

Larger buffer size, up to a certain limit, generally improves the IO performance. However, there is a trade-off between speed-up the the memory usage. For file copying, a large buffer is certainly recommended. But for reading just a few bytes from a file, large buffer simply waste the memory.

Example 3: Copying a file with Buffered Streams

```
import java.io.*;
public class FileCopyBuffered {
   public static void main(String[] args) {
      File fileIn;
      BufferedInputStream in = null;
      BufferedOutputStream out = null;
      long startTime, elapsedTime;  // for speed benchmarking

      try {
         fileIn = new File("test-in.jpg");
         System.out.println("File size is " + fileIn.length() + " bytes");
         in  = new BufferedInputStream(new FileInputStream(fileIn));
         out = new BufferedOutputStream(new FileOutputStream("test-out.jpg"));
         startTime = System.nanoTime();
         int byteRead;
         while ((byteRead = in.read()) != -1) {
            out.write(byteRead);
         }
         elapsedTime = System.nanoTime() - startTime;
         System.out.println("Elapsed Time is " + (elapsedTime / 1000000.0) + " msec");
      } catch (IOException ex) {
         ex.printStackTrace();
      } finally {            // always close the streams
         try {
            if (in != null) in.close();
            if (out != null) out.close();
         } catch (IOException ex) { ex.printStackTrace(); }
      }
   }
}
File size is 417455 bytes
Elapsed Time is 61.834954 msec
```

In this example, I chained the `FileInputStream` with `BufferedInputStream`, `FileOutputStream` with `BufferedOutputStream`, and read/write byte-by-byte. The JRE decides on the buffer size. The program took 62 milliseconds, about 60 times speed-up compared with example 1, but slower than the programmer-managed buffer.

DataInputStream & DataOutputStream

The `DataInputStream` and `DataOutputStream` can be stacked on top of any `InputStream` and `OutputStream` to filter the streams so as to perform I/O operations in the desired data format, such as `int` and `double`.

To use `DataInputStream` for formatted input, you can chain up the input streams as follows:

```
DataInputStream in = new DataInputStream(
                        new BufferedInputStream(
                           new FileInputStream("in.dat")));
```

`DataInputStream` implements `DataInput` interface, which provides methods to read formatted primitive-type inputs, such as:

```
public final int readInt() throws IOExcpetion;
public final double readDoube() throws IOExcpetion;
public final byte readByte() throws IOExcpetion;
public final char readChar() throws IOExcpetion;
public final short readShort() throws IOExcpetion;
public final long readLong() throws IOExcpetion;
public final boolean readBoolean() throws IOExcpetion;
public final float readFloat() throws IOExcpetion;
public final int readUnsignedByte() throws IOExcpetion;   // [0, 255] upcast to int
public final int readUnsignedShort() throws IOExcpetion;  // [0, 65535], same as char,
upcast to int
```

Similarly, you can stack the `DataOutputStream` as follows:

```
DataOutputStream out = new DataOutputStream(
                          new BufferedOutputStream(
                             new FileOutputStream("out.dat")));
```

`DataOutputStream` implements `DataOutput` interface, which provides methods to write formatted primitive-type input. For examples,

```
public final void writeInt() throws IOExcpetion;
```

```
public final void writeDoube() throws IOExcpetion;
// others similar to DataInput interface
```

Network IO

[PENDING]

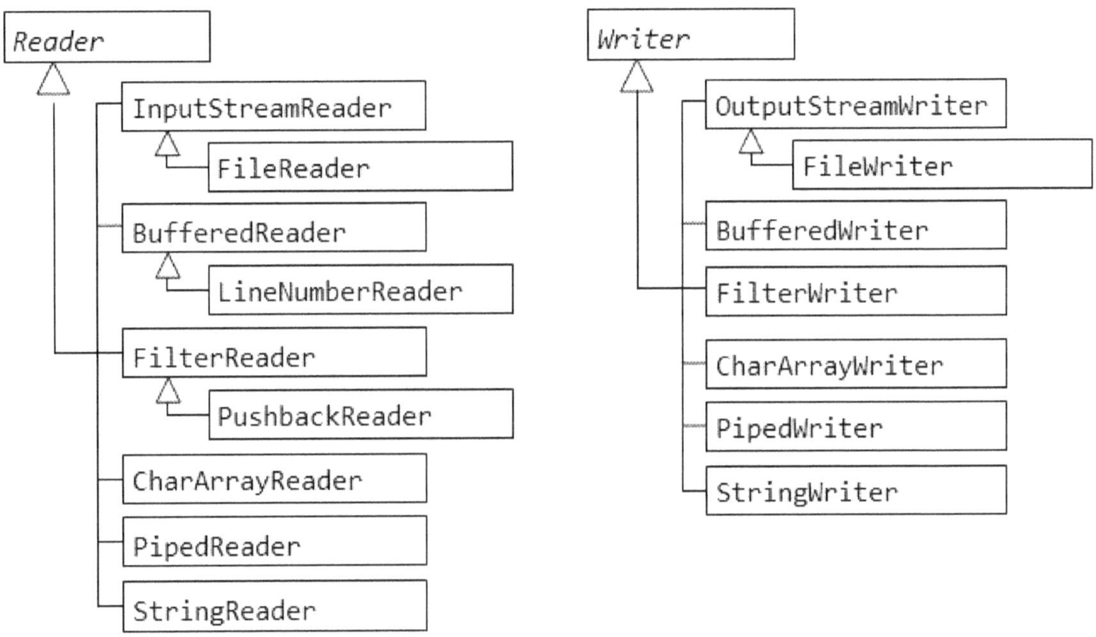

Character-Based IO & Character Streams

Java uses 16-bit character set internally, instead of 8-bit character set. Hence, it has to differentiate between byte-based IO (for binary data), and character-based text IO. Other than the unit of operation, character-based IO is almost identical to byte-based IO.

Instead of `InputStream` and `OutputStream`, `Reader` and `Writer` shall be used for character-based IO.

The abstract superclass `Reader` operates on characters (primitive `char` or unsigned 16-bit integer from 0 to 65535), it similarly declares an abstract method `read()` to read one character from the input source, and convert the `char` to an `int`; and variations of `read()` to read a block of characters.

```
public abstract int read() throws IOException
public int read(byte[] bytesBuffer, int offset, int length) throws IOException
public int read(byte[] bytesBuffer) throws IOException
```

The abstract superclass `Writer` similarly declares an abstract method `write()`, to write a character to the output sink. The lower 2 bytes of the `int` argument is written out; while the upper 2 bytes are discarded.

```
public void abstract void write(int aChar) throws IOException
public void write(byte[] bytesBuffer, int offset, int length) throws IOException
public void write(byte[] bytesBuffer) throws IOException
```

Example:

```
import java.io.*;
public class FileCopyCharBased {
   public static void main(String[] args) {
      BufferedReader in = null;
      BufferedWriter out = null;
      try {
         in  = new BufferedReader(new FileReader("in.txt"));
         out = new BufferedWriter(new FileWriter("out.txt"));
         int charRead;
         while ((charRead = in.read()) != -1) {
            System.out.printf("%c ", (char)charRead);
            out.write(charRead);
         }
      } catch (IOException ex) {
         ex.printStackTrace();
      } finally {              // always close the streams
         try {
            if (in != null) in.close();
            if (out != null) out.close();
         } catch (IOException ex) { ex.printStackTrace(); }
      }
   }
}
```

Java Internal Character vs. External Devices

The byte/character streams refer to the unit of operation within the Java programs, which does not necessary correspond to the amount of data transferred between the program and the external IO devices. This is because the extenal IO device may store a character in 8-bit format (e.g., ASCII file) or 16-bit format (e.g., UCS-16) or encoded (e.g., UTF-8 or UTF-16). When character stream is used to read an 8-bit ASCII file, an 8-bit data is read from the file and put into the 16-bit char location of the Java program. You can run the above example on a 8-bit ASCII text file and a 16-bit Unicode text file and observe the result.

Unicode Files (UCS-2, UTF-8, UTF-16)

Java programs use 16-bit raw Unicode (or UCS-2) internally. But external Unicode files could be unencoded (i.e., UCS-2) or encoded in UTF-8 or UTF-16 format. Read "Data Representation: Character Encoding" for details about Unicode character set and Unicode encoding.

Two classes `InputStreamReader` and `OutputStreamWriter` can be used to convert unencoded UCS-2 used internally in the Java program to UTF-8 byte-stream for the external file. [Can `FileReader` and `FileWriter` handle it automatically??]

You can specify the character set in the `InputStreamReader`'s contructor:

```
public InputStreamReader(InputStream in)   // default charset
public InputStreamReader(InputStream in, String charsetName) throws
UnsupportedEncodingException
public InputStreamReader(InputStream in, Charset cs)
public InputStreamReader(InputStream in, CharsetDecoder dec)
```

The supported and commonly-used charset are:

- "US-ASCII": 7-bit ASCII (ISO646-US)
- "ISO-8859-1"
- "UTF-8"
- "UTF-16", "UTF-16BE" (big-endian), "UTF-16LE" (little-endian)

Example of writing Unicode texts to a UTF-8 file,

```
FileOutputStream fos = new FileOutputStream("test.txt");   // byte-based stream
Writer out = new OutputStreamWriter(fos, "UTF8");   // convert UCS-2 character to UTF-8
byte-stream
out.write(str);
out.close();
```

Example of reading Unicode texts from a UTF-8 file:

```
FileInputStream fis = new FileInputStream("test.txt");       // byte-based stream
InputStreamReader isr = new InputStreamReader(fis, "UTF8"); // convert UTF-8 byte-stream
to UCS-2 character
Reader in = new BufferedReader(isr);
int charRead;
while ((charRead = in.read()) != -1) { ... }
in.close();
```

Example: The following program writes an UTF-8 file, and reads it back via character-based input and byte-based input.

```
import java.io.*;
public class UnicodeFileIO {
   public static void main(String[] args) {
      try {
         FileOutputStream fos = new FileOutputStream("TestUTF8.txt");
         Writer out = new OutputStreamWriter(fos, "UTF8");   // Output file UTF-8 encoded
         out.write("Hello, 您好\n");
         // UCS-2: 您(60A8H), 好(597DH)
         // UTF-8: 您(E6 82 A8), 好(E5 A5 BD)
         out.close();

         // Character-based (or text-based) input
         FileInputStream fis = new FileInputStream("TestUTF8.txt");
         Reader in = new InputStreamReader(fis, "UTF8");
         int charRead;
         int charCount = 0;
         while ((charRead = in.read()) != -1) {
            charCount++;
            System.out.printf("%c(%02XH) ", (char)charRead, charRead);
         }
         System.out.println("\nNumber of characters read = " + charCount);
         in.close();

         // Byte-based (or stream-based) input
         fis = new FileInputStream("TestUTF8.txt");
         int byteRead;
         int byteCount = 0;
         while ((byteRead = fis.read()) != -1) {
            byteCount++;
            System.out.printf("%02XH ", (byte)byteRead);
         }
         System.out.println("\nNumber of bytes read = " + byteCount);
         fis.close();
      } catch (FileNotFoundException ex) {
         ex.printStackTrace();
      } catch (UnsupportedEncodingException ex) {
         ex.printStackTrace();
      } catch (IOException ex) {
```

```
            ex.printStackTrace();
        }
    }
}
H(48H) e(65H) l(6CH) l(6CH) o(6FH) ,(2CH)  (20H) 您(60A8H) 好(597DH)
(0AH)
Number of characters read = 10

48H 65H 6CH 6CH 6FH 2CH 20H E6H 82H A8H E5H A5H BDH 0AH
Number of bytes read = 14
```

OBJECT SERIALIZATION AND OBJECT STREAMS

Object serialization is the process of representing a particular state of an object in a serialized bit-stream, so that the bit stream can be written out to an external device (such as a disk file or network). The bit-stream can later be re-constructed to recover the state of that object. Object serialization is necessary to save a state of an object into a disk file for persistence or sent the object across the network for applications such as Web Services, Distributed-object applications, and Remote Method Invocation (RMI).

In Java, object that requires to be serialized must implement `java.io.Serializable` or `java.io.Externalizable` interface. `Serializable` interface is an *empty* interface (or *tagged* interface) with nothing declared. Its purpose is simply to declare that particular object is serializable.

`ObjectInputStream & ObjectOutputStream`

The `ObjectInputStream` and `ObjectOutputStream` can be used to serialize an object into a bit-stream and transfer it to/from an I/O streams, via these methods:

```
public final Object readObject() throws IOException, ClassNotFoundException;
public final void writeObject(Object o) throws IOException;
```

`ObjectInputStream` and `ObjectOutputStream` must be stacked on top of a concrete implementation of `InputStream` or `OutputStream`, such as `FileInputStream` or `FileOutputStream`.

For example, to write objects to a file:

```
ObjectOutputStream out =
    new ObjectOutputStream(
        new BufferedOutputStream(
            new FileOutputStream("object.dat")));
out.writeObject("The current Date and Time is "); // write a String object
out.writeObject(new Date());                      // write a Date object
out.flush();
```

```
out.close();
```

To read and re-construct the object back in a program, use the method `readObject()` which returns an `Object` and downcast it back to its original type.

```
ObjectInputStream in =
   new ObjectInputStream(
      new BufferedInputStream(
         new FileInputStream("object.dat")));
String str = (String)in.readObject();
Date d = (Date)in.readObject(new Date());
in.close();
```

Example: Object serialization

```
import java.io.*;

public class ObjectSerializationTest {
   public static void main(String[] args) {
      ObjectInputStream in = null;
      ObjectOutputStream out = null;
      try {
         out = new ObjectOutputStream(new BufferedOutputStream(
                  new FileOutputStream(«object.dat»)));

         // Create an array of 10 SerializedObjects with ascending numbers
         SerializedObject[] objs = new SerializedObject[10];
         for (int i = 0; i < objs.length; i++) {
            objs[i] = new SerializedObject(i);
         }
         // Write the 10 objects to file, one by one.
         for (int i = 0; i < objs.length; i++) {
            out.writeObject(objs[i]);
         }
         // Write the entire array in one go.
         out.writeObject(objs);
         out.close();

         in = new ObjectInputStream(new BufferedInputStream(
               new FileInputStream(«object.dat»)));
         // Read back the objects, cast back to its original type.
```

```
            SerializedObject objIn;
            for (int i = 0; i < objs.length; i++) {
               objIn = (SerializedObject)in.readObject();
               System.out.println(objIn.getNumber());
            }
            SerializedObject[] objArrayIn;
            objArrayIn = (SerializedObject[])in.readObject();
            for (SerializedObject o : objArrayIn) {
               System.out.println(o.getNumber());
            }
            in.close();
         } catch (Exception ex) {
            ex.printStackTrace();
         }
   }
}

class SerializedObject implements Serializable {
   private int number;

   public SerializedObject(int number) {
      this.number = number;
   }

   public int getNumber() {
      return number;
   }
}
```

Primitive types and array are, by default, serializable.

The `ObjectInputStream` and `ObjectOutputStream` implement `DataInput` and `DataOutput` interface respectively. You can used methods such as `readInt()`, `readDouble()`, `writeInt()`, `writeDouble()` for reading and writing primitive types.

Notes on Serialization:

- `static` fields are not serialized.
- To prevent certain fields from being serialized, mark them using the keyword `transient`. This could cut down the amount of data traffic.
- The `writeObject()` method writes out the class of the object, the class signature, and values of non-`static` and non-`transient` fields.

Random Access Files

All the I/O streams covered so far are one-way streams. That is, they are either read-only input stream or write-only output stream. Furthermore, they are all sequential access streams, meant for reading and writing data sequentially. It is sometimes necessary to read a file record directly as well as modifying existing records or inserting new records. The class `RandomAccessFile` provides supports for non-sequential, direct (or random) access to a disk file. `RandomAccessFile` is a two-way stream, supporting both input and output operations within the same stream.

`RandomAccessFile` can be treated as a huge byte array. You can use a file pointer (of type `long`), similar to array index, to access individual byte or group of bytes in primitive types (such as int and double). The file pointer is located at 0 when the file is opened. It advances automatically for every read and write operation by the number of bytes processed.

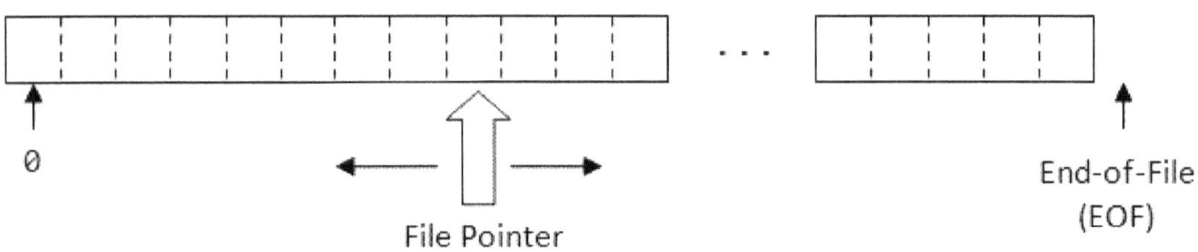

In constructing a `RandomAccessFile`, you can use flags `'r'` or `'rw'` to indicate whether the file is "read-only" or "read-write" access, e.g.,

```
RandomAccessFile f1 = new RandomAccessFile("filename", "r");

RandomAccessFile f2 = new RandomAccessFile("filename", "rw");
```

The following methods are available:

```
// Position the file pointer for subsequent read/write operation.
public void seek(long pos) throws IOException;
// Move the file pointer forward by the specified number of bytes.
public int skipBytes(int bytes) throws IOException;
// Obtain the position of the current file pointer, in bytes, from the beginning of the file.
public long getFilePointer() throws IOException;
// Returns the length of the random access file.
public long length() throws IOException;
```

`RandomAccessFile` does not inherit from `InputStream` or `OutputStream`. However, it implements `DataInput` and `DataOutput` interfaces (similar to `DataInputStream` and `DataOutputStream`). Therefore, you can use various methods to read/write primitive types to the file, e.g.,

```
public int readInt() throws IOException;
public double readDouble() throws IOException;
public void writeInt(int i) throws IOException;
public void writeDouble(double d) throws IOException;
```

Example: Read and write records from a `RandamAccessFile`. (A student file consists of student record of name (String) and id (`int`)).
[PENDING]

COMPRESSED I/O STREAMS

The classes `ZipInputStream` and `ZipOutputStream` (in package `java.util`) support reading and writing of compressed data in ZIP format. The classes `GZIPInputStream` and `GZIPOutputStream` (in package `java.util`) support reading and writing of compressed data in GZIP format.

Example: Reading and writing ZIP files

[@PENDING]

Example: Reading and writing JAR files

[@PENDING]

FORMATTED TEXT IO (JDK 1.5)

Formatted Text Input via `Scanner`

JDK 1.5 introduced `java.util.Scanner` class, which greatly simplifies formatted text input from text files or keyboard (or `System.in`). `Scanner`, as the name implied, can scan for texts from an input source. It can also scan and parse text into primitive type. It first breaks the text inputs into *tokens* using a delimiter pattern, which is by default whitespace (blank, tab and newline). The tokens may then be converted into primitive values of different types using the various `nextXxx()` methods (such as `nextInt()` and `nextDouble()`). Regular expression can optionally be applied for matching.

The commonly-used constructors are:

```
// Scanner piped from a disk File
public Scanner(File source) throws FileNotFoundException
public Scanner(File source, String charsetName) throws FileNotFoundException
// Scanner piped from a byte-based InputStream
```

```
public Scanner(InputStream source)
public Scanner(InputStream source, String charsetName)
// Scanner piped from a New IO's channel
public Scanner(ReadableByteChannel source)
public Scanner(ReadableByteChannel source, String charsetName)
// Scanner piped from the given source string (NOT filename string)
public Scanner(String source)
```

The last constructor pipes the text input from the `String` given in the argument. The string is not used as a filename. For example,

```
// Construct a Scanner to scan a given text string.
java.util.Scanner in1 = new Scanner("This is the input");
// Construct a Scanner piped from a file.
java.util.Scanner in2 = new Scanner(new File("in.txt"));  // need to handle
FileNotFoundException
```

Example 1: The most common usage of `Scanner` is to read texts and values of primitive types form the keyboard (`System.in`), as follows:

```
java.util.Scanner in = new Scanner(System.in);  // piped from standard input device,
default to keyboard
// Use the default delimiter of whitespace (blank, newline and tab) to break up tokens
String str = in.next();           // reads the next token as String
int anInt = in.nextInt();         // scans and parses the next token as int
Double aDouble = in.nextDouble(); // scans and parses the next token as double
```

The `nextXxx()` methods throw `InputMismatchException` if the next token does not match the type to be parsed.

Example 2: Reading from a text file.

```
import java.util.Scanner;
import java.io.File;
import java.io.FileNotFoundException;

public class FileScanner {
   public static void main(String[] args) throws FileNotFoundException {
      Scanner in = new Scanner(new File("input.txt"));
      double d;
      while (in.hasNextDouble()) {   // iterate thru the input source
```

```
            d = in.nextDouble();
            System.out.println(d);
        }
    }
}
// input.txt
// 1.1 2.2 3.3
// 4.4
```

The `Scanner` class implements `iterator<String>` interface. You can use `hasNext()` coupled with `next()` to iterate through all the `String` tokens. You can also directly iterate through the primitive types via methods `hasNextXxx()` and `nextXxx()`. `Xxx` includes all primitive types (`byte`, `short`, `int`, `long`, `float`, `double` and `boolean`), `BigInteger` and `BigNumber`. `char` is not included but can be retrieved from `String` via `charAt()`.

Instead of the default whitespace, you can set the delimiter to a chosen string or a regular expression via these methods:

```
public Pattern delimiter()
public Scanner useDelimiter(Pattern pattern)
public Scanner useDelimiter(String pattern)
```

Example 3: Customized token delimiter

```
import java.util.Scanner;
public class ScannerWithDelimiter {
    public static void main(String[] args) {
        Scanner in = new Scanner("one apple 2 apple red apple big apple 5.5 apple");
        // Zero or more whitespace, followed by 'apple', followed by zero or more whitespace.
        in.useDelimiter("\\s*apple\\s*");
        // The delimiter breaks the input into tokens {"one", "2", "red", "big", "5.5"}.
        System.out.println(in.next());
        System.out.println(in.nextInt());      // parses text into int
        System.out.println(in.next());
        System.out.println(in.next());
        System.out.println(in.nextDouble());   // parses text into double
    }
}
```

You can use the following methods to find the next occurrence of the specified pattern using regular expressions:

```
public String findInLine(Pattern pattern)
public String findInLine(String pattern)
public String findWithinHorizon(Pattern pattern, int horizon)
public String findWithinHorizon(String pattern, int horizon)
public Scanner skip(Pattern pattern)
public Scanner skip(String pattern)
```

Example 4: [PENDING]

Formatted Text Printing with `printf()`

JDK 1.5 introduced C-like `printf()` method (in classes `java.io.PrintSteam` and `java.io.PrintWriter`) for formatted-text printing. `printf()` takes this syntax:

```
public PrintStream|PrintWriter printf(String format, Object... args)
public PrintStream|PrintWriter printf(Locale l, String format, Object... args)
```

`printf()` takes a variable number of arguments (or varargs). Varargs was introduced in JDK 1.5 (that is the reason Java cannot support `printf()` earlier).

`printf()` can be called from `System.out`, as `System.out` is a `PrintStream`. For example,

```
System.out.printf("Hello %4d %6.2f %s, and\n   Hello again\n", 123, 5.5, "Hello");
Hello  123   5.50 Hello, and
   Hello again
```

Format Specifier: A format specifier begins with '`%`' and ends with a conversion-type character (e.g. "`%d`" for integer, "`%f`" for `float` and `double`), with optional parameters in between, as follows:

`%[`*`argument_position`*`$][`*`flag(s)`*`][`*`width`*`][.`*`precision`*`]`***`conversion-type-character`***

- The optional *argument_position* specifies the position of the argument in the argument list. The first argument is "`1$`", second argument is "`2$`", and so on.
- The optional *width* indicates the minimum number of characters to be output.
- The optional *precision* restricts the number of characters (or number of decimal places for float-point numbers).
- The mandatory *conversion-type-character* indicates how the argument should be formatted. For examples: '`b`', '`B`' (`boolean`), '`h`', '`H`' (hex string), '`s`', '`S`' (string), '`c`', '`C`' (character), '`d`' (decimal integer), '`o`' (octal

integer), `'x'`, `'X'` (hexadecimal integer), `'e'`, `'E'` (float-point number in scientific notation), `'f'` (floating-point number), `'%'` (percent sign). The uppercase conversion code (e.g., `'S'`) formats the texts in uppercase.

- Flag: `'-'` (left-justified), `'+'` (include sign), `' '` (include leading space), `'0'` (zero-padded), `','` (include grouping separator). `'('` (negative value in parentheses), `'#'` (alternative form).

Examples:

```
System.out.printf("%2$2d %3$2d %1$2d\n", 1, 12, 123, 1234);
12 123  1
System.out.printf(Locale.FRANCE, "e = %+10.4f\n", Math.PI);
e =    +3,1416
System.out.printf("Revenue: $ %(,.2f, Profit: $ %(,.2f\n", 12345.6, -1234.5678);
Revenue: $ 12,345.60, Profit: $ (1,234.57)
```

Formatted-Text Output via `Formatter`

JDK 1.5 introduced `Scanner` for formatted text input. It also introduced `java.util.Formatter` for formatted text output.

The `Formatter` has the following constructors:

```
public Formatter(File file)
public Formatter(String filename)
public Formatter(OutputStream os)
public Formatter(PrintStream ps)
```

The `format()` method can be used to write formatted text output:

```
public Formatter format(String format, Object... args)
public Formatter format(Locale l, String format, Object... args)
```

Notice that the method `format()` has the same syntax as the method `printf()`, using the same set of format specifier as `printf()`.

Other methods are:

```
public void flush()   // flush out all the buffered output
public void close()
```

Example:

```
import java.io.File;
import java.io.FileNotFoundException;
import java.util.Formatter;
import java.util.Scanner;

public class FormatterTest {
   public static void main(String[] args) {
      try {
         Formatter out = new Formatter("out.txt");  // override existing file
         out.format("%3d %s\n", 12, "Hello-world");
         out.format("%3d %s\n", 345, "Hello");
         out.format("%3d %s\n", 6789, "again");
         out.close();

         // Set up text file input using a scanner and read records
         Scanner in = new Scanner(new File("out.txt"));
         while (in.hasNext()) {
            int id = in.nextInt();
            String name = in.next();
            System.out.printf("%4d %s\n", id, name);
         }
      } catch (FileNotFoundException ex) { // for Formatter and Scanner
         ex.printStackTrace();
      }
   }
}
```

Formatter vs. PrintWriter/PrintStream

[PENDING]

New IO (java.nio) (JDK 1.4)

New IO package was introduced in JDK 1.4 to support:

- High-performance file IO
- Scalable network IO
- Characters sets

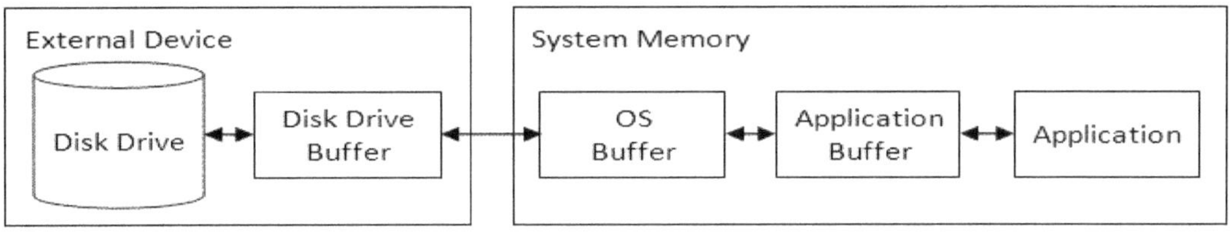

Physical IO operation is thousands times slower than memory access. Hence, a chunk of data is often cache or buffer to improve the throughput. As illustrated from the above diagram, many layers of cache exist between you Java application and physical disk.

- Disk Buffer is RAM that is built into the disk drive to store a block of data from the disk. The cost of transferring data from the disk surface to the disk buffer is by far the slowest and the most expensive operation, because it involves physical movement of the disk.
- OS Buffer: OS does its own buffering as it can cache more data and manage it more elegantly. This buffer can also be shared among the applications.
- Application Buffer: Application may optionally buffer its own data.

Channels (`java.nio.channels.Channel`)

Channel represents a connection to a physical IO device, such as file, network socket, or even another program. It is similar to Standard IO's stream, but a more platform-dependent version of stream. Because channels have a closer tie to the underlying platform, they can achieve better IO throughput. The types of channel include:

- FileChannel
- SocketChannel: support non-blocking connection.
- DatagramChannel: Datagram-oriented socket (i.e., UDP).

A `Channel` object can be obtained by calling the `getChannel()` methods of classes such as `java.io.FileInputStream`, `java.io.FileOutputStream`, `java.io.RandomAccessFile`, `java.net.Socket`, `java.net.ServerSocket`, `java.net.DatagramSocket`, and `java.net.MulticastSocket`.

For example, you can obtained a `FileChannel` as follows:

```
FileInputStream fis = new FileInputStream("in.dat");
FileChannel fc = fis.getChannel();
```

A `FileChannel` obtained from a `FileInputStream` is read-only; while a FileChannel obtained from a `FileOutputStream` is write-only. The Standard IO's stream is read/write into a byte-array buffer; while `FileChannel` uses a `ByteBuffer` object.

Example: Copying a file using `FileChannel`

```
import java.io.*;
import java.nio.ByteBuffer;
import java.nio.channels.FileChannel;

public class FileChannelCopy {
   public static void main(String[] args) {
      File fileIn;
      FileInputStream fis;
      FileOutputStream fos;
      FileChannel fic = null;
      FileChannel foc = null;
      ByteBuffer bytes;
      long startTime, elapsedTime;  // for speed benchmarking

      try {
         fileIn = new File("test-in.jpg");
         System.out.println("File size is " + fileIn.length() + " bytes");
         fis = new FileInputStream(fileIn);
         fos = new FileOutputStream("test-out.jpg");
         // Construct channels from streams
         fic = fis.getChannel();
         foc = fos.getChannel();
         bytes = ByteBuffer.allocate(4096);

         startTime = System.nanoTime();
         while (true) {
            bytes.clear();
            int bytesRead = fic.read(bytes);
            if (bytesRead <= 0) break;
            // flip the buffer which set the limit to current position, and position to 0.
            bytes.flip();
            foc.write(bytes);
         }
         elapsedTime = System.nanoTime() - startTime;
         System.out.println("Elapsed Time is "
               + (elapsedTime / 1000000.0) + " msec");
      } catch (IOException ex) {
         ex.printStackTrace();
      } finally {            // always close the streams
         try {
```

```
            if (fic != null) fic.close();
            if (foc != null) foc.close();
         } catch (IOException ex) { ex.printStackTrace(); }
      }
   }
}
File size is 417455 bytes
Elapsed Time is 6.955283 msec
```

Remark: It is slower than the 3 msec reported using IO streams with a programmer-managed buffer of the same size (4 KB)?! [May need to look into it!]

Buffers (java.nio.Buffer)

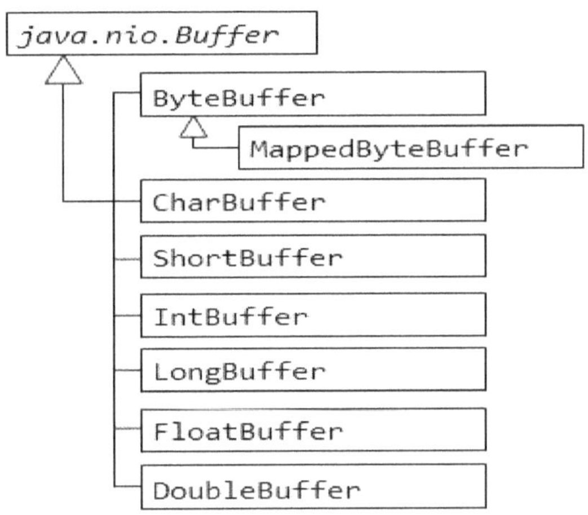

There are buffers for each primitive type. Buffer is similar a byte array, which represents a contiguous chunk of data with a fixed capacity. The fundamental difference between a byte array used in Standard IO and Buffer is that array are always *non-direct*, whereas Buffer could be *direct*. This will be explained later.

A Buffer is allocated once and reused. A Buffer has a capacity, position, limit, and an optional mark:

- The capacity must be specified when the `Buffer` is constructed and cannot be changed. You can retrieve it via method `capacity()`.
- The position indicates where the next piece of data is to be read or written. You can retrieve the current position via method `position()` or change the current position via method `position(int newPosition)`.
- The `limit` specifies the current occupancy, i.e., the uppermost position that contains valid data. You can retrieve the current limit via method `limit()` or set the `limit` via method `limit(int newLimit)`.
- The mark provides a positional marker. You can mark the current position via the method `mark()`.

Several methods are available to manipulate the `Buffer:`

- `clear()`: set the `position` to 0, `limit` to the `capacity`, and discard `mark`.
- `flip()`: set the `limit` to the current `position`, then `position` to 0, and discard `mark`.
- `reset()`: set the position to the previously-marked position.
- `rewind()`: set the position to 0, and discard mark.

java.nio.MappedByteBuffer

`MappedByteBuffer` is a so-called *direct* buffer that is managed by the OS, instead of the Java application. In other words, `MappedByteBuffer` can be used to wrap a region of OS buffer. Application can allocate different direct buffer to *view* the different portion of the OS buffer.

[PENDING] New IO to be continued...

[PENDING] Network IO

REFERENCES & RESOURCES

- PENDING
- Latest version tested: JDK 1.6
  Last modified: August 29, 2008

Part VIII:
Job Prospect and Career Path

Part VIII: Job Prospect and Career Path

INTRODUCTION

Many times students wonder about the job prospect for computer programmer after graduating with a degree in the area of studying. This article gives a comprehensive view on this issue. It focuses on several areas of this discipline– types of programming, career path, educational requirements, job experience, and financial compensation. These are critical points that one needs to; at least have some answers to, before investing in a degree in this discipline.

Programming

BY WETFEET

OBJECTIVES

After reading this article you will be more educated to:

1. The nature of programming
2. The expectation/responsibility of programmers
3. The career opportunities for programmers
4. The educational and job experience requirements of a programmer
5. The financial compensation at present

TERMINOLOGIES

Application Programmer • System Programmer • Database Administrator • Web Programmer • Project Manager • Software Engineer • Quality Assurance

OVERVIEW

Programming—writing instructions to be carried out by a computer or other programmable device using a given programming language (such as Java, C++, or Perl)—combines elements of math, science, and engineering.

Computer programmers are at the center of the information technology (IT) field. These days, we rely on all kinds of programmable devices—our laptops, personal computers, personal digital assistants (PDAs), in-car global positioning systems, factory robotics systems, and more. None of these things would function without programmers, though, who give programmable devices specific, accurate instructions on how to perform their various functions. Your PC, for example, is nothing more than a dumb box without the input of programmers. It can't solve even a simple math problem without a series of programming commands to tell it how to do so.

Programming languages are not languages in the traditional sense of the word. Instead, they are series of codes that instruct computers how to operate. Most programmers know several languages and must also be willing to learn new ones as they develop.

WHAT YOU'LL DO

Early in their career, programmers may be responsible for writing code for specific, discrete portions of the overall software program. Later on, they may become more involved in devising the overall shape and organization (or architecture) of software programs, as well as managing teams of lower-level programmers as they write the code for the various program modules. (Some programmers prefer writing code to managing, though, and choose to stay in positions that allow them to continue doing that.) The opportunity for doing more macro-level programming work—determining the overall architecture of a given software program, for instance—will typically come earlier in your career at smaller companies than at larger companies, where in some cases you might spend your entire career working on only a specific aspect of larger programs.

Programmers may also test, repair, and maintain software programs.

Typically, programmers work in a single language, or just a few languages. They also typically write code for a specific type of programmable device, such as mainframe computers or servers. However, during the course of his or her entire career, a programmer is likely to have to know a variety of languages; the programming world is evolving constantly, and to stay up to speed (and remain in demand in the employment marketplace), programmers must update their knowledge on an ongoing basis.

Often, programmers are referred to as being one of two types: applications programmers or system programmers. Applications programmers write code designed to complete specific tasks; the programmers who wrote the code for Adobe Acrobat and Microsoft Word, for instance, are applications programmers. Systems programmers, on the other hand, write the system software that runs other software, such as Microsoft's Windows or Apple's Mac OS X.

In addition, because Web surfers are increasingly accessing the Internet via wireless devices, be they Wi-Fi or Bluetooth-enabled computers, cell phones, or personal digital assistants, programmers are increasingly facing the need to optimize the software they write for wireless devices.

WHO DOES WELL

There are several personality traits you can usually find in successful programmers. Because much of their work involves abstract concepts and complex mathematical formulas, programmers need to be analytical thinkers. They have to approach a problem in many different ways until they find the ultimate solution.

Patience is another important characteristic. Each line of code must be written with exacting attention to detail. Any mistakes can cause a system to come to a crashing halt. Some IT departments have employees whose sole purpose is to painstakingly search through previously written programs to seek out and eradicate bugs.

In today's business world, teams composed of programmers from various disciplines usually work together on projects. Consequently, companies place an increasing emphasis on strong writing and communication skills. The most successful programmers are not only competent code writers, but well liked among their peers.

REQUIREMENTS

Most computer programmers have a four-year degree in computer science. However, a degree from a related technical field, such as math or engineering, is acceptable. Around 20 percent have an advanced degree in computer science or engineering. A limited number of programmers are self-taught. Certification programs, available through technical schools or community colleges, offer another route to employment.

While degrees are important, employers usually place more emphasis on actual work experience. Many recent college graduates with sparkling report cards can't find work because they lack portfolios. A programmer who has a limited formal education but a strong knowledge of several programming languages has a better chance of finding employment. Take advantage of all available work opportunities and internships. The more experience you can show, the better your chances of finding a position after graduation.

It's important that computer professionals continue to update their skills. Software development tools and technologies are always advancing and evolving. Programmers have to seek out trade shows, seminars, periodicals, and professional education classes to help programmers stay abreast of changes in their industry.

JOB OUTLOOK

The picture for programmers has changed drastically over the past couple of years. Firms are consolidating and centralizing their computer systems and often outsourcing programming overseas, where salaries are much lower. Off-the-shelf software is becoming more sophisticated and is reducing corporate reliance on IT. Over the last few years, many programmers have seen their wages decline, and raises have been the exception rather than the rule.

While these factors have put pressure on jobs, the information age has created an ongoing need for skilled programmers. Quick studies who know the latest programming languages inside and out, who "get" how business needs determine programming priorities, and who work well in teams should be able to find opportunities.

The Bureau of Labor Statistics projects that opportunities for programmers will grow at about the same rate as the average for all occupations between 2004 and 2014. Computer software engineers, though, who count programming among their responsibilities, but are often more involved in software design than straight-ahead programmers, have better prospects, with BLS estimates showing better-than-average growth in opportunities in this specialty through 2014.

CAREER TRACKS

You can find computer programmers in all types of industries. While the working environment may change, the goal of all programming is to make computers come to life. Usually, programmers work within a company's IT department. Organizations sometimes bring in skilled contractors to work on specific projects. Smaller businesses may outsource part or all of their programming needs. Following is a list of the most common programming job titles.

Application Programmer

Application programmers develop the software we are most familiar with. Examples include word processors, video games, and accounting packages. Programs may be written to reach a wide audience, such as with off-the-shelf software, or for a specific function within an organization.

Most application programmers work with a product from its inception through its final testing. At the start of a project, they meet with designers and management to understand the nature of the program to be developed. Several strategies are designed, outlining the best ways to proceed. Any potential flaws or design complications will be noted for future reference. The options are then presented to the project manager who selects the best one. At this point, programmers can begin writing code. After the program is completed, the applications team works with the systems programmers and quality assurance personnel to remove any bugs.

Application programmers need to have strong communication skills, as well as technical expertise. Most have experience working with multiple computer languages. Specialization in a specific industry, such as finance or health care, is common. Most companies require a four-year degree, but having recent experience in the industry and knowledge about a particular programming language can open up opportunities.

System Programmer

If computer programming is a war, then systems programmers are firmly in control of the trenches. They develop programs that control computer hardware and how it will interact with peripherals such as terminals, disk drives, and printers. At a fundamental level, systems programmers design and construct operating systems, which communicate directly with computers' central processing units.

Also in this group are programmers who develop software that controls computer networks and lays out the paths along which data is routed. In a telephone company, for example, the system programmer writes programs that direct millions of phone conversations across a network of wires and fiber-optic cables.

Systems programmers may work on a number of projects simultaneously. They are frequently brought in at the end of the development cycle to find hardware glitches that prevent a program from operating properly. Their input is an important part of the troubleshooting process.

All systems programmers have substantial technical backgrounds. They must have an intimate knowledge of the entire computer system. Almost all systems programmers have four-year degrees. A significant number have advanced degrees in computer science.

Database Administrator

Database administrators, or database engineers, create software that controls and maintains massive databases. Large corporations, including online retailers and financial firms, typically use such programs. The computer systems involved are usually very large and can encompass a vast network.

Web Programmer

Writing pages in HTML is a relatively simple process. Until recently, self-taught HTML programmers could use this to their advantage. The bar of entry into Web development was easily crossed. But, currently there is an increasing demand for Websites that interact with users. Developers of these sites must have extensive knowledge of Perl and other object-oriented languages such as Java. These languages create Web pages that not only interact with users, but tap into information stored in large company databases connected to the Website.

Project Manager

The project manager (PM) oversees the work done by members of the programming team. She takes on numerous responsibilities during the course of a project. The PM ensures that programmers finish their assignments on time and within the specified budget. Since the team reports directly to the PM, it is her responsibility to make sure all members are cooperating with one another.

The project management role is part technical consultant, part manager. PMs must understand all of the technical components used in the development process. They work with upper management to make the final decision on how a project advances. PMs must also be expert negotiators, have excellent communication and time-management skills, and have financial forecasting experience.

Corporations say this is the hardest programming position to fill. Qualified applicants are difficult to find and many do not last through their first PM assignment. However, individuals who can successfully work under these conditions are always in demand. Educational background is not as important as getting the job done right. That said, many PMs have bachelor's degrees in computer science and sometimes MBAs.

Software Engineer

Software engineers are concerned with the overall structure of a project. They typically apply general engineering practices—such as quality assurance and failure analysis—to the process of software production. They work directly with Quality Assurance to develop quantitative tests to identify programming shortfalls.

Usually, a software engineer has several years of experience as a general programmer or a traditional engineer. A few lucky ones have been hired directly from undergraduate programs. Many have advanced engineering degrees.

Quality Assurance

The quality assurance (QA) team has the final look at a program before it's released to users. They work with the software engineers, systems, and applications programmers to find bugs that could halt a computer system. QA develops testing procedures that simulate the many ways in which a program could be used. They are the last line of defense. If any errors remain, users will find them.

Most technical organizations have QA teams who search through previously written code to find and fix errors. Smaller companies or nontechnical-based businesses may outsource this function.

COMPENSATION

Compensation varies widely in computer programming jobs depending on skills, company size, and industry. However, the following are typical salary ranges:

- Software engineer: $45,000 to $105,000
- Web programmer: $45,000 to $80,000
- Programmer: $50,000 to $90,000
- Software architect/designer: $90,000 to $120,000
- Quality assurance specialist: $50,000 to $90,000
- Application development manager: $70,000 to $140,000
- Software project manager: $80,000 to $110,000
- Database administrator: $60,000 to $105,000

References

1. Object-Oriented Programming Fundamentals
   Booth, Jim Booth : http://www.jamesbooth.com/OOPBasics.htm

2. Object-oriented language basics, Part 1
   Learn how to declare classes and create objects
   By Jeff Friesen, JavaWorld.com, 04/06/01
   http://www.javaworld.com/javaworld/jw-04-2001/jw-0406-java101.html

3. Object-oriented language basics, Part 2
   By Jeff Friesen, JavaWorld.com, 05/04/01
   Declare and access fields and methods
   http://www.javaworld.com/javaworld/jw-05-2001/jw-0504-java101.html

4. A Pedagogical Approach to Discussing Fundamental Object-oriented programming Principles – using the ADT Set
   Ragonis, Noa: ACM Inroads, June 2010, Vol I, No 2

5. Polymorphism – Prose of Java Programmers
   Splawski, Zdzislaw: http://www.proceedings2005.imcsit.org/docs/38.pdf

6. Polymorphism and Interfaces
   Artima, Inc 1996–2009:
   http://www.artima.com/javaseminars/modules/PolymorphInt/index.html
7. AP Computer Science – Curriculum Module: An Introduction to Polymorphism in Java
   Umbarger, Dan: http://apcentral.collegeboard.com/apc/public/repository/Intro_to_Polymorphismin_Umbargar.pdf

8. Java Loops - for, while and do …while
   Copyright © tutorialspoint.com http://www.tutorialspoint.com/java/java_loop_control.htm

9. Arrays
   All material in this Arrays is copyright 2010 Webucator. The purpose of this Website is to help you learn Java on your own and use of the Website implies your agreement to our Java Tutorial Terms of Service.
   http://www.learn-java-tutorial.com/Java-Arrays.cfm#h1.5

10. Java Notes: Algorithms: Binary Search
    Swart, Fred: 2006 Fred Swartz MIT License http://leepoint.net/notes-java/algorithms/searching/binarysearch.html

11. Java Notes Bubble Sorts
    Swart, Fred: 2005 Fred Swartz MIT License http://leepoint.net/notes-java/data/arrays/32arraybubblesort.html

12. Programming
    WetFeet: http://www.wetfeet.com/careers-and-industries/careers/programming.aspx

13. Implementing Lists Using Linked-Lists
    http://pages.cs.wisc.edu/~vernon/cs367/notes/4.LINKED-LIST.html

14. The Essence of OOP using Java, Exception Handling, September 3, 2002
    http://www.developer.com/print.php/1455891

15. Exceptions in Java This story appeared on JavaWorld at
    http://www.javaworld.com/javaworld/jw-07-1998/jw-07-exceptions.html

16. Understanding Java Exceptions
    Understanding Java Exceptions

17. JAVA EXCEPTIONS
    http://pages.cs.wisc.edu/~hasti/cs368/JavaTutorial/NOTES/Exceptions.html

18. Stacks and Queues
    http://www.cs.princeton.edu/introcs/43stack/

19. Java String
http://codingbat.com/doc/string.html

20. Java If and Boolean
http://codingbat.com/doc/ifboolean.html

21. While and For Loops
http://codingbat.com/doc/loop.html

22. Arrays and Loops
http://codingbat.com/doc/array.html

www.ingramcontent.com/pod-product-compliance
Lightning Source LLC
LaVergne TN
LVHW082345011026
849160LV00024B/1132
* 9 7 8 1 6 2 1 3 1 2 5 6 7 *